This book is dedicated to the Behi Dual Champions, Field Champions and Amateur Field Champions responsible for helping me accumulate the knowledge to write this book.

ACKNOWLEDGMENTS

All pictures not taken by the author are credited in the captions where used. Picture captions are by the author.

Larry Hanna, DDS, Bryan, Ohio reviewed and proof read the final work copy.
John Ingram, DOGS UNLIMITED, Chillicothe, Ohio proofed the printer's blue print.

This book was produced for camera ready reproduction on an Epson QX-10 Computer, Peach Text(TM) Word Processor and Comrex II Printer. The pages were set-up and pasted-up by the author.

Succeeding with pointing dogs

FIELD TRIALS & HUNTING TESTS

by Bernard C. Boggs

1989

GLENBRIER PUBLISHING COMPANY
P.O. BOX 1844
CHILLICOTHE, OHIO 45601

Printed in the United States of America, by BROWN & KROGER PRINTING CO., Dayton, Ohio 45414.

FOREWORD

A bird dog standing on a rigid, picturesque, point is a beautiful sight. It is the catalyst for the many emotions experienced by its hunting and non-hunting owners who are drawn into field trials and hunting tests.

Pointing bird dog training can be simple or complex while being progressive for both the dog and its owner/trainer. There are many ways to train using pen raised birds which are now a necessity. The man-dog relationship is complex where one intelligent creature learns to work with another as a team that competes in a sport against many other like pairs, or braces.

Not all dog owners become good trainers or handlers of pointing (bird) dogs. Many who have the desire still find it difficult to learn what is required to be successful so that they can thoroughly enjoy the sport and become dedicated field trialers.

This book gives a comprehensive in-depth treatment of pointing dog training for field trials and hunting tests, and how to compete and how to conduct them. It should help the novice and marginal trainer as well as those who are first starting as handler, chairman, secretary, marshal, gunner, bird planter and spectator. It should also be interesting reading for those having more experience.

The field trial sport has been established at many different levels of competition which is now in its second hundred years here in this country. Yet, it keeps changing, expanding and adapting to new or different requirements, rules and standards. It is dynamic--never static.

Field trial trainers and handlers are divided among those who prefer to work from a check cord or not; to retrieve, or not; to allow chasing during puppy/derby ages, or not; to collar and lead dogs off the flush, or not; to foot handle or horseback handle; to have birds shot by handlers or official gunners, or not; to shoot birds on course or just in a bird field, or not; to have dogs steady to wing, to shot, and/or to kill; to have dogs back naturally or by command; to allow scouts, or not; to ride off the course to keep a dog in sight, or not; or, to range out of sight for long time periods or check back frequently with its handlers. These are some of the many things which divide and separate trainers and handlers. Fortunately, there are organizations which satisfy the desire of every dog owner who wants to belong to a club and compete with his prized pointing dog, participate in hunting tests, or not belong and enter trials and tests.

It requires many different levels of expertise to compete in any one trial, or in the different kinds of pointing dog field trials of which all are covered in some detail in this book, although the greater emphasis is on trials held under license by the American Kennel Club. The training applies equally well to hunting tests. It has field representatives who go out to its licensed and member field trials. They are there to learn and help guide the committees in the proper application of the rules and assist in any way possible.

It makes no difference which organization an owner chooses to join and compete in because a good dog will stand out, and if the handler learns the variations in procedures and rules his dog can become competitive in most different kinds of gun dog or shooting dog stakes, but not necessarily in all-age, and can pass hunting tests.

The basics remain nearly the same for all. The hunting test for derby age dogs requires no formal training, because it is intended to evaluate natural ability and not be competitive. Thus, any owner can enter hunting tests and enjoy his dog. They offer titles which are the real incentive to participate, yet anytime dogs are braced together competition or problems result and true natural ability cannot be ascertained.

Trainers provide many innovations for gadgets and training aids to overcome problems with individual dogs. Those who invent these are enthusiastic enough to make them work on their dogs. I would never downplay any gadget or artificial method used to solve a problem in the absence of an abundance of wild birds. In fact, I encourage innovation and variations in training methods and conditions while observing the basic fundamentals. There is always a way, even a better way, if we look for it, which can bring out the best in any dog. Patience is the dog trainer's greatest asset, and he must also learn when to quit a training session or when to change methods or locations.

Too many trainers/handlers give up for a multitude of reasons. It helps to win once in awhile to help them learn to appreciate the real benefits the sport offers.

No book has all the answers, but a lot of the old time dog trainers could not write books. Some of these trainers and handlers still captivate the attention of owners and handlers at field trials.

CHAPTER HEADINGS

FIELD TRIALS & TESTS
PART I

These are the organizations in the United States which hold various kinds of field trial competition and testing for pointing dogs. The way field trials are conducted is also explained to help new and existing clubs.

FIELD TRAINING & TRIALING

FOR EXCELLENCE

PART II

Techniques for developing the maximum potential for any pointing dog and how to win field trials and pass hunting tests are explained in considerable detail.

CONTENTS

PART I

PART II

PART I
FIELD TRIALS
&
TESTS

BERNARD C. BOGGS

(Photo by John Ingram)

Chapter 1

Introduction

Thirty four years ago, I was given a non-descript pointing dog which was supposed to be pure-bred. It had the wrong coat color. Pheasants were plentiful and I did not care about his pedigree. He learned to hunt, point, retrieve and find crippled pheasants shot by others, for I was a poor wing shot then.

A few years later I bought what was claimed to be another versatile pure-bred hunting dog with similar success. It was a pure-bred Vizsla bitch and I have not owned any other breed since that day. Times have changed. The birds and the habitat essential to their propagation and survival are gone--maybe forever in my state, along with others. I still own several Vizslas, but my hunting is mostly training and field trialing.

I believed then like so many potential owners do that pointing dogs did not have to be trained--just taken hunting, and they knew what to hunt and how to hunt. True, most pointing breeds have the instinct and desire go out and look for something, but they must find game to develop their instincts. They need help. The problem for many dog owners is that wild game birds are very scarce even where there is good habitat and hunting seems to be something in the past.

Perhaps once in a blue moon an inexperienced trainer will get a dog that will do well for hunting, but not for field trial competition which demonstrates the apex of the skill for pointing breeds. It takes work, and while a trainer can teach dogs to be steady to flush, shot and retrieve much like basic obedience training by working a few minutes a day three to five days a week on pen raised birds, these dogs are seldom capable of winning field trials without blending in the extra work required to develop their maximum hunting potential in order to win consistently in competition. That is even more difficult now with so few wild birds to work dogs on.

This book is mostly about developing and training pointing dogs for competition in American Kennel Club (AKC) trials, but is equally applicable to all others including those which test dogs. There are comparisons made to other organization and association trials, and it has been my experience that dogs trained to win AKC trials can also be competitive in all other kinds while the reverse is not always true without specific knowledge of what is required. I recommend that each and every dog owner check out all the different organizations to find which suits him the best. There is a great variety available and every owner can enjoy ore than one type of competition or test activity.

The new AKC Hunting Tests may solve one problem in field trials for derby age dogs. Traditionally their owners could not compete with them after two years of age until they were broke gun dogs or all-age and expect to win or place. Some owners were thus encouraged to break their dogs entirely too soon—often with disastrous or poor results.

These dogs can be entered in Junior Hunter Tests and permitted to mature. With some training, they can be entered in Senior Hunter Tests. These "Hunting Tests" cannot evaluate a dog's natural hunting ability, because they brace dogs, have horses present, follow a prescribed course, use man-handled birds and bird fields as examples. Dogs exclusively trained on birds having man's scent may not even point wild birds until having several encounters with them.

Few participant sports allow an individual to be competitive all his life and what makes field trials stand out above all the rest is that they are so complex, exciting and interesting, because trainers and handlers have to develop their own knowledge and skills, and then use these to train and develop a dog that works in perfect harmony with them in a team effort under many uncontrolled variables.

Field trials are popular all over the United States, in Mexico, Japan and most European countries, although Europe has different standards which demand a more versatile dog—not one just restricted to pointing game birds. In the United States most trials are seasonal with spring and fall periods most active, although they can be found somewhere year round.

People and dogs behave different under the stress of competition and it does not always bring out the best

3

in them although good sportsmanship predominates. I
would be easy to gloss over the problems dogs and
people cause in the sport, distort the truth or ignore
it, but I do not. Beginners should know what they face
in the sport which should not lessen their enjoyment
from training or competition.

Every sport must have rules. They are necessary and
essential to the well-being, continuity and enjoyment
for all who participate. Field trials have no paid
officials and depend largely on voluntary compliance in
the spirit of fair play and good sportsmanship to make
it a safe, enjoyable, sport.

Field trials serve as the primary recreation for many
people and even the entire family. More and more women
are participating in all aspects of field trials and
are respected as competitive winners. When wives
become interested in their husbands' sport it helps
cement a marriage and makes them better companions and
friends. Many women love horses and this is a sport
that offers a variety of other interests too.

The field trial sport is for old and young alike and
the dogs encourage their owners or trainers to walk
with them in the field which provides the best exercise
for good health and long life.

There are human emotions experienced in competition
which serve to lessen or deepen the bonds of the many
friendships developed over the years. Sometimes egos
interfere with the ability to learn or to be well
liked, but everyone has that problem and must learn to
deal with it. Dog owners are proud, like to brag, show
their dogs off to willing or unwilling patrons, and
most seem to put winning first. Winning does bring the
most reluctant participants to life.

4

There are pointing dog owners in different rganizations who frown on those who participate with ertain breeds, but there are excellent dogs in every reed capable of beating each other on any given day ith all things being equal.

This is an exciting, thrilling, healthy, wholesome nd skilled activity. Bringing a dog along in training hen developing its maximum potential where it can win ield trial stakes requires a long term program. This akes patience, flexibility and correct feedback, so hat correction and redirection are done with a minimum f undesirable effects which allows the dog to mature ith good training experiences and a minimum of istress.

There is a difference in **training** as opposed to **eveloping** pointing dogs. The problem is with trainers nd not dogs. It requires hard work, time, onsistency, repetition, patience, flexibility and etermination. The question comes down to what is best hen a problem develops as some may take years to vercome. Is it better to get a new dog or to stick ith a problem dog? A step by step training procedure, cook book method, a mechanical method, or a trial and rror method will all accomplish some level of erformance short of perfection when done over a long eriod of time. A person with little or no knowledge r experience can eventually train a pointing dog to do is bidding no matter how many mistakes he makes in the rocess. And, there will be mistakes made regardless f the proficiency of the trainer or handler. But, the eed has existed for more information which can be used o develop a class pointing dog steady to wing and shot hich will retrieve properly and win field trial stakes

with style and class. This book goes several step
beyond the average book and provides information neede
to develop the other essential ingredients for clas
bird dog development, knowledge and understanding. I
also gives the information necessary to set-up an
manage field trials which is also applicable to huntin
tests.

Quick and easy solutions to training field tria
pointing dogs are used every day by amateurs an
professionals alike. They even win stakes and titles
but are not class pointing dogs and are normall
short-lived in competition which does not happen whe
developed to their maximum potential while bein
trained. Some dogs are ruined by inept training, an
there is no guarantee for the amateur that sending hi
dog to a professional for certain parts, or all, of it
training will succeed either. There are risks.

A well **developed** , healthy, pointing dog withou
arthritis or hip dysplasia should be capable of winnin
up to twelve years of age while a **trained** dog will bur
out at a much younger age. Somewhere between the goa
of finishing a dog in field trials before it is full
mature or at an older age, there is a BEST age fo
finished training and developing for it to be at th
maximum competitive level for each individual dog i
any breed.

Books are not written for full time professiona
trainers, but sometimes by them, for they are usuall
proficient and successful to the degree needed to mak
a full time living. But, a new pointing dog owne
starts thinking about either sending his dog to
professional trainer, or trying to learn how he can d
the training himself. I was once in that position an
I searched everywhere trying to find books whic

rovided the information and education I needed to rain for meat hunting and competition. There were everal books on this subject, but they had big holes hich did not bridge the gap between training a dog and raining me on what was really important. Now I elieve that a dog's development is more valuable than raining. Confidence comes with knowledge and xperience and it became evident that this was a long erm learning situation. Therefore, I tried to find xperienced field trialers who could help. I walked very brace at weekend trials. Eventually I got my own orses and began to ride, but it was many years before begin handling from horseback.

No matter what or how much a person reads, it takes uch time and hands-on work, knowledge, experience and onfidence. Some never master the finer points and ubtleties in working with and understanding their ogs. Knowing when to stop at times is more important han knowing how to do a given task. Books teach othing. They provide information which must be known nd are important references for solving problems. ideo tapes and movies on pointing dog training are nportant teaching mediums available from magazines and ail order firms engaged in dog supplies. College urriculums do not include pointing dog training which s probably more complex than most study fields.

The methods I could have learned and used to best dvantage are in this book. I have used short quotes om several people in other breeds, organizations and ational publications which provide information and etailed accounts about handling, scouting and ompeting in field trials to emphasize certain points d discussions. Perhaps I could have written the same ings myself, but these people seemed to say it so ich better.

7

Socializing at field trials is as important as runnin dogs, especially on a nice warm day for the people. Thi group is at the Indian Creek Wildlife Area, Fayetteville Ohio.

Here is a group of field trialers waiting to hear th secretary announce the judges' placements for a stake wher the level of excitement can be very high for some owners This is at the Branched Oak Recreation Area, Nebraska.

8

My breed turned me toward American Kennel Club trials, although I entered local trials held under American Field rules where I was advised in a nice way to use a horse to ride and handle which would increase my dog's range. Unfortunately, although these people were, and are still well meaning, that is not the best advice for beginners. They must learn to walk and handle before they can ride and handle.

Not many handlers can take the time to help beginners during competition in trials, and when I started there was no place else to find help and there were fewer trials. Some beginners just lived in the wrong place or had the wrong friends. Those days are hopefully past now and we are better informed, and there are more trials locally to practice what can be learned. It is easier now for a beginner to learn to train by himself, although it helps to have someone else to work with as it heightens one's interest and enjoyment. What good is it to work hard to reach a goal and win without having anyone to share our emotions with? It is hollow. When new owners and trainers lose sight of the fun, excitement, satisfaction and sense of accomplishment, and sometimes even glory, they probably have put the quest for winning out of its proper perspective in the sport.

Many people are nervous and excited when their dogs go on point which affects their dogs in a negative way. These people should work to minimize this problem which is similar to stage fright. It is not easy but it can be done.

The greatest satisfaction for a trainer is being able to solve a problem dog's behavior. Yet, the real thrill is to confirm it in competition and win.

Wild birds are scarce or do not exist in many states
but they have provisions for trainers to train dogs or
special areas year round. This is the salvation fo
pointing dog owners and trainers interested in fiel
trials. Wild birds are important to a dog'
development, but effective training can be done usin
pen raised game birds even if less practical an
perhaps more expensive.

Most pointing dog owners buy their first dog becaus
they believe it will help put more meat on the table
They are dedicated hunters who have no intention o
engaging in field trials. In fact, they bad mout
field trials as a rule. Yet, field trialers usuall
come from meat hunters, just as horseback handlers com
from foot handlers. I know. I did that myself. But
some field trialers have never hunted. They onl
became interested because they knew someone who fiel
trialed and were brought into the sport by them.

There is no doubt that field trials and hunting test
are poorly publicized and seem to be secretive to thos
not in the know. Each one is open to the public at n
charge as a spectator, and they need not even own
dog. The problem is how to find out about field trial
and hunting tests which are held weekends within
short distance of most dog owners.

The best way to learn about area pointing dog fiel
trials is by writing to the American Kennel Club an
ask for information, or subscribe to *The American
Field* weekly publication. The American Kennel Club i
located at 51 Madison Avenue, New York, New York 10010
and the American Field Publishing Company at 542 Sout
Dearborn, Chicago, Illinois 60605.

Field trials are held in all kinds of weather and are seldom cancelled because of bad weather. They are more fun in nice weather.

11

Chapter 2

The American Kennel Club

THE ORGANIZATION

The American Kennel Club, first formed in 1884, i
unusual when compared to the other dog organizations
The State of New York by special act of its Legislatur
incorporated The American Kennel Club (AKC) to regulat
the conduct of persons involved in dogs owned and bre
under its registry. It has powers through law.

It was empowered to: adopt and enforce uniform rule
regulating and governing dog shows and field trials, t
regulate the conduct of persons interested i
exhibiting, running, breeding, registering, purchasin
and selling dogs; to detect, prevent and punish fraud
in connection therewith; to protect the interests o
its members; to maintain and publish an official stu

book and an official kennel gazette, and generally to do everything to advance the study, breeding, exhibiting, running and maintenance of the purity of thoroughbred dogs.

For these purposes, the American Kennel Club was given the power to adopt a constitution, by-laws, rules and regulations, and enforce the same by fines and penalties, the right to collect and enforce by suit, or by suspension or expulsion from membership, or by a suspension or denial of the privileges of said corporation.

These powers were granted to regulate and control dog shows at which pure-bred dogs are exhibited and given an opportunity to compete for prizes and enabling their breeders and owners to show progress made in breeding for type and quality, and for holding of field trials at which pure-bred dogs are run in competition for prizes and to enable their breeders and owners to show the progress made in breeding for practical use, stamina and obedience.

The booklet, "Registration and Field Trial Rules and Standard Procedure for Pointing Breeds, Dachshunds, Retrievers and Spaniels," is updated periodically and is available free from the American Kennel Club, Inc., 51 Madison Avenue, New York, N.Y. 10010.

The American Kennel Club has breed member clubs which were formed, with its help and direction, that meet the requirements of its legislative charter. They are called "parent" clubs under which local breed clubs in each state must obtain approval for competitive activities. Parent clubs usually publish monthly publications of activities for members. It can hold trials and shows as a member club, and is only responsible to the local clubs for keeping trial dates

13

such that there is a minimum of conflict within a certain distance (radius) on given dates. Local field trial clubs are formed under direction and approval of the American Kennel Club. Each one must have enough members with experience in breeding, showing, obedience trialing and, or, field trialing to be approved. Local breed clubs are under their complete jurisdiction and control. They may hold a maximum of two field trials each year under license.

At these field trials, the field trial committee has the full powers of the American Kennel Club to control activities and is expected to promptly handle any problems which may arise that are not in the best interests of pure-bred dogs, or the sport itself.

The running rules and standards of performance are reviewed periodically and updated as necessary. Representatives of each pointing breed member club meet with officials of the American Kennel Club to discuss and vote on changes. It may also change rules without meeting with these representatives. The most recent unilateral change was in rescinding the privilege of handlers shooting birds over their own dogs. Official gunners must now be used for all shooting.

Field trial results are published monthly in the *American Kennel Club AWARDS*. The dogs which win shows, field trials, obedience trials, tracking tests and hunting tests and new titles are listed each month.

There has been much misunderstanding by the dog owning public about the purposes and enforcement of events held under the American Kennel Club license than is deserved. Most owners do not take time to understand the tremendous responsibility the American Kennel Club has to the pure-bred dog owners. Pure-bred dogs registered with it are more likely to be pure-bred than those registered with any other registry. Considerable effort is made by AKC to assure that breedings are pure, and the dog buying public has protection against indiscriminate breeders and sellers. This does not exist in any other organization.

Whenever a dog is bought and registered with the American Kennel Club, the purchaser automatically has the organization at his service whenever there is a need. Most all criticism heard against this body has been unwarranted and without merit. True, at times it may be too autocratic and this causes resentment or misunderstanding. It is aware of its lawful requirements since no other dog organization has any legal authority.

Its **Standards of Performance** prescribes the training needed in competition, and how it is to be judged at field trials. These are simple and concise, and should be easily understood by everyone, yet they are complex. The understanding and application requires considerable knowledge and experience to master. The standards and rules are often read and re-read by owners who are most interested in training, competing and judging to know and understand them and to keep current on changes. Other people may read them once and consider that they are always fixed. Not so.

Chapter 4 explains one way of interpreting these standards which is relative, because oftentimes the meanings are subject to the reader's practical experience in training, competition and success.

DISCUSSION OF TRIALS

The two major registering organizations in the United States for pointing breeds are the American Kennel Club, the largest in the world, and the American Field. Both approve and keep records of the winners and championship titles awarded.

The American Kennel Club recognizes ten pointing breeds and controls the championship requirements—which may be different for each one. For regular field and amateur field titles in some breeds a dog does not have to retrieve and handlers may collar their dogs and lead them away from a flushed bird. The German Shorthaired Pointers, German Wirehaired Pointers, Vizslas and Weimaraners require retrieving for part of the championship points. Open titles give points only for first place, but amateur points can be for three places. The individual breed championships are tailored to the requirements of member breed clubs designated "Parent Clubs."

A champion can be named in a single stake under American Field rules and the number of these is large and also include specific breed championships. The American Kennel Club permits Parent Clubs to hold one trial each year for open and amateur championship titles. These are yearly titles. They need not be held at the same time. Regular championship titles under the American Kennel Club are based on dogs winning a total of ten points, with conditions.

In American Kennel Club trials, amateurs can compete in any stake. The professional handlers are restricted to open stakes. The ten point requirement for field champion and amateur field champion titles must have at least one major win of three to five points of which four points must be from retrieving stakes for German

16

Ch. Smokerise First Edition—Brittany owned by Charles
Kreger (Michigan).
(Photo by Jeannie Wagner)

Field Champion Cider Mill Prairie Schooner.   Owned by
Regis R. Cantini (Ohio).
A beautiful English Setter AKC Field Champion.   English
Setter owners seldom attend AKC trials which require
retrieves, but this one does.

17

Hot Rock Diamond Janie--German Shorthaired Pointer owned by Dale Pickens (Ohio)

Jim Kaths High Roller. German Wirehaired Pointer owned by James P. Yates and Kathleen A. C. Yates, DVM (Michigan).

Shorthaired Pointers, German Wirehaired Pointers, Vizslas and Weimaraners. Only four points can be used from puppy, and derby. All points may be earned in the gun dog or all age stakes, or a combination including puppy and derby. A minimum of three trials are required, and all ten points may be earned under the same judges.

The old *American Kennel Club Show, Obedience and Field Trial Awards,* January through December 1985 listed 337 pointing breed trials with approximately 25,200 entries. These trials produced 139 field champions and 89 amateur field champions with less than one title (2/3rds) for each trial, but many points are won by dogs already having champion titles which reduces the points available for dogs competing for their titles. Field Champion breed titles for 1985 are listed in the order of their ranking with Amateur Field Champions in parenthesis: Brittanys 54 (34); German Shorthaired Pointers 46 (36); Vizslas 9 (4); Weimaraners 7 (4); English Setters 8 (2); German Wirehaired Pointers 7 (2); Gordon Setters 3 (3); Irish Setters 3 (3); Pointers 2 (1); and, Wirehaired Pointing Griffons 0 (0).

Brittanys and German Shorthaired Pointers dominate the statistics and either one outnumbers all other breeds combined. Brittanys have very large all-age stakes with 92 the largest in 1985 which was a five day trial with 233 entries at Raymond, Nebraska.

The January to December statistics contain part of 1984 trials and 1985 trials. The last two months are usually printed in January and February issues, but some may be delayed until the March issue, but the 1985 monthly issues are representative of the calendar year.

These entries were down from those issued by the American Kennel Club in 1981 with 471 licensed and

Smokerise Day Tripper--Gordon Setter owned by Pam Bachman (Connecticut).
(Photo by Jeannie Wagner)

Amateur Field Champion Karrycourt's Rose O'Cidermill--Irish Setter owned and handled by Jeannie Wagner (Ohio)

member trials. The ten breeds held the following number: Brittanys 159; German Shorthaired Pointers 132; Weimaraners 52; Irish Setters 38; Vizslas 33; German Wirehaired Pointers 28; Gordon Setters 15; English Setters 7; Pointers 6; and, Wirehaired Pointing Griffons none. It is estimated that the entries totaled over 40,000.

The American Kennel Club trials are usually limited to weekends. A single course trial may be limited to about 72 entries although some clubs do manage to run as many as 90 entries when the days are long. Two course trials are often run simultaneously and can accomodate about 150 entries on a weekend.

Entry fees vary widely depending on the stake. Championship stakes are two or more times the cost of regular stakes, depending on the kind of championship stake and the purse offered.

Judges in American Kennel Club trials must be 21 years of age and in good standing. Nothing in the rules require them to have ever owned, trained or handled a dog in competition. The check and balance is with the trial giving club.

In an effort to improve judging through education, the American Kennel Club used Gene Shultz, California, to hold seminars for the German Shorthaired Pointer breed in 1984 and 1985. As a result of this work, judges for that breed must meet new criteria to judge these trials except for those fitting the "grandfather" status. A meeting of pointing breed Parent Club presidents held in the fall of 1985 resulted in all agreeing to require the same education for judges in their breeds.

Better efforts are needed to educate handlers and judges. This is being done for Hunting Tests which may

Field Champion The Pepsi Challenger. Pointer owned by William Kleener (Michigan). This pointer is also a winner in American Field Championship stakes.

Dual and Amateur Field Champion Paradox Title Chase of Behi. Vizsla owned by David and Nancy Boggs Heinold, DVM's (Michigan).

Birtzel's Alberfelda Duchess--Weimaraner **owned by** Sondra
Langen (Ohio)

Wirehaired Pointing Griffon--owned by Royal Hunt Kennel,
Halifax, Massachusetts. (Photo by Joe Di Santis)

have a beneficial fallout for regular trials.

Clubs can hold several different stakes in the normal two day weekend trial, and can limit entries for the trial or for individual stakes. Also, non-regular stakes can be run for which the results are not recorded.

The braces are normally thirty minutes duration at a foot handler's pace and fast riding is forbidden and is seldom ever necessary. Handlers are not allowed to run their horses except by direction of the judges. The distance normally traveled for a brace is between two and three miles along a prescribed course which starts out and ends up near the same place.

In these trials a dog can compete in puppy stakes from six to fifteen months of age, in derby from six to twenty four months, but is eligible to compete in all other stakes at six months of age without respect to training or experience. The dogs can compete until the day they die if their handlers choose. Entries may be solely to compete for Top Ten dog of the year after a championship title is earned.

Hunting seldom sours out dogs, but intensifies desire although the exact opposite can occur in field trials. Some stakes are worse than others. A good mixture of stake conditions is important where dogs compete in three or more stakes in a single weekend.

An American Kennel Club field trial giving club can hold stakes for puppy, derby, gun dog and all-age as it chooses in which points are awarded toward championship titles. Non-regular stakes can be set up anyway a club wants if they do not conflict with its rules. No championship points are awarded and placements are not recorded. It also has **Hunting Tests** for pointing breeds providing competition in three categories:

24

Junior, Senior and Master. The dogs are **tested** against a hunting performance standard without placements (similar to obedience trials.) It is pass or fail. Dogs which meet all the requirements of each level have the highest title (JH, SH, or MH) added as a suffix to their names.

Each stake, except puppy and derby, can be either open or amateur, and additional gun dog and all-age stakes can be "limited" which requires dogs to have placed in gun dog or all age stakes previously, or a first place in open derby. Brace time for any stake can be the minimum specified time or a longer time period.

The minimum age of six months should be changed for gun dog or all-age stakes. Occasionally a beginner, or novice, will enter a puppy in finished gun dog stakes and the entry must be accepted as long as it is properly filled out. An owner will say, "Put my dog in the best stake," implying a puppy could compete with and beat the best trained older dogs. In remote cases this may occur in non-retrieving stakes.

There is no apparent restriction on a handler's age. A baby just past the crawling stage could handle a dog. I suppose a club's out is the provision where it can print in the premium whatever additional rules it considers necessary which do not conflict with published rules.

Horseback handling is permitted in any or all stakes according to the wishes of the club and must be stated on the premium.

Shooting must be done by official guns on course or in a designated bird field.

Bitches can be run when in season on courses that will not be used again that day and must be the last braces run. The premium must state which stakes bitches in season may be entered.

A club may have any type course and can hold additional stake series according to what the club puts in its premium. Judges may call for additional running after a first series, or second series to decide winners. Any game bird may be used, but pigeons are permitted only in puppy stakes.

Money prizes may be offered. The important provision is that a club must describe its stakes completely in the printed premium. Only unknowledgeable people find fault with the American Kennel Club rules, but most everyone can find fault in how its rules are sometimes applied by those in the sport.

Judging is based on control and correct manners of dogs on game. Style, application and range are important considerations, but it must be understood that these vary for different breeds. Twelve o'clock tails may be practical for pointers and setters but they are mostly man-made in ways unknown to most dog owners over several generations. Range seems to be paramount by all those who judge and in stakes having several different breeds there is no consideration specified for range or application for the individual breeds.

Any established American Kennel Club breed pointing dog club which opens all its stakes to other breeds continues the practice when their breed wins most of its stake placements. Some clubs must have other breed entries to warrant holding trials.

Water tests are considered by some national breed clubs to be important enough to warrant proof of a dog's ability in water before receiving the field champion title under American Kennel Club rules. The

German Wirehaired Pointer and Weimaraner are the only two having this requirement. The German Shorthaired Pointer Parent Club recently rescinded this requirement. The qualifying water test is held at a licensed or member club trial and is simple and requires little training. Much less than it should be when compared to the performance these dogs can do in water.

Owners and handlers should read and understand the **special** requirements for their breed for earning the field champion titles.

DUAL CHAMPION

The American Kennel Club is exclusive in the use of the **Dual Champion** title which indicates that the dog has a show (conformation) title and an open field champion title.

Pointing breed owners and breeders should strive to retain both form and function as they work in field trials. The dual champion title is intended to reward them for doing that, but a show title is no assurance of a field title or vice versa.

In some of the pointing breeds, any owner can get a show title on a dog, even if it is not worthy, by entering enough shows under many different judges. Eventually he can win the two majors (3-5 points) and a total of fifteen points. But, field titles must be won in an entirely different form of competition and it is not so easy. A first time show handler can in a very short time learn how to show and win a title. The first time field trialer will learn that dogs are more difficult to train and also learn that titles are more difficult to earn. It is possible for a show dog to win a champion title in three shows in one weekend under two different judges if they are all five point shows. But, to do this in the field it requires a trained dog to win stakes and some trials have the same judges for all stakes. A field champion title is seldom earned under two years of age. Most professional trainers, if not all, will start breaking derby dogs or just as they come out of derby stakes.

Some breeders want to work both in field and show, but it varies among the different pointing breeds. Brittany owners seem to have the most success in earning dual titles; however, most breed owners put a low priority on the value of shows in their program.

The American Kennel Club has no published record of Dual Champions and it requires a very close familiarization with a given breed to know how many duals it has. The only example available is Vizslas which have earned 49 dual titles in the first 20 years since accepted by AKC in 1960 and approximately 2,000 show titles. That is a significant difference and could be an indication of the difficulty in earning a field title, but data to prove that would be very difficult to document.

Work on showing dogs should begin shortly after a puppy is born in setting it up and gaiting. The field training should follow the schedule in Chapter 7, Part II.

For field trial owners, the best time to concentrate on showing is just as soon as the dog is twenty four months old and/or just out of derby stakes. It is possible to finish show titles at less than a year of age and some do. Yet, the dogs are not yet mature, but the sooner the better for work toward a dual title.

28

It is more difficut to win a show title by waiting until after winning the open field title, but some have done it. Younger dogs usually always go over the older ones and those with no muscle which are plump win over those heavily muscled. This is why it is difficult to win with a field trial dog while it is being campaigned.

TRIPLE CHAMPION

The triple champion title is for dogs having won open field, show and obedience champion titles. This title is ideal for the single dog owner. It is beyond the reach of most owners because it is difficult enough for them to earn a dual title on one or more dogs. Field and obedience champion titles should not be made easier to give more quantity. The obedience champion title is perhaps more difficult to win than a field title since it is done against all AKC breeds and the requirements are just as demanding. Many of the all breed owners are specialists in training obedience dogs. Although arguments could be presented as to which of the two is the most demanding, most dogs are not capable of winning a dual title much less a triple title because of their physical and mental makeup before being altered by environment.

Field trialing costs the most money for the same number of entries if that helps solve an argument.

The first Triple Champion in any breed was a Vizsla, Cariad's Kutya Kai Costa owned by Bob Costa, New York out of a show breeding. He was well along on the road to success when this title was established. There may be others, but the number will be low in all the

pointing breeds. It requires a special dog and a
special dog owner.

AKC field representatives attend trials to watch and to
help solve problems, offer guidance or help improve
procedures. This is Seymour Green at a Pittsburgh German
Shorthaired Pointer Trial.

HUNTING TESTS FOR POINTING BREEDS

The AKC entered in an entirely new operation in 1986 when it approved sanctioned, licensed and member Hunting Tests for Pointing Breeds. This was followed shortly thereafter with a bi-monthly newspaper type publication, *"The Hunter's Whistle."*

The idea was to provide an outlet for hunters and pointing dog owners who did not particularly like competitive activities where they could demonstrate that their dogs **could** hunt and find birds.

These tests were launched for AKC with existing field trial clubs, but it is hoped that it will encourage new clubs to form for Hunting Tests. Eventually some owners with Hunting Test titles will want to compete in the regular field trials. So far, existing field trial clubs have taken this on as an extra activity using previously prime field trial dates at the same locations they have traditionally held field trials. The net effect is that there has been a big increase in entries for Hunting Tests and an apparent drop-off in regular field trial entries.

Some field trialers are upset with the hi-level promotion of this new activity without AKC providing a publication dedicated to field trial activities, or a section in its publication *"Pure-Bred Dogs/American Kennel Gazette."* That policy alone has failed to bring in many new people to traditional field trials.

While is is true that most AKC field trial clubs favor horseback handling, it is optional. Horseback handling is beneficial for some handlers. All the new Associations require foot handling.

AKC has a special program to help educate judges for Hunting Tests. I believe that judges trained for the Shoot-To-Retrieve Association are ideally suited for this work. Any person in good standing with AKC can be approved to judge.

These tests bring in a variety of dog owners not experienced in hunting or field trialing which may cause more disgruntled people than there are with field trials. Hunting Test handlers will compare scores, and that is competition whether we like it or not.

It is set-up to be non-competitive, yet dogs are run in braces in all tests. The judges can ride horses to officiate and the marshal can also ride. This in itself tends to negate the results because few hunters ever consider hunting from horseback. This and bracing are both stress indicators which introduce factors which affect a dog's hunting ability. A gallery makes it even worse. But, as everyone will admit, all dogs have basically the same conditions to run under. Bitches in season cannot be entered or run.

Clubs must provide a Hunting Test Committee of at least five members and a Hunting Test Secretary, and must provide a premium the same as for a regular field trial.

The standard for Junior Hunter is similar to the AKC field trial Derby Standard and the Senior Hunter and Master Hunter uses the Gun Dog Standard with a few different rules.

There must be two dogs in each brace. Handlers in Junior Hunter must use a blank pistol. All shooting of game in the Senior and Master Hunter is by Official Guns with live ammunition. But, in Master Hunter the handler must aim an empty shotgun at the birds in flight. Shooting can be on course or just in a bird field. Handlers must fire a blank pistol in the absence of an official gun. The Senior Hunter must retrieve but need not be steady to wing and shot, and must honor if it encounters a dog on point. The handler can hold the dog by the collar after it has honored.

The Master Hunter must give a finished performance--positive steadiness to wing and shot, retrieve promptly, tenderly and absolutely to hand and honor without a command of any kind. A dog meeting this level should be able to win field champion titles easily if it can reach out to objectives.

Scoring for Junior Hunter is on HUNTING, BIRD FINDING ABILITY, POINTING AND TRAINABILITY. Senior Hunter and Master Hunter are rated also on RETRIEVING. SH and MH must also be given the opportunity to honor and retrieve if the scores in the other four abilities indicate a potential qualifying score.

Scoring is from 0 to 10 for all levels and dogs cannot have a score below 5 and need an average of 7 to pass. It requires four different test passing scores to earn the title JH, five for SH and six for MH to earn the suffix after the dog's name.   The SH and MH test are reduced by one for titles earned in JH and MH.

There are no placements or order of finish. Scores of the two judges can be averaged.

It should be noted that this program, as well as all others, is subject to change to improve its value to dog owners.

Anyone interested in this program can write to the American Kennel Club, 51 Madison Avenue, New York, NY 10010 and request a free copy of "Regulations For AKC Hunting Tests For Pointing Breeds" for complete information.

Chapter 3

American Kennel Club
Pointing Breed Dog Clubs

FORMING CLUBS

Any small group of dog owners of a given pointing breed accepted in the American Kennel Club registry may form a club specifically for field trials by meeting its requirements. That same club can also expand to other activities.

The American Kennel Club has a booklet "The Formation of Dog Clubs," available to dog clubs. It also furnishes a "Sample Constitution and By-Laws" and a "Guide for Field Trial Committees In Dealing With Misconduct At Field Trials & Hunting Tests."

Only **MEMBER** clubs, through the elected delegates, elects its Board of Directors and helps determine its policy.

Individuals and groups wanting information should contact the American Kennel Club, Attention: Show Plans--Field Trial Clubs.

The American Kennel Club requires clubs to actively engage in the promotion and protection of the sport specializing in, e.g. field trials. It will not help or recognize any club that conflicts with an existing club, or recognize two clubs of the same type in the same local area.

A club's approval is based on the American Kennel Club's evaluation of the membership, relative popularity of the breed and population density. In areas having low population density, members from more distant locations are acceptable, where heavily populated areas will require membership to be much closer. The most important consideration is that the members be dedicated enough to travel whatever distances are necessary to meet regularly for purposes of working to further their breed and sport. Husband and wife are considered as one member, so it is better to count addresses instead of names for a total membership number.

Rare breeds cannot normally cover entire states or regions so that others of the same breed clubs can form at some future date. Clubs in heavily populated areas may become too large and cannot function effectively, and it may be necessary to form another club from that membership.

The job of collecting names of breed owners and calling them together for the first meeting to organize usually falls on the shoulders of one or two families having considerable interest and initiative in the breed. They should use the guidelines furnished by the

American Kennel Club to complete their organization and adopt by-laws, etc. Good record keeping from a club's inception is essential for all meetings and competitive activities. There is no need to wait for approval before becoming firmly established and well organized as a club. Such clubs can hold fun field trials and training clinics as often as they can be supported effectively, or hold events under the **Minimum Requirements** of American Field or its affiliated organizations until well enough established for American Kennel Club acceptance. These activities can be used later as evidence of the club's activities and leadership. The important consideration is to select **one** central city for all meetings and activities with support from as many local and area owners as possible. Activities should be planned for the entire year. This practice is difficult to do and takes a lot of special effort by a few dedicated individuals to succeed. The most important function of any dog club is to prepare monthly newsletters. Communication is very important to success and growth.

A club name may not seem too important on the surface, but the American Kennel Club will not accept a name that does not adequately describe the localized area where the club is formed. Cities, rivers and valleys are the more common names accepted, sometimes including two or three of these. A good guide for names is to look at the pointing dog breed clubs names of those already accepted as published periodically in the *Pure-Bred Dogs/American Kennel Gazette*. It should be noted that some of the existing names would no longer be accepted for newly formed organizations and some are forced to change names after being approved and having operated for several years.

Members of new clubs trying to form under the American Kennel Club complain that it is too arbitrary and inconsistent. Rejections result from inadequate preparation, misunderstanding, or because the clubs do not always follow the guidelines that are available.

How long should a club be in operation before applying to the American Kennel Club for a sanctioned field trial? There is no set time. Applications are reviewed whenever they are received by the American Kennel Club and adequate explanation usually given to the club for rejection along with suggestions for acceptance. A club without sustained interest of its active members will probably be turned down. Clubs are expected to be perpetual.

The American Kennel Club approval of a field trial club is based on an acceptable name, constitution and by-laws, an indication it has functioned as a club for a period of time, held several "fun" field trials, has a membership list of several member addresses—twenty is enough as a rule—and a record of the club's development.

One member should be appointed by the club at its inception to compile records of all members as they join about their past dog activities and specifically those under the American Kennel Club. The club's record keeper should maintain records up to date each year on the members. Information should include name, address, date joined, other club memberships, number of dogs owned, litters bred, shows entered, obedience and field trials entered and titles earned, if any.

How many fun field trials should a club hold before applying to the American Kennel Club for the

"Application for Advancing to Hold Sanctioned Events?" The usual minimum requirement has been three fun field trials over a year or more at least six months apart. This is not to imply that a club cannot hold one more often than that. A high level of interest and activity is important.

Once a club is accepted and has become **a club of record** for sanctioned field trials, most of its problems of being recognized are over. The club must then work to prove its leadership and management capability for holding licensed trials. It is possible that a club would never be approved for licensed trials that cannot be supported by its own breed entries. This is what the American Kennel Club tries to guard against in its acceptance process. One important reason for closing a breed field trial to other breeds is to build up a strong following in the breed giving club. The American Kennel Club expects new clubs to grow in their membership and active support. Many clubs experience decreased support and interest with age and cannot support activities from within and must increasingly look to other breeds to make expenses for trials. There are already too many breed field trial clubs with this problem that do not have enough workers to effectively put on a field trial. Part of the reason is that a minority of members with the greatest influence insist on competing against **all breeds** to prove their breed "equal or better." This is not the purpose of breed field trial clubs, and there may be no real harm done if that particular club's breed wins most all the time in its own trials. Once other breeds regularly win all or most of the placements, many members will quit trying to learn or compete with the other breeds. This sport rewards **winners**, not losers

Winners want to continue, but losers quit. The trick is to make every member a winner. The club has a responsibility to do that, but few bother to make the effort.

Fortunately, there are many other rewards besides **winning,** but not all club members ever come to learn what they are and distort the sport's image. Many people do enjoy working at the various trial jobs without having to compete or win, and some never do, but continue to work for years. Breed clubs which are to continue indefinitely must have good workers to help out on field trials, and must maintain a high level of interest and activity.

Parent Clubs are national breed clubs that are **Members** of the American Kennel Club and must coordinate approval of the different field trial breed club field trials although this is their only responsibility they have to them. These parent clubs have no jurisdiction over the breed clubs with all control held by the American Kennel Club. The parent club cannot prevent a club from holding a field trial, but the coordination process can bog down making timely approval difficult.

Parent clubs provide forms to coordinate dates. The club or field trial secretary fills out the form in multiple copies and mails it to the parent club's designated person for approval. This is followed by requesting an application form from the American Kennel Club for a licensed trial which is then submitted for approval with the required fee. Once approval is received at the American Kennel Club from the Parent Club, the license is approved. The Field Trial Questionnaire forms are mailed to the secretary who provides **all** the particulars for the field trial and mails it in at least eight weeks before the trial date. The premium list can be printed for a fee by the American Kennel Club or done privately. Shortly after that the field trial secretary will receive a package which includes pamphlets, "Guide For Field Trial Committees In Dealing With Misconduct At Field Trials & Hunting Tests," "The Status of a Judge of Licensed Field Trials & Hunting Tests," judges books and a list of suspended owners. Similar material is provided for a Hunting Test secretary.

PARENT CLUBS

Of the ten recognized pointing dogs only the Wirehaired Pointing Griffons have no national organization.

1. American Brittany Club
2. English Setter Association of America
3. German Shorthaired Pointer Club of America
4. German Wirehaired Pointer Club of America
5. Gordon Setter Club of America
6. Irish Setter Club of America
7. American Pointer Club
8. Vizsla Club of America
9. Weimaraner Club of America

LOCAL CLUBS

New local pointing dog field trial clubs are forming all the time. These clubs were those recognized by the American Kennel Club through July 1985.

Brittanys

1. North Alabama Brittany Club
2. Greater Phoenix Brittany Club
3. Sahauro Brittany Club
4. California Brittany Club
5. Central California Brittany Club
6. Golden Empire Brittany Club (CA)
7. Northern California Brittany Club
8. San Diego Brittany Club
9. Sierra View Brittany Club (CA)
10. Southern San Joaquin Valley Brittany Club (CA)
11. Skyline Brittany Club (CO)
12. Southern New England Brittany Club (CT)
13. Central Florida Brittany Club
14. Central Gulf Coast Brittany Club (FL)
15. Greater Atlanta Brittany Club
16. Aloha Brittany Club (HI)
17. Eastern Idaho Brittany Club
18. Idaho Brittany Club
19. Heart Of Illinois Brittany Club
20. Illinois Brittany Club
21. LaSalle Brittany Club (IL)
22. Southern Illinois Brittany Club
23. Greater Indianapolis Brittany Club
24. Hoosier Brittany Club (IN)
25. Iowa Brittany Club
26. Midwest Brittany Club (KS)
27. Neosho Valley Brittany Club (KS)
28. Kentucky Brittany Club
29. Red River Brittany Club (LA)
30. Central Maine Brittany Club
31. Maryland Brittany Club

32. Northern Virginia Brittany Club (MD)
33. Central New England Brittany Club (MA)
34. Eastern New England Brittany Club (MA)
35. Michigan Brittany Club
36. Michigan Saginaw Valley Brittany Club
37. Western Michigan Brittany Club
38. Minnesota Brittany Club
39. Greater St. Louis Brittany Club
40. Missouri Brittany Club
41. Ozark Brittany Club (MO)
42. Missouri Valley Brittany Club (NE)
43. Nebraska Brittany Club
44. Northern Nevada Brittany Club
45. Southern Nevada Brittany Club
46. Northern New England Brittany Club (NH)
47. Del Val Brittany Club (NJ)
48. North Jersey Brittany Club
49. Central New Mexico Brittany Club
50. Southern New Mexico Brittany Club
51. Sunland Brittany Club (NM)
52. Brittany Club of Upper New York
53. Hudson Valley Brittany Club (NY)
54. Long Island Brittany Club (NY)
55. Niagara Frontier Brittany Club (NY)
56. Southeastern Brittany Club (NC)
57. Tar Heel Brittany Club (NC)
58. Buckeye Brittany Club (OH)
59. Ohio Brittany Club
60. Northern Oklahoma Brittany Club
61. Sooner Brittany Club (OK)
62. Stillwater Brittany Club (OK)
63. Oregon Brittany Club
64. Anthracite Brittany Club (PA)
65. Pennsylvania Brittany Club

66. Susquehanna Brittany Club (PA)
67. Hawkeye Brittany Club (SD)
68. Ringneck Brittany Club (SD)
69. Volunteer Brittany Club (TN)
70. Alamo Brittany Club (TX)
71. Fort Worth Brittany Club
72. Lone Star Brittany Club
73. Texas Coastal Brittany Club
74. Top O'Texas Brittany Club
75. Waco Brittany Club
76. West Texas Brittany Club
77. Wasatch Front Brittany Club (UT)
78. Rapahannock Brittany Club (VA)
79. Tidewater Brittany Club (VA)
80. Inland Empire Brittany Club (WA)
81. Washington Brittany Club
82. Whid-Isle Brittany Club (WA)
83. Badger Brittany Club (WI)
84. Greater Milwaukee Brittany Club

English Setters

1. Michigamme English Setter Club (MI)
2. Monterey Bay English Setter Club (CA)

German Shorthaired Pointers

1. Desert German Shorthaired Pointer Club (AZ)
2. Southern Arizona German Shorthaired Pointer Club
3. German Shorthaired Pointer Club Of California
4. German Shorthaired Pointer Club Of Central California

5. German Shorthaired Pointer Club Of Northern Sacramento Valley (CA)
6. German Shorthaired Pointer Club Of Orange County (CA)
7. German Shorthaired Pointer Club of Riverside County (CA)
8. German Shorthaired Pointer Club Of San Diego
9. German Shorthaired Pointer Club of Southern California
10. High Sierra German Shorthaired Pointer Club (CA)
11. San Joaquin German Shorthaired Pointer Club (CA)
12. German Shorthaired Pointer Club Of Colorado
13. Northern Colorado German Shorthaired Pointer Club
14. Nutmeg German Shorthaired Pointer Club (CT)
15. Diamond State German Shorthaired Pointer Club (DE)
16. German Shorthaired Pointer Club Of North Florida
17. German Shorthaired Pointer Club Of East Idaho
18. German Shorthaired Pointer Club Of Idaho
19. German Shorthaired Pointer Club Of Magic Valley (ID)
20. Fort Dearborn German Shorthaired Pointer Club (IL
21. Gateway German Shorthaired Pointer Club (IL)
22. German Shorthaired Pointer Club Of Illinois
23. German Shorthaired Pointer Club Of Indiana
24. German Shorthaired Pointer Club Of Central Iowa
25. German Shorthaired Pointer Club of Eastern Iowa
26. North Iowa German Shorthaired Pointer Club
27. Quad-City German Shorthaired Pointer Club (IA)
28. Heart of America German Shorthaired Pointer Club (KS)
29. Sunflower German Shorthaired Pointer Club (KS)
30. German Shorthaired Pointer Club Of New Orleans
31. Mason-Dixon German Shorthaired Pointer Club (MD)
32. Mayflower German Shorthaired Pointer Club (MA)

33. German Shorthaired Pointer Club Of Michigan
34. Lansing German Shorthaired Pointer Club (MI)
35. Saginaw Valley German Shorthaired Pointer Club (MI)
36. German Shorthaired Pointer Club Of Minnesota
37. Heart Of America German Shorthaired Pointer Club (MO)
38. German Shorthaired Pointer Club Of Lincoln (NE)
39. German Shorthaired Pointer Club Of Nebraska
40. German Shorthaired Pointer Club Of Reno
41. Easter German Shorthaired Pointer Club (NJ)
42. German Shorthaired Pointer Club Of Las Cruces (NM)
43. Yucca German Shorthaired Pointer Club (NM)
44. Finger Lakes German Shorthaired Pointer Club (NY)
45. German Shorthaired Pointer Club Of Western New York
46. Hudson Valley German Shorthaired Pointer Club (NY)
47. Long Island German Shorthaired Pointer Club (NY)
48. Buckeye German Shorthaired Pointer Club (OH)
49. German Shorthaired Pointer Club Of Ohio
50. German Shorthaired Pointer Club Of Oregon
51. Willamette German Shorthaired Pointer Club (OR)
52. German Shorthaired Pointer Club Of Greater Pittsburgh
53. Schuykill Valley German Shorthaired Pointer Club (PA)
54. Ringneck German Shorthaired Pointer Club (SD)
55. El Paso Del Norte German Shorhaired Pointer Club (TX)
56. German Shorthaired Pointer Club Of San Antonio
57. Gulf Coast German Shorthaired Pointer Club (TX)
58. Lonestar German Shorthaired Pointer Club
59. German Shorthaired Pointer Club Of Utah
60. Four Lakes German Shorhaired Pointer Club (WI)

61. Fox Valley German Shorthaired Pointer Club
62. German Shorthaired Pointer Club Of Wisconsin
63. Southeastern Wisconsin German Shorthaired Pointer Club

German Wirehaired Pointers

1. Delaware Valley German Wirehaired Pointer Club (NJ)
2. Fort Detroit German Wirehaired Pointer Club (MI)
3. German Wirehaired Pointer Club Of Central Iowa
4. German Wirehaired Pointer Club Of Eastern Nebraska
5. German Wirehaired Pointer Club Of Illinois
6. German Wirehaired Pointer Club Of Northern California
7. German Wirehaired Pointer Club Of Southern California
8. German Wirehaired Pointer Club Of Wisconsin
9. Seattle Tacoma German Wirehaired Pointer Club (WA)

Gordon Setters

1. Gordon Setter Club Of Hawaii
2. Paumanauk Gordon Setter Club (NY)
3. Tartan Gordon Setter Club (CT)

Irish Setters

1. Irish Setter Club Of Arizona
2. Irish Setter Club Of Central California
3. Irish Setter Club Of Sacramento

46

4. Irish Setter Club Of The Pacific (CA)
5. Irish Setter Club Of Colorado
6. Irish Setter Club Of Central Connecticut
7. Western Irish Setter Club (IL)
8. Potomac Irish Setter Club (MD)
9. Irish Setter Club Of New England (MA)
10. Irish Setter Club Of Michigan
11. Irish Setter Club of Greater Kansas City (MO)
12. Irish Setter Club Of Greater St. Louis
13. Eastern Irish Setter Association (NJ)
14. Irish Setter Club Of Ohio
15. Multnomah Irish Setter Association (OR)
16. Irish Setter Club Of Houston
17. Irish Setter Club Of San Antonio
18. Irish Setter Club Of Milwaukee

Pointers

1. East Seattle Pointer Club (WA)

Vizslas

1. Rio Salado Vizsla Club (AZ)
2. Central California Vizsla Club
3. South Coast Vizsla Club (CA)
4. Vizsla Club Of Northern California
5. Vizsla Club Of Southern California
6. Connecticut Valley Vizsla Club
7. Vizsla Club Of Illinois
8. Hawkeye Vizsla Club (IA)
9. Vizsla Club Of Eastern Iowa
10. Boothill Vizsla Club Of Kansas

11. Conestoga Vizsla Club (MD)
12. Vizsla Club Of Central New England (MA)
13. Vizsla Club of Michigan
14. Twin Cities Vizsla Club (MN)
15. Nebraska Vizsla Club
16. Vizsla Club Of Northern New Jersey
17. Vizsla Club Of Greater New York
18. Miami Valley Vizsla Club (OH)
19. Vizsla Club Of Greater Cleveland (OH)
20. Vizsla Club Of Utah

Weimaraners

1. Valley Of The Sun Weimaraner Club (AZ)
2. Orange Coast Weimaraner Club (CA)
3. Sacramento Valley Weimaraner Club
4. Southland Weimaraner Club (CA)
5. Weimaraner Club of San Diego
6. Mile High Weimaraner Club (CO)
7. Weimaraner Club Of The Washington D.C. Area
8. Weimaraner Club Of Northern Illinois
9. Weimaraner Club Of Greater Louisville
10. Yankee Weimaraner Club (MA)
11. Weimaraner Club Of Greater Detroit
12. North Star Weimaraner Club (MN)
13. Weimaraner Club Of Greater St. Louis
14. Garden State Weimaraner Club (NJ)
15. Weimaraner Club Of Albuquerque
16. Hudson Valley Weimaraner Club (NY)
17. Long Island Weimaraner Club
18. Cincinnati Weimaraner Club
19. Weimaraner Club Of Columbus
20. Weimaraner Club Of Greater Cleveland

21. Willamette Weimaraner Club (OR)
22. Delaware Valley Weimaraner Club (PA)
23. Weimaraner Association Of Greater Pittsburgh
24. North Texas Weimaraner Club
25. San Antonio Weimaraner Club
26. Western Washington Weimaraner Club
27. Wisconsin Weimaraner Club

Miami Valley Vizsla Club

A.K.C. LICENSED

INDIAN CREEK WILDLIFE AREA, FAYETTEVILLE, OHIO, ONE-HALF MILE SOUTH OF FAYETTEVILLE ON ROUTE 68, AND EAST ON CAMPBELL ROAD ONE AND ONE-HALF MILES

APRIL 8-9, 1989

OPEN GUN DOG AND OPEN LIMITED GUN DOG OPEN TO ALL A.K.C. REGISTRABLE
POINTING BREEDS
OPEN PUPPY, OPEN DERBY, AMATEUR GUN DOG, AND AMATEUR LIMITED GUN DOG
OPEN TO VIZSLAS ONLY
BITCHES IN SEASON MAY COMPETE IN THE AMATEUR LIMITED GUN DOG, OPEN PUPPY,
OPEN GUN DOG AND OPEN LIMITED GUN DOG STAKES

This Field Trial is held under Rules and Procedures of the
AMERICAN KENNEL CLUB

MAIL ADVANCE ENTRIES WITH CHECKS TO: BERNARD C. BOGGS, FIELD TRIAL SECRETARY,
51 CHERRY DRIVE, SPRINGFIELD, OHIO 45506
PHONE 513-325-2095

ENTRIES WILL CLOSE AT 7:00 P. M. (LOCAL E.S.T.), TUESDAY, APRIL 4, 1989, WITH THE
FIELD TRIAL SECRETARY AT 51 CHERRY DRIVE, SPRINGFIELD, OHIO 45506

Drawing Will Take Place At 7:00 P. M. (Local E.S.T.), Tuesday, April 4, 1989,
At 51 Cherry Drive, Springfield, Ohio 45506

JUDGES AND STAKES TO BE JUDGED
John W. Hoover, 3727 Route 757, Felicity, Ohio 45120, Amateur Limited Gun Dog,
Open Gun Dog, and Open Limited Gun Dog
William J. Kuehnhold, 3178 Mt. Olive-Pt. Isabel Road, Bethel, Ohio 45106, Amateur Gun Dog,
Open Gun Dog, Open Derby, and Open Limited Gun Dog
Deborah Fridlund, 717 North Riley, Indianapolis, Indiana 46201, Amateur Gun Dog, Open Puppy,
and Amateur Limited Gun Dog
John Ingram, 207 Boy Scout Road, Ray, Ohio 45672, Open Puppy and Open Derby

FIELD TRIAL MARSHALS
Holly Hanna   Martha Lipscomb

David Kayser

OFFICIAL GUNS
Thorny Lipscomb   Jerry Campbell
Jim Ervin   John Ingram

STAKES, SCHEDULE AND ENTRY FEES

Amateur Gun Dog	7:00 A. M., Saturday, April 8, 1989	$28.00
Open Puppy	To Follow Amateur Gun Dog	$18.00
Amateur Limited Gun Dog	To Follow Open Puppy	$28.00
Open Gun Dog	To Follow Amateur Limited Gun Dog	$26.00
Open Derby	To Follow Open Gun Dog	$22.00
Open Limited Gun Dog	To Follow Open Derby	$26.00

Dogs which first qualify at this trial will not be permitted to enter the Limited Stakes.

THE FIELD TRIAL COMMMITTEE reserves the option to rearrange the running order of the stakes should conditions warrant.

★ ★ ★

COURSES AND BIRDS

OPEN GUN DOG AND OPEN PUPPY—SINGLE COURSE WITHOUT A BIRD FIELD
ALL OTHER STAKES—SINGLE COURSE WITH BIRD FIELD
QUAIL, CHUKARS AND/OR PHEASANTS WILL BE USED IN ALL STAKES
A BLANK CARTRIDGE WILL NOT BE FIRED IN THE PUPPY STAKE
SHOTGUNS WITH BLANK SHELLS PERMITTED
AMATEUR GUN DOG AND AMATEUR LIMITED GUN DOG ARE RETRIEVING STAKES
HORSEBACK HANDLING WILL BE PERMITTED ONLY IN THE AMATEUR GUN DOG, AMATEUR
LIMITED GUN DOG, OPEN GUN DOG, AND OPEN LIMITED GUN DOG STAKES
HANDLERS' HORSES WILL BE AVAILABLE FOR RENT BY THE BRACE

★ ★ ★

PRIZES

STANDARD A.K.C. ROSETTES TO ALL PLACED DOGS
TROPHIES TO ALL FIRST PLACE DOGS

★ ★ ★

OFFICERS

Wayne Leis, President, 3072 East Pitchin Road, Springfield, Ohio 45502
David Kayser, Vice-President, 616 Mercury Drive, Cincinnati, Ohio 45244
Clara Kayser, Secretary, 616 Mercury Drive, Cincinnati, Ohio 45244
Bernard C. Boggs, Treasurer, 51 Cherry Drive, Springfield, Ohio 45506

★ ★ ★

FIELD TRIAL COMMITTEE

David Kayser, Chairman, 616 Mercury Drive, Springfield, Ohio 45244

Wayne Leis	Patty Leis
Larry Hanna	Holly Hanna
Don Keeton	Denny Keeton
Ed Schaefer	Margaret Schaefer
Carol Feder	Paul Rothan
Diane Shell	Clara Kayser

OFFICIAL AMERICAN KENNEL CLUB ENTRY FORM

Note: This Entry Form Must Be Completed in Full

FOR FIELD TRIALS/HUNTING TESTS

Miami Valley Vizsla Club

INDIAN CREEK WILDLIFE AREA, FAYETTEVILLE, OHIO, ONE-HALF MILE SOUTH OF FAYETTEVILLE ON ROUTE 68, AND EAST ON CAMPBELL ROAD ONE AND ONE-HALF MILES

APRIL 8-9, 1989

I SUBMIT $_____ for entry fees.

Enter in Stake/Test (Use a separate form for each stake/test.)

NAME OF DOG (Print)	CALL NAME	
A.K.C. Reg. Number	**Or** A.K.C. Litter Number (If Dog Not Reg.)	
Or Foreign Reg. Number	**And** Country of Registry	
Breed	MALE ☐ FEMALE ☐	Date of Birth
Sire		
Dam		
Breeder		
Name of Actual Owner (Print)		
Owner's Address Street		
City	State	Zip Code
Name of Handler (Print)		

FOR RETRIEVER TRIALS ONLY: THIS IS TO CERTIFY THAT		
THIS DOG IS ☐	IS NOT ☐	QUALIFIED FOR A LIMITED ALL-AGE STAKE
THIS DOG IS ☐	IS NOT ☐	QUALIFIED FOR A SPECIAL ALL-AGE STAKE

I CERTIFY that I am the actual owner of this dog, or that I am the duly authorized agent of the actual owner whose name I have entered above. In consideration of the acceptance of this entry, I agree to abide by all the rules of The American Kennel Club and the Standard Procedures governing this Field Trial and any decisions made in accord with them, and I further agree that the dog is entered in and will be at this trial at my own risk and that I will hold the trial giving club, its members and agents free from liability for any claims arising out of the entry of the dog or its presence at the trial.

SIGNATURE of Owner or His Agent Duly Authorized to Make This Entry _____

Address of Agent (If Any Signs Above Line for Owner)

Street _____ **Phone No.** _____

City _____ **State** _____ **Zip** _____

52

Chapter 4

Analysis of American Kennel Club Performance Standards

GENERAL DISCUSSION

The present Performance Standards should be supported by better rules with definite, precise meanings for pointing dog breeds, to improve training and handling dogs and judging field trials the same as any other sport. It would be the responsibility of the judges to understand and enforce them, and this would help eliminate or minimize loose application or interpretation. Present rules are inadequate, and more uniformity is needed for fairness to dogs and handlers.

The spotting system of judging is used to select the best dog in the stake considering all positive and negative performance factors related to the standard.

Judging will always be more negative than positive, and there is nothing evil about it. Every rule is made for fairness, but some work that dogs do should give them less of an edge toward winning just as some things they do should give them a better edge to win. Some of the rules should be so specific that failure to comply would result in dogs either not being placed or ordered up for infractions related to interference.

Almost every sentence in the field trial rules by the American Kennel Club involves usage of verbs such as "must" and "shall" in second and third person which imply a command—no other choice. The word **shall** should be eliminated except that shall is less strong and gives some leeway. Because of this, trainers, handlers and judges should understand the exact meaning of the words used in each rule.

Some handlers and judges like to understand and visualize a broad or narrow meaning and application of a standard provision. Others consider dog owners and trainers who have a narrow view as being pedant. The narrow view is exactly what I am against, but I believe in the value of rules developed from standards for the sport. **There can be no sport without rules and officials to enforce them.** Most handlers and judges are inconsistent in this department, and are loose in setting down exact values to some of their observations when being much more fixed in others.

I will try, in my own way, to break down the Standards and Procedures in the American Kennel Club pointing dog rule book and explain each one from my own experience and the association with many other trainers and handlers who are also the judges. By so doing, my own powers of understanding can be improved upon, and others might benefit as well. Under no condition do I

54

claim to be the authority. Other people will have differing interpretations and opinions.

We must first understand what a "standard of performance" is, and then learn ways to measure it. Within a standard there is a wide range of performances possible from failure to the best in excellence. A standard is **only** a guide.

As an analogy to a dog's performance evaluation, let us consider a standard which applies to a foot race. A distance and a line of travel are set with a start and finish line visibly marked. Individually, each contestant is judged. "How is he judged?" Against a stop watch which may not be as accurate as needed to separate winners? Maybe we need three judges so that individual reactions can be averaged, or we could make the mechanics of measurement entirely electronic. The rules have defined the conditions for the contest. The standard states that any contestant failing to cross the finish line in ten seconds has failed. The only winner is that one with the fastest time. All others, with ten seconds or less time, know they did well enough to continue in training for future competition. Not too unlike field trials except that those who do not make it across the "finish" line in field trials may be worthy of further training. We could further complicate this standard if we choose.

This happens when evaluating dogs using a standard of performance which also includes intangible, subjective levels and values. Each person sees these values differently. Specific rules for standards could improve interpretation and judging.

PUPPY STAKES

"Puppies must show desire to hunt, boldness, and initiative in covering ground and in searching likely cover." (Ages 6-15 months.)

Consider first a six month old puppy. What he demonstrates is a product of his training or experience up to that age. He must be trained--by prior exposure to like conditions--in the sense that he has been out in the field and shown how much fun he can have using his natural instincts. His nose has sampled many different odors and has experienced some form of pleasure, if unrestrained, with each one. But he can be helped in enjoying the smells in the field most of all. He learns to identify and like a particular odor associated with a bird. He likes it, instinctively, or is encouraged to like it, and now he knows this place with the lovely smell can be found again. The puppy then hunts **(desire to hunt)** for it. He is oblivious to anything else **(boldness)**. In addition he remembers **(intelligence)** where he found the bird scent. He looks out and sees what to him is that place **(searching likely cover)** and goes quickly to it demonstrating he is learning to use natural intelligence.

"They should indicate the presence of game if the opportunity is presented."

Now if a puppy cannot identify the smell, he may just decide to check it out anyway out of curiosity. Often he will seem to ignore it simply because he does not know its meaning. If he is taught the scent-bird meaning he will most likely indicate its presence in a positive manner, and thereby satisfy this portion of the performance standard. If the puppy has never been

56

taken out, he will most likely do nothing except seek the security that being near the owner or handler means. Or, he might like to follow his brace mate around as it hunts, out of curiosity and the desire to play.

"Puppies should show reasonable obedience to their handler's command. . ."

He should want to stay out in front of his handler without being commanded to do so, but should show some sign of minding when told to leave his brace mate alone. His handler should be able to exercise some obedience with commands such as "NO" and "COME." A "WHOA" command should cause him a moment of indecision. Except for these two commands it is questionable why this standard is included since it is identical to the derby requirement.

In recognizing that a six month old dog is qualified to enter derby and gun dog stakes does not seem to justify its inclusion here. This could cause novice trainers early problems in the pup's training. A most important concern is that a puppy should always be happy in what he is doing. If he does not have this characteristic all other standards are not going to better his potential for field trial work and essentially the trainer has failed before he got started. Most all problems with dogs are caused in their first two years which is also the time they should be learning the fundamentals.

". . . but should not be given additional credit for pointing staunchly." (Stopping.)

Which means that the judge **can** and usually will give additional credit. Now the standard says nothing about the puppy chasing game, but it is a known beneficial requirement in building desire. It should start in the puppy stage and continue through derby age. This standard will usually put the beginning field trialer at a disadvantage.

"Each dog shall be judged on its actual performance as indicating its future as a high class Derby dog."

This also puts the beginner at a disadvantage for the literal meaning is "all-age." So, if a puppy does not drive out front and stay there searching diligently and intelligently at a fast pace, he is a "loser." Such a standard encourages judges to fault the puppy doing the better job at thirty to one hundred fifty yards. The only actual difference then between puppy and derby performance is staunchness on point. The standards should not intend this to be the primary difference between the two stakes.

The remaining puppy standard requires no further discussion.

DERBY STAKES

"Derbies must show a keen desire to hunt, be bold and independent, have a fast, yet attractive, style of running, and show not only intelligence in seeking objectives but also the ability to find game." (Ages 6-24 months.)

All that has been written about the puppy's early exposure to field conditions also applies here. Additional experience in creating intelligence and desire is based on having more bird contact under actual field conditions and better obedience to the handler learned under controlled conditions when using planted birds. Each time the derby dog points he **must** be prevented from catching the bird, as with puppy, yet allowed to and encouraged to chase. He should be praised at the spot the bird was pointed upon his return. This experience will generally give the desire, boldness, independence and obedience required. Sometimes a dog must be jealous of another dog to inspire the fast searching, but selective breeding of top field trial dogs may be the best method of getting a fast style of running. Whether it is attractive or not is a subjective opinion. Independence should be demonstrated with the brace mate although not to the extent it is in gun dog stakes.

The process of searching in front to objectives is improved by putting birds there initially and is then crystallized when wild birds also are found at the same objectives. Finding game is a must for the derby dog in field trials. The dog must point and the handler must inform the judges that his dog has a point by calling point or raising an arm or hat.

A derby's entire future is dependent upon early development and capability. His nose is one key. Speed of search, quality and speed with which he discriminates scent and sifts out the various scents are all important in derby dogs. If he always runs like the wind and never finds game he is a failure--perhaps he has been pushed too much toward running and not allowed time on his own to recognize weak scents that are so important in his natural development. If he finds game at the expense of running, then he is an apparent failure only as a derby **all-age** dog. Since some dogs in every breed are slow to mature it is not unusual for one to be pushed too soon in attempting to achieve certain desired or prescribed levels of performance. This can ruin some dogs at an early stage of development. So the standard cannot prescribe solutions for these problems.

A high class derby performance that fits the standard prescribed in the first sentence is perfection personified. Few dogs are ever capable of this level of performance, and, if so, they seldom repeat it. But, the owners will remember it for a lifetime and the remembrance will stimulate them to always strive for a repeat with each new derby dog.

"Derbies must point but no additional credit shall be given for steadiness to wing and shot."

This part of the standard tells us what? What is a point? When is a point more than a flash and bump. A staunch point (stopped dog) is probably defined as one in which the handler can trust his dog to remain on point when the bird stays or until the handler flushes it. But the standard does not require this. Therefore, both **"steadiness to wing and shot"** is a logical extension of the staunch characteristic of a point. There are no problems here, although some judges ignore this part of the standard and will award a higher placement to a derby dog steady to wing and shot. This could be wrong according to the standard although it would be correct to give greater credit to the intensely staunch dog with all other areas of performance equal.

A derby dog which is steady to wing and shot violates the permissiveness for chasing.

"Should birds be flushed after a point by handler or dog within reasonable gun range from the handler, a shot must be fired. A lack of opportunity for firing over a derby dog on point shall not constitute reason for non-placement when it has had game contact in acceptable derby manner."

This stresses the importance for a judge to observe the derby being shot over as opposed to puppy which is optional. It further establishes that a derby dog need not stay on point after showing that he has established point. Because of this, it behooves some handlers to observe the practice of not shooting over a puppy indiscriminately. Exposure to firing at the wrong time, under the wrong conditions with a sensitive puppy/derby aged dog can create a serious obstacle to its future training and competition in field trials.

Some handlers, for whatever reason, allow, some insist, that their derby dog back its brace mate. A dog on a backing situation can easily move in too close to the other handler who may have a habit of kicking up a bird when holding his blank pistol down and behind his back to fire. He can shoot a backing dog in the face which is called "smoking a dog." Some dogs will not accept this "punishment" and they can only react to the gun unfavorably in the future. No back is required for puppy/derby age dogs and it would be better for the handler, if possible, to go to his dog and hold him by the collar when the other handler works his bird. This is permissible for all derby pointing breeds. It is very important for trainers to know their derby dogs and to advance them properly as individuals. A derby dog, not shot over, otherwise under consideration may be called back and put on a bird for a shot.

"Derbies must show reasonable obedience to their handlers commands."

This again signifies that a derby should chase its bird, but the handler must be able to bring it back into the area of the find and onto the course in an acceptable time and effort. It means that the handler must prevent his dog from bothering or interfering with its brace mate by command when necessary. No judge is interested in seeing a derby so obedient and subservient to its handler that it overshadows his natural inherited capabilities or potential. To put it a different way, a derby should be on the edge of being **out of control.** That represents an all-age type standard which is what most judges seem to require in derby although the standard does not state this. A derby should whoa on command but not necessarily stay long after the command. It is probably preferred that the handler should have some difficulty in stopping his derby from hunting when time is called. Reasonable? That word leaves a lot to the imagination here.

"Each dog is to be judged on its actual performance as indicating its future promise."

This may imply that it is better for the judge not to see the same derby dog run more than once. It is a human trait to compare the same dog's performance at one trial to the next or he might overhear others tell how great one is before he judges. It can also be construed as meaning an "all-age" run. What is intended is that a judge only consider what he sees during that heat and only use that in judging its **"future promise "** as a field trial or hunting dog. This is a difficult requirement for any person to undertake as a judge to predict **"future promise".**

When judging there is a strong tendency for me to look for that all-age run and a strong chase after the flush. Both of these preferences could cause one to overlook a better derby performance in the stake, which can make judging more difficult when judging with a person having an opposing viewpoint. Each judge has preferences in different ways--some are stronger than

62

others regardless of their experience.

Some dogs are perfectly capable of accepting the sound of a gun at any age, depending on their temperament, environment and introduction. Others are not. This brings us to the added optional condition of derby retrieving stakes.

"Retrieving is required in all Retrieving Stakes and counts as an important part of a dog's performance. After the shot, the handler shall not command or signal the dog to retrieve until the dog's steadiness to wing and shot has been positively demonstrated. The dog must retrieve promptly and tenderly to hand."

Most dog clubs do not believe in retrieving derby stakes so it is not of great concern. If the flushing and shooting go wrong an undesirable and harmful experience happens to the dog.

This requirement serves to encourage owners to break their dogs to wing, shot and retrieve before two years of age which is much too soon for best long term results.

The conditional proviso for derby is that he does not have to give a finished retrieve, but the one which does will most likely receive additional credit. The prompt retrieve is expected, but the application of this is loose whenever the dog finds the bird whether it is marked or not. The word "prompt" will be covered in more detail under gun dog standards.

Many derby dogs will retrieve better before they are broke. The drawback is not the retrieve, but the potential for a bad experience where the handler is not able to control his dog, the brace mate or over-eager gunners. If a dog is taught to chase, he will, but he often jumps off the ground trying to catch a bird.

Gunners normally do not expect this and do not make a mental note of it unless it is drilled into them. A dog which is not too staunch can develop a bad habit in these stakes which can be difficult to correct.

Experienced field trialers learn the patience necessary to wait for a top performing dog to mature which is always beyond the derby age of two years. Those first learning are the ones most apt to accelerate training and over-exposure to field trial conditions and stress to the dog's detriment. Retrieving derby stakes offer no advantage to its long term training and development.

GUN DOG STAKES

"A Gun Dog must give a finished performance and must always be under its handler's control."

What is a finished performance? Many experienced trainers must think about it. Should it be error free? We could say that a dog that puts it all together with perfect control and whose manners on game, before and after shot, are above reproach with a positive mark on killed game with a fast retrieve to hand fits this standard to a tee. "Must" means that this is the way it is, judges are **commanded** to be satisfied that they saw a **finished** performance. Any judging that strict cannot be positive. There are no perfect dog performances for we can always see something that could have been better. Not every conceivable circumstance which might involve a test of a dog's training and experience can occur in such a limited time. If that happened, it is possible that a miracle would be the only way that a dog could give a finished performance.

64

There are both handlers and judges who seem to forget that a dog is not a machine.

There are handlers who honestly believe that the judging of an amateur stake should be more lenient than the judging of an open stake. Sometimes there are no professionals entered which allows both stakes in effect to be amateur. The standard makes absolutely **no** distinction except that an open stake is for both amateurs and professionals. There are some who believe that open judging should be more lenient to favor the professional who cannot devote as much training time to each individual dog in his string.

The standard states that the dog must be under **its handler's control at all times.** This makes no exception for one dog handling to the wrong handler or whistle. Oftentimes both handlers have voices that sound the same or both dogs are in the mood to handle to the same voice or whistle. Surely if that dog handled properly, he would be able to discriminate between the two handlers, but for some reason does not. Is the dog or handler to be faulted? It is better for the judges to ignore it, but one handler is usually upset with the other when it does happen.

Neither should the dog be handled by the gallery or scouts though it is done at times and is unchallenged by the judges. For instance, if the dog needed scouting but was not found on point, that dog's handler should be able to bring him around. The scout was sent out for no good reason. He should just report where the dog is at the time and what he is doing. Unnecessary scouting may indicate the dog is out of control. When the brace enters the bird field the handlers should be able to keep their dogs away from the parking lot and gallery and continue hunting.

"It must handle kindly, with a minimum of noise and hacking by the handler."

The problem is simply keeping the dog to the front and not too wide. If the dog is accustomed to working the wind, a cast-off downwind could result in the dog going behind. Unfortunately, this is one reason that field trial dogs get bad mouthed because they must be trained to handle first and use the wind second in many situations. A dog which is behind the judges and gallery all the time gives everyone a stiff neck. Field trial dogs are trained to ignore the wind at their backs when staying in front of the handler, judges and gallery. This will put fast running dogs in inadvertent flushes which can cause their elimination from the stake by some judges. A dog properly introduced and brought along at field trialing should be capable of working without hacking by his handler, but it is the vogue, and unfortunately will most likely continue in the walking Hunting Test stakes too. Such handling should be penalized even to the extent that the handler's dog is disqualified. Harsh judgment, but it is becoming more and more a necessity if field trial dogs are to remain viable hunting dogs. Nothing can be more aggravating or frustrating than one handler's hacking to the handler in a brace who does not engage in this practice. Some handlers drive their dogs around the course and are rewarded with wins or placements.

". . . A Gun Dog must show a keen desire to hunt, must have a bold and attractive style of running, and must demonstrate not only intelligence in quartering and seeking objectives but the ability to find game."

This statement is almost verbatim for part of the derby standard except that it does not require individual boldness (except in running) and independence. A gun dog should show independence to his handler and brace mate. Who wants a follower or a leader type brace heat? Does this then leave room for handling wherein the dog is directed to objectives by his handler?

". . . The dog must hunt for its handler at all times at a range suitable for a handler on foot, and should show or check in front of its handler frequently."

Maybe we could take this to mean that a handler should require his dog to hunt for him by voice, whistle, or hand signals, or by using all three, without it being defined as hacking. Then it becomes a challenge to define hacking. Many dogs **look** back to the handler without stopping and judges assume that the dog is looking for instructions. Many dogs will conduct their search activities without uncovering anything of interest and automatically hesitate, look back, then go the next objective. Is this not what this part of the standard requires? The tendency for this behavior does not indicate a lack of boldness, nor does it necessarily appear that the dog hunts in spurts. Sometimes a dog runs with such boldness and determination in wet cover that he atomizes the moisture causing his trail to appear foggy or smoky. This is much more than the standard requires even if he at times hesitates, stands up in cover, checks to his handler and takes a new direction.

The range of a gun dog is most controversial. Considering the maximum effective range of a shotgun is less than sixty yards, but mostly twenty five to forty yards, it might seem that a dog should be within this range, and learn, or be trained, to hold birds on point for long periods of time for the handler. A dog which

67

works a bird for a long distance before pointing is expected to hold it there until the handler arrives.

The requirement for showing or checking in front frequently could mean once or twice on a twenty two minute back course or once every five minutes, yet a dog can be disqualified if he is out of sight more than one-sixth of the time, or five minutes in a thirty minute stake unless found on point, for example. When does a judge arrive at the decision that **now** is the time to start timing a dog's absence? When should he permit a dog to be scouted in a gun dog stake? It is possible that a dog can be within a hundred yards or less during the entire heat yet not be seen in heavy cover. He could even be on point and the judges and gallery pass by at close range and find him there still on point in the next brace.

"It must cover adequate ground but never range out of sight for a length of time that would detract from its usefulness as a practical hunting dog."

It would be easier to judge this stake if this sentence did not appear. This inasmuch allows a judge wide latitude. It is also a hedge which favors a wide ranging dog in a gun dog stake. This means that one owner is forced to tolerate a wide range in his opinion of what is useful and practical. Covering adequate ground could be construed as a straight line with the dog following the horse tracks (to the bird field). Such a performance by any dog in a stake should be cause for disqualification. Efficiency should be the catch word here. Does it go to all objectives or just the ones its brace mate misses? Does it rework the same ground or fence line? Dogs which yo-yo or run a long way out and come straight back in are performing

68

poorly and these are serious faults.

**"The dog must locate game, must point staunchly, and must
be steady to wing and shot."**

Note that game is all inclusive which means it could
be a skunk, but not necessarily a bird, and when he
points, is staunch, and steady to "flush" of the game
and shot, he should be properly credited. Dogs have
pointed ducks out in a lake where the handler could not
get to them. However, there are those among us who
judge and will only give credit to points on the basic
game birds used in field trials. Some contend that a
pigeon is not a game bird. This is a tragedy, when
some clubs use pigeons in puppy stakes and these birds
are pointed later in gun dog stakes with dogs not
getting credit. Some judges will not give credit, but
will mark a dog down if he handles furred game
improperly. Some judges will wrongly allow a dog a
short run on deer without faulting it.

Pointing staunchly is a loosely define phrase in its
application. The setting of game would be a better
one. It should mean a dog with every muscle tensed in
his body and immobile as if hypnotized. But for some
people it is a loose, soft, stop near a bird. Some
breeds of dogs point such that it is impossible to
tell. Is the bird there? If not, the point is
meaningless. The dog **must** know. Does it describe a
dog with his tail wiggling to signal something
interesting is closeby or is it pointing a bird with
man scent on it? We can assume that if a dog stops,
has a minimum of body motion without moving from its
place, and stays until the handler flushes a bird that
this is a staunch point. But, a dog can have a solid
intense point and still move in on a bird until he pins
(sets) it or moves when pointing a moving bird. Dogs

69

should relocate automatically when a bird moves off from its point. Many field trial dogs are not allowed to develop this talent and are consequently charged with many non-productives.

". . . Intelligent use of wind and terrain in locating game, accurate nose, and style and intensity on point, are essential."

This means that these qualities are fundamentally inherent in a pointing dog and that if the dog does not make correct use of the wind and terrain, he will miss much of the game or find none. But once his super sensitive sensor locates game, he must know what the bird is doing and handle the situation properly. When style and intensity on point are not always amenable to being essential, they must exist to qualify the dog as a pointing dog. We may not all agree that these things must be present to have a good one. Dogs can use the wind correctly and waste time where birds are unlikely to be found, or point at an extreme distance and the bird does not even know a dog is in the vicinity. This does not represent a **finished performance.**

A good field trial dog is expected to hit heavy cover boldly and sparse cover like a streak of lightning. If the terrain is completely flat with weed or stubble fields, there can be little **intelligence** used except to keep to the front and quarter.

It is much easier for us to be satisfied that a dog is using **intelligence** in covering the terrain, when checking properly to the handler, when it is not flat but with copses, fence lines, tree lines and brier patches at different intervals. What about the combination? Should a dog waste time in the open field or cast on to the objectives? In a sea of sage brush which one should he go to for game? If he uses his

intelligence according to the standard he should know when the birds are in heavy cover, feeding in corn fields or lounging around in the cover that borders the fields sunning themselves. Ridiculous? Maybe, but we can find dog owners who claim to have owned dogs that smart.

Experienced dogs automatically adapt their range based on the terrain, wind and scenting conditions as they search for game. If they overrun, or inadvertently flush a bird, they will become more cautious and run less swiftly to adapt to the conditions which is a mark of intelligence.

Accurate nose can mean many things, but first and most important is that when he points, the bird should be so accurately located that it is a simple task for the handler to find and flush. An accurate nose does not prevent a dog from running over birds and not smelling them or causing them to flush. Dogs cannot control the weather conditions and vagaries of scenting.

Intensity on point is important. We like to believe that our dog has forced a bird to a distant eyeball to eyeball confrontation with the bird immobile for fear of being caught and the dog staying put for fear any movement will cause the bird to fly. A charge of dynamite set off nearby would not cause the dog to bat an eye. Yet, many dogs fail to keep their tails still or in the wrong position and are severely penalized. They are faulted for turning their heads or for relocating without being ordered to move on. A dog with the **intensity** required must believe he is seeing the bird in heavy cover and refuses to move to prevent flushing. Softening on point is evidence of a training syndrome, and should be penalized, but not ordered up.

All-AGE STAKES

"An All-Age Dog must give a finished performance and be under reasonable control of its handler."

There is a true story of a pointer being cast off in a field trial and found a week later nearly one hundred miles in a line to the front of his cast off. This is too much range for an all-age dog and neither the handler or judge can tell if he can give a **finished performance** or that he was even hunting. Not many all-age dogs have an extended range problem even though they consistently become lost from the handler and field trial party. Dogs like these are out of control and must not be placed. A dog can be out of sight for a time, but if the judge asks that the dog be shown to the front, the handler is expected to bring his dog in before grace time expires and there is a tendency to be more lenient in all-age stakes as opposed to gun dog stakes although the standard does not make this provision. Also, a handler should be able to keep his dog to the front and negotiate all turns on the course. When found on point the dog should be as mannerly as a gun dog with or without a backing dog present.

There is somewhat of a paradox in all-age judging, for if the dog is out of sight the judge cannot judge what he cannot see, and if the dog finds too much game, then he is not showing the judges an all-age run.

A finished performance in itself is paradoxial. Both judges base their opinions and decisions on dogs for placement which they have seen for just a few minutes of the heat. A dog when out of sight can make many

72

mistakes, and nobody is the wiser unless "official" watchers are staked out which is not permitted although it used to be for bird fields.

An all-age dog must by the nature of his range remain on point until found. If the handler calls his dog he should remain on point, but some will leave and come to the handler and go back and point again, or bark and return. It happens sometimes that the time needed to find a dog on point may exceed the limits of the brace time and grace period. Scouting then is all important in all-age stakes. An all-age dog that handles and does not show will likely be on point somewhere. The problem is to find him. Before the grace period is over, the handler should call point which means that if he is not found on point, he is out of the stake. It then behooves the judge, handler and scout to find him before the stake time and grace period have expired. But, until a handler makes that decision the judge should not ride off course looking for a dog. If a bird flies in the distance and the dog is nearby, seldom can a judge be positive that it is a game bird or if the dog was responsible for it taking wing. If an all-age dog is to be competitive, he must be visible part of the stake which means that he will learn to leave pointed birds after waiting awhile for the handler to find him. This is not what is intended for a **finished performance** but sometimes necessary to get around the course.

"... It must show a keen desire to hunt, must have a bold and attractive style of running and must show independence in hunting. It must range well out in a forward moving pattern, seeking the most promising objectives, so as to locate any game on the course. Excessive line-casting and avoiding cover must be penalized."

The derby standard is nearly identical except that the derby dog requires that intelligence be demonstrated. For the most part the good all-age dog thumbs its nose at his handler on cast-off as he takes off for parts unknown. As he is lost from sight his handler must experience an inner feeling of nostomania. An all-age dog should not become involved in side or back casting without being heavily penalized. The astute handler will usually allow his dog to go to the outer limits of what he believes will satisfy the judges, but no more. If his dog does handle kindly, he can be helped by the handler "singing" for the dog's benefit to keep it oriented to the direction of travel and position of the field trial party. This is not considered hacking and may be desirable if the dog is out of sight. Experienced all-age, and even gun dogs, handle to the field trial party and need no singing to remain oriented.

The standard implies that if game is on course the dog will locate it based on reaching the proper objectives. If he did not reach out to all the accessible objectives in his view, then he did not show what is required for placement. This pitfall analysis is obviously faulty as with much judging.

Most judges are more interested in a dog's application, range and style on the back course for single course stakes with designated bird fields. They recognize the difficulty in testing and judging dogs under simulated conditions and settle with how a dog handles birds in the bird field. A back course find for a promising dog made "way out on a limb" as the saying goes, is just extra gravy.

Many field trial courses have wide paths mowed

through the cover to help the field trial clubs and handlers. On either side of these paths is a variety of cover--weeds, copses, ditches, fence rows, woods lines and woods which the dog should cast out to work. Some field trial-wise dogs know the system and how long they will run (hunt). In single course stakes having a designated bird field, these dogs cast to the front, stay on course by following the horse tracks and are standing on point in the bird field within a few minutes. Some will point for a short time, find and point the other birds, then return to the course and wait for the field trial party to enter.

They learn other tricks on continuous courses when using the field trial party as a check point to line out and maintain contact. They may lose contact for awhile and loop back and behind to pick up the horse tracks to come back to the front, but no matter where or how far away they go, they still have learned how to find the field trial party when they are ready.

". . . The dog must respond to handling but must demonstrate its independent judgment in hunting the course and should not look to its handler for directions as where to go."

This says it perfectly. A dog which does this is hunting. But many dogs respond to handling in different ways when handlers force or drive them out against their will. We know that some dogs respond beautifully only to get out of the handler's sight and lay in the shade of a tree, or take a stimulating and refreshing swim or wallow in a mudhole, or to ground scent or urinate with no purpose in mind. These dogs are smart enough not to get caught in the act for they remember past physical punishment for such behavior, and they can see a field trial party in time to move farther on without being under the slightest suspicion of this behavior.

Heat and excess humidity is hard on dogs. Handlers will soak and chill their dogs down at the starting line, and stop or call them in at intervals along the course, and faithfully ask permission to water not for the protection of dogs, but with the belief that it provides an advantage. It is often carried to excess. Does this represent a **finished performance** considering that all other aspects of the dog's performance were superior when compared to an average performance by a dog not watered and protected?

An all-age dog looking for direction is probably just another gun dog. There is a shade of difference between a dog looking back for contact as opposed to looking for direction from its handler.

"Intelligent use of the wind and terrain in locating game, accurate nose, and style and intensity on point, are essential."

This is identical to the requirement for a gun dog, but we expect an all-age dog to use wind current different by the nature of his range and speed. He should slam into point upon contacting bird scent with all muscles rigid when his momentum almost causes him to fall over. We would not expect a good all-age dog to slow up, make game, then sneak into a point. All-age dogs need a better and more accurate nose than gun dogs to excel.

". . . At least 30 minutes shall be allowed for each heat."

This does not matter whether the stake includes a bird field or not. The test time is 30 minutes. It does not say that if there have been better dogs run and the present brace, or one dog in the brace is not

up to the performance of dogs in previous braces, that for expediency the judges can order handlers up. Yet, this is done even if it is wrong. Judges also are known to cut time short with some dogs in a stake and overlook the 30 minute time limit. Some handlers are picked up for protection in a bird field with the first retrieve. Dogs which are given placements in stakes with brace time of less than 30 minutes could fail the test in the last minutes and win out over a dog that could go the 30 minutes with a **finished performance.** It is essential that field trial committees not patronize judges who are too lazy to follow braces to the time set or are indifferent in their judging. The judges should be instructed to judge dogs the full 30 minutes or be replaced.

BACKING IN GUN DOG, ALL-AGE, LIMITED GUN DOG AND LIMITED ALL-AGE STAKES

"A dog encountering its brace mate on point must honor. Failure of a dog to honor when it sees its brace mate on point must be heavily penalized, and the intentional avoidance by a dog or a handler of a backing situation must be heavily penalized. A dog that steals its brace mate's point must be ordered up by the judges."

The standard no longer states that a time period for backing is required such as waiting until it has demonstrated complete steadiness to wing and shot, as in the one this revised standard replaced, nor does it say a dog cannot be cautioned, even whoaed, to back. An even earlier standard required that the first and second placed dogs must have a back. This caused many

77

problems with handlers and dogs.

Dogs that appear to be backing another dog may in reality be pointing the bird or dog's odor when stopped. It is impossible to tell which dog was the first to point in a divided find, or why one dog is so close to the other dog in an open area. Many dogs appear to be trained only to back in a position behind the pointing dog. These dogs do not avoid a back but fail to meet the standard's requirement of backing on sight. The question is should the dog be penalized and how much?

How long should a handler be required to hold his dog on a backing situation? Usually he is expected to hold his dog until the pointing dog's bird has been flushed, or retrieved and sent on or sent to relocate. A long wait for a pointing dog to complete its work is never justified.

Handlers should never stop at the brace mate's point and wait for his dog to check in and be forced into a backing situation. He should never interrupt his dog's performance to get a back and his dog should never be penalized. He should continue on course after his dog with one judge following his progress. Dogs win stakes by finding birds, not by backing.

Dogs with training syndromes do avoid their brace mate's points and sometimes come is too close to smell and blink the bird being pointed, but do not steal point if it is any consolation.

A **finished performance** should include a back, but this is not the intent of the standard where one ⁻ forced on a dog. Therefore, two dogs of near equal equal, performance, but if one had a back, he woul the dog with the best demonstrated **fini performance.** Many dogs while earning champion t never have backs which is better than forced artificial backs.

The standard requires that a dog **must** be ordered up by the judges for only one breach of manners--stealing point! Unfortunately, many of the divided finds in field trials are stolen points. The difference is that the judge did not see the act occur. It is hard to believe that all judges do not know what a stolen point is, but from experience I know they do not. A judge must see a dog deliberately move in and go in front of the pointing dog in most every case. Observation of pointing dogs in these situations shows that they are being interfered with by the dog stealing point which is bad for their mental balance.

RETRIEVING FOR GUN DOG, LIMITED GUN DOG, ALL-AGE AND LIMITED ALL-AGE STAKES

"Retrieving is required in all Retrieving Stakes and counts as an important part of a dog's performance. . . The dog must retrieve promptly and tenderly to hand. In a Retrieving Derby Stake the dog must also retrieve, but steadiness to wing and shot and a finished retrieve are not required for placement."

This standard is easy to interpret and understand. Yet, many dogs are placed without a finished retrieve. Nothing is mentioned regarding the bird's condition after being shot whether it has been blown to bits or is still alive and kicking or running.

What is the natural behavior with a dog in retrieving a bird shot to pieces? Is the retrieve of a wing adequate? Should a dog be excused for failing to retrieve all or part of the bird?

It is a natural behavior for dogs to kill game before retrieving, but maybe they should point again if the bird is alive. Yet, some experienced dogs can tell the bird is injured by smelling blood or the smell of powder. Inexperienced dogs will point crippled birds or be unsure of what to do, and the continuity of a retrieve is interrupted. What should a dog do when the crippled bird takes to wing? Chase? How far? A dog sent for a retrieve must not come back empty handed, nor chase a bird when sent. Dogs with tender mouths have difficulty picking up and holding pheasants for a retrieve and lose their grip several times on the retrieve. Are they to be faulted?

Dogs often point a different bird on the way to or from a retrieve. What about the dog which urinates when going for a retrieve or upon the return? Dogs retrieve to the gunner who is not the handler. How do we judge these dogs?

Killing, then chewing up the bird, or picking feathers, when refusing to bring the bird usually represents a training problem and these dogs are normally never placed. It is preferred that a dog retrieve a bird in the same condition as found, yet killing live game is instinctive. Dogs can be ruined by trying to retrieve live pheasants if they do not learn to kill.

The primary purpose of the retrieve is for a dog to mark the flight, locate the dead or crippled bird or game, and deliver it to the handler which is mostly a convenience to him. A dog is more adept at catching and killing crippled game. We would be foolish to do it ourselves when we have a dog.

Dogs obviously like the feel of holding a bird in

their mouths and sometimes are reluctant to give it up. We expect puppy and derby dogs to run away and refuse to give it up, but not gun dogs in a field trial.

A finished retrieve's quality varies at each trial, is weather dependent, and many are not done to the letter of the standard, but are accepted by the judges for placing dogs. There are judges who have trained many dogs and understand the problems with some retrieves when others have little experience or understanding. Dogs which have run hard on the back course may be so hot and thirsty they are near exhaustion and cannot breathe with a bird in their mouths and must drop it. Feathers spring off the bird into their dry hot mouths and gag them when they first pick up the bird. But, there are dogs which seem to overcome all obstacles and even pick up all the pieces and guts of a bird for a retrieve and deliver quickly to hand. These are the happy dogs which are proud of their accomplishments and show it.

Retrieving quickly and tenderly to hand should dispel the idea that the handler can move about and help his dog find the game without penalty. Pointing dogs are not trained like retriever dogs, but they should have been trained to take directions by voice, whistle or hand to the bird and the handler should remain where he flushed the bird. They need not put the birds in the handlers' hands, but should bring them close enough where handlers can pick the birds up. There is latitude for acceptable retrieves other than where the dogs runs full speed, grabs the bird in his mouth, and races back, stands in front and waits for the command to GIVE. A handler who finds the bird for his dog should not get credit for a retrieve.

"Regulations and Supplement To the Regulations For

Hunting Tests For Retrievers" gives detailed rules for acceptable retrieves for those breeds. Perhaps some detail should be included in "Registration and Field Trial Rules and Standard Procedures for Pointing Breeds," to provide more specific instructions to handlers and judges. Within the broad scope of subjectivity, pointing breed judges make their decisions using some of these same retriever rules, but there is too much inconsistency. It needs corrected by having more specific written rules for pointing breed trials.

There are other rules and standards of performance which must be studied and understood for use in training and competition. Trainers, handlers and judges must also keep up with changes made from time to time to remain current. The most important standards of performance have been discussed.

The American Kennel Club's pointing breed advisory committee helps make rule and standard changes periodically. Some changes are major, but many are minor. The education of field trial judges is difficult, but is a subject for future change which will not be done by this committee. The assumption that an owner with placements in trials or a field champion titled dog (trained by others) can judge is oftentimes wrong. Judges should have special training.

The three setter breeds pointing and backing. Ch. Halcyon
Bealltainn WC owned by Anita Listenberger (New York)--Gordon
Setter; Dual Ch. and AFC Karrycourt's Rose O'Cidermill owned
by Jeannie Wagner and George Clark (Ohio)--Irish Setter;
and, Fld. Ch. Jagerlust's Judge owned by Charles and Hernine
Lowe (Michigan)--English Setter. (Photo by Jeannie Wagner)

Chapter 5

The American Field

The American Field Publishing Company and the Field Dog Stud Book, 542 South Dearborn, Chicago, Illinois 60605 started in 1876 is the most active field trial organization in the world. It publishes *The American Field* weekly which reports on hundreds of championship stakes and thousands of regular field trials each year. All trials are listed in its **Kennel** columns and its pages cover just about everything of importance to the field trial sport, its dog registrations, advertising of dogs, game birds, horses, equipment, trials, boarding and training and dog food.

NOTE: American Field not italicized refers to the "organization."

The American Field provides a registry for all breeds, not just bird dogs. Application blanks and breeders certificates are available on written request with postage included. Actual dog registration is mainly pointers and English Setters, although several other dog breeds are registered each year.

The American Field sponsors trials under its **Minimum Requirements** for any bird dog club, but again most clubs reporting trials and trial results are heavily weighted to pointer and setter breeds. There are many Championship Associations working under the American Field umbrella. The trials and wins of all clubs are recorded and a pedigree will show all wins of a given dog and its ancestry.

The American Field Hall of Fame is for famous men and outstanding winning dogs which dates back to 1954. There is a fifteen day nomination period which closes on August 1 each year. Voters (subscribers) may nominate candidates for **Distinguished Dogs** which are no longer living and **Distinguished Persons,** living or dead, who have made important contributions to the field trial sport.

The official ballot form printed in *The American Field* must be used by voters, and election to the Hall of Fame is a permanent honor.

The Election Committee is comprised of officials of specific field trial clubs, persons having judged certain important field trial stakes, and persons having positions with leading sporting journals. There is a minimum of fifteen members required and thirty two were used in 1981.

The sporting public determines the leading candidates by their votes in both categories. The top ten nominees are given to the Election Committee. Each one casts only one vote each for two dogs and two people from the list. The two dogs and two persons having the highest number of votes are elected for that particular year.

All trials are run under **Minimum Requirements** as adopted by the Amateur Field Trial Clubs of America, The American Field Publishing Company and the Field Dog Stud Book. It is up to the judges, club officials, owners and handlers to know, understand and use them. The club secretary attests that the trial was run in compliance with them when filling out the Essential Data forms for the trial. Failure to comply may place the club standing in jeopardy and nullify the placements awarded at the trial. Any known violations may be reported to the American Field Publishing Company. Owners and handlers are responsible for providing all pertinent information on the entry form regarding registered name of the dog, FDSB registration number, breed, sex, date whelped, name of sire and dam, and name and address of the owner and handler.

Trial results are to be reported no later than thirty days after the event.

Effective September 1, 1989, the number of placements awarded in a recognized stake are **one** for six dogs started, **two** for eight dogs started and **three** for twelve dogs started. Championship stakes must start **fourteen** with **twenty** or more started for a runner-up.

A club's acceptance for listing in the Kennel columns is for a fee and it is sent the Essential Data Forms for reporting the results.

Clubs may advertise their trials with ad copy sent well ahead of the trial dates so that potential competitors can make plans to enter or attend.

Where age affects the entry, clubs may require prior

registration of a dog and they may refuse entry to any dog if proof of age is not given.

MINIMUM REQUIREMENTS FOR FIELD TRIALS FOR ALL POINTING BREEDS

As Adopted by Amateur Field Trial Clubs of America, The American Field Publishing Company and the Field Dog Stud Book

Wins will not be recognized and recorded unless the trial and/or each stake in which such win is made conforms to the following conditions:

1. The name of the club, place and date of the trial, and the secretary's name and address must be announced in an issue of THE AMERICAN FIELD bearing a publication date at least fourteen (14) days before the trials are to be run, and entry blanks, with complete description of each stake, be available to owners and handlers at least six (6) days before the date of the drawing.

2. Recognized Stakes are:
PUPPY STAKES--From January 1 to June 30 in each year for dogs whelped on or after January 1st to December 31st of each year for dogs whelped on or after June 1st of the year preceding.
DERBY STAKES--From July 1st to December 31st in each year for dogs whelped on or after January 1st of the year preceding, and from January 1st to June 30 in each year for

87

dogs whelped on or after January 1st of two years preceding.

ALL-AGE STAKES--For dogs or any age.

An "Open" stake is one in which there are no limitations with respect to either dogs or handlers.

An "Amateur" stake is one in which all handlers are amateurs as defined by the By-Laws of the Amateur Field Trial Clubs of America. Winners in Members' and Shooting Dog All-Age Stakes will be recorded but winners of Children, Ladies , Brace, and other stakes not conforming to the foregoing definitions will not be recognized.

CHAMPIONSHIP WINNERS STAKES AND FUTURITIES--Wins will be recorded only in such Amateur events of this character as are recognized by The American Field Publishing Company and the Field Dog Stud Book.

3. The minimum length of heats for all stakes other than Puppy Stakes shall be thirty (30) minutes on the basis of the time that an average brace takes to negotiate the course. In the case of one-course trials, no more than eight (8) minutes of the thirty (30) shall be spent in the birdfield. Minimum length of heats for Puppy Stakes shall be fifteen (15) minutes.

4. A stake must be drawn no later than the night before the day the stake is advertised to be run.

5. Dogs shall not be substituted after the draw.

6. Braces shall be run, and handled, as drawn, unless given prior consent of the judges, which consent must not be given for the purpose of accomodating owners, handlers or dogs that are not available when reached in the regular order of the draw. In the case of withdrawals, the bracemate of such withdrawn dogs may be run together at the discretion of the judges. Bitches which come in season, braced with a male, are scratched.

7. No entry shall be accepted after a stake is drawn.

8. No more than one brace of dogs shall be run on a course or any part of a course at the same time, irrespective of whether the dogs are in the same stake or in different stakes.

9. Stakes shall be run only on recognized game birds whose flight shall not be impaired by caging, hobbling, wing clipping, brailling or in any other manner.

10. Bitches in season shall not be permitted to run in one course trials. In multiple course trials they may start only if, in the opinion of the judges, it can be accomplished under conditions which will insure absolute fairness to other entries. Bitches in multiple course trials must be drawn in season and braced with a female.

Wins will not be recorded, or if recorded, will be cancelled if made at a trial or in a stake not conforming to the above requirements.

It is recommended that courses contain sufficient bird cover and suitable objectives to induce intelligent searching by the dogs. Birdfield, if used, should be of adequate size to permit a dog to hunt without excessive hacking and with cover sufficient to hold birds. A variety of cover and objectives is desirable. Five (5) acres is suggested as a minimum area for a birdfield.

In *The American Field* space is available to any club for reporting its trial when a **Kennel** fee has been paid. With paid advertising of trials, writeups are printed.

Except for major circuit trials, as a rule, American Field trials are open to any dog in its registry, or eligible for registration. Some clubs hold restricted breed stakes where pointers and setters cannot enter.

The American Field records over 7,000 field trials each year which includes championship stakes of every description on every type game bird on the North American Continent, Hawaii and Japan.

The American Field organization is noted for its pointer and setter trials and its name is synonymous with these two breeds.

Many of its stakes are open to all pointing breeds, but clubs must meet its **Minimum Requirements** to hold trials that are entered in the record. Most of the championship stakes are for pointers and setters only and have various restrictions for eligibility. Several futurities are sponsored through the American Field.

Sizes of trials and stakes vary. The American Field championship stakes sometimes have large entries and huge galleries. On one Saturday in 1985, there were nearly one thousand horseback riders in the gallery at Grand Junction, Tennessee. This stake is not run on Saturday as of 1986 because of the large gallery. Miles and miles of trial ground are needed for the continuous course stakes, otherwise the cover would be tramped flat if a single course were used. These trials may last two weeks or more with brace times up to three hours. Some stakes may have more than one hundred entries.

Major circuit trials are big business for the professional handlers who compete for large cash purses. In *The American Field*, February 8, 1986 John Criswell tabulated the winners and cash purses for twenty two of the prestigious championship stakes with 995 total entries. They paid $105,202 in cash purses to twenty one handlers. The biggest purse was $8,260 and the biggest winner was Robin Gates with $12,000, and the winningest dog was High Fidelity with $12,924.

These handlers are the established and elite of the sport. Reporters for these trials are articulate, and unequalled, whose writings provide prestige to dogs, owners and handlers alike. The American Field **Hall of Fame** is filled with the great men past and present, and outstanding dogs of years past.

Although there is no conscious intention of discriminating against any of the other breeds, it might appear that way. They are so engrossed in their own dogs that they are not even conscious of other breeds even existing or being of any value to the sport. It is somewhat like a "class" system where the "other breeds" are inferior. This is also the lot of any newcomer in the sport before becoming accepted, and is even more difficult with an "odd" breed.

Major circuit handlers and galleryites are usually mounted on the finest Tennessee Walkers noted for their seemingly effortless fast walk which requires other horse breeds to trot or gallop just to keep up. This horse is a necessity for anyone if they are to keep in sight of the dogs all day long, several days in a row and be comfortable. It can be a gruelling test for rider and horse over sometimes dangerous terrain which can cause serious injury to horses and riders.

Dogs in major circuit trials, at normal speed cover more miles than their handlers who ride fast to keep them in sight. Judges, scouts and gallery may ride as fast as twenty five miles per hour to keep the dog in sight for short periods of time. This requires good sound, healthy, horses and accomplished riders. Handlers and scouts may use more than one horse in trials lasting several days. In the continuous course trials which go cross country all day long to some end point, a rider is committed to follow the marshal. Only the marshal, experienced handlers, scouts and some judges know how to get back to the assembly area without wandering aimlessly or becoming lost.

Pointer and setter trials can be thrilling, exciting, punishing or boring depending on the dogs and weather conditions. It is not unusual for riders to be hurt when riding fast over unknown ground conditions causing horses to fall. Handlers, scouts and gallery sometimes become lost and may wander around all day.

This may be just one of several reasons that causes

new organizations to form with different rules and standards. Most dog owners prefer to see their dogs continually, and not have to hunt all over creation hoping upon hope to find them somewhere. Some of these dog owners want the pointed birds shot and retrieved and have formed organizations to emphasize retrieving.

Four of these organizations have become associated with the American Field in recent years: National Bird Hunters Association; American Bird Hunters Association; National Shoot-To-Retrieve Association; and, the United States Complete Shooting Dog Association.

The first, second and fourth are similar to regular field trials with shooting of birds on course, but some shoot them in a designated bird field. The National Shoot-To-Retrieve Association's stakes are held in an area of approximately 20 acres. Braces are 30 minutes with specific rules and the winner has the highest score on the most pointed birds and retrieves.

American Field trials are held almost exclusively on quail and grouse, although national championship trials on pheasant, chukar, woodcock and prairie chickens are held regularly each year.

It should be noted that the English Setter is considered the grouse specialist and is to the grouse hunter what the pointer is to the covey quail hunter. Several large southern plantations are still being used for trials on wild quail with emphasis on covey finds. Probably most of the trials use released quail with dependence on wild birds where possible. In these trials, the scouts might do as much handling as the handlers and anyone can be appointed the handler if a dog comes to the gallery without the handler or scout being present.

The American Field major circuit judges are the elite

"old timers." The stakes are normally for large money purses, and it is more difficult to become accepted as a judge in these prestigious stakes. These judges are the "bird dog gentlemen" in the sport, and they frequently judge the same trials every year.

Amateurs in these stakes are encouraged by the Amateur Field Trial Clubs of America to accept a certificate of win instead of money for placements. It is under the umbrella of the American Field.

Chapter 6

Amateur Field Trial Clubs
of America

The Amateur Field Trial Clubs of America, Inc. has its corporate charter in the District of Columbia.

The business and objects of the corporation cover a wide spectrum of activities in ornithological sciences, knowledge of upland game birds on the North American Continent, restoration and management of upland game birds and their habitats, grant of awards and scholarships, and other things to support functions promoting, regulating, controlling, advising and conducting field trials on upland game birds.

It is a non-profit corporation run by a Board of Trustees with power to change and amend the by-laws.

Membership in the organization is by clubs,

sustaining members and honorary members. There is a membership fee for clubs and sustaining members. A member refers to a field trial club, not an individual.

The Board of Trustees has established fifteen Regions composed of the different states from east to west with Region 10 including British Columbia, Region 13 Ontario and Quebec, Region 14 Alberta and Saskatchewan and Region No. 15, Japan. Each Region must have no less than five member clubs.

National Amateur Championship stakes are: National Amateur Quail Championship (1 1/2 hr.) since 1896; National Amateur Pheasant Championship; National Amateur Shooting Dog Championship; National Amateur Chicken Championship; National Amateur Grouse Championship; International Amateur Woodcock Championship; National Amateur Invitational Championship; National Amateur Pheasant Shooting Dog Championship; and, the National Amateur Chukar Championship.

Each has a one hour first series. They are held each year at a time and place set by the President.

The National Shooting Dog Championship is an Amateur Free-For-All Championship run by the National Shooting Dog Championship Association at Union Springs, Alabama.

Breed Championships may be held by parent organizations offering Amateur Championships for a fee to the Amateur Field Trial Clubs of America.

Wins at these club and regional trials to be recorded must conform to the conditions required by the Amateur Field Trial Clubs of America, Inc., The American Field Publishing Company, and the Field Dog Stud Book.

The name of the club, place, and date of the trial, and the Secretary's name and address must be announced in an issue of *The American Field* bearing a

View of riding gallery and judges from the gallery wagon at the inaugural Region 3 Amateur Field Trial Clubs of America Walking Shooting Dog Championship. The stake was hosted by the United States Complete Shooting Dog Association at Pinelake Shooting Preserve, West End, North Carolina.

publication date at least fourteen days before the trials are to be run; and entry blanks with a complete description of each stake shall be available to owners and handlers at least six days before the date of the drawing.

Recognized stakes are Puppy, Derby and All-Age Stakes. Open stakes have no limitation for dogs or handlers. The Amateur Stake is one in which all handlers are amateurs as defined by the Corporation. Winners in members and Gun Dog or Shooting Dog Stakes are recorded and win certificates issued as well as Championships, Winner's Stakes and Futurities.

Minimum length of heat for a puppy stake is fifteen minutes with all others thirty minutes. Bitches in season can compete only in multiple course trials where in the opinion of the judges conditions insure absolute fairness to other entries. They cannot be kenneled or transported near other starters.

The sponsoring club must have a license from the Corporation, have a Stake Manager to oversee the running of the trial and certify its winners to the Corporation within thirty days after the trial. Winners certificates will not be issued in amateur or open stakes where a cash purse is accepted by the handler.

Individual handlers must be designated at the time of the drawing. That handler must handle the dog if present and physically able. Anyone under suspension by the Corporation or barred from competition in trials, shall not handle or scout a dog.

Judges have the power to disqualify handlers and dogs where handlers do not conform to the rules and regulations, or can refer the matter to the Stake Manager. Judges must rigidly enforce a strict rule upon the interference of handler, scout or dog with the brace mate's dog.

The Stake Manager has authority to bar participation for anyone who impugns the action of a judge, or has annoyed him when doing his official work during or after the running of a trial. It can be made permanent by later action of the Board of Trustees.

No electronic device can be used during competition. Only the handler can give a command to a dog in competition except with permission of the judges. Live ammunition is banned in all member and championship stakes.

Anyone acting in a manner contrary to good sportsmanship and detrimental to the best interest of field trials generally may be barred from attending, handling or entering any dog in competition.

A professional handler is any person who receives or has received, either directly or indirectly, compensation for training or handling dogs, or has accepted a cash prize or prizes, or other valuable consideration for handling dogs other than his own in field trial competition, or any person who works for or has worked for a professional handler in the training of dogs, or any member of the family of a professional handler, age fifteen or over, who assists him in the training of dogs. All others are amateur handlers. It requires three years of amateur status after being declared a professional to be reinstated.

It is contrary to the rules of the sport for judges to order dogs up that in their opinion do not have a chance to place. The owner is entitled to the length of the heat as advertised unless there is deliberate interference with a brace mate or is likely to hurt his chances. A judge does not have the authority to order up a dog because it has no chance of winning.

The American Field is much more informal than the American Kennel Club regarding member clubs. Whenever a club is formed for sportsmen with dogs that can be registered in the Field Dog Stud Book, and pays a Fixture fee, and runs the trial according to the **Minimum Requirements**, the trial results will be recorded and published.

The "Standard of Judicial Practice and Field Trial Procedure" was prepared by several prominent judges in 1947. It was printed but not endorsed by the trustees of the Amateur Field Trial Clubs of America, Inc. and was endorsed by American Field.

It has been replaced in 1988 with the "Guidelines To Field Trial Procedure and Judicial Practice." This time it was adopted by the Board of Trustees and it is available from Ventre Vision, Inc., P.O. Box 350122, Brooklyn, NY 11235-0003 at a modest cost.

It is in a question and answer format and very few changes were expressed by the forty noted judges, handlers and authorities in 1988 over the 1948 version. Its purpose is to provide systematic guidelines for conducting and judging of field trials.

The major reason there has been no licensing of judges in the American Field (American Kennel Club) is that there are too many judges who hold contrary opinons of rules or procedures. Subjective opinions in a great many instances are not always in the best interest of the sport, but they cannot be legislated. Judging remains a flexible and fluid art.

The qualities desired of a judge are different in the 1988 publication, but I will quote the 1948 version which is:

100

"He should, first, be honest, fearless and absolutely impartial; wholly without prejudice for or against any particular breed, dog, style or type of performance or individual. Secondly, he should have the mental ability to quickly analyze a situation and properly interpret it. Third, he should be calm and dispassionate in temperament; not easily ruffled and not willing to risk snap judgment. Fourth, he should be physically able to withstand long hours in the saddle without impairment to physical or mental alertness."

With all those attributes and requirements no two people watching some action occur will "see" the same things.

Judging is not appreciably any different between the American Field and American Kennel Club trials because both use the spotting system. Other association judging is different in given situations.

Chapter 7

American Bird Hunters Association

The American Bird Hunters Association, Inc. was recognized by the American Field Publishing Company, the Amateur Field Trial Clubs of America and the Field Dog Stud Book in 1983. It must observe the **Minimum Requirements.** It holds Open Puppy, Open Derby, Amateur Shooting Dog and Open Shooting Dog stakes with shoot to retrieve requirements. State and National Classic stakes are held each year. Member clubs are in Texas, Missouri, Louisiana, Mississippi, and Oklahoma with other regions being established in additional states. It is an offshoot of the National Bird Hunters Association because several owners were interested in amateur stakes and shorter range of the dogs for its foot handlers.

Its purpose is much the same as that of the Amateur Field Trial Clubs of America and was established by several veteran field trial clubs that were interested in Amateur Stakes and events being judged on walking shooting dog standards beginning on the club level and then to the classic and championship levels. It was incorporated by Art Lasseter. **Members** are clubs which are active members of the corporation and may be state or regional. The country is divided into seventeen Regions which have a minimum of five clubs with provisions to change the boundaries.

It holds regional Walking Dog All-Age Championships or Classics on one course under natural conditions of one hour with whatever additional series the judges require. Money as a reward is prohibited. State championship stakes are also an hour duration with the national two hours and the President of the corporation is the Stake Manager.

The minimum length of brace time for all stakes is 30 minutes, except puppy which is fifteen minutes, with no more than eight minutes in the bird field. Bitches in season cannot run in its trials.

Scouting is not permitted in a Walking Dog Stake, but the judges may appoint someone to go see if a dog is on point at a specific location but he cannot handle the dog. Judges are not required to ride off course to locate a dog.

Dogs must have a back to place and dogs which refuse are ordered up. Backs must be obtained before dogs leave the bird field and judges will when necessary call back dogs in contention. The back must be natural and no dog can be held while backing when called back for a mandatory back. At other times with permission of a judge the handler may collar his backing dog and wait for flush or take his dog on ahead.

Puppy and derby dogs are not required to back for placements and no additional credit is given for backing. Derby dogs should whoa on command as they can be disqualified for interfering with a dog on point.

In the Shooting Dog Stakes, dogs must have one actual retrieve to hand to be placed, and the judges can request that a bird be planted, flushed and shot by the handler before he leaves the bird field.

Shooting is done by handlers and permission to load guns on course must be given by judges and permission requested when to load guns in bird field. Anyone shooting unsafely is cause for disqualification of the handler and his dog. When birds fly toward a judge, participants or gallery, a shot is not to be fired and the handler is given an automatic retrieve.

A Shooting Dog is expected to break point at flush by its handler with no additional credit given for staying any longer. Judging is based on the quality of finds and not the number.

Derby dogs in the fall are expected to make a partial retrieve if the opportunity is presented and in the spring they should retrieve to the handler's feet to be placed.

Dogs are expected to hunt their way out with very little handling, and are expected to keep track of their handlers without assistance except when the course turns while maintaining range suitable for foot handling. Those that quit hunting the last few minutes are not to be considered for placements since endurance is being stressed. A dog out of sight for ten consecutive minutes should be disqualified no matter if it is a qualifying, classic, national classic or championship stake.

Horseback handling is never permitted and handlers must be in good to top physical condition to handle the one and two hour stakes as well as their dogs.

Judges are expected to evaluate dogs as the stake progresses and once a dog is selected with an acceptable performance then all others are rated against that standard whether they are better or worse and the judges should be prepared to announce winners as soon as the stake is finished or name dogs for additional series.

A booklet is available which has "Articles of Incorporation By Laws and Running Rules, Standards of Judicial Practice and Field Trial Procedures for ABHA Sanctioned Trials." Refer to *The American Field* Kennel columns for a current name and address to obtain information.

Chapter 8

National Bird Hunters Association

This organization was formed by Dan Smith, Arkansas, with a few other hunters initially, and with his hard work within a few years he was able to build it into a strong national organization. Its walking retrieving stakes offer something interesting and challenging to pointing dog owners.

Any field trial in effect extends the hunting season whether a dog is being trained for one or is in trial competition.

The primary purpose of the National Bird Hunters Association is to evaluate a complete walking shooting dog. Its trials have a back course to measure the dogs' ability to handle covey finds, and a bird field to see how well they handle a single quail when shot and retrieved.

These trials are run as open stakes on weekends with the drawing held on Friday evenings--the day before the trial. Publication of the trial must appear at least two weeks before the running in *The American Field*.

Puppy, derby and all-age stakes are offered. Shooting is restricted to the bird field. The length of the back course is twenty two minutes with each dog allowed eight minutes in a bird field of between five to ten acres. The four corners of the bird field are marked.

Fifteen birds are put out before each stake and those flushed that fly outside the field for each brace are replaced. At the noon break one half that amount are put out.

Judging is done by the spotting system. The all-age dog must point, back and retrieve to be in contention, and if those opportunities in total, or part, do not occur during the heat, the judges may call a dog back. A dog called back that fails any one of these three requirements is removed from contention. Puppy or derby dogs are not required to back or retrieve but if one does, he sets the standard for the stake all other things being equal, or better.

Dogs need not be steady to wing and shot (hunter stake requirement), but the handler and not his dog must flush the bird.

The dog having the best performance should win the stake. If, in the eyes of the judges, two dogs are considered absolutely equal in the back course race, style, amount of bird contact, etc., then the dog steady to wing and shot would break the tie. A dog which holds only to flush with a better performance is expected to win the stake.

Trials sanctioned by the National Bird Hunter Association are for bird hunters who do not, as a rule, break their dogs to wing and shot which should appeal to the average hunter.

The trials must conform to the **Minimum Requirements** and are reported in *The American Field* for recording wins. The Association recommends that dogs be registered before competition, although it is not essential.

Trophies are awarded to three placements--first through third. Win certificates are issued by the Association which qualifies dogs for sanctioned All-Age, Puppy and Derby Regional Classics. Derby wins qualify dogs for the All-Age Classic and Puppy wins only for the Puppy Classic. Dogs placing first, second or third in All-Age or Derby in state or regional classics are qualified to run in the National Walking Shooting Dog Classic. The winner of this stake is equivalent to that Association's Champion.

All state classics are run in one hour heats with a minimum of eight minutes in the bird field. The National Walking Shooting Dog Classic is run in two hour heats with a minimum of eight minutes in the bird field. A National Invitational stake was started in 1985.

Anyone interested in the National Bird Hunters Association may obtain copies of the by-laws and running rules by checking the address of the current President in *The American Field* Kennel columns.

Chapter 9

United States Complete Shooting Dog Association

The United States Complete Shooting Dog Club was formed by Jack Myrick, Gerald E. Shaw and R. E. Lee from North Carolina in 1980. It was a grass roots effort. They were not aware of the American or National Bird Hunters Association. As more people became interested in forming clubs, rules were drawn up and the Associaton was formed in 1983.

The Association was first listed in *The American Field* in 1983. A championship stake has been authorized which requires a Certificate of Win from the American Field to enter. It uses the **Minimum**

Requirements as adopted by the Amateur Field Trial Clubs of America, The American Field Publishing Company and the Field Dog Stud Book as do all the other associations. The organization now has entire states as Regions and as clubs form within the states they will be sub-divided. North Carolina and South Carolina represent current Regions.

There are some differences between this Association and the others but it expects to award wins to bird dogs that can be seen. It believes that a good field trial dog is only an outstanding bird dog on display. The dog should exhibit range, stamina, good style, intensity and finished manners.

The stakes are single course without a bird field and are 20 minutes for open puppy and 30 minutes for open derby and the open or amateur complete shooting dog. Official gunners accompany the handlers on foot. Judges ride horses. Scouts must be named at the start of the brace and walk or ride the gallery wagon and cannot handle dogs. If the gallery wagon cannot be used on state grounds in some states, the gallery would ride horses.

Complete Shooting Dog means pointing, backing and retrieving. Backing is important in derby and the Complete Shooting Dog. Dogs not having the opportunity to back on course are called back only if in contention for a placement. A need for a retrieve is handled the same way.

Official gunners follow the handlers and must shoot safely in killing birds for the dogs to retrieve. When a handler sends his dog for a retrieve he cannot move from his position unless allowed by a judge.

Dogs are permitted to be absent without disqualification for one fourth of the brace time.

There are ten birds put down before each stake and additionally there are four birds per brace for puppy, six for derby and eight for the Complete Shooting Dog. The only birds used are quail and are distributed along the course. There is no bird field although the Association would not prevent clubs from using one.

Puppy dogs are not required to back or point staunchly and are to be judged on actual performance showing potential for a high class shooting dog. They are fired over when conditions permit. They are not required to retrieve but should display a strong interest in doing so.

Derby dogs should show more speed and endurance than puppy dogs, hold point until the handler arrives (no credit given for being steady to wing and shot), shot over, and retrieve. A finished retrieve is not yet required but the derby dog must have that potential. They must be reasonably obedient and respond to the handlers' commands on ground patterning. The winning derby should be the one judged best to succeed as a finished dog.

The Complete Shooting Dog is not required to be steady to wing and shot, but credit is given for this refinement. He must have a good nose to accurately locate game, point staunchly and retrieve to hand.

He must show a strong desire to hunt boldly, be independent, go to birdy objectives, show consistency of pattern as related to range and not look to the handler for directions to birdy objectives. The pace should not vary from beginning to end.

Competition in these trials requires a handler be in good health and have the physical stamina to walk under many different conditions for thirty minutes. Unquestionably, this eliminates some field trial

competitors who cannot walk and handle dogs. These
trials should be more natural than horseback handled
trials, but dogs considered for placement must be
called back if they did not have a retrieve or back in
their regular braces which causes judges, club
officials, handlers and dogs some problems. Official
gunners who flush birds for the dogs change the balance
when compared to the handlers flushing and shooting
their own birds as in the American Bird Hunters
Association, Inc.

Refer to *The American Field* Kennel columns for a
current name and address to obtain information.

**Gallery wagon used by the United States Complete Shooting
Dog Association at Pinelake Shooting Preserve, West End,
North Carolina.**

Chapter 10

National Shoot-To-Retrieve Association

The National Shoot-To-Retrieve Association (NSTRA) was formed in 1967 by a group of sportsmen in Indiana and expanded into a national organization in 1977. It included clubs from forty states and three foreign countries at the time of its official affiliation with the American Field organization July 1981.

The trials must meet American Field **Minimum Requirements.** They are listed in the Kennel columns for a fee and the Association has access to the Field Dog Stud Book, with reporting space and advertising space in *The American Field* for its trials. Record keeping is an additional coverage specifically for this Association.

The National Shoot-To-Retrieve Association remains a separate entity responsible for the entire scope of its operations and activities. Its affiliation with American Field makes it a solid, permanent organization for pointing dog owners, and is fast growing with a solid foundation for the future.

It holds a National Invitational Dog Of The Year Championship at Amo, Indiana in October each year for dogs having won Regional elimination trials. Two top dogs are selected from each day's competition and are then braced for a final series of one hour. This event has grown to a four day 96 dog trial.

Also at Amo each April beginning in 1982 the National Trial Of Champions is held for National Shoot-To-Retrieve Association Champions. This title is won by an accumulation of 18 points of which nine must be first place in trials approved by NSTRA and the American Field. Dogs also must demonstrate backing before certification. It is run the same way as the Invitational Championship.

Winning records of dogs registered in the Field Dog Stud Book were recorded back to 1977 for the owners who took time to provide the essential information on their winning dogs.

All pointing dog owners, men and women, are eligible to enter one trial without being a member of the Association. The one day trials are limited to the first thirty two dogs entered. Two trials can be run on one weekend by the same club. Owners or handlers who live 100 miles or more away who enter Saturday's trial are guaranteed a place in Sunday's trial.

Shoot-To-Retrieve trials put maximum emphasis on bird finding and clean bird work, although dogs do not have to be steady to wing and shot, but are required to retrieve. This is a hunting dog trial for hunting dog owners where the dog having the most finds and retrieves in thirty minutes is the probable winner.

Competing with dogs that break at wing or shot does not require too much stressful training, and the stress on dogs at these trials is much less than with dogs trained steady to wing, shot and required to retrieve to hand. My own experience in these trials is that dogs steady to wing and shot are not scored any higher on their obedience in any judging category.

It is true that handlers can score lower by not following the rules exactly. One such example is on a natural back. In American Kennel Club rules, the handler cannot hold his dog by the collar in a backing situation except in puppy and derby stakes, but it is a firm requirement in these trials.

It is the only trial where a pointing dog owner without any previous experience in trials can enter a good hunting dog and earn a respectable score, and may on occasion win. Supposedly training is not a prerequisite to post high scores, but trained dogs post higher scores consistently when not braced with one their equal. Handlers with the best dogs score higher when braced with poor dogs.

Shoot-To-Retrieve trials have definitely added to the sport's variety, and provide an opportunity for many pointing dog owners to satisfy a basic need. The Association is composed of members who are hunting oriented with the opportunity to extend their hunting season under simulated conditions.

This is a blind where the handlers and their dogs must
stay in while birds are being put out in a Shoot-To-Retrieve
stake.

When is is not possible to get horses for judges, these
ATV's solve the problem for Shoot-To-Retrieve trials on
private grounds.

The trial area is a marked field of twenty acres or more. Six birds are put out for the first brace and five thereafter are guaranteed for each brace. Each brace is turned loose for thirty minutes to hunt game birds much like in a preserve hunt except each handler has a judge who usually rides a horse. All handlers and gunners walk and poor shooters are at a marked disadvantage because retrieves add measurably to the total score. Handlers may use gunners of their choice, or shoot their own birds, but the gunner must flush the birds.

The intent of these trials is for the ordinary hunter, but specialized handlers who are superior gunners with well trained dogs have evolved where the beginner stands a poor chance of winning. The specially trained dogs are superior bird finders and work quickly, with great intelligence, for this type hunting situation. These skilled handlers have also learned every trick to their dog's advantage.

Birds are released, usually from a motor bike, when the handlers and dogs are out of sight in a blind.

A handler never intentionally leaves a bird that might accrue to the score of the next brace. The marked bird (three minutes) routine used to work to one's advantage to card more finds. That has changed some. Now, for example, if a bird is pointed and not shot, but scored as a find by the judge, it cannot be scored by that dog again or its brace mate. Marked birds are birds not scored as a find by either dog. If a dog points this bird in less than three minutes, the gunner must shoot it for no score. Running to a dog on point is no longer permitted which improves safety and training.

Judges switch handlers after fifteen minutes, so each handler is judged part of the time by two different judges. This seems fair enough. The two score cards are added at the end of the brace with ground race and obedience judged by each one at half the value. The total score of each dog is posted on a blackboard so that every one can see the scores as the dogs compete throughout the day. This gives handlers a current high score which they must beat.

The class bird dog exists in these trials as much as in any type field trial. The owners have managed to control the big running dogs by keeping them in the designated bird field and make winners out of them. These dogs have extremely beautiful style, intensity and class on point.

The real danger as I see it is the potential for gunners to shoot the dogs on poor flying birds. Many of these dogs break at flush with the gunner shooting the bird close to the chasing dog, sometimes just a few feet in front of the gun. It may appear that gunners shoot the birds before they leave the ground. The danger is evident, but I have not seen or heard of any accidents. The advantage to breaking dogs to wing and shot are many, but in these trials it seems necessary for a dog's safety, yet requiring this would defeat much of the Association's purpose. At one time, birds were shot that were flushed by the dogs making for many scary situations, but this became evident and was changed where the gunner must flush.

These trials have the same breeding of pointers and setters as major circuit trials, but somehow they are trained to stay in the designated bird field and must do so to post high scores. A find is scored when a dog points from inside the marked boundary on a bird outside it, but not when the dog is outside the boundary. Finds on dead birds and marked birds are not given a score.

Handlers must call point each time and the judge must acknowledge each one. A relocation requires that handlers call point again.

There are many other rules handlers must learn to maximize their scoring. Some seem to be tricky. Habits once learned are not easily broken and puts the handlers who change from one type trial to this one at a disadvantage. Handlers who become addicted to these trials stay with them exclusively, but they are good training for American Kennel Club retrieving stakes.

The gap has been bridged for hunters and field trialers who sampled other organization's trials before and were disenchanted with the big running dogs having little, if any, bird work to win. These trials provide the opportunity to show superior bird finding abilities, and these dogs do just that. My own experience has shown that my American Kennel Club trained trial dogs are just as competitive and are seldom out of the top scores, and have won too.

Pointing dogs that are specifically trained for Shoot-To-Retrieve trials hunt honestly to a high degree of perfection in the specified hunting area. Sometimes they need considerable hacking to keep them inside it, but in due time these dogs learn the limits.

Dogs usually adapt to the terrain and their handlers' control regardless of different standards of performance. These bird fields are polluted, saturated, with bird, dog and man scent. An abundance of bird scent excites any dog.

My experience in American Kennel Club trials has

confirmed that dogs may show little interest in hunting on a sterile back course, but are changed to super hunting dogs upon entering a bird field where much bird scent is present. It starts their adrenalin flowing and brings out the natural drive in dogs. The lack of bird scent creates boredom and maybe even distress.

Just about every breed has won in Shoot-To-Retrieve trials. Winning dogs are eligible for Regional Elimination Trials each October and for possible eligibility and selection for Dog of The Year Trial finals.

Points toward a champion title are awarded for the local, regional and national placed dogs. A total of eighteen points are required of which nine must be first place and the dogs must demonstrate they will back for certification as a champion.

A dog must also be enrolled in a recognized breed or field dog registry, approved by the National Shoot-To-Retrieve Field Trial Association, Inc. officers and Board of Directors, to be awarded the certificate of champion. Both AKC and FDSB registration are accepted.

Points are based on the number of dogs in a trial and points may be awarded for first through third place. A trial must have a minimum of twelve and a maximum of thirty two dogs for the points to be awarded.

All judges must attend a judging seminar and pass a written test to be certified as a judge.

Judging rules and the scoring system are the same for all trials. The winning dog must prove that he will point, back and retrieve. They may be called back to show one of these before naming the winner.

JUDGING REQUIREMENTS

GROUND RACE: Score 0-100 points
   To achieve a 100 score, dog should have good speed, style, spirit and intensity on game. Consideration can be given for normal traits of the individual breeds.

OBEDIENCE: Score 0-75 points
   To achieve a 75 score, dog must display immediate response to every handler command, such as return to bird field, come in, etc.

   BACK: Score 0-75 points
   To achieve a 75 score, dog must back immediately when seeing a dog on point, being intense with good style, remaining this way until handler reaches dog to control him when pointing dog completes his retrieve.

   RETRIEVE: Score 0-100 points
   To achieve a 100 score, dog must have good speed, quick location (based on conditions), quick pick-up, return directly to handler, willing release of bird with tender mouth.

   FIND: Score 0-100 points
   To achieve a 100 score, dog must have quick location, outstanding style, be intense and maintain his composure until bird is flushed by handler/gunner.

   The rules related to these five judging requirements are specific and attempt to correct some obvious problems experienced in competition under the spotting system used to judge course type field trials.

   Dogs cannot be put on leash or taken from the bird field without being replaced by a standby dog for the duration of the heat, and then only on permission of the judge. There are no bye dogs except those braced with a standby dog. This rule eliminates the advantage or disadvantage for a dog running by itself (bye dog).

Judges' scoring decisions are final, but not the addition so handlers should check the addition if they are close to the highest scoring dog. This scoring system does not nullify complaints registered against the spotting system, because judges in these trials also must make subjective judgments for points given for various levels of performance. This human element, or failing, is always present, but is usually compensated for by a dog getting the most points and retrieves.

Shoot-To-Retrieve trials are no less expensive than stakes in any other trial. There is only one stake and each handler is restricted to a maximum of three dogs, except in the Dog of The Year Trial.

Trophies are awarded to the three highest scoring dogs. Ties are run off in fifteen minute braces. The value or cost of the trophies depends on the number of entries. This type trial is much simpler to conduct as compared to course type trials having several different stakes.

The entry fee may vary with the game bird used, but most clubs use quail for practical reasons. Pheasants and chukars are difficult to keep in the designated bird field area very long after being released which makes quail the ideal bird to use.

Most dog owners become involved in their particular brand of field trial sport and remain locked in permanently. A few do try other kinds of trials whenever they become disenchanted for various reasons. The opportunity is available for whatever variety best suits the individual and all the organizations enhance the development of pointing dogs. Some dogs are better trained than others which depends on the trainers' personal preference or training ability.

There is the human tendency to look at another man's type of field trial sport as being inferior. This feeling is typical of hunters toward field trials. It is an honest one, but is born from ignorance which interferes with their opportunities to fully enjoy their dogs year round. The Shoot-To-Retrieve trials should convert some hunters from their self-induced isolation and prejudice. Any one who owns a fully trained dog knows how much better the relationship is between man and dog when engaging in the field trial sport. Both learn to enjoy it more.

A Championship rotating trial will enable more dog owners to participate and travel less distance to compete starting in 1989.

Hunters and field trialers interested in these trials should write for information about membership and judging standards to the National Shoot-To-Retrieve Association, Inc., 226 N. Mill Street #2, Plainfield, IN 46168, or check the **Kennel** column in *The American Field*.

Chapter 11

North American Versatile Hunting Dog Association

The North American Versatile Hunting Dog Association (NAVHDA) is a non-profit organization and its purpose is to foster, improve, promote, and protect the versatile hunting dog breeds in North America. It is meant to supplement the activities of other organizations and breed clubs by providing a standard for testing and a measure for evaluating dogs of all versatile breeds through sanctioned trials using standardized scoring methods.

NAVHDA's main focus is on versatility and game conservation by having a well-trained dog to hunt with in field, water, woods and marsh. It encourages owners

124

to train to a high level of perfection. Reports of its activities and articles of general interest are published in its monthly newsletter.

Most sanctioned activities in the field are sponsored by regional chapters. Training and judging clinics are given, and a data bank maintained for scores of all dogs tested. A registry is also offered for individual dogs, litters and kennels.

First formed in Canada, its organizers sought to perpetuate the Europeans' emphasis on breeding, training, and use of the versatile breeds for their inherent capabilities on a variety of game, both fur and feather. As conceived this North American program recognized the different nuances of hunting in Canada and the United States versus the European Continent.

The development of the versatile breeds resulted from a desire for dogs that could handle a variety of game before and after the shot, and on land or in water. Basic breeding objectives included a keen nose, a strong pointing instinct, a lively temperament, eagerness to retrieve from land and water, stamina, and a durable coat to enhance work in cold water or heavy brush. Other characteristics included intelligence and ease of training, and a character compatible with living in or near their master's home. Although the resulting breeds have different physical characteristics, they all share the desired hunting characteristics.

The common versatile breeds are the German Shorthaired Pointer, German Wirehaired Pointer, German Longhaired Pointer, Weimaraner, Brittany, Vizsla, Wirehaired Pointing Griffon, Pudelpointer, Large Muensterlander Pointer and Small Muensterlander Pointer.

A trained dog is a better hunting companion and returns more game to hand.
(NAVHDA Photo)

Dogs are judged for pointing intensity during both Natural Ability and Utility Tests.
(NAVHDA Photo)

NAVHDA officials recognize that as a group, the different breeds were not designed to compete against each other or the specialty breeds (pointers, setters, and retrievers). It emphasizes that versatile breeds are different from the specialty breeds because they were bred to be that way. Also, it proclaims that these breeds were not intended to improve upon the specialty breeds. Selective breeding is encouraged such that they remain useful both on land and in water.

NAVHDA is making a determined effort in North America to unify versatile hunting dog enthusiasts. Until the formation of NAVHDA in 1969, there were no strong versatile gun dog clubs. Tests tailor-made for the breeds were rare. No standard rules existed for rating the breeds.

NAVHDA offers Natural Ability Trials and Utility Trials. In the former, dogs sixteen months of age or younger are judged only on their hereditary hunting characteristics: nose, search, tracking, pointing, waterlove, desire, gun shyness and cooperation. The latter test is designed to judge the dog's usefulness as a hunting companion for the on-foot hunter. There is no age limitation in it. There is no competition among the dogs in either test. All dogs could conceivably receive a perfect sore or no score.

The Natural Ability Test consists of three phases: (1) The dog is hunted for about 20 minutes over a field where birds have been planted. (2) Dummies are thrown into water of swimming depth to determine if the dog will enter the water and swim without hesitation twice. (3) The dog is introduced to the track of a flightless running pheasant and must display eagerness and perseverance on the track. The scoring system has an importance index of 2-6 with a maximum judging score of

Puppies are tested for water love—a requirement for later training for waterfowl hunting.
(NAVHDA Photo)

Tracking tests determine if a puppy has the nose and concentration for tough work later on with cripples.
(NAVHDA Photo)

0-4, which is then multiplied together to give a total score in each judging category. A maximum of 112 points can be given in Natural Ability Tests.

The Utility Field Trial Tests simulates actual hunting conditions. The test is divided into two groups, field and water. The Water Group includes walking at heel, remaining in blind, behavior in blind, retrieving a duck and search for a duck. In the Field Group, the dog is hunted over a field that has been planted with at least two species of birds for thirty minutes. Dogs are judged on search, pointing, steadiness on game, retrieve of a shot bird and retrieve of dragged game (feather or fur, depending on the handler's wishes). Nose, cooperation, handling and obedience, desire to work and stamina are judged thoughout both groups. Backing another dog is not required. The index is also from 0-4, as in the Natural Ability Test, for a total of 204 points maximum.

Conformation is examined in both tests but does not affect the score or prize. Passing dogs are awarded a Prize I (highest), Prize II or Prize III based on their scores and minimum ratings in specific areas (for example, for a Prize I in either test, a dog must achieve a rating of "4" in nose).

Every dog tested is evaluated by a judging team consisting of three judges. NAVHDA's judgeship program is an aspect of NAVHDA that distinguishes it from most other dog tests or trials. NAVHDA judges are graduates of a rigorous training and apprenticeship program. NAVHDA is extremely demanding on its judges because the NAVHDA test program is based on a defined set of standards that must be uniformly applied to all dogs tested. This is difficult because the versatile breeds

Utility testing includes simulated waterfowl hunting, complete with blind and decoys, with the retrieve of a duck. (NAVHDA Photo)

All NAVHDA tests are scored by three judges who have successfully completed an intense training and apprenticeship program. (NAVHDA Photo)

have different characteristics and because tests are conducted throughout North America in different climates and terrains. Since the results and usefulness of the test program are only as good as the judges' program, NAVHDA has stringent and exacting requirements for judgeship. NAVHDA judges are appointed only when they have trained and qualified a dog in a Utility Test and apprentice-judged until it is deemed by the organization that the prospective judge has demonstrated good hunting dog knowledge and ability, and a thorough understanding of the NAVHDA test program and standards. Once appointed, a judge is reviewed and evaluated annually.

Training or work days are held by the regional chapters to help owners prepare for these tests and/or train for hunting. In preparing a dog for the Natural Ability Test, NAVHDA makes a strong point of distinguishing between training and exposure and, in fact, discourages against certain aspects of training that could detract from the evaluation of natural ability. Dog owners are encouraged to introduce their natural ability candidates to field and game, water, and tracking to help develop their dog's searching, pointing, desire, confidence, concentration, swimming, and other abilities, which mature independently at different times in different pups.

Training of a dog for hunting or Utility Testing is geared toward giving a dog and handler the best natural advantage. The highest scoring dog in a test, for example, will point and remain steady until the game is flushed, shot and has fallen. Dogs must deliver to hand and not drop game to avoid loss of cripples. Dogs are expected to use their intelligence and capabilities to find and retrieve game. A dog fetching a duck

Steadiness, before and after the shot, earns a high score in a Utility Test.

downed in water taking a land route in his retrieval is not downgraded, since the land route in the dog's mind could be the most expeditious. Dogs **are** expected to hunt for their master, not themselves. During training days, two of the most common areas of work in achieving the performance described above are force retrieval training and teaching the dog the "Whoa" command.

As mentioned, there are Regional Chapters in Canada and the United States. NAVHDA has experienced considerable growth over the last few years. Between 1981 and the end of 1985, membership increased from 500 to over 1000, and the number of chapters from 12 to 30. There also was a significant increase in dogs tested: 242 in 1981 versus 586 in 1985.

Materials, such as training books, standard booklets on rules, training and judging, and decals are available from NAVHDA. Advertising information is normally found in *Gun Dog* magazine or other dog publications. Further information on NAVHDA is available by writing NAVHDA, 1700 N. Skyline Drive, Burnsville, Minnesota 55337.

Handlers need dust masks at some field trials when riding in the gallery as evidenced here in the Mojave Desert. The author uses a bandana which is of little help.

Chapter 12

Conducting Pointing Dog Field Trials

GENERAL DISCUSSION

Pointing dog owners should join a local field trial club. The clubs are usually organized by one or more dedicated individuals with a strong interest in field trials.

They should be organized to operate into perpetuity and not for short time periods. It helps to have hard core dedicated bird dog owners.

Clubs often try to make a profit on trials, but trials should be operated for the benefit of the members and the field trial fraternity, whether local or national in scope. The best managed trials break even or turn a small profit, so clubs generally use other means to make money to support their club operations through membership dues, raffles or calcuttas at trials.

A field trial can break even or make a slight profit by running about thirty two dogs per day. It depends on the cost of birds and horses. Fun field trials need much less money and entries, because they are informal and have less expense—the primary cost is birds.

Some clubs have survived for nearly one hundred years and have grown stronger when others wither away or last for only a short time.

New clubs usually get off to a good start but it is not long before the jockeying for "power" begins. Some members become angry with each other, do not like certain members, get disgruntled with the operation, make a big fuss over little things, criticize members' dogs and handlers which is counterproductive even with good leadership. Members are disappointed to learn that other members do not share their views, or do not have similar values about their dogs. The average member lasts about five years, but many owners, trainers and handlers spend all their lives in one or more field trial organizations, and serve with apparent distinction.

It is important that clubs and responsible officials stress that trials should command the best manners and conduct from the owners and handlers while they display the highest competitive spirit possible—and have fun when doing it. They should enjoy the opportunity it provides to meet both old and new owners and handlers when watching different dog breeds, training and handling methods.

This is why bird dog clubs exist and they usually do a good job of providing outstanding recreation and socializing also.

STAKES FOR DIFFERENT BREEDS

What breeds should be allowed to enter a trial? For many clubs that has been long established. The American Kennel Club recognizes only ten pointing dog breeds, and individual pointing dog clubs for these breeds determine whether they will permit any other breeds to enter their local trials.

The general philosophy is that if the club's breed can almost always beat the other breeds entered, they are no threat, and are allowed to enter to help defray the trial costs. Generally, there is usually no real problem when a trial is open to all pointing breeds as a rule. Each breed group has its own schedule of activities from one weekend to the next and tend to stay in their own area of competition or breed.

The actual situation varies geographically in trials, but German Shorthaired Pointer clubs, German Wirehaired Pointer clubs, English Setter clubs, and Pointer clubs do not limit breeds which can enter. Irish Setter club policy varies, Gordon Setter clubs always have some stakes open, Brittany clubs may have one stake open and Vizsla clubs usually have one or more stakes open. Some of the Weimaraner clubs open a few stakes to other breeds. There are no clubs at present for the Wirehaired Pointing Griffons.

The philosophies of individuals vary in clubs from one geographical area to another. American Kennel Club pointing dog standards encompass all its recognized pointing breeds, so theoretically all are equal in performance, and one can compete equally with any other. In practice it does not work out that way, but the standard does serve each breed well. The difference is usually in range and application.

Members of a breed club having Breed X want to promote that breed and are usually friendlier and accept its owners as "family" more than other breed owners at trials. Potential owners of a breed should be invited to that breed's club trials to convince them that is the best for their purposes. Once a potential owner is sold on a breed, he must be sold on field trial competition. Some people may not enjoy it.

If a breed trial is open to other breeds and those breeds and their handlers are too advanced, the new owners become reluctant to get their feet wet in a sport where they have no knowledge or opportunity to win. Fun field trials serve them well in the beginning, but they must still face the day they decide to compete with their "special" dogs, and if they never place in trials open to other breeds they are quickly discouraged.

The obvious solution in promoting growth of a given breed is to close all stakes, or all but one stake, to other breeds to serve the best interests of the owners and their breed. There is room for everybody to learn and compete, but it takes hard work to become a consistent winner.

The experienced handlers with the best dogs often compete in other breed trials and tougher stakes if they feel a need to prove something about themselves and their breed.

FIELD TRIAL COMMITTEE

It is important for the field trial chairman and secretary to have had previous experience in running a trial, yet it often happens that both are "volunteered" into a job they know nothing about. At least one should know and be familiar with the rules and procedures for conducting the trial to help the other one learn.

The check lists for chairman and secretary, and the American Kennel Club "Standard Procedures For Pointing Breeds" should be used as a guide to solve problems which occur from time to time.

Fun field trials are less complicated, but they should be the place used to learn these things and used as a place for new competitors to learn. Owners and handlers assemble at a specified hour and gather entries for each stake as it is run. They select two of those present to judge and have others plant birds for each stake without regard to dog ownership, handling or conflict of interest. Everyone should get involved in the work and different handlers should be used to judge each stake. The fun trial entry fee should include the cost of birds and minor extra expenses. Some clubs can afford to offer training for its members at no cost. The idea is to make it a regulated and enjoyable training session where experience is gained for the dogs and handlers at the least expense. This helps create a better form of togetherness and teamwork, and does a better job of improving dogs than haphazard training without a specific goal.

A field trial committee should come from just such a group of club workers who enjoy working together, and who like to work voluntarily under difficult circumstances. Each should have one or more jobs assigned by the field trial chairman, and be willing to do the job efficiently and in a timely manner in conjunction and in coordination with all other committee members, gunners, marshals, bird planters and judges. Each person should be experienced in his assignment and dependable enough to go ahead and do his work and pitch in where others need help too.

Conducting a formal licensed (or sanctioned) trial means much work for a few people before the trial and for several people at the trial. It becomes increasingly more difficult when two or more stakes are run simultaneously. This creates more than twice the effort and causes timing problems when one handler is running on one course and is up on another course at the same time. The temptation then is for the committee or the chairman to adjust the order of running to avoid delays. This is illegal. The American Kennel Club allows naming of more than one handler for the drawing and nobody really is concerned who eventually handles the dog. But, if two dogs are drawn for the same brace with two or more handlers named on one entry and a same name on the other entry, they are braced together.

Entries may be sent to the field trial secretary when the trial date is published in the *SUPPLEMENT TO: PURE-BRED DOGS/AMERICAN KENNEL GAZETTE EVENTS CALENDAR*. Premiums may be mailed before the date is published though and the drawing precedes the trial a few days to allow for plans and printing of a running order.

It is the field trial committee that uses specific rules promulgated by others in the sport, and they may add some of their own as necessary which do not conflict with existing rules. The committee interprets and enforces the rules that are required to run the trial.

140

DUTIES OF THE FIELD TRIAL CHAIRMAN

1. Has charge of the trial, and may select grounds.
2. Selects field trial committee members and instructs them on their duties.
3. Along with the Field Trial Secretary, coordinates the running conditions of the trial and stakes using the American Kennel Club's "Registration and Field Trial Rules and Standard Procedures for Pointing Breeds" and any other special club rules in filling out the American Kennel Club's field trial questionnaire by the Field Trial Secretary once the Club Secretary has obtained approval for the trial and grounds location, or American Field **Minimum Standards** or special association or national organization standards which may be in addition to these or entirely separate.
4. Assigns duties and obtains the following people:
    a. Judges, and alternates.
    b. Field trial marshals, assistants and alternates.
    c. Captain of guns and gunners.
    d. Game steward to obtain birds. (Usually Chairman.)
    e. Horse steward and hostler.
    f. Bird planters.
    g. Trial communications (CB, PA, etc.)
    h. Hotel or motel accommodations and reservations for judges and others.
    i. Food steward or food arrangements.
    j. Banquet, special speaker, and general arrangements.
    k. Social steward or hostesses.
    l. General facilities on the trial grounds.
    m. Individual course layouts.

n. Field trial headquarters in town and at trial grounds.
o. Special meeting rooms if needed.
p. Placement and removal of direction markers and field trial signs.
q. Time keeping (stopwatches) for judges and marshals.
r. Dog training or exercise area at or near trial grounds.
s. Trophy and rosette steward.
t. Publicity.
u. Policing of the grounds after trials.
v. Coordinator of stakes and braces.

5. Instruction of the judges on special judging requirements and awards if any.
6. Insures that Field Trial Secretary performs duties in a timely manner.
7. Instructs marshals, gunners and bird planters.
8. Maintains discipline on the grounds and enforces rules.
9. Handles all complaints quickly.
10. Convenes trial board as **the** American Kennel Club from field trial committee if required.
11. Acts as ambassador of good will and does all things necessary to insure the excellent conduct of the trial.
12. Makes final report of the trial to the next Field Trial Chairman and to the Club Secretary.

DUTIES OF THE FIELD TRIAL SECRETARY

1. Determines stakes that will be run each day and

142

the order of running.

2.   Sets drawing of stakes for location, date and time.

3.   Checks with Club Secretary to make sure that Parent Club approval and an American Kennel Club license has been obtained. Or, for American Field documentation of wins, pays for a listing of the trial in the **Kennel** columns. Advertising in *The American Field* is paid for four to six weeks prior to the trial. Trials can be held under both organizations.

4.   Obtains American Kennel Club field trial questionnaire or American Field "Essential Data" forms, or other organization's forms and completes all essential data for the trial and its running.

5.   Obtains trial sign imprinting, trial markers, course markers, judges books and other materials needed.

6.   Obtains special permits from State where required for facilities grounds and birds.

7.   Orders ribbons or rosettes for either the three or four placements and judges awards of merit from supplier.

8.   Sends publicity for trial to newspapers and club news media.

9.   Advertises in national publications if required.

10.   Obtains suspension list from the American Kennel Club and checks against entries if running under its rules.

11.   Answers all correspondence relating to trial, ntries, and other business promptly.

12.   Signs American Kennel Club form certifying having read and understands the rules. (Judges must also sign form if first time judging.)

13.   About one month before trial mails premiums to

each club member, other interested clubs and handlers.

14. Collects all money for entry fees, accounts for all expenses and pays all bills unless payment is handled by Club Treasurer.

15. Mails two premiums to the American Kennel Club after making necessary changes or corrections. Four are required if club prints its own premiums.

16. Does not accept entries after the advertised deadline. Accepts telephone entries unless prohibited by premium list.

17. For thirty minute trials, the average time used is forty five minutes. Limits entries according to daylight hours and courses used for the total days advertised for trial.

18. Promptly notifies individuals when entry form is refused for any cause.

19. Makes sure that the Field Trial Chairman has notified all officials in plenty of time and makes all the arrangements including gifts for judges.

20. Contacts any person with errors on entry form and obtains corrections and entry fees before dog runs.

21. Holds the drawing at the time and place designated.

22. After the drawing (supervised by Field Trial Secretary) fills out judges books for each stake. (Two books for judges and one for marshal.)

23. Provides field trial catalog or order of running to all participants.

24. Awards rosettes and trophies to winners at the end of each stake or at other designated time or place as pre-arranged. Four placements for American Kennel Club trials and three for American Field and other organizations. Awards the special trophies or traveling trophies.

144

25. Fills in the judges books and obtains judges signatures after the stake is completed and/or essential data forms.

26. Takes pictures of the winners.

27. Obtains judges comments on winners.

28. Reports winners and provides trial write-up for local and national news if appropriate and the club news medium.

29. After the trial, double checks entries for correctness, checks judges books for accuracy and completeness, writes American Kennel Club's Field Trial Secretary's Report, and makes sure that all materials are in the office by seven days (maximum) after the last advertised date of the trial.

30. When a change of judging or running of the stakes has occurred, he reports immediately after the trial to the American Kennel Club.

31. Sends essential data forms and trial write-up to the American Field. Trials can be held under American Kennel Club and American Field rules at the same time.

32. Sends trial report and all records to Club Secretary after all details are completed.

33. Makes certain that all bills have been paid, preferably before leaving the trial grounds.

GROUNDS

There are some field trialers who claim that "Sassafras Junction" grounds are the **best** in the United States. No grounds are ideal for organized field trials as opposed to hunting.

The best public field trial grounds in the state of Ohio is Killdeer Plains Wildlife Area. It has modern

Outstanding field trial facilities at Killdeer Plains Wildlife Area, Harpster, Ohio

The field trial building at Assunpink Wildlife Area, New Jersey.

146

facilities (service center, kitchen, rest rooms, showers, horse barn and dog kennels) with flat ground having fence rows, tree lines and woods edges. It also has the massasauga rattlesnake which is troublesome from late April until mid-September. Part of the area is a Canadian goose preserve and off limits. There is an abundance of mice and owls. Some of the prestigious trials are run at Killdeer during the months of April and October. When it rains, it is wet even though efforts are continuing to provide better drainage to eliminate much of the standing water after heavy rains by creating small ponds in strategic places. The ground is firm and horses do not sink in more than three inches when it is muddy.

The Ames Plantation is claimed to be the best, but is not used by American Kennel Club breeds. I have ridden both courses there and consider some of the creek crossings and cuts through the woods too narrow for the gallery and one creek crossing is probably impossible to negotiate during periods of heavy rainfall. The largest gallery in field trials assembles at Ames. Otherwise, the grounds are excellent although a dog must handle to do well and remain in contention. The facilities are adequate by some standards, and a new handler's barn has been built at the morning course with toilet facilities. Bryan Hall is open usually only for lunch and special events. The plantation is operated in trust by the University of Tennessee and is private and available primarily for certain prestigious pointer and setter trials.

Most all states have public areas for field trials, but facilities are usually limited or primitive. Field trialers depend heavily on the use of state grounds.

Private grounds are available for some clubs and a

The Ames Plantation handlers' barn at the morning course.

The morning breakaway at the National Championship at Ames Plantation.

A luxury facility for field trialers at Withalacoochee
State Forest near Brooksville, Florida.

The camping area at Withalacoochee State Forest.

149

few clubs own grounds. There are less restrictions when using private grounds as a rule.

The grounds at Withalacoochee State Forest in Florida are second to none, and a considerable amount of work is spent burning and cutting to maintain more wild quail covies. The facilities there are outstanding in every respect.

Some other good grounds are at Baldwinsville, New York, Branched Oaks in Nebraska, Bong in Wisconsin, Des Plaines in Illinois, Crane Wildlife Area in Massachusetts, Assunpink Wildlife Management Area, New Jersey, Ionia Recreation Area in Michigan along with many others. These are adequate--some better than others especially in the spring time. There are many state areas available and private grounds are being used for both all-age and gun dog stakes.

Most breed clubs use whatever grounds are convenient and available. State grounds generally have the better facilities where the usage rate is high. The national breed clubs make every effort to find and use quality grounds.

Few are ideal for running both gun dog and all-age stakes but are used anyway. It is important that the grounds used fit the type of dog and stake being run. A big edge running dog cannot be judged properly where there are no edges, nor a gun dog where there are no objectives.

Most field trial grounds are primitive, but pose no particular inconvenience with today's recreation vehicles used by many field trialers.

State grounds sometimes have little care or upkeep and no grooming for field trials as compared to Killdeer and Withalacoochee. Cover is high in the midwest and east in the fall and the grounds are usually wet and muddy in the spring. Most grounds are

Many field trial areas have primitive camping facilities. This is a championship field trial at the Ionia Recreation Area, Michigan.

Field trial building and parking area at Sandhills Game Management Area, Hoffman, North Carolina.

marginal for all-age stakes in the fall because of heavy cover. All have some hazard or minor irritation for dogs, horses and people.

The west has cactus, the mid-west has sand burrs, some areas have spear grass or similar weeds, there are swampy areas in the south, deer and poisonous snakes are most everywhere, and there are other hazards that may deter from an otherwise satisfactory performance or safe experience. Field trialing is not much different from hunting when it comes to problems and hazards except few hunters use horses.

Field trial grounds should be treated as if they were one's own private property without littering. Empty cans, bottles and wrappers should be picked up and taken back to the assembly area and disposed of properly.

A broken bottle or sharp tin can cut dog pads. A dog might miss winning a prestigious stake or two when he is out of action because of someone's carelessness and lack of consideration in litter disposal.

State officials may have to tolerate the littering and spend money cleaning up without taking away privileges, but the private land owners will not. If field trialers care for their sport, they should never litter. Handlers and gallery should be asked not to litter and admonished whenever they do.

COURSES

The arrangement and kind of courses which are set up by field trial clubs, committees or stake managers are extremely important to handlers and dogs. The stake requirements are equally important to the handlers and judges and must be known before a stake is started.

Field trials are held on every kind of cover and terrain. This trial is on the Mojave Desert near Edwards Air Force Base in California.

The riding gallery is shown watching a brace on a clear, beautiful, day at Assunpink Wildlife Area, New Jersey.

153

Frozen horse tracks cause dogs difficulty when running in trials. Some entire field trial grounds are pocked with horse tracks. A few dogs adjust quickly and pay little attention to this problem, but many do. That is unless they are filled with thin frozen water which cuts feet and pads.

Mid-day morning coffee break and dog wagon used at Southeastern Brittany trial at Sandhill Game Management Area Hoffman, North Carolina.

154

The two most common courses are single and continuous of not less than thirty minutes duration. Multiple courses are usually just single courses in which each brace starts at the same place and ends up at about the same place in a cloverleaf pattern or out and back.

A single course starts and stops at or near the same place. A continuous course generally means that no other brace will run over that course for a specified period of time. This depends on the number of braces that must be run and the size and scope of the grounds. Braces continue one after the other until there is no more ground to run on, or the course returns to the original starting point. New braces are started at any point along a designated route which usually requires that a dog wagon follow the gallery.

On a continuous course the field trial officials either assume there is enough natural game available, or birds are released along the planned route of travel.

Single and multiple courses can be set up with or without bird fields, and the bird field may be anywhere on course--beginning, middle or end. Multiple courses can have separate or common bird fields. Birds may be released on course in stakes having bird fields also. Birds must always be released on single courses without bird fields, and contrary to opinion, no dog should be placed that has not had acceptable bird work in a stake. Yet it is done occasionally in American Kennel Club trials although against the performance standard, and frequently in American Field trials. Judges assume that a class run equates to class bird work which is not always true. Where judges know that the field trial officials have been negligent, they may or should

155

call for a second series in which they require birds put out for the dogs they have selected to see on game. Then a birdless run or poor bird work will give a justifiable reason for not being placed. Running of additional series is always an option for judges in every stake.

Field trial officials may use second series call-backs for pointing and retrieving requirements, but it is mostly done in retrieving stakes where birds are not shot on course, or because of safety reasons a dog considered for a placement did not get a retrieve.

Trials must be run within the state laws and within the rules of the sponsoring or licensing organization. Some states limit the places birds may be shot. Certain states do not permit the killing of birds in field trials on state lands and suitable private grounds must be used for shooting birds to satisfy retrieving requirements. Many states permit handlers to shoot birds without a state hunting license at field trials, and some require a handler's own state hunting license to compete in trials.

A first series can be run without a bird field and a second series consisting of just bird field work for the dogs. This variation is useful for some retrieving stakes to break up the routine of a back couse with a bird field where many dogs learn to cut the course to go directly to the bird field.

American Kennel Club rules require that no less than two birds be put out for each brace except in puppy stakes. If a bird field is used at least two birds must be released for each brace.

Whenever practical birds should be released on course in conjunction with the two or more birds in the bird field. Most clubs use three in the bird field retrieving stakes which is the fairest to dogs and handlers.

Time may or may not be called in the bird field depending on what club officials require in the premium list. All-age and gun dog stake bird fields are for eight minutes. If time is called the brace mate must be stopped, or back, until the pointing dog has been released or retrieves.

Stakes having bird fields must be for 30 minutes, or for a longer time, if specified. No dog in a 30 minute stake should be left down longer than 30 minutes unless he is obviously working a bird or is on point. This is a common mistake where a dog gets behind and the judges then allow it a full eight minutes in the bird field after the 30 minute brace time has expired. It is unfair to all the other contestants in what is a **limited** competitive experience for each one. Nothing should be done that creates unfair advantages or disadvantages to a dog in a stake. Cutting brace time for expediency or any other reason is wrong and a violation.

Field trial officials are derelict whenever they run all the stakes over one single course when there are other choices. Sometimes there is no alternative and little opportunity to have multiple or continuous courses. Dogs that run over the same course in each stake may be hurt in their later performances. Some dogs do better each time on the same course and others do worse, but it invariably teaches them bad habits.

AWARDS

Field trial clubs and associations furnish the prizes

for handlers and owners who win and place. The awards can be cash, trophies, hat pins, traveling trophies, merchandise, or paintings and rosettes.

Most American Kennel Club stakes offer championship points, trophies and rosettes. A few clubs offer a money stake--usually these are the limited stakes, but money is not the amateur's quest. Scouts usually receive ten percent or more of the purse, but very few are in the employ of professional handlers in the American Kennel Club.

Most trophies are given by clubs or donated by field trial patrons, although a few are given by makers of dog products.

Futurity money comes from fees for nomination of dams, registration of eligible dogs and entry fees. Except for expenses the money received is divided between the winners and breeders of the winning dogs.

Calcuttas are sometimes used to make money for the club where dogs are auctioned off to the highest bidder. This helps create interest in the individual dogs and the winners. The dogs do not change hands. Usually half of the money goes to the club and half distributed to first to third placements.

STAKE MARSHAL

Field trial marshals have the authority to control the behavior of the gallery and spectators without the force of law. Cooperation is generally good. The National Championship held annually at Grand Junction, Tennessee uses special deputies with arrest authority, or has the authority necessary to remove unruly spectators and gallery along with their horses from the trial grounds. The gallery at this trial is huge and many of those in the gallery have no interest in the running or the outcome.

Marshals should know the course used and guide the handlers and judges with a minimum of instructions. They usually mark the courses with bright streamers before the stake. Marshals regulate and control the gallery, follow special instructions issued by the judges as required, and prevent the gallery from talking to or distracting the judges or handlers. They keep the gallery separate from and behind the judges and scouts. Marshals can be ex-officio judges and when a judge cannot continue, the marshal can step in and continue the stake. For that reason, the first marshal should "judge" the dogs, and the position provides an opportunity to see the dogs almost as well as the judges. It is a job from which to learn judging as well as observe how well others judge.

Large galleries require more than one marshal and many clubs use line marshals to insure that the dogs and handlers for each brace are available and on the starting line at the appropriate time, although it is the handler's sole responsibility.

Marshals normally lay out the courses or are already familiar with established courses and help the stake manager or field trial chairman in other ways.

Some stakes have essentially no gallery riders and after the judges learn the course, or already know established courses, they may agree to forego a marshal where help is short in the club. Many clubs have difficulty getting qualified marshals. Unfortunately, many local clubs use raw novices who in reality are just a number in the gallery, or may be the only one.

Anyone who enters or handles a dog cannot marshal.

In bird field retrieving stakes, the marshal usually keeps time for the judges, and can appoint someone in the gallery to take over his duties and keep it in a position of relative safety from the guns until the bird field time is over. He may direct the gallery to a fixed position each time to wait.

On course, the marshal follows the front dog and handler and does whatever is necessary to direct the lead handler to the bird field at the proper time when one is used. Handlers become separated when one dog goes on point and the other dog is not in a backing situation and its handler goes on. In stakes without a bird field a marshal will keep to the course for the brace time. He can appoint someone from the gallery when a dog goes on point to stay with the gallery when he continues on with the other judge, dog, handler and scout.

In some championship stakes, the gallery is permitted to follow the dog of their choice, but in most local club trials this is not permitted. Again, clubs can make whatever rules they consider appropriate. The duties vary with different associations and they should be known by the gallery.

Marshals may be used to replace birds on course. They should be good horsemen and horsewomen with full control of their horses as they are asked from time to time to take a handler's horse which may not always be an easy or safe task.

DOG WAGON

Most clubs use single course stakes of thirty minutes and never require the use of a dog wagon to transport dogs back and forth from the starting lines to the pickup points.

Dog wagons are used mostly in single course out and back stakes and continuous course stakes. Sometimes it is necessary to shuttle horses back and forth.

There are several precautions the dog wagon driver should observe. He should insist that the owners, handlers, helpers or scouts be responsible for loading and unloading their dogs. Drivers have been bitten when trying to load or unload strange dogs.

Since experienced continuous course dogs often come to dog wagons, the driver should try to time his arrival at the designated points just as the brace is finishing up, or arrive early on a route not likely to intersect a dog in the brace.

Some trial locations permit dog wagons to follow the gallery which seems to be the most effective method. All type vehicles are used including horse drawn wagons. Most clubs holding weekend trials do not own dog wagons, but must depend on the loan of a suitable private vehicle and driver. In these, the crates may not be fastened down and bounce around which can upset dogs, and can affect their performances. Hostility between strange dogs crated, or loose, may also affect their performances.

GALLERY

The gallery is not a part of the official field trial brace activity. They are spectators and should always be well behaved. It might be acceptable for a person in the gallery to call "standing dog" when it is obvious that neither the handler nor judges are aware of it, or call "dog coming up" to alert other riders to

161

protect the dog from the horses. Riders should place the palm of their hands on the horses' rumps and put their weight on it until any danger to the dog is over. Otherwise, they should only follow and watch and not engage in anything that would compromise the running and handling. Galleries should refrain from making loud noise.

A scout should know where his handler's dog is all the time, but it is not possible for the handler, judge or scout to have the dog in sight constantly because of the cover and terrain. But, this does not justify self-appointed **handler coaches** from the gallery shouting out such things as, "Get on your dog," "Your dog is at one o'clock," or "Call your dog," and many other instructions to handlers. The next step is double handling which requires that the dog be disqualified, yet scouts can be observed handling dogs and unless this practice is corrected and penalized, a new bad habit will be formed if unchallenged by the judges. Bad habits can be easily and incipiently formed that are difficult to correct.

In gun dog stakes, dogs will be out of eye contact for short periods of time and are expected to handle. The dogs usually know where their handlers are and will show periodically when not on point. Handlers usually know their dogs well enough to dispatch scouts effectively without using them to handle or intimidate their dogs. Handlers will ride herd on their dogs if permitted by the judges which is nothing more than intimidation. Being close to the dogs keeps them from making mistakes which they do when out of sight of their handlers.

The argument that the handler must show his dog to best advantage is a ploy. The American Field handlers who ride breakneck speed after dogs to keep them in sight or to intimidate them by being in sight of them are only kidding themselves, and it has become a too common practice in Brittany all-age stakes.

THE CAST-OFF

It is natural and healthy for puppies to play. But there is a time and place for everything. Some dogs play all their lives, but if done on the cast-off, or breakaway, it detracts from the performance and can be detrimental to a dog's acceptance of field trials.

A handler should not permit his puppy or derby age dog to play at cast-off, but they usually give it up shortly and go on hunting. But, not always, for some learn to love playing, bumping, tagging, wrestling and trailing more than hunting and these are the dogs which cause problems to every brace mate, and once the habit is fixed they never quit of their own volition.

This behavior must be stopped the **first** time it happens. Male dogs start most of the undesirable playing. These dogs usually belong to beginners, but a few experienced amateur and professional handlers see no real harm in a puppy being a puppy and are guilty of helping ruin many dogs.

Dogs with strong hunting instincts will not permit any interference from brace mates. They have methods of putting fear into the offending dogs without fighting them. Others do not fare so well and become problem dogs with males often learning to fight, or they become so distressed they will not leave the starting line and if they do, will not hunt.

Male dogs historically do not like to back down or break off from a challenge with a strange dog. Some will not and pick a fight causing other problems.

Present rules require that judges report dogs which start fights, and after only two separate fights are disqualified permanently from competition. This rule came about because judges and handlers were ignoring the problem and permitted the guilty dog to continue on in the brace.

It is unfortunate that an otherwise potentially great dog suffers because of a handler's ignorance or poor training of a young dog. A handler with a problem dog will often take his dog over to the brace mate on the starting line on the pretense of "getting acquainted." This is a sure sign that he has a problem on cast-off and the bracemate usually gets the worst end of it. This is not a suggested training method to solve it, and may only serve to exacerbate that very problem.

BIRD FIELDS

A bird field is normally set up at the end of a course. It gives all dogs in the stake an equal opportunity to find birds and show their pointing style, manners and control on flush, shot and retrieve when required.

When single course stakes are used, native birds are driven off after the first brace or two along with most other game. There may be an occasional bird that wanders across the course during the day. For economy, a club may not release pen raised birds on course, but place them only in the designated bird field. It is always best for the dogs to have opportunities to find birds on the back course.

Bird fields should be between five and ten acres in size, and may be anywhere on course and marked at the

Bird field stakes allow the gallery to watch all the braces working the bird field in relative comfort.

Professional handler, Daniel Burjan, is watching his father work a dog in the bird field at the Vizsla Club of America National Championship.

four corners with flags. The location is a factor in the working difficulty for club officials and gallery when it is not placed at the end of the course.

Whenever horseback handling is permitted, bird fields should be at the end of the course. It is difficult to have someone take handlers horses at the bird field and lead them in to the stable or starting line. When handlers have scouts they do this task, but many times there is nobody in the gallery to take a handler's horse. For that reason, some clubs would be better off having walking stakes.

Most handlers agree that it is unfair to have bird fields at the beginning of a stake. Dogs must **always** urinate and defecate the first hundred yards or so out, and this really fouls up the bird field in a hurry. Another reason is that the dogs are usually eager to run at cast-off as fast as their legs will go and could overrun birds, push them out unintentionally, or make other mistakes which could eliminate them from competition in the first minute.

The gallery can create problems in bird field stakes. Instead of staying together at the entry point of the handlers, or another designated location, they string out all along one or two sides of the bird field in their eagerness to go into the assembly area on the other side. The gallery compromises the safety and ability of the gunners to kill birds no matter where they are located.

The gallery is important to field trials as most of the people are handlers, owners or interested patrons of the sport. Many are there to evaluate the dogs independent of the judges.

One duty of the marshal is to direct the handlers around the course so they enter the bird field together at the proper time. If handlers become separated it cannot be done.

Bird fields for gun dogs are eight minutes duration. A normal single course stake is thirty minutes which means that the dogs should enter at twenty two minutes. This is different for puppy and derby stakes, since puppy stakes can be fifteen to thirty minutes and derby stakes twenty to thirty minutes. A puppy stake has a maximum bird field time of six minutes and derby of eight minutes.

STAKES

Even when suitable grounds are available for continuous courses, some field trial clubs never plan stakes to use them. Any experienced field trialer knows that in order for a dog to do his best he must be hunting on new ground in his casts to the front--not along a string of dog and horse urine and manure.

Most clubs set up courses for the convenience of their workers and to satisfy the maximum number of dogs in a limited amount of daylight hours on a weekend. Efficiency and quantity are the criteria to run the maximum dogs, not what helps make the dogs do their best. Continuous courses tend to do that for dogs and better simulates real hunting conditions.

Most field trialers realize that theirs is a weekend sport. Recognizing then that it is not always possible to run on continuous courses, the basic philosophy should be to set up running conditions to satisfy the maximum number of entries and to simulate natural hunting conditions without giving undue advantage to one handler over any other.

Every possible consideration should be made so that bitches in season can run if their handlers choose.

There are two classifications for handlers: open stakes for both professional and amateur handlers; and, amateur stakes which are for amateur handlers only.

There are no amateur stakes for puppy and derby age dogs in AKC trials contrary to what some owners/handlers believe, but rules are never cast in concrete. All stakes, except puppy, can be for retrieving killed birds.

for German Shorthaired Pointers, Brittanys, Weimaraners, Vizslas, Irish Setters and German Wirehaired Pointers. The remaining breeds have not qualified through national clubs.

The AKC licensed stakes are: Open Puppy; Open Derby; Open Gun Dog; Open All-Age; Open Limited Gun Dog; Open Limited All-Age, Amateur Gun Dog; Amateur Limited Gun Dog; Amateur All-Age and Amateur Limited All-Age.

A club may run any or all these stakes in a weekend trial with no entry limitation if it chooses. An unlimited entry means that two, three or more courses may be run simultaneously if entries require. In practice this never works because the same dog can be entered in all the gun dog and all-age stakes and results in conflicts in the running where one stake waits for a handler who is running in another stake. It is impractical to run more than four regular stakes on a weekend in addition to puppy and derby, but it is done by a few clubs.

German Shorthaired Pointers, German Wirehaired Pointers, Vizslas and Weimaraners require a minimum of four of the championship points to be won in retrieving stakes. It is sometimes difficult for an owner to find retrieving stakes close enough to home that he can win and finish his dog. Therefore, those breed clubs

168

should provide more than one retrieving stake at each trial.

Another point of contention with some field trialers is that dog breeds requiring retrieving points should be tested in retrieving stakes all the time. A dog can have puppy and derby points for a total of four points (maximum), then win an amateur retrieving stake of four points and win a three point non-retrieving stake for an open champion title by an **amateur** handler. Some argue that an amateur stake lacks the quality of competition of open stakes with professional handlers.

It is possible to finish a dog's champion title in less than top quality competition with only six gun dog points where three points must be won in an open stake (major) and three in an amateur stake and four in puppy and derby stakes. A Brittany must win a major stake held by a Brittany club. Retrieving stake points must be won in retrieving stakes held by a specialty club for the four breeds mentioned.

These clubs can make it difficult for professional handlers to finish their dogs by holding non-retrieving open stakes. Somewhere between the two extremes of holding all retrieving stakes and all non-retrieving stakes there are ways to insure that only quality dogs finish their field champion titles.

REPORTING

Every owner wants to see the name of his dog in print and revels in a favorable writeup which does wonders for his ego and gives good advertising. Unfortunately, not enough is written about dogs in most trials which would be helpful to breeders, future breeders and potential buyers of top performing field trial dogs.

The field trial secretary is responsible for making a complete report but, trial writeups are not a requirement.

Sometimes a field trial secretary or chairman will report trials in detail for their local club or national club publications with no guarantee that it will be published. Some owners do not like to read the truth about the performances of their dogs, so it is just as well that writeups about each dog in a brace are not done. Reporters who write about poor performances, as they see them, are often verbally abused.

The National Championship was reported by Albert F. Hochwalt from 1904 until 1937 for *The American Field*. He became ill and had to leave the trial in 1936. He attended and reported twenty to thirty major circuit trials each year which was no easy task considering the type transportation available. He was both a prolific writer and author and maybe he was the best reporter in history for these kinds of field trials.

William F. Brown succeeded him and reported the results of the National Championship until 1982, and some of his friends think he was the greatest field trial reporter.

Both men have contributed immensely to the prestige and value of this stake and to the field trial sport in every way possible.

The pointing dog followers and breeders need access to information of dogs currently in competition. The American Kennel Club publications are derelict, and place little or no importance on reporting of the running and bracing. It lists judges, number of entries, number of points, placed dogs and owner's

170

names in *The American Kennel Club Show, Obedience and Field Trial Awards* monthly publication. Once in awhile it will report on a National Championship trial for one of its Parent Clubs in *Pure-Bred Dogs/American Kennel Gazette*. Until just recently both publications were together.

The German Shorthaired Pointer News, a private publication, provides coverage of the smooth and wire coat field trials. Otherwise, individual breed club national publications and local club newsletters give results of some, but not all, trials. It is hit and miss mostly. Therefore, there remains a great thirst for information and knowledge about field trial activities among pointing dog owners, and the general public is not even exposed to field trial writeups except by accident. Newspapers seldom ever carry results because club secretaries do not know how to prepare and submit such information, or have been previously discouraged. They usually do not meet the timeliness necessary for newspapers.

Most all newspapers have an 800 number and sport editors will accept collect calls for trial reports. It is a nice practice to call a national winner's home newspaper so his friends can congratulate him.

Field trial reporters usually ride with the judges and use a tape recorder to keep a running account of each brace. Reporters may or may not wish to discuss their writeups with judges because what they see and write may not be what the judges saw. Where judges write reports of the placing dogs for clubs, the reporter might wish to compare notes. Enough dissension is created without a conscious effort to do it, and reporters normally do not want conflicting writeups with those judging.

RULE INFRACTIONS

Most people are not interested in causing problems or distress to themselves while field trialing, but some consume more alcoholic beverages than they can comfortably handle and become boistrous or insulting. It is important that the field trial committee understand that undesirable behavior should be stopped and action taken by the field trial committee to discipline offenders for serious offenses. This includes all social events and activities which are a part of the field trial.

Poor sportsmanship is a rule infraction which can result in being suspended from future trials. Beating and any other mistreatment of dogs can result in suspension of privileges in the American Kennel Club.

The field trial committee is the American Kennel Club for the duration of its trial and must act against unsportsmanlike conduct, abuse of dogs and other rule infractions that are harmful to the sport's image. Anyone can bring charges before a field trial committee. This is not to say that such charges will always be handled properly or promptly, because many people on these committees prefer to gloss over or ignore the complaint, or fault the one who complains.

Procedures for disciplining field trialers is given in Chapter 15, in the American Kennel Club's "Field Trial Rules and Standard Procedures for Pointing Breeds," available free. It also furnishes a "Guide For Field Trial Committees In Dealing With Misconduct At Field Trials & Hunting Tests."

Field trial committees are guilty of rules

infractions and nothing much is done about it. The American Kennel Club has field representatives who visit selected trials periodically throughout the year. They are on the road every weekend. They usually act in an advisory capacity and leave enforcement to the field trial committee.

Field trials are on the honor system and the clubs are responsible for policing themselves. It is a fact that some field trialers believe that rules are not needed, and if they are, then they are for everyone else. Rules are necessary to every sport and the enforcement is an established requirement.

Many field trialers reject rules by ignoring they exist. They dare anyone to do anything about them. In spite of all this, field trials are being run every weekend all over the country and self-policing works well most all the time. There is no substitute though for education, even when some people refuse to be educated.

UNETHICAL BEHAVIOR

Everyone who first starts out in the sport of field trialing, as a rule, is naive, innocent, pure in thought and purpose, and is not looking for problems.

Field trials have rules which are intended to instruct, inform, control, regulate and sometimes discipline those who participate and are offensive to other participants, dogs and the sport.

So, if there is a problem with dogs, other competitors, or spectators what relief, if any, is possible? We must consider those laws, rules or regulations for the sport which are in addition to

173

those which protect life and property under established state laws for the area.

The stake manager or field trial chairman is required to act on all complaints without delay, even if it means stopping the trial. He or she may or may not elect to help, but it is his or her responsibility to make an investigation and take it to the field trial committee if necessary and resolve it as quickly as possible. This requirement is in effect from the start of the trial to the end including all social functions.

For conduct alleged to have been prejudicial to the best interests of field trials, an owner, handler or spectator can be expelled from the stake, organization or grounds. The American Kennel Club has the power to levy fines and suspend clubs and individuals from further competition. Therefore, problems which are ignored by the chairman or field trial committee should be sent to the American Kennel Club. Sometimes it may be necessary to protest against an ineligible dog in a stake or trial.

Usually, the abuse or mistreatment of a dog by his handler results in fewer charges than should be made. Abusive treatment of judges is always a problem. Fights are detrimental to the sport and should not go unpunished.

County Sheriffs or State Police are available to handle crimes to participants and their property when in their area of jurisdiction. Sometimes their services may be needed. They should be used when necessary, for sometimes it does not pay to be too forgiving for the sake of harmony in the sport.

TRIAL COSTS

The field trial sport is expensive but there is no other sport that gives the knowledge, exhilaration, joy, clean exercise and rewards. A one dog, one stake, weekend outing might not cost anymore than a weekend fishing trip, but it is useless to make a comparison to any other sport. There **is** no other sport that can compare in its depth, breadth, knowledge and skill for success and physical well being.

Field trials and gambling are similar. Once started it may be impossible to quit.

Game birds and horses used for field trials are expensive and pace field trial costs. A few years ago a pheasant could be bought for two dollars and horses rented for ten dollars a day, but those days are gone. Pheasants cost up to ten dollars and fifty dollars a day for horses. Entry fees reflect these costs.

Another cost driver is judges—even though most accept only expenses, or pay their own. Costs can be kept lower by using local field trialers for judges.

Transportation, training equipment, dogs, horses and birds are a big part of field trial costs in preparing for competition. Each dog owner progressively becomes more and more involved over the years and slowly accumulates whatever is needed. These costs are never dissected and added to the entry fees in figuring the total cost of the sport.

Field trials are not for people who have problems meeting daily needs, but a person does not have to be rich either. I know people who make many sacrifices to compete with their dogs which may mean there is not always enough food on their tables. We would prefer that did not happen, for there are other ways to be involved in the sport other than by competition. There is considerable satisfaction in working as chairman, secretary, marshal, bird planter, gunner, judge or spectator. All have something of interest and require certain enjoyable skills.

Some handlers and owners spend weeks and months on the field trial circuit. They are the professionals mostly–and men and women with means.

Entry fees depend on the type field trial stake. A club which runs on native birds has the least expensive stakes. The cost increases with inflation and is dependent on whether the stakes are pop–gun, retrieving or more than 30 minutes. Costs vary with the kind of bird and the number used per brace. The cost to an amateur depends on the number of stakes entered. Half–hour gun dog stakes cost about $30 in 1989.

One solution to a trainer's bird expense is to build a pigeon loft and keep recall pigeons. Where state laws permit, he can use quail recall pens. The birds used this way are not normally killed and are able to return and be used over and over. Chukars and pheasants are difficult to recall by comparison.

There is a mortality rate from birds of prey, wild predators, neighborhood cats and the birds dogs catch in training. Some birds never return.

For every pigeon that returns to the loft, a trainer can take one dollar from one pocket and put it in another. For every quail he can put in two dollars and fifty cents the same way.

The number of birds used for a given dog will depend on the training methods used and the progress it makes.

It takes many birds to develop young dogs. Experienced trainers make every effort to prevent them

176

from breaking point and catching birds. This is the best reason for using pigeons. Once flushed, they fly away and are less likely to light nearby (as quail do) and be caught.

I have read ads where the trainer claimed he worked each dog seven days a week several times a day which is entirely too much, if true. A reasonable alternative is half that many days per week once a day on birds. This is not to say that other things should not be done each day with the dogs. Trainers should do several obedience and fun things.

The number of birds used accumulates quickly. Three birds a day will approximate ten birds a week per dog. Five hundred twenty per dog per year. It would be costly to feed those for a year. Keeping ten in the loft for one dog and twenty for three dogs is adequate. The more dogs the less birds need be kept per dog as many return quickly to be used again.

Once a dog is ready to be broke, it should take twenty to fifty birds a month to be killed. It is important not to miss killing any of the birds at the start of breaking, or the breaking can be extended as a result. Once a dog is broke on pigeons, quail should be used, followed by chukar and pheasants in that order. Polishing a dog into a top notch performer after the breaking takes a lot more time. Some dogs lose their range and drive after being broke but in time regain it after the stress has decreased. A distressed dog needs no accelerated training after being broke.

The quantity and method given for breaking relates to dogs broke to wing, shot and retrieve. The dogs are not being trained to retrieve. That is incidental to breaking. The dogs are being taught to stay when a

177

bird is shot and killed. They may or may not be allowed to retrieve the birds depending on how excited they are to break without a command. Retrieving should be allowed only after the breaking to kill is firmly fixed. The reason so many trainers have retrieving problems is that they are trying to teach the dog two things at once. Each training exercise should be done singly. Obviously, it is easier to break a dog to wing and shot when the birds are not killed. The difference between a bird dog and a **bird dog** is retrieving.

Quality field trial stakes require that a dog retrieve. Otherwise, a dog can finish his champion title and never be a proven performer. This is not to suggest that a dog will not work in a way that he will not appeal to the esthetic senses of his. owner and handler. A retrieve is not required for that. Such a dog is not a **complete** bird dog but a delight to watch work.

The use of horses for handling in AKC trials has increased until hardly anyone walks any more. Also, the pace has been increasing, making it very difficult for the walking handler. The cost of rental horses is now as high as $50 dollars per day with brace costs of four and five dollars.

After a dog is broken steady to wing and shot he can be entered in three or more stakes each weekend for ninety dollars or more during the normal eight week spring and fall trial season in most sections of the United States. It is possible to field trial year round by traveling south and west. Entry fees add up to over twelve hundred dollars a year for each dog, and field trial champion titles do not always come quick or easy. It takes two or three years, or even longer, and some never finish. Many things happen other than the luck of the draw and weather to extend the time required. Yes, it is true that some dogs do finish in a spring or fall trial season, but that does not happen too often.

AKC dog owners can only get two titles in trials--Field Trial Champion and Amateur Field Trial Champion. These dogs can continue to compete in all gun dog or all-age stakes, and, when possible, should also begin serious competition in another association's trials. Except for health reasons, these dogs should not be retired, but trialed and hunted.

A dog entered in both puppy and derby stakes every weekend for two seasons, spring and fall, and in all the derby stakes every weekend for another season will have run in a total of twenty four trials. The dog will be about two years old then. Owners will spend over forty dollars a weekend in entry fees. The cost of transportation, food, lodging, horse rental and incidental expenses for two days and nights each week will vary for each person. The total cost in entry fees will be about eight hundred dollars.

Once both open and amateur field titles are won in American Kennel Club trials and a prestigious breed national championship title for the year, there are other kinds of trials put on by other associations. Some owners might want to compete against other breeds if they are interested in proving how well their dogs will do in them.

BIRD PLANTING FOR FIELD TRIALS

Clubs should find a good reliable, dependable, source

This is the method used to fold and lock the wings of a
pigeon so it will stay in place without flying away. Each
method of keeping birds in place is no substitute for
working dogs on wild birds.

A bird releaser should be placed down in heavy grass
(cover) where the outline cannot be seen by a dog. The bird
should be facing into the wind as the dog will point from
downwind with a better possibility that the bird will fly
away from it when flushed.

Bird planters should stay upwind when planting birds and
then wipe the bird in a circle and put it down on the upwind
side of the circle with the bird facing into the wind so the
dog is helped with the scent and flush.

locally for strong flying pen raised birds. They should be reserved in the approximate number needed for spring and fall trials during the breeding season. It is usually difficult to buy birds in the spring of the year unless clubs have made previous arrangements. Bird breeders in the south usually have a supply year round, but shipping by air can be inconvenient.

A field trial is never successful when a club skimps on the number of birds it uses. Many clubs do not use any birds for their puppy stakes, but charge a big entry fee. It is important for a puppy to have bird contact in its formulative stages in the sport. Puppies should have strong flying birds that they cannot catch. Pheasants are not as suitable as quail or chukar for puppy stakes, but are better for derby stakes.

Puppies need not point, but it is essential for derby dogs. The vagaries of field conditions associated with the weather conditions makes the pheasant the most practical bird for derby stakes. Chukar are good too and provide reasonable scent under wet conditions, but both birds have a tendency to run out of the bird field early. So, it is important to use experienced trainers to put out birds.

Quail and chukars are best for putting out on courses. Pheasants can run a mile away in a few minutes, and are noted for running from a dog that has established point. It is possible to set up conditions for quail so that they remain in the general area for an entire trial and be worked several times by dogs in different braces.

When the ground is wet or it is raining, there is not much advantage in using quail. They do not fly well and cause dogs to break with their grasshopper jumps

into the air trying. This is especially troublesome
with pointing dogs accustomed to retrieving, for this
situation nearly duplicates those conditions where the
dog is expected to retrieve. Dogs then have difficulty
figuring out what to do, and become confused because
they are already overly eager to retrieve and are on
their tip toes ready to go.

Sometimes the weather conditions are such that birds
planted in the bird field will not stay down,
especially in high winds. This is particularly true
with pheasants. When it is wet, or rainy, they should
never be dizzied as they will not be able to fly.
Because there is no formal training for bird planters
they are slung up and down, around and around and
practically pounded into the ground. Sure, these birds
stay--dead birds always do.

One man I knew took pride in putting birds down in
the bird field where dogs had a difficult time finding
them. He dug a hole and buried them alive if they
survived his method of dizzying.

Some pheasants when dizzied, if strong enough to
survive, will not stay down. Their body chemicals are
stirred up too much.

Pheasants, chukars and quail can be put out on course
without getting down from a horse, and they will stay
put most of the time. Quail can be thrown upside down
in the grass and stay put. The other two birds may
need slept slightly, not dizzied, and dropped in place
where most will not fly off. If they do, they usually
fly on course in an even better location.

Some people are more effective in putting birds down
using identically the same methods. They should be put
down long enough for the human scent to be diminished,

but not so long that they get up and walk out of the bird field. It is important that they be in the bird field for the eight minutes the dogs are hunting in it. Ten minutes should be the earliest they are put down before the dogs arrive. It is preferable that a person be used for each pheasant and each one put down and leave his bird at the same time as all others. Quail can be planted by one person by throwing them upside down in a clump of grass or placing their heads under a wing and tucking them head first in a clump of grass. They should never be dizzied. The same method can be used for chukars. Three birds should be used for each brace, and two used when there is a bye dog. Motorized vehicles are not permitted for bird planting on state grounds.

GUNNING

American Kennel Club stakes require that official gunners be used when on course and in bird fields for retrieving stakes. They cannot flush birds. Gunner-handler stakes were stopped on advice of its lawyers. That was an unfortunate turn of events for this provision helped remove much of the artificiality in field trial stakes.

It is impractical to use gunners on course, except for the most prestigious stakes, simply because of the mechanics and costs of running them. It requires two extra horses and, believe it or not, most gunners cannot ride and they have no saddle scabbards. There is too much confusion of gunners trying to control their horses, carry their shotguns, and get to a dog on point as others ride up to hold their horses.

This shows a field trial callback second series which requires the use of two official gunners in AKC trials.

Shooting in a regular bird field retrieving stake where only one official gunner is required.

Sometimes not enough people are in the gallery to be helpful. Oftentimes it leaves a marshal to take a handler's horse and a gunner's horse when trying to stay with the advance judge and handler at the same time.

A handler should position his gunner so that he can have a safe clean kill at the proper distance for the retrieve. Nobody really wants the bird shot at the end of the gun barrel. Gunners should never shoot from behind or over dogs for they have sensitive ears.

Handlers do lay down on the ground at times to keep from getting shot or to make a "safe" shot for their gunners. I saw my fellow gunner in a call back stake nearly shoot the handler because he **walked** into the path of the gun from the side as the bird flushed. He had a habit of moving in the direction of the flushed bird. He primarily competed in American Field trials and did not know proper, safe, procedures in retrieving stakes.

There are many flushed birds in retrieving stakes where the gunner should never shoulder his gun. He should not mount his gun until after the bird is flushed. Some are so tense and nervous and at ready, one would think they were expecting a tiger charge. Nothing is that important in bird shooting.

Bird fields should be selected and laid out, where possible, to take advantage of all conditions and factors which contribute to safe shooting. Special attention should be given to how the riding and walking galleries are controlled at the bird field. Sometimes it is better for them to go to the starting line. Other times it is better to stay in one place on the edge of the bird field in one group.

The location of bird fields should be a consideration

for the gunners. Therefore, most bird fields are at the end of a course.

A gunner can make or break both dog and handler through ignorance of his duties at a field trial. The **best** gunner is not the person who can shoot a hundred straight in trap or twenty five staight in skeet, although given a choice between the two, I would choose the skeet shooter. The best gunner is the trainer having shot birds over dogs and trained them to be steady to killed birds. That person has had to be better than a fair shot and has learned when **not** to shoot. Simply taking a trap or skeet shooter and placing him in a field trial situation can give bad results. Usually he has not been properly coached for his work. He can be trained to do the job--although it takes special effort.

I have had several personal experiences with gunners who have caused my dogs to lose everything several different times. I have observed other gunner situations far worse than what I have experienced for usually I can help the gunner do a good job. Most handlers are at the mercy of the gunner and, even worse, judges who have no real knowledge of what a proper gun should do.

The easiest and simplest explanation of what a gunner does is that he does **nothing** but shoot (only one shot preferably) when the bird flushes properly in a safe direction and all previous training instinctively tells him to shoot, or is prevented from doing so by the judge or handler who will call out "NO," if time permits.

The best gun to use is an over/under or double barrel shotgun. The action should never be closed until the handler is prepared to flush the bird. The gun should be unloaded immediately after shooting and left broken down.

The gunner should never shoulder his gun until he has determined that the bird is taking a safe line of flight for the shot.

The gunner must remember that it is the handler who must flush the bird and handle his dog in AKC stakes.

The gunner must always be with and keep up with the handler, right behind him, and if he cannot keep up he should be replaced. Sometimes gunners need to be track stars.

A gunner must work in such a manner that the handler is never aware that he is with him. The gunner should **never** ask the handler or judge anything during the time he is in the bird field following the handler.

The gunner does not direct the activities in the bird field like a traffic cop. He should never even make light conversation.

The duty of the gunner is to kill birds without danger to anything or anybody.

The gunner should never be in a position that he has to fire over top of the dog or handler. If he cannot get into a different position he must not shoot.

The gunner should avoid being in a position that he has to have the handler drop down on the ground for him to have a safe shot at the bird.

A good gunner will never interfere with the dog and should move to a location to one side and slightly ahead of the pointing dog.

The gunner should make it a practice to be invisible to the dogs when waiting at the edge of the bird field, whenever possible.

The gunner should observe where the birds are planted and be aware of potential points, but not go to the general area beforehand or tell the handler where the birds are located.

Experience for wind conditions and pattern of flushed birds will quickly teach the gunner which way to expect the birds to fly and always position himself with this in mind, or that the birds cannot fly because of the weather conditions.

Gunners should be informed on how and what shooting will be done in each stake. If the stake calls for pheasants then a quail may not be shot or vice versa. The gunner should fire into the air upon flush when it is unsafe to shoot the bird, so that the handler will not have to make a decision to fire his blank much too late. But, he should make special note of what the handler is doing to be sure that he is not firing too. The gunner always defers to the handler.

A bird running on the ground should not be shot except at the direction of the judges--not the handlers.

The Captain Of The Guns should determine whether judges want the second gunner when not occupied to be back up gunner after the brace mate has been eliminated. Most gunners do not understand the purpose of a back up gunner and make a mess out of the attempt to kill the bird. In bird field stakes only one gunner should be used with a handler in all fairness to all other handlers.

A gunner must not fire directly over a dog such that the muzzle blast can ruin the dog's pointing intensity.

The gunner must keep an eye on the judges, the other handler and his dog, and the standing and riding galleries. A bird flying toward any of these must not be shot.

It never keeps a clean dog from being placed when a

gunner misses or cannot shoot a bird if the dog is in
contention for a placement. At the end of the stake
the judges will request additional bird work for that
dog, and will request a back up gunner.

Field trial clubs should train their gunners based on
demonstrated judgment, safety, natural or trained
ability to evaluate the total instantaneous situation,
and the ability to make one-shot clean kills at a
proper retrieving distance.

The official gunner should work and make decisions as
though he were acting in the place of the dog's handler
without ever becoming directly involved. He is an
extension of the handler.

After the shot, the gunner should move to a position
directly behind the handler because dogs used to
hunting often retrieve to the gun.

Gunners must remain emotionally uninvolved with the
conduct of the handlers, gallery, judges and dogs and
concentrate only on safe shooting.

PERSONAL SAFETY

Every activity has hazards and dangers to a person's
health. Field trials are no exception. Fighting dogs
may be the single worst danger to handlers, although
injuries from horses may be more severe and disabling.

Dogs learn to pick fights on stake out chains, and
every once in awhile they are treated to a loose dog
coming into their "territory" and the fight must be
stopped or allowed to continue to its logical end. We
tend to frown on that. Dog fights occur at cast-off
which can ruin one or the other's performance.

A dog can move with lightning speed when fighting and

190

it should be left to experts to break them up, but they are seldom around when needed. Fighting dogs cause serious injuries to their owners, handlers or good Samaritans when breaking them up. It might be wiser to stay out of the fracus.

Walking handlers are subjected to tripping over uneven ground, holes, ant hills, being clipped from behind by a dog, other ground obstacles and fall breaking bones. The situation to avoid is when a dog gets behind and in coming by to get ahead runs full speed into a handler. This also happens frequently when owners exercise their dogs off lead for elimination. Broken bones are incapacitating for a long time.

The walking handler also has to contend with poison ivy, stinging insects, poisonous snakes at certain times of the year and rabid animals. He should be careful in taking a supposedly dead fur animal from his dog. Handlers should watch where they put their hands and feet, and should be extremely wary when flushing over point—it may be something other than a bird and skunks are no fun to kick up either.

Horse tack should be checked often to be sure it is safe, and that the girth strap is in good condition and tight. If not, a handler can cause the saddle to shift when mounting. When this happens out in the field, the horse often panics and runs off. A broken rein can also cause problems with some horses. Bird shot may not be fatal, but it can bring blood when hit from a distance. And, if one is on a horse not accustomed to being shot with bird shot, it could be dangerous.

PART II
FIELD TRAINING &
TRIALING
FOR EXCELLENCE

Chapter 1

Field Trial Pointing Dogs

DEFINITION

There are two **kinds** of field trial dogs--**male** and **female.** Although there are striking similarities, there are also distinct differences that must be understood in their development and training.

A **field trial dog** is one used in field trial competition. He or she may or may not be competitive which may be from poor training and handling.

Field trial dogs are bred and trained for all-age, shooting dog, gun dog, hunting dog or shoot-to-retrieve stakes. Although puppy and derby aged dogs are normally entered in separate stakes, they are juveniles which will later develop into one or more of the above

192

categories, although some have all-age range and independence at a young age.

I have selected descriptions by a few of the many notable field trialers writing in *The American Field,* who relate to pointers and setters. Nobody else can say it any better or more completely no matter what rules, standards and stakes they run under in any of the other organizations. American Kennel Club publications are not field trial oriented and ideas from individual writers cannot be expressed, so I have used quotations from several other publications.

Paul Walker wrote in *The American Field,* March 15, 1975:

"Unless your dog will hunt for you and stay with you, he is not a true field trial dog."

For some owners, an all-age dog is historically the only **true** field trial dog. All age dogs are at the apex of field trial competition, and glory, in the minds of many owners and trainers because the maximum desire and potential is brought out by avoiding the stress of retrieving.

Preferences though do not define a field trial dog. Whoever toots his own horn-the loudest in this argument wins. Extensive public relations by special groups or individuals can make a big difference in opinions and public acceptance. Minority breeds are seldom mentioned by established writers in this field. The Vizsla is just one breed. When they were first introduced into the United States in the early 1950's every sports magazine carried ads and articles. Hardly any do anymore, yet this breed is in field trials regularly in numbers greater than many of the older more established breeds.

David Grubb writes that:

"too many people have the misconception that field trial dogs are not gun dogs. All too many hunters think that all the field trial dog does is run, run, run. The field trial dog is a gun dog with class."

Consider for a moment all the thousands of dogs that are in field trial competition year in and year out. Who is to say that they are not all "field trial" dogs? Some seldom place or win, but their owners must believe they are to keep entering them year after year. Many usually suffer from poor training and development. Many are not even good gun dogs. After all it is difficult, if not impossible, for beginners to learn a systematic method of training a **complete** field trial dog.

Paul Walker writes that:

"A true field trial performer is one whose potential has been unhampered, yet developed and intensified to a high degree. His performance must be more than that of a good hunting companion. A top flight field trial dog must be brilliant, eye catching, as well as fully trained. That is where the trainer comes in."

I believe that paragraph is adequate, but Paul continues:

"A field trial dog is a dog of substance and temerity along with characteristic ability and accomplishment. Above all, perhaps, he is a happy dog. He loves his work. He must take joy in it to be good at it. With experience, it is quite possible he even knows he is in competition and revels in it."

There are many more definitions of a field trial dog and there is disagreement on many of its attributes. Some writers present their observations and opinions with descriptions better than others. Some breeds may really show more desirable qualities than others but

194

lack owners having the money and the ability to promote them in the same way.

Range is always the one most magnified performance characteristic which varies from that of a boot-licker to a renegade self-hunter that runs until he collapses from exhaustion many miles away. Somewhere between these two extremes is the right dog for each breed and owner.

The best dog is one which had the best potential and training based on the trainer's distinct personality and interest in a class bird dog.

There is always one failing we have when describing dogs. It is difficult not to refer to them in human terms, although temperament is the one best descriptive word for a dog's behavior--not personality. I use the words most common and familiar which describe the dog's actions and behavior even if anthropomorphic sounding.

Another way to understand different ideas of what is best in a field trial dog is to observe all dogs that compete in field trials and select the breed which best suits an individual's personality. This is important to success. Not all have the range, style, handling, desire and temperament that suits everyone's personality. Not all are the same size in each breed which is minor by comparison to the other important requirements.

There are long hair, wire hair, short hair, large and small dogs with both long and short tails. Cockleburrs and stick-tights do cause serious problems with long haired dogs and some may spend more time chewing on cockleburrs or looking for a mud hole to wallow in to cool off instead of hunting.

Certain breeds and individual dogs within a breed establish a close relationship with their owners.

Some never do. Trainers may spend more time hunting dogs than handling and being competitive in field trial stakes.

What breeds get lost or lose contact? The pointers are most famous of all, but several strains of German Shorthaired Pointers, English Setters, Red Setters and Brittanys in the all-age classification are often lost in field trial stakes. Some are found still hunting on and about the course and taken in tow in later braces, but some are never found or are found dead along a road.

Many owners prefer big running dogs and accept the inconvenience of hunting for them as a condition of ownership. Used car salesmen are a different "breed" from new car salesmen. Each one is born to his job as are the owners who own all-age dogs. I have no desire to have my field trial interrupted to look for a dog.

It should be easier to pick out a "field trial" puppy in a litter than to pick out what some consider the "pick of the litter." Like begets like, so one should go to a breeder who is active in field trials with an established reputation of always having competitive dogs. We do not have to take anyone's word. Field trials are open to the public free of charge. Potential dog owners should go to trials and watch the breeds in competition to make a more intelligent choice.

Puppies should be seven weeks of age when taken from the breeder where the first few weeks should be spent housebreaking and making necessary adjustments. Toys can be bought to occupy the puppy's time and save valuable furniture or anything else it happens onto if kept in a home. The other choice is putting it out in the elements in a kennel. Some are well built and heated which provide excellent conditions for the

196

puppy. There are obvious advantages and disadvantages to both methods.

It will be a few weeks after the puppy is in its new home before he adapts to his new environment and is socialized enough to take into the field.

When is the best age? It depends on an owner's experience and background. A puppy must learn to hunt. An inept owner can damage a puppy's natural desire.

Puppies may be worked shortly after they are weaned at something related to field work, if nothing more than putting a dead bird in with them and introducing them to the wing and string game. Some breeders may be better off to wait until their puppy is older, but they need to begin early so that their dog will be mature enough to accept things in its environment and learn how to live and cope with them. There is that age in many young dogs where an experience can be positive or negative. Dogs exposed to something which creates a negative reaction will cause trainers to regret it, or they may blame it on poor breeding.

A field trial puppy should be introduced to horses when old enough to get out of the way of one intent on doing it harm. Too much trust by being only associated with a "safe" horse can spell trouble later at field trials where hooves fly in a dog's direction when the horse feels threatened. Some seem to do it for sport.

A good field trial prospect must be healthy, free of external and internal parasites and disease, have no structural deformities and be fed a daily diet that best suits its individual needs. Most important of all is that it should be able to reproduce. Hip dysplasia is one example of structural deformities, and a dog should have its hips x-rayed at two years of age, or older, by the local veterinarian, and the film sent to

197

the Orthopedic Foundation For Animals for analysis and clearance. Dogs should not be bred if dysplastic.

Histoplasmosis is just one disease--seldom diagnosed--that destroys a dog's stamina and endurance, and it goes hand and glove with field trials since it comes from bird droppings. X-rays of the lungs will show that a dog has had it, but the sympthoms may not be associated with the disease when he is suffering from it. Anytime a dog appears out of condition or cannot get into top condition, this disease might be the problem, but nothing is really known about it. Dogs do recover and return to normal health, although they might not have the endurance they would have had without it, and they may build up an immunity. This disease also occurs in humans.

A field trial dog has **class**. What is class? It is one of many intangible qualities that are possessed by good field trial dogs. **These** dogs are not run just to make one more entry, they are entered to **win**.

There is no question in my own mind that class dogs know they are in competition. They know that they need to beat their opponent from the cast off on, or maybe they just detest backing another dog on point. I suspect that being competitive is hereditary after seeing different types of behavior repeated in several generations of my own dogs.

Three different generations of my Vizslas, those trained from horseback since giving up foot handling, kiss my horse before casting off. Something that could be hazardous to one's health if on the wrong horse. No one to my knowledge had ever seen another dog do it. I believe they are indicating that they accept the horse as part of the team making the heat competition a triad--handler, dog and horse. This is purely a guess.

Art can best describe training of pointing dogs for field trials. The individual owner-trainer or professional trainer develops, or destroys, a dog's ability to learn and progress in training. Some use the chauffeur (mechanical) approach in which they will not permit their dogs to think for themselves and must submit totally to the handlers demands. This approach does not make for good **class** field trial dogs.

Once we agree on what a **field trial** pointing dog is, we must differentiate between the all-age, shooting dog, gun dog and hunting dog.

All-age stakes began for all ages of dogs which included puppy and derby age. All-age now means a dog with unlimited range and superior speed. Every dog owner or trainer describes the all-age dog based on his own perceptions and experiences. Derby age dogs often win all-age stakes in American Field stakes and one has won the National Championship.

John S. Gates in *The American Field*, March 29, 1980 maintains that the dog and handler are a team and

". . . that the ideal field trial performance is an exhibition that brings out brilliantly all the superior qualities of the brainy, bold, tireless bird dog." He also writes that the handlers with the most success **". . . virtually allow these dogs to train themselves, applying only such restrictions as are necessary in steadying of a dog on point and back, but allow the dog almost absolute freedom in other respects so that he is not hampered in the development of his natural qualities (which are all that can be perpetuated)."**

There is no question that this is the ideal way, but forcing a dog to retrieve stifles freedom to develop

199

along the same lines. It is what is called a new ball game.

William F. Brown in *Field Trials: History, Management and Judging Standards* wrote:

"Bird finding is the desideratum, but the manner and quality of the performance round out the simple finding of game. To measure up to field trial standards a bird dog must possess speed, range and style. He must be endowed with stamina and a good nose. He must exhibit initiative and enthusiasm; he must demonstrate methodology in negotiation of terrain. He must display character, animation, independence, intelligence. His work must be incisive, merry. He must show intensity and steadiness on game. He must handle and demonstrate biddability. The ideal bird dog, in short, is the finished <u>product</u>, a high-class thoroughly broken performer which excites constant and persistent admiration by the excellence of his works."

The all-age dog almost runs off as he raises the hackles on one's neck when experiencing electrifying tingles up and down the spine. Range is the horizon and beyond. His staunchness is that of a statue until his handler finds him on point.

It takes much more work and risk to train an all-age dog than a shooting dog and takes more skill and stamina. They get lost and are difficult to find whether on point or when hunting. These dogs usually have accomplished trainers, handlers and outstanding scouts. Dogs can have all the stellar genetic qualities for becoming top field trial competitors, but fail because of poor training and handling.

Gun dogs and shooting dogs are for all practical

purposes the same thing. The American Kennel Club uses "gun dog" and American Field uses "shooting dog." Sometimes there is an effort to differentiate between horseback and foot handling where the dog handled from horseback is expected to range out farther but not to all-age range.

Gun or shooting dogs are field trial dogs having most of the same characteristics found in the best all-age dogs. The primary difference is range, independence and handling. Gun dogs are more practical for the average person engaging in the sport.

A gun dog should range out according to the cover and conditions necessary and remain aware that he is hunting in partnership with his handler, and to the gun for retrieving stakes. That range may be self adjusting from fifty to three hundred yards or more depending on the terrain and cover.

A dog spends more time hunting for birds than finding and pointing them. It is only logical that more emphasis is placed on his hunting qualities especially from an esthetic point of view. Therefore, the dog finding the **most** birds will not always win. The method and manner of bird finding is important.

In Shoot-To-Retrieve Association trials the **reverse** is true, but the dogs that win the most often also have many of the great qualities of **class** dogs. Although the emphasis and score is based upon the number of finds and retrieves, they are gun dogs in the truest sense, but practically speaking are **hunting** dogs.

Retrieving is an important requirement for field trial dogs--hunting dogs--before their true character can be known or evaluated. Maybe they would be even better dogs if they were required to flush on command as is done in Australia, for example. It is less hazardous for the handlers. I have read where John Rex Gates teaches his gun dogs to flush on command and I have seen it done.

Many field champions win titles in all-age and gun dog stakes without ever demonstrating backing or retrieving. Yet, they met the standards for the stakes and breeds to win the titles, or the standards' options.

Range has always been a controversial subject, but Alvin H. Nitchman put it in proper perspective in *The American Field*, page 751, 1981:

"It has been my observation, in the last fifty years, that the consistent winners have been dogs with moderate range that hunt hard and point the most birds. Range in shooting dog stakes has increased along with the speed, style and class of dogs.

"The growth of walking shooting dog stakes in the last few years indicates the desire of many owners for dogs with less range."

Nitchman also writes that heredity, environment, speed, gait and training are responsible for the range of a finished dog.

There is no doubt in my mind that the better field trial dog will hunt at a faster pace and greater range than that preferred by most hunters. A great many owners **do** hunt their field trial dogs regularly, and grouse hunting does the most to develop the range and independence in my own dogs. A few professional handlers will not allow owners to hunt their dogs when in competition.

The primary consideration in hunting a field trial dog is that speed and range not be diminished by hunting so long that he learns to pace himself. I have had no problems when hunting and field trialing in the

202

same week in American Kennel Club trials. A well trained dog will do well in both areas, but I do not insist on perfect manners when hunting. It all depends on the individual dog. Good dogs learn the difference without having a problem when running in field trials.

Probably the potentially greatest field trial dogs were never field trialed and were always hunting dogs. We will never know.

One most important quality in a pointing dog often overlooked is beauty. I believe the **best** dogs have excellent conformation and are pleasing to look at.

Race horses do not come from plow horses, and it is often said that all-age dogs only come from other all-age dogs, and the best gun dogs come from them also. There are exceptions to truisms, but no knowledgeable person would buy a dog for hunting from a show breeder. Yet, the first American Kennel Club Triple Champion dog (field, show, obedience champion titles) came from a show breeding.

Beauty is in the eyes of the beholder, so there is a big variation in what is considered as a **successful field trial dog.** Some which win field champion titles at the time are not much more than green broke, and were intimidated to stay at wing and shot or into retrieving. They may later on become well trained. Yet, they were successful, and their owners were just as happy as if they had the **one** great dog of the century. Some are satisfied with no more than that level of training, and we may all know some well trained dogs which lacked that little something which kept them from winning a field champion title.

BUYING A FIELD TRIAL OR HUNTING DOG

Breeders may not always produce dogs to their breed standard. There are field dog owners who want **performance**--not looks. Yet, their dogs are pure bred. But a few breeders have cross-bred their dogs for greater range in an effort to win more stakes.

Pure bred dogs are used to create more of the same and the ideal is to always create better dogs whether used for field trials or hunting.

It behooves any potential owner to go to a field trial dog breeder for a new puppy. He will produce better hunting dogs no matter what they will be used for. These breeders have selectively proven and then bred their top performers that generally produce the intrinsic qualities so essential to a class field dog. Too much time and money are involved for them to keep and produce poor dogs as a rule. Intelligent buyers know that the same amount of money and time, or more, are required to feed and develop poor dogs.

What we see is not always what we get. Phenotype and genotype are two technical terms having important meaning to responsible breeders.

Phenotype is what we see when looking at a single dog. Genotype is what is hidden from view in his genetic makeup. Therefore, it is possible to have a dog that meets the most discriminating criteria, but when bred to another dog with like phenotype characteristics will not reproduce the parent's desire for hunting. One or both are not genotypically compatible. It may come out eventually in the wash which, if not both, do not breed true in looks or performance. I know of great performing male dogs bred to many different bitches that failed to produce field trial winners.

Buyers should watch performances of offspring bred from more than one bitch, or one dog, in an effort to see if they breed true. When proven dogs come from a long line of proven performers with high inbred quotients, they generally breed truer to phenotype and genotype.

Performance for searching, range, application, stamina, guts, endurance, pointing, backing, retrieving, manners, handling, intelligence, speed and others of importance must be genetically strong and be unrelated to environmental changes.

The effect of environmental variations must be reduced in predicting results where the heritability traits are low. Environment exerts a high degree of influence on the outcome of traits in dogs having low inherited aptitudes for hunting. What we see may be due more to training than natural ability.

Knowledge of all dogs in a pedigree, and how they are related to one another, can help breeders. It is important that all dogs in the pedigree have demonstrated trainability. This may not be learned in the American Kennel Club registry, because nothing much is ever in print about their exploits, but major circuit dogs' exploits are printed in *The American Field* every week. Some are in great detail. Its pedigrees show all the wins of all listed in it.

Unfortunately, personal likes and dislikes bear on one's selection of a dog. If one does not like the breeder, chances are he will not consider breeding to his dogs or buying a puppy from him. This attitude may be unfortunate, but is generally true.

Only **proven** dogs should be bred. Puppies should only be bought from reputable and responsible breeders. New owners should attend field trials and watch the particular breed they are interested in, or take a look at every pointing breed. They should learn who the responsible breeders are with a reputation of winning in competition for all-age or gun dogs.

Breeders are usually interested in the progress and performance of puppies they sell and guarantee them. Better breeders x-ray for hip dysplasia. They, in effect, collect a "family of owners" who develop a special interest in one another and how they fare in competition, and sometimes develop lifetime friendships.

Puppies should be eligible for registration in the American Kennel Club, the largest dog registry in the world, or American Field, or both. The "papers" are not a pedigree, but a slip of paper with which a dog can be registered for a fee. A buyer should never pay for a puppy without first getting the necessary registration form from the breeder.

Buyers should be aware that an American Field registration does not equate to an American Kennel Club registration for the same dog, but one with American Kennel Club registration can be registered in the American Field registry where a dog does not have to be a "recognized" breed.

Buyers should be wary of the breeder who offers something **new**--such as a cross breeding between two pointing breeds. They should steer clear of such experimentation if planning to field trial. Too much money is spent on poor dogs from established breeds that cannot be made competitive in field trials without buying an unknown.

Dog buyers should stay with pure bred dogs and their individual standards and improve, if they can, on what they have. Pride is not a substitute for honesty.

Buyers expect breeders to be in business for a long time.

Everyone must not forget that the best part of a breeding equation is the bitch. Stud dogs impregnate. Bitches teach puppies to deal with their environment the first and most important weeks of their young lives. She **has** to be the best of the two.

Temperament is extremely important in a bitch used for breeding--even more than for the male, for she transmits her characteristics genetically and environmentally. An owner should never breed to a shy, timid or vicious dog no matter how many great stakes he or she has won.

Gun shyness is a man made fault, but some dogs have a weakness for it. It goes beyond poor training. Their temperament and trainability are suspect. The cause of gun shyness should not be confused with excessive submissiveness. Any dog can get that way. It all depends on how the puppy is treated and disciplined the first weeks and months of its life.

Which sex makes the better field trial bird dog--male or female? Records in American Field trials show that it is the female, all things considered. They handle better, are easier trained and do not waste time and concentration covering every stinky spot on the course with urine.

Both sexes win in field trials. Males are generally more consistent because they do not come in season, have false pregnancies, become pregnant, whelp or nurse puppies. They have the easy life. But, they have other kinds of problems. They try to dominate other males, urinate a drop or so a great number of times in training and trials, and are more stubborn. Females are easier to work and live with, but are **part-time**

207

field trial competitors, otherwise they would most always beat males.

One particular advantage in owning a male is that he is not discriminated against as are females. When properly trained and conditioned, it is easier to keep male dogs that way and make them more consistent winners. They usually win more because more males are campaigned for longer periods of time.

Lip service is given to breed improvement when bitches are generally restricted from most field trials whenever they are in season. Something is wrong in the sport. It is an archaic practice of no particular value. Women and black people were put down by men until just recently because they were supposed to be dumber and less responsible. Pure bunk! In World War II, black men were claimed to be incapable of learning to fly for combat. The experimental program with a black squadron in Italy proved that humans have generally the same capacity to learn and do an excellent job. Some a little better than others which does not relate to skin color.

Every knowledgeable dog trainer-handler should know that restricting bitches in season from running is unwarranted and discriminatory. Male dogs can and should be taught to leave bitches alone in trials or when hunting. Their desire to hunt should eclipse their desire to propagate, and they must be taught to wait until they quit hunting. It may be difficult to do sometimes because some females can be real bitches and the same should be true of them.

There are many factors which trigger what may seem natural sexual behavior that when left uncontrolled will cause a dog's downfall in trials. This can and must be controlled in order to have a competitive dog.

A male dog has heritable characteristics that a female dog does not have. He **can** be stopped from staking out territory, canceling the urine of another male, or covering a female's urine when in competition. A male if left undisciplined can become so possessed with marking and canceling other's marks that he lives to do nothing else. The reason is not because some bitch left her mark. The cause is most likely too much stress from poor or improper training or the lack of training.

Excitement and stress is the cause of excessive bowel movement. It is instinctive to empty bowels before the "chase," and the anal glands can become irritated which results in a dog trying to obtain relief, but the more he tries the more difficult and painful it is. The judicious use of Preparation H(TM) a short time before the brace is helpful if a dog is susceptible to this problem. Vaginal discharge from infection arouses a male's interest more than one in estrus, yet these bitches cannot be prevented from field trial competition. It can do more harm to male performances than when a bitch is in standing heat.

Male dogs are notorious for intimidating brace mates as they leave the starting line, and they do not always limit their objectionable behavior to male dogs.

Field trial committees can control the running so that bitches can compete without undue hardship on themselves or create "unfair" conditions for males. The normal practice is to brace with another female and run last. The American Kennel Club rules say no dog can run on a course until the next day where a female in season has competed, or they can be run in the last stake of the trial.

Dogs should hunt all the time, both male and female,

and no excuses should be offered, nor rules promulgated for dogs that do otherwise. There is never any reason to run males with females in season, but until the rules change so that owners will declare they have bitches in season this will continue to be done. It is cheating much like speeding is in breaking the speed limit. Those who do it have no guilt feelings whatsoever.

In his book, *Bird Dogs and Field Trials*, Jack Harper wrote:

"Ches (Harris) handled a long succession of champion trial dogs. . . . He did much of his good winning with bitches, claiming that on the average a bitch could do better work than a dog, and that a bitch would only be in heat two weeks out of a field trial season while a dog was in heat at all times."

That may sound like rationalization because they should be in season for three weeks. The real problem, if it is one, is that many handlers **cheat**. They say nothing about their bitches being in season and run them anyway even when braced with males. Normally nobody is any wiser.

NOSE

A field trial dog's nose is its most important sense organ. A dog **thinks** with its nose and it is the basic source of intelligence, reasoning and knowledge for its brain. In the relationship with man, touch is also extremely important. A dog reacts to being touched as well as by sight and sound, but relies on its nose to confirm friend, foe, good, bad or to ignore something.

A dog uses his nose to tell where its owner has been,

who he visited and what he did when he was away. If another dog was involved where he was, he is even more interested in learning more about his owner's experiences with his nose. Nothing can be hidden, and nothing is moved or added in his environment without it being detected and checked out.

In the field, it is extremely important to allow a puppy or young dog to examine all scents as much as he chooses in order that he can decide their affect on his future actions. Once he has examined them over a period of time and still persists, that scent should be one that means something--game for instance, not just bird droppings, urine or something of no value. Bird dogs tend to put less emphasis and interest on foot scent as opposed to body scent, but will learn that foot scent means game is closeby and can be found by tracking.

There is plenty of time to decide whether a young dog should pursue a given scent situation in the field. Trainers can usually tell if it is the urine or excretement of another dog or animal. At some time in his puppyhood the owner or trainer should show his displeasure. In time he will learn to leave those scents alone the same way he loses interest in non-game birds as he grows. That is something most dogs quit on their own without discouragement from the handler.

It would be interesting to list all the different scents a dog learns in his lifetime if we only could. Everything has a different smell and he is able to detect it, and in time can discriminate between the scents that are important and those that are to be ignored.

This is one reason we see so many different reactions and eventual acceptance of man-scent on birds used in training. Some dogs learn to ignore all other scents except game birds and remain staunch and stylish when others go through all sorts of unacceptable behavior patterns when the birds are man handled.

It is difficult to be sure that a dog has a good or poor nose when he is only worked on planted game. Over a period of time in many different situations, a dog's trainer learns how good it really is. The ability to smell without good experiences on birds renders a dog's nose practically useless. A dog that does not use the wind properly cannot use his nose effectively to find game. I have had experienced dogs point birds upwind a considerable distance on wild birds. Dogs show us miraculous accomplishments with their noses.

They have to learn to ignore hundreds upon hundreds of scents that have no meaning for them as they run or hunt. I have had dogs sprayed full in the face by skunks and when they got the nasty taste rubbed out of their mouths in the grass, they would immediately point a pheasant. We have seen many dogs that go out to retrieve a bird and point another bird on the way out or in. A dog's nose used properly with its brain is truly a miracle of nature.

DESIRE

Extreme desire is a quality that all field trial dogs should have in training and competition. They should have a one-track mind to seek game when at top speed to the exclusion of just about everything else. Desire can be developed by the trainer and dog together, or independently through self-hunting.

Desire is the quality that keeps a dog going when all

his physical drive has been exhausted. Guts get him up one more time. He still wants to continue hunting when his trainer wants to quit, or believes his dog has run his heart out. Once on leash, or safely back in his crate, he still wants to continue hunting. This quality separates the winner from the also rans. Without desire a pointing dog will never make a great competitor.

This desire extends to competition with its brace mate where the dog is keenly aware that the trick is to find the most birds the quickest.

There may be negative connotations to desire where it leads to jealousy, refusing to back, stealing point, breaking to retrieve before being sent or in challenging the brace mate on cast off.

RATINGS

Whether it is the TOP TEN or TOP TWENTY rating of field trial dogs there are handlers and owners who become fanatical about its value to them, their clients or their ego.

I know professional handlers who do an injustice to many of their clients by continuing to run consistent winners in their strings in **every** stake just to make them the top dog in the rating schemes. The bridesmaid clients are wasting money.

First, the owner with money to hire the best professional handler to run his dogs in the maximum number of stakes and trials every weekend will usually always win out, unless there happens to be a hot shot dog with another professional handler in those same trials.

Of all the schemes devised so far, none accurately determines the **best** dog each month or year in any breed. The dogs listed in the top ten or twenty represent the dogs winning that were entered and run in the most stakes.

For the most part, the TOP TEN is counterproductive and serves no useful purpose, yet we all like to make comparisons. This is what field trials are all about and it is important.

It is unfair to combine all-age and gun dog wins in the same rating tally for TOP TEN. Other schemes split up gun dog, open and amateur and limited stakes in an effort to make the ratings more meaningful.

Some of the winning dogs may not be really worthy, but these rating systems will never indicate that. The top dogs may not even be broke to wing and shot--just intimidated by the nearness of the handler.

It is difficult, if not impossible, to list all the times these particular dogs were put in stakes and did not place. The owner or handler is the only one with that information or knowledge.

Rating schemes tend to give the professional "status," and an advertising lever in getting new clients and retaining those already in his fold.

Handlers campaign dogs at great expense after having finished field champion titles in point trials just for the TOP TEN rating. Some cannot afford to do it anymore than a poker player who is on a losing streak in a no-limit game. Those wins only delayed some of the better dogs in earning their titles costing their owners more money and in the final analysis had to beat **those** dogs to earn titles. Experienced handlers know that no dog can win all the time.

Some owner-handlers have just one dog and learn to

love the sport and the competition and want to remain part of the action when their dogs are competitive. Some with male dogs continue to compete because it is good advertising for stud service assuming the dog continues to win regularly.

The best dogs do not always rise to the top and those doing the most winning are not always a measure of greatness unless they can pass the potential to their get. Like cream, some dogs sour out shortly after winning American Kennel Club champion titles, especially those which were never developed fully or were intimidation trained.

Chapter 2

Field Trial Equipment

The amount and types of equipment a trainer uses in his work will vary with the individual. The list may be much more than the average owner or trainer would ever use. The cost of each item keeps changing each year. There are several excellent mail order firms supplying dog and field trial equipment.

Dog ownership, for field trial competition, can be inexpensive when participating at the minimum level, but full bore it can cost a hundred thousand dollars or more.

An expensive motor home alone can cost over a hundred thousand dollars and horse trailers with living quarters cost tens of thousands of dollars. Obviously most owners will not become that involved or cannot afford the best.

The equipment listed is alphabetical.

Adhesive or electrical tape--Used to fasten dog boots or short sections of bicycle tube to protect the dog's feet from cactus, sharp stones, sand burrs, thorns, briers, course sand or lava.

Bell--Fastened to a dog's collar in order for the handler to know the approximate location of the dog in woods or heavy cover. Mostly used in grouse trials.

Bird pens--For holding training birds for short time periods. Usually made of wire galvanized after weaving. Top can be nylon netting. Quail and chukar must be kept on wire. Pheasants after a certain age can be kept on the ground. Pens can be whatever size suggested for the type bird which varies depending on the age and type bird. Mature pheasants need four square feet per bird, chukars one square foot per bird and quail one square foot per three birds. Flight pens are recommended to condition birds. Quail should be sprayed with water periodically in warm weather.

Bird scents--Pheasant, quail, duck, etc. scents are used on dummies, pigeons, bird wings, and other objects as training aids.

Bird wing--A wing from a game bird is used on a fishing pole, or hidden in various places for the dog to find and point or retrieve.

Blank shells--Most field trial shooting is done with blank pistols or blank shotgun shells and are used in training where killing the bird is not important to that phase of training. A great many shells are used in training each dog.

Collar, choke--A choke chain is used mostly in obedience training and is not recommended for field work. A handler can lose fingers from a dog twisting and thrashing around to free itself to chase. Some are made of leather and tend to shut off the dog's air to get response.

Collar, leather or nylon--Should always be on the dog's neck with owners name, address and telephone number. Used with leads or check cords for all training and control.

Collar, spike--The collar has sharp spikes that dig into the dog's neck to control him on lead or check cord. Not a practical tool for bird dog training except for extremely difficult dogs to control.

Check cord or strap--Used to control dogs when training or roading from foot or horseback. The length should be at least twenty five feet and if made of rope it should be of large diameter, and if the check strap is used it should be at least an inch wide. Shorter check cords, straps or leads may be used when roading from a bicycle or motorized vehicles.

Dog boots--Molded rubber, bicycle tire tube or leather that cover dog's feet which are used for protection on adverse terrain. A bicycle tube can be used in short sections or leather tailored to fit the feet.

Dog crate--Used to house or transport dog. It can be made of welded wire, aluminum, wood or fiberglass. It is made in various sizes and shapes for different size dogs.

Dog toys--Useful in cutting down on boredom and assisting in play and early retrieving. Made of semi-indestructible rubber, nylon or plastic.

Duck decoys--Used in water retrieving training. Some pointing dog owners also like to use their dogs in water and for duck hunting.

Dummy launcher--Shoots a dummy using .22 blanks of various power levels up to one hundred yards. It relieves hand slinging of dummies, is more natural, and dogs love it. Must be handled the same way as a loaded gun.

First aid kit--First aid book, rectal thermometer, scissors, tweezers, adhesive tape, gauze pads, gauze bandage, bandaging tape, Topazone, Bitter Apple, Panalog Ointment, Boric Acid solution, Kaopectate, Opthalmic Ointment, Tincture of Merthiolate, Preparation H, Vaseline, etc.

Fishing pole--Used to play with puppy or dog with wing on line. Stiff casting rod or bamboo pole with monofilament line is best.

Flea spray/dip/powder--Used to kill and control fleas.

Flushing whip--Used by trainers in American Field trials to flush birds or whip dogs.

Food pan--Best material for feeding is stainless steel in two quart size.

Game bird releasers--Use to hold birds in one place in teaching pointing, stop to flush and breaking a dog. Helps control unproductives. Use with foot, string, flushing whip, electric or electronic release methods.

Game bird harness--Made for quail, pigeon or pheasant used with fishing pole to control bird and saved for many training sessions.

Heartworm medication--Used either daily or once a month to prevent heartworm in dogs in all North American climates.

Horse--Used to train and handle dog. Helpful when working several dogs, one at a time, and conserves energy when handling at field trials in muddy or slick terrain or in snow.

Horse blanket--Used to keep horse warm after a hard day when temperature is cold or windy.

Horse tack--Equipment needed to use horse properly: saddle, bridle, halter, lead rope, tie-out, brush, curry comb, hoof nipper, hoof file, hoof knife, leather punch, water bucket and feed bucket.

Horse trailer--For taking horse to field trials and training grounds. Also may be combined with dog boxes.

Insect repellent--To cut down on insects bothering horses or dogs. Some dogs will turn to fight insects when on point.

Jacket/vest--Worn always when training and field trialing. Dogs can see white and light blue the best. They are able to pick out the handler better when it is worn and helps prevent dogs from coming in too close to check with the handlers.

Kennel--For keeping dogs outside the house. Command KENNEL for dog to enter crate or dog box in truck. Also fenced area with dog house which can be placed outside or inside a kennel building.

Lead--(leather or nylon six feet long) Normal length for taking dogs to cast off, obedience training, short check cord training and walking dogs.

Pigeon loft--Small building used for pigeons to return when used for training. Regular barn pigeons can be kept inside for three weeks minimum, then shown how to get though bobs (entrance) and most will make it their permanent home. Homing pigeons should be raised in the loft for best results.

Pistol, blank--A .22 caliber or larger for pop gun dog training and field trials. A .32 caliber pistol can be modified for use with shotgun shell primers at a great savings using spent cartridges.

Pistol holster--For carrying pistol. Use with cord attached to gun to prevent loss. Fasten cylinder pin with safety string or rubber band.

Plastic jug--Used to carry water in training or trials to give dog a drink or wet him down for cooling.

Quail call--Used to locate quail.

Quail recall trap--Used with about one dozen quail. Half are released at a time and return through a cone in the trap to be used over and over.

Rawhide or nylon chews--Used to help relieve boredom and to prevent tartar on teeth.

Recall Pen--Used to feed, water and hold quail where part are released for dog training and they recall back into the pen to be used over and over.

Retriever dummies--Used for play and teaching dog to retrieve from land and water.

Riding chaps--Used when training or field trialing off horse-back in flushing birds in briers. Prevents chaffing when riding.

Roading harness--A special harness for roading with a single check cord or can be used for pulling weights to build up muscles, stamina and endurance.

Saddle bag--To carry extra clothing, rain gear, water, food, drink, etc. when on horseback.

Scabbard--Leather holster for carrying shotgun on horseback fastened to saddle.

Shock collar--An electronic device having a transmitter and receiver which when actuated shocks the dog with the collar to control bad habits or undesirable behavior. Can be used for obedience training exercises.

Shotgun--For killing birds or using blanks in training or field trials. Maximum safety comes with the use of a single barrel, double barrel or over/under in a gauge suitable to individual's preference.

Station wagon, truck, van or motor home--used to transport people and dogs to and from training grounds and field trials. Special vans, horse trailers with living quarters and motor homes can be self contained and save on living expenses. Also, a great convenience at field trials since they can be kept on grounds.

Stopwatch--Used by marshal, judges and handlers to keep time of brace or bird field.

Tie out chains--For dog elinination, exercise, eating, or lying down and resting. Horse tie-outs have a rope threaded through the center of a short length (10-20 feet) of water hose.

Toe nail clipper--To trim dog's toenails to prevent cracking, breaking or tearing off when too long.

Training cap--Can be used for better visibility by dog the same as the training jacket.

Visibility collar--Used as an aid in seeing dog when hunting or when on point and to identify the dogs in a brace. Available in several reflective colors.

Water canteen--For handler or dog to quench thirst or to wet dog down in training or in trials. Also safety measure if dog gets too hot.

Water pan--Used to water dog in kennel or on tie out chain.

Whistle--Used to train, direct or control dog in training and field trials. Excellent for those with inadequate voices.

WEARING APPAREL

The best way to endure the weather at field trials and be comfortable is to take summer, winter and rain clothing to every trial. They are held in every type weather from scalding hot to bitter cold temperatures, tornados, windstorms, thunderstorms, snowstorms, blizzards, hailstorms, sleet, downpours of rain and sometimes even beautiful weather. Fog, ice, severe thunderstorms, drifting snow or a tornado are about the only things which delay the trials.

If the weather is good for people, it may not be for dogs; and, if it is good for dogs it is not always good for people. Horses seem to manage in most kinds of weather conditions better than man or dog.

Horseback riders wear leg protection to prevent chaffing and usually use leather, nylon or naugahide chaps. Panty hose are used by some judges.

Saddle bags are necessary for continuous course trials moreso than single course trials to carry rain clothing and other essentials.

It is important that handlers wear stockings and foot wear that will keep their feet warm and dry, but some just grin and bear wet and cold feet without a whimper.

I prefer a combination of leather boots with two pair of socks, one pair cotton and one pair wool, and a rubber pullover boot or artic boot over the leather boots for wet and cold weather. The light pullover rubber boots can be carried in a game bag or saddlebag and used only when needed.

Handlers should wear something their dogs can recognize quickly when on foot or handling from horseback. Light blue or white is most visible, but I now wear a blaze orange vest, not because dogs can see it better, but it is more useful for me.

Clothing should always be worn in layers. Face protection is important in cold windy weather and lip chap should be used as needed. Leather gloves help when handling from horseback whether it is warm or cold.

No matter what is worn, it can get filthy dirty and covered with mud the first time out in the gallery when it is muddy. Cockleburrs, stick tights and some other weed seeds stick to most materials and are a nuisance.

WHISTLES

A whistle is of significant help to some handlers who

are unable to project their voices or who have difficulty hollering loudly at a dog.

If a whistle is not used in training and trials, dogs must be trained to ignore it. Some dogs handle, or react, to a whistle even when not trained to one the same way they do to certain handlers' voices. In some kinds of training and competition, the use of a whistle is the best option.

Handlers use standard toots on the whistle for stopping, coming in, changing directions, etc. I do not and have never used one in training, and cannot advise anyone on its use except that from my experience whistles are over used and appear to be ineffective by most users.

It is possible for two handlers to use identical whistles and not affect the other's dog. Dogs can learn to recognize their own handler's whistle blowing technique.

More and more women are taking up the sport of field trials every year, and they should learn to train and compete using whistles. Not many have the voice to carry and command dogs. Whistles can be heard farther than the average human voice. Unfortunately many handlers overuse and misuse them. Jack Harper believes that no handler should do anything that handicaps another competing handler or dog, but it happens and there is really nothing ever done about it by the judges.

Havilah Babcock in his book *Tales of Quail'N Such* wrote:
". . . And most of them are great whistle blowers. I sometimes think a whistle has hindered more dogs than it has helped–especially a whistle in the wrong mouth. The best dog trainers I ever watched were the least noisy."

Handlers who walk or ride right adjacent to another handler delight in bursting his ear drums and have no consideration for the harm or pain it causes. I would like to ban all whistles in field trials for that reason, but there are others. Some horses dislike a handler blowing a whistle, so it behooves the smart handler not to get on a horse he does not know or that does not like a whistle blast in its ears.

CHECK CORD OR CHECK STRAP

Trainers should have check cords/straps of various lengths to suit the type training they are doing. For close work, a long one only gets tangled up and in the way.

Some trainers prefer round (nylon braided) ropes. Others find the strap better suited. The rope should be of large diameter, at least one half inch or larger, and a strap at least one inch wide of soft nylon material.

Both the rope and strap have an affinity for wrapping around the arms or legs. A strong dog taking off after a bird can cause severe rope burns. The strap has more area and causes fewer or less severe burns. Gloves should always be used to protect one's hands.

It is best to use the check cord or strap for control--never discipline, but some handlers will do whatever suits their temperament at the time.

A young puppy should be started in the home and field with a short check cord tied to its collar and left on for two or three months. It is very useful in teaching leading, control and timely discipline.

227

In working a young dog on dizzied or slept birds to teach pointing, or for putting hands on the dog on point, a check cord or strap six to ten feet long is long enough for leading downwind to the bird.

I prefer the strap over the rope as there is more surface area (friction) to hold when standing or walking on it to the dog. If the dog tries to change position with the trainer standing or walking on the strap he does not normally associate the restraint with his handler. He will if the handler picks up the cord or strap and gathers it in as he approaches. It can cause softness or other undesirable behavior.

The check cord or strap is a useful tool in teaching the young dog to whoa, stay and come.

Dogs of different breeds and dogs within a given breed require different levels of persuasion or force to learn. Contrary to what some writers or trainers claim, a dog should not get to the end of a check cord or strap and be dumped forcefully the first time he chases when starting to break him. Some dogs can be ruined by doing this. Like anything else, one trainer can use the exact same techniques and ruin a dog when another will not. The novice trainer should never use the check cord forcefully until well along in the dog's training regimen if it is deemed necessary. The trainer must use whatever persuasion or force at the absolute minimum level necessary to maintain control in training.

He should start out by standing on the check cord or strap when the dog is on point even though a strong dog will pull it out when he breaks, but the trainer will be better able to chase him down and stop him either by voice or by getting his hands or feet on the check cord or strap. No discipline or punishment is required and none should be administered initially. It takes time and repetition for a dog to learn to want to do what is asked of him. Patience is paramount for the trainer in the beginning as at other times too. Praise or sweet soft talk must follow all training activities.

A young dog should run with a check cord of twenty five feet, or longer, to become accustomed to it before it is ever used in forceful training. It should be used on older dogs once in awhile when training, even if it is not normally used. Yet, it is helpful to the trainer in preventing a dog from breaking as he approaches. A dog tends to jump in and attempts to catch the bird as the trainer approaches the point. When he is broke from this habit of breaking point as the trainer approaches, then he must also be broke of it when other dogs approach his point. This is normal. It just takes a little time and repetition for the dog to understand that he must obey the trainer and allow him to flush.

On approaching the pointing dog, the trainer should simply step on the cord and walk up to him and pet and praise him when pointing. He can remove the check cord before flushing and then encourage him to chase as a puppy and derby age dog.

Trainers must remember that it is unwise to allow a big running dog to run free or without constant supervision. Check cords will become tangled around bushes, or other objects, and the dog must be found and freed by someone.

BELLS

Mechanical gadgets, such as bells, may eventually be replaced by electronic devices in trials. They are now being used in training and hunting to keep track of dogs.

The little "cow" bell is and has been the only device used to keep track of dogs in field trials. It is a mainstay of grouse hunters and for those who hunt in heavy cover.

When the bell stops ringing, the dog may be out of hearing, on point, smelling some enticing odor or eliminating. Sometimes the handler can tell.

There are several different kinds and shapes of bells sold with types of sounds varying from a clang to a tinkle. Some are easier to follow and maintain the approximate location of the dog. I expect each person's hearing is different too, so it is best to experiment some to find the bell best suited to an individual. The dog should be accustomed to a bell on home grounds first.

Dogs braced together learn to use the other's bell to maintain contact which probably helps each other's searching pattern. It lets handlers know if their dogs are moving and adds confidence.

The bell can be considered a training aid just as much as a whistle, and both are permitted in all field trials. This is not to say that the other handler in the brace may not be irritated. He may be ignorant of the rules. It may affect the brace mate's performance if he is not accustomed to it, and the other handler may become angry.

Horses can learn to follow a dog bell, when used extensively in training and trials, and a few horses seem to know where a dog is better than its handler.

Young dogs should be introduced to check cords and roading harness early but they should not be roaded too young. This puppy uses a Frisbee as a pacifier.

At Iams Seminar and Clinic handlers are being shown how to use a check cord properly.

231

BIRD RELEASERS

The manual, electric or electronic bird releaser is as important to dog training as was Er M. Shelley's work with planted, dizzied, pigeons in the early 1920's. His method is still in use and of great value. Some trainers fold a pigeon's wings so it cannot fly, and others tie a small square of cardboard on a short string to control the distance it flies which aids in its recovery and reuse.

Bird dog training requires that the trainer have certain tools to help him. An important one is the bird releaser. Some trainers swear by the check cord and some scoff at artificial aids, but more and more trainers are beginning to learn how valuable the bird releaser is for controlled training. Nowhere is there the number of birds available to do the total training job under wild hunting conditions. So, the trainer must buy birds and give his dog situations which simulate that in the wild. Some trainers do this using quail recall pens and some use homing pigeons or common pigeons trained to return to a loft. Oftentimes good use can be made of several devices when training. Each workable device or method for use in keeping a bird in a fixed known location when a dog is freely hunting, keeps training costs bearable and simplifies training. It must assure the trainer that indeed his purchased bird will be there for his dog without concern for the time taken to find and point it.

The spring actuated bird releaser is nearly foolproof and holds the bird mechanically until intentionally released by the trainer, or accidentally by the dog. Some are more effective than others. There are writers who have seen one used, maybe improperly, and condemn all such devices.

A baby sock can be effective to keep birds down such as
this pheasant, but it is sometimes difficult to keep on
their heads.

Electronic and manual bird releasers are very effective in
breaking dogs to wing and shot and stop to flush. Helps
prevent unproductives by keeping bird in place.

Each different design of bird releasers on the market influences the amount of scent available for the dog as well as the nature the scent. This in itself determines the relative effectiveness of different releasers as does the amount of retained human scent left.

A bird, awake and alert, surely provides a different scent pattern than one which is asleep and relaxed. It also varies with wind conditions. It is evident that different releasers provide different qualities of scent when used on any given day with the same dog. The best releasers cause the dog to point from a greater distance where best results in flushing and controlling are obtained. Accuracy of location presents a different area of experience for a dog and this is normally not learned under artificial situations if the trainer interferes in any way in its freedom of search.

Dog trainers need a practical device that serves as well as a wild bird hiding from a dog. The Behi Bird Releaser designed and built by me and my son from welded wire provides the maximum amount of scent as evidenced by the distance dogs point birds in it. But, this is not to say that dogs will not learn to creep in further if not controlled properly. Too often, dogs know a releaser holds a bird, and certain ones will creep in where they can see the bird. This then becomes a bad habit which is difficult to stop.

The reason the mechanical bird releaser was first invented and developed by Jack Stuart and improved on by various dog trainers was that no other method of putting birds down kept them in place until found and pointed.

The use of a baby's sock is partially effective. It

234

is placed over a bird's head, but sometimes a pigeon flies off with it. A pigeon can be used just a few times before it learns how to remove it. Pigeons cannot be dizzied and put down many times until they get wise and will get up and fly away.

Most artificial methods require an unnatural act by the trainer to put the bird to flight. These methods cannot be used many times without causing problems to some dogs. Bending over to release a bird must be avoided for it can affect a pointing dog. Problems vary from one dog to another, but the astute trainer will be able to see them in time to stop and use other methods or variations.

The bird releaser can be used effectively for a long time with each dog in several different ways. Hitting the trigger with a flushing whip can present the same picture to the pointing dog as with a whipped flush. The foot release method is good. I kick around the releaser area pretending to put up the bird, which serves to keep some dogs alert, and at an appropriate time depress the foot lever and the bird flies off or drops back on the releaser screen to be flushed.

Whenever a dog becomes releaser-wise and fails to point quickly or properly, the string release, electric or electronic actuated releaser should be used. The bird should be released at about the same time the dog smells it and at the time it should normally point. They are also useful in training dogs for stop to flush and to prevent dogs from creeping up after first pointing.

The worst problem in using artificial devices is the residual human scent. After a certain time, the pointing dog begins to point the retained human scent and the residual bird scent. Then dogs begin to point the human scent. This is easily proven. Trainers should go into the area they normally train using bird releasers and walk around making many tracks, then bend over and touch or handle an object and leave. A dog under training using releasers should be released and the trainer then watch it work. If he is pointing human scent it will be easy to observe him point the object previously handled.

The worst faults come from the trainer not trusting his dog. When he sees his dog working game, he immediately interferes with the process. This is often seen when a trainer gets off his horse and his dog immediately starts hunting a short pattern when remaining almost at heel. Another handler may call out "birds" which is a signal to his dog to play the game of finding something which has been put out by some **man**. In a sense the handler is leading his dog to the game. None of its natural ability is developed. The handler and dog never learn mutual trust. The dog never learns to function on his own.

It takes different methods to train pointing dogs and even individual dogs in a breed. Mechanical gadgets may work better for one dog and planted birds may work better for another when breaking them.

The bird releaser can help weld the mutual trust of trainer and dog, for the trainer need not fear about the bird being gone, and he can allow his dog full command of the situation where he can evaluate the process of his dog's finding and pointing in a natural manner. If the dog tries to get at the bird in the releaser, he can actuate it himself without injury or it can be secured such that he cannot release it. Obviously, no dog can be adequately broken to wing and shot when not staunch on point. The releaser is not

236

advocated for teaching a dog to point, but to help staunch up a dog that already points well and when breaking it to wing and shot.

A puppy should not be started on a bird releaser until he has had some experience **with** hunting and birds not so restrained. This is not to say it cannot be used as a "game" using a ball or dummy around the house and then on birds later.

Somehow the puppy has to learn, or be taught, that it is not his business to try to catch birds on the ground. It is possible to cause a young dog to blink birds in a releaser when improperly introduced to birds just as it is to make him gun shy from indiscriminate shooting.

The trainer should have a helper following along to recover each releaser so that it is not there for his dog to find and point again. They can be left out if the trainer does not pass through that area again with that dog during that particular training session.

The releasers have enough scent remaining that some dogs will return and point them with intensity and style after birds are released. A trainer should not create artificial situations that increases a dog's chances of learning to false point. Some dogs will even point where the releaser was for some time after it has been picked up, and it is important that the trainer encourage his dog to go on. This then becomes a valuable lesson in the dog's gaining confidence and the ability to discriminate scent. Some dogs learn to sight point releasers or may even stop pointing altogether when releasers are used.

We want dogs to learn that a particular smell **always** represents a bird hiding so that they will not develop bad habits such as creeping, false pointing or blinking.   There is no method known which will always allow the handler to get to a dog when he points a wild bird every time to staunch it up.   Dogs learn faster when a situation develops in which we do not want them to learn.   Under these wrong conditions it may be permanent the first time.

Rote in training is essential, but rote in the placing and using of bird restraining devices can be damaging to a dog's development.   They should be used differently each time.   Some dogs like this type work and accept it as a game requiring their best performance each time.

Bird releasers are the one most important training device available to the trainer.   With a little experience he will develop better trained dogs having intense natural desire, but improperly used the training will show no improvement or the dog can be ruined.   There are many different breaking processes that are effective, but the bird releaser offers the most potential for producing the most uniform conditions time after time.

ELECTRONIC DEVICES

Electronic technology has thankfully invaded the world of dog trainers.   With radio transmitters and microprocessors, there is no end to the different kinds of dog training devices possible to design and manufacture.   Can you imagine programming a dog collar device to give voice commands and corrections to your dog?   It is not here yet, but it could be someday.

Jack Stuart invented and pioneered the electric operated bird releaser and dog collar transmitter in the 1940's which operated by proximity. The electronic signal to the dog collar actuated the releaser when the dog got too close. His releasers were also made to operate electrically using a foot or hand switch on a long electric cord. Stuart patented his releaser and manufactured it for several years. His invention is now manufactured with permission by Tri-Tronics, Tuscon, Arizona.

Tri-Tronics manufactures three remote trainers: Correction; Avoidance; and, Relaxation. Other manufacturers manufacture similar devices.

The Correction Trainer can give a strong or variable shock to a special (receiver) collar worn by the dog. Its purpose is to stop undesirable behavior or bad habits. It is manufactured in different models for use on one or more dogs selectively or simultaneous.

The Avoidance Trainer administers correction training and avoidance of correction. It has two buttons. One produces a warning sound followed by electrical shock and another button produces the sound warning alone. It comes in one and two dog models.

The Relaxation Trainer administers correction training, avoidance and relaxation. One button produces the warning sound followed by electrical shock, then by another tone which the dog learns is the same as praise (relaxation), the second button produces the sound warning, and the third button produces the relaxation tone. It has variable intensity for dogs overly sensitive to electrical shock. (Tri-Tronics uses the word <u>stimulation</u> for shock.)

These same transmitters are now designed for use with the Tri-Tronics game bird releasers. All have rechargeable batteries and work for about five years before batteries need replaced. One model operates over a long range.

The Tri-Tronics receivers are free from extraneous signals. Other models in the past have been activated by police transmitters. Nothing is said about one transmitter actuating a shock collar on another man's dog being worked in the same immediate area since there are just so many frequency variations possible in the assigned range.

Sensitronix, Houston, Texas manufactures remote control electronic trainers which work like the Tri-Tronics Correction Trainer and has an adjustable shock feature. Another model has six channels of which three can be used for shock and the other three for remote control devices. It also has adjustable shock features.

The shock collar produced by these two manufacturers are water resistant and operate in cold weather conditions.

There are other shock collar manufacturers and these were cited just as examples of their performance.

Electronic collar technology is improving each year, but the collar is too expensive for the average one or two dog owner. This business is highly competitive and some manufacturers will be replaced. The electronic collar is an indispensible tool for most professional dog trainers.

Dr. Daniel F. Tortora, author of *Understanding Electronic Dog Training*, by Tri-Tronics wrote the book especially for use with Tri-Tronic remote training collars. The instructions though are applicable to other shock collars. This book is recommended reading for **every** dog trainer even if he has no intention of using remote electronic shock collars. It is "out of print" because models used in the text are outdated and replaced with newer models. It can only be purchased from Tri-Tronics. It was not written for bird dog trainers, but its treatment of the scientific and behavior concepts are applicable. This material may be included in future publications sold with Tri-Tronics' products.

Anyone who plans to use shock collars in training pointing dogs should have some experience in dog training first. A dog must really be already properly prepared and trained for the shock collar to become an effective tool in solving problems. In the wrong hands, it can cause unsolvable problems that would never have existed without its use. Unfortunately, these electronic devices are often used as toys at the expense of the dogs by their owners. It would not surprise me to see one around a dog's neck and flank at the same time. No trainer should rely solely on these devices, and they should be used primarily when all other methods fail in training. There are some dogs that can only be trained by electronic shock collars or brutality, but may be of questionable value once trained.

Electronic devices are effective tools when properly used. No training device is any better than the person using it.

The electronic collar with a buzzer can be used to teach trainers to time their corrections. The student carries the shock collar in his hand and the teacher presses the buzzer button at the time the student should make a voice or whistle correction or signal to his dog. It gives the advantage of an instant signal without the teacher yelling or hand signaling for a correction. Timing of correction is critical in a dog's learning and progress. The time it takes to tell a handler to make a correction is usually too late. It also demonstrates to the student that correction must be anticipated before it is required. The dog may think the trainer is reading his mind which is exactly what is required for best results.

Many other electronic devices are on the market which do special jobs such as keeping track of a dog and what it is doing such as moving or pointing (stopped). Electronic devices and collars are made to stop or control barking.

Electronic beepers having different beeps and tones are made to replace bells and can be used in heavy cover or woods for grouse dogs. Some of us are old fashioned and like the tinkle of a bell while others prefer the electronic beepers.

Bird buckets keep birds in better shape than gunny sacks for planting on course or in the bird field.

The whoa post can be used to teach whoa or to stop chasing. A pinch collar is being used. The check cord has a knot to whip into the dog's chin to reinforce the command.

Chapter 3

Handlers

HANDLING

It may sound like a simple truism, but the best handlers do have the best dogs. Some handlers are fortunate to have the benefit of guidance and help from experienced dog trainers and handlers, but many come up from the school of hard knocks. Their experience and expertise must come from their day in and day out work with dogs. It would be helpful if every beginner could find and use experienced help.

The best handlers will admit to making mistakes at times where it caused their dogs to work poorly or lose a stake. They catalog these mistakes in their brains

244

and try to improve, but none are ever perfect.

Handlers psyche themselves up before the competition, and become so nervous they lose complete control of their thinking process and are incapable of remembering what to do next. Sometimes this may be triggered by the desire to excel, or to have their dog excel, but often times they lose all control of themselves and goof up their dogs. Yet, I expect these people enjoy their sport more than handlers with ice water in their veins.

Nobody apparently understands why some dogs instinctively like and work for some handlers better than others. Some people are just born dog handlers.

A good trainer is flexible and adaptable in his thinking and the way he works. He provides successful solutions to problems as they appear which in turn improves his capacity and ability to solve all the more difficult and challenging ones.

Trained dogs will often work for strange or inexperienced handlers until they learn new limits and handlers' weaknesses, or make errors which would not happen with their regular handlers. Usually good handlers win the respect of strange dogs and win with them.

The mechanical, chauffeur approach, **me boss--you obey or else,** trainer usually does not do well. There must be rapport such that a team effort and a harmonious relationship develops between a handler, dog and horse.

A good handler has a thorough knowledge of the sport and knows how to get the most out of his dogs. He reads their actions and reactions quickly and correctly. He sees changes in his dog's conduct, attitude and performance and does something constructive to change it when needed.

Paul Walker said:

"It is a revelation how a really good dog responds to proper handling. If the handlers, the judges and the gallery proceed at a proper pace, the dogs will work the course intelligently, have time to hunt and get results, and withal show spectacularly, handling responsibly."

There are many things a handler must learn in competition and the above quotation is a most important one to remember. Most problems stem from a handler's ignorance or inexperience. But, there are experienced handlers who will not play the game straight and will test the limits of other handlers, dogs and judges.

A handler can ruin his brace mate's performance in many different ways. He notes that his brace mate responds to his voice or whistle when handling his own dog and mis-handles the brace mate.

Proper handling should allow the other handler to get to his dog to control it in a backing situation. Flushing over a pointing dog and sending it on before the brace mate's handler has control will most likely eliminate it from the stake. This is the worst example of poor sportsmanship other than running a horse too close to the brace mate on a point or back.

In retrieving trials, a great many handlers know how to cause a backing dog to break as they send a dog for the retrieve. A loud command and arm motion is usually all that it takes for the brace mate to leave.

Handlers intentionally flush a bird so that it will fly into the backing dog's face or run close to him. Gunners who intentionally shoot birds so they fall close to a backing dog will cause the dog to fault. Some gunners have a "bone to pick" with a handler and deliberately empty their guns at a bird, and shoot the bird even after it has fallen to the ground. These gunners hurt the sport and are not asked back after the damage is done. A few hotheaded handlers vow revenge for such tactics and such handlers are not long in the sport, but also create a bad image.

A professional handler may have several dogs which can beat each other and the competition on any given day. A select few are not above using one of these dogs to take out any competition.

Clients should make a point of visiting and watching their dogs, and all others in the professional handler's string to see if he is being fair and that the dogs are really competitive or are being used as fillers or worse.

A professional handler may offer to buy out his competition or offer to campaign the dog for practically nothing. Beware! Unethical handlers will do most anything to win or keep a good dog from winning. What better way than have that dog in his own string if he is a professional?

Dogs must be trained to withstand all the additional pressure in field trials from unethical handlers. Handlers should make a point of helping the other handler, for in so doing, they help their own dogs. Some handlers are never smart enough to figure that out and winning is compulsive and excludes good behavior. Dogs develop enough problems from training and competition and none need to be added by using a dog improperly in a brace. Bad situations, whether created deliberately or by accident which results in trauma, stress, jealousy or any adverse reaction are counterproductive. Dogs are not immune to these happenings.

Experienced trainers, as a rule, do not enter dogs

Whoaing a dog after a flush to mount the handler's horse causes problems with some dogs and handlers. The new AKC rule allows the scout to set up and hold the dog while its handler mounts his horse.

Judges should stay behind handlers and never override or block a dog's view of its handler.

which interfere with a brace mate, yet this happens at most every field trial. This problem occurs mostly with novice handlers who are working with their first dog in trials, but not always.

When braced with a dog that interferes, or fights, the handler should stop his dog and express his concern to the judges, if it appears they are not going to correct the situation quickly. He can get the problem resolved by picking his dog up (with permission). This is much better than allowing the adverse behavior to continue.

It is true that dogs will play, some play more than others, but a properly developed independent dog will resent the interference. Affected dogs hesitate to leave the starting line, are indecisive, or will hold back to see what his brace mate is going to do to him. Male dogs eventually learn to fight and become worthless for field trial competition without corrective measures.

Foot handlers set the pace. With two foot handlers in the brace there is usually no restriction on the pace, but if one is handling from a horse, he must stay behind the foot handler. The horseback handlers set whatever pace the judges allow. The horse is to be used only for conveyance and not an active handling aid, and it must be always kept at a walk (most walking horses have a deceptive walk). If a foot handler is going entirely too slow for the normal pace of a horse when one handler is handling from horseback, the judges or marshal should ask the foot handler to speed up. If he refuses, or cannot, they can do whatever is necessary at the time to be fair to the other handler. How slow is too slow?

There are handlers who do not give a damn about

messing up the brace mate by their own misbehavior or that of their dogs. Novice handlers are guilty because they may not know any better. Others do it in subtle ways such as giving their dog the WHOA, or HO command over and over which is intended for the brace mate.

Finding and producing a bird over a dog's point can be difficult depending on how he has been trained and the handlers own emotional state at the time. Whenever time is not called in a bird field, a handler should keep his dog away from the brace mate when he goes on point and avoid a backing situation so he can continue hunting. Some handlers will spend more time than necessary "looking" for a bird when the clock ticks away at the other dog's expense if time is not called.

Sometimes it is difficult to locate a pointed bird. A dog may be pointing where a bird was placed in a prior brace, or the bird ran off. If the dog is trained properly, he will figure it out and avoid unproductives.

If a dog has pointed and the bird escapes the handler, he can send the dog to relocate or heel it away to continue hunting. The choice is his. The handler knows his dog better than anyone else and must be willing to accept the judges' decisions on his performance even if it is not to his liking.

The way a dog is approached on point can make a big difference in the outcome. If a pheasant is suspected, it pays to go a long way in front of the dog and work back toward him. Sometimes this backfires, but it can prevent a relocation with the potential for the dog to push out a bird and be eliminated. Sometimes a bird flushes over top of the dog, and it takes experience and maturity before a dog can be expected to resist such temptations to grab the bird. Also, the handler can force a bird to run under his dog with equally bad results. Handlers need to keep a positive attitude and do everything in their power to keep control and always flush the bird **away** from the dog. It is difficult.

All this is further complicated with a poor horse. He can interfere with the process if he does not ground tie and there is nobody in the gallery available to hold him.

What qualifies a horse as a handler's horse? He breathes! But, established wranglers take pride in furnishing good horses for field trial officials. Far too many inexperienced handlers, and a few experienced ones depend on a club to furnish horses. Some clubs require handlers to deal directly with the horse wrangler. Handlers never know how the horse they get will behave. Sometimes horses are unmanageable, hurt riders, and clubs are sued. Wranglers have been known to buy horses at auction for a trial to satisfy a large demand for a particular trial and sell them back to a horse trader after the trial.

It is distressing to see a handler dismount to work his dog on point, only to have his horse follow and interfere with the dog, or bolt away through the area of the dog forcing it to abandon point.

Professional handlers have horses trained to ground tie, or have helpers who hold their horse when working their dog on point.

Remounting to cast a dog on to hunt can be equally troublesome. The girth strap may be loose and inexperienced handlers are not too adept at mounting, and their dogs are not properly trained and run around the horse causing it then to misbehave. This can be dangerous to both dog and handler.

Many experienced dogs key off the horses and it does

not matter to them where their handlers are. For the best working relationship the dog and horse should learn to work together.

Every handler should strive for the maximum performance possible from his dog whether he is on foot or horseback. With a well trained dog it does not matter. Dogs usually extend their range when handled from horseback, but it is too complex to generalize.

Amateurs should not enter a trial and then decide at the last minute to handle from horseback for the first time. The dog may heel or circle the horse because he is distressed and some dogs refuse to accept their handlers on a horse.

Some handlers' health and age make horseback handling the only reasonable alternative, so their dogs need to be accustomed to horses early in their training. It is true that some dogs never object to their handlers getting on a horse the first time. These dogs have the right temperament for field trials.

A handler can do a better job for his dog from horseback. He can see and follow its movements better and is better able to handle any situation. If he has to dismount to work his dog, he is not winded or tired. The horse also extends his useful field trial life.

Handlers should never stop and wait for dogs to urinate, defecate or make game. A dog that makes game should be able to locate and point without his handler standing on top of him. It encourages dogs to potter and the results are disastrous. Dogs must be taught to be decisive and positive in their work.

THE BEGINNER

Many factors influence a beginner's acceptance and eventual love of the sport. Most important he should experience some early success with his dogs.

The future of the sport depends on new converts. Clubs which fail to bring in new members have a hard core of old timers who soon become too old to do the work needed for a successful field trial.

Therefore, it is essential that a club's older members make every effort to work and help train new members. Too often new people are accepted into membership and ignored. They are not accepted, or fail to learn to like the hard work associated with competition and allow their memberships to lapse. New members must be made to feel wanted, needed and to belong.

How is that accomplished? First, not everyone who shows interest in the sport will be suited for it. And, in any random group of people seemingly having a common interest, there are those who cannot, or will not, get along with others in the club and create conflict. Herm David says there are psychotic personalities in dog clubs. They must be dealt with and are hard to ignore. Club officers often fail to discipline when required and these people disrupt or cause clubs to fail.

Field trialing is a strenuous sport and those not in the best physical condition must depend on using a horse or the services of a professional handler.

Everyone considering entering the sport, other than walking trials, should be able to ride a horse with some level of proficiency and confidence. Inexperienced riders should avoid English or plantation type saddles. Most wranglers use western saddles which are best for inexperienced riders, but are more difficult to get out of in an emergency dismount, and day in and day out are harder on the rider.

My experience leads me to believe that a rider is safer staying on a horse that misbehaves and runs out of control. They do spook and are prone to run back to the barn or horse trailer. The inexperienced riders who bail off usually break bones in their panic dismount when those who stick with the horse and ride him down are seldom hurt.

Every beginner who sticks with field trials for five years and has never ridden a horse before will eventually come around to riding and handling.

New applicants are not screened. Members who sponsor new members usually do so because they have sold them a puppy or older dog, and know little or nothing about the applicant. These members then have a major responsibility in making them welcome, introducing them to other members, and working to make them effective members, trainers and handlers.

There never is a guarantee. A member can take them under his wing, work hard training them and their dogs, take them hunting, break their dogs, campaign and win with them and they will still lose interest. Winning is a worthy goal, but **never** losing is not realistic. Some owners cannot remain interested when they lose. They are not willing to dedicate themselves to the work necessary to winning. They never learn to appreciate the basic values available in the sport other than winning which all veteran trialers have learned to love and appreciate. Wins without enjoying the many other esthetic values available are hollow wins at best.

Far too many beginners overwork their young dog and

at less than a year of age are doing everything perfect, but then take them into competition and they behave as if they never had any training. These owners are never seen in competition again. Some have the peanut, potato chip, popcorn, syndrome. If one dog is good two, three, four and more are better. They become bogged down with too many dogs and spend all their time feeding and little, if any, time training.

FOOT vs HORSEBACK HANDLING

Every pointing breed handler began handling on foot and those in the American Field trials changed over early, but it was not until 1961 that the American Kennel Club rules permitted horseback handling.

R. J. Schweiger wrote in *The American Field*, Christmas issue, 1979:

"I vividly recall my field trial debut. I was paired with a mounted handler who was skillfully guiding a pointer that seemed to glide over the ground. Afoot, I moved at a hard trot, and although out of breath at the twenty minute mark, I managed to reach the end of the course along with the judges and gallery. To a man the group complimented me on my dog's performance--field trialers are kind--and to a man they suggested that it would be advantageous for me to handle from the back of a horse in future contests."

The change in range of gun dogs and all-age dogs can be traced back to the use of horses in training and handling.

Handlers were in better physical condition before they began working from horseback, but required more "sudden" bursts of energy to get a dog under control or to chase it down for correction. Horses are advantageous for stakes with bird fields for the handlers are fresh and not tired and sweaty (no matter what the temperature is) and can work their dogs better.

Handlers can see their dogs and follow their movements much better and easier from horseback. Most dogs range out farther when accustomed to horseback handling.

For handlers with bad hearts, who are overweight not strong physically, or old, horses are a godsend, provided they become experienced riders.

Handlers who arrive at trials without ever having ridden a horse or have never accustomed their dogs to horses will try to handle from them which is a mistake. The handler and dog must be prepared beforehand. Some dogs that have never been handled from horseback do not react unfavorably but many do.

Horses can be dangerous even to experienced riders, and often there is a kicking horse in the gallery which can cause injury to men, dogs and horses. Those horses should have a ribbon tied at the base of their tails and kept outside of the gallery. Horses may be reliable over strange ground without a rider, but riders have a habit of trying to **see** for their horses and cause them to stumble or fall. Horses spook for the dumbest reasons.

R. J. Schweiger also wrote:

"Careless or reckless action around horses are direct shortcuts to a hospital. A horse in pain, or frightened, or even angry, will react violently. Since horses will outweigh their riders about ten to one, and dwarf their

Nothing is any more embarrassing than the "long walk" back after one's dog makes a serious mistake and is ordered up. All professional and experienced amateur handlers teach their dogs to road back on a long check cord. Dogs usually make their mistakes at the back end of a course.

Trainers should avoid trying to handle two dogs on foot where commands to a dog which makes a mistake will be misunderstood by the one doing nothing wrong. This is exacerbated when working from horseback alone with an untrained horse. Trainers trying to control their horses make commands to horses that are misinterpreted by their dogs creating situation or place stress.

master's physical strength, it's impossible to bend their will with brute force. When a "war" occurs between horse and man a horse can be badly injured, but more often it is the human who becomes a battle casualty! What frightens a horse today will go unnoticed tomorrow. What angers your mount today will be quietly accepted tomorrow. What seemed painful to your horse yesterday is well received today. Horses are indeed difficult to figure out and the expert horseman selects and uses methods that work in given situations. Horsemanship is a science and an art!"

When handlers dismount, horses will run off. They kick dogs, lay down on the ground and in the water to roll over on riders, girths break, or slip, losing riders, they throw riders and may be gun shy. They truly are dangerous to people's and dog's physical well being, but we need them. Horseback handlers should have someone to hold their horses whenever they dismount to flush birds. Ideally handler's horses should ground tie. Usually scouts go to the handlers and take control of their horses when they dismount for any reason. Like everything else, there is an art to taking and leading handlers' horses. Done improperly there is more danger than is necessary and dogs can get in the way of a horse and be injured. The person going to take a handler's horse should approach from the right side to take the horse and deliver the horse back in the same way.

Handlers often lose in competition because of problems with dismounting and remounting their horses. Dogs take liberties to delay chase as their handlers remount.

Handlers learn techniques for individual dogs. Some

may stop their dogs, remount and cast on, or walk with their dogs and horse a given distance, cast the dog on and remount, or remount and then cast the dog on.

Foot handling is not completely safe either for the ground conditions cause tripping and result in broken bones. Poisonous snakes can cause as much or more of a problem than when on horseback. Briers, nettles, heavy cover, burrs, thorn bushes, flies, mosquitoes and bees are nuisances. The muddy, wet, thick cover, snow and ice make walking hazardous. Standing water often goes over boots and wet feet are common.

A dog can be controlled easier when handled from foot and he makes a more honest hunting dog. This is a good reason for the emergence of the new foot handling field trial organizations with hunting dog stakes. Some clubs in the American Kennel Club hold walking stakes, non-regular hunting stakes, and its new walking Hunting Tests for pointing dogs may help some dog owners enjoy their dogs more.

Both foot and horseback handling can be enjoyable, and we must not lose sight of this as we age. It helps keep us in the sport with those who are younger and abler. Courses are normally gaged for speeds of two to five miles per hour and few foot handlers will maintain the fast pace for long under muddy or snowy footing, and some cannot sustain the slower pace.

AMATEUR HANDLERS

Amateur dog owners are responsible for all field trials. They organize the clubs and set up and conduct trials all over the world for amateur and professional handlers. Professional handlers may help in some small way, but it is better if they stay completely out of the business of running clubs and field trials.

There have been many great amateur handlers in the past, and even now, who do not receive the credit and publicity that comes more naturally to the professional handlers.

One definition of an amateur handler is that he does not accept money for prizes offered in trials. Another is that he does not accept money or renumeration in any form for training and handling pointing dogs--but can accept money offered in prizes in trials.

The amateur handler is in the sport for his own personal enjoyment and recreation. He is the backbone of the sport contrary to popular belief in some quarters which varies with the different kinds of bird dog field trials. He may not always be admired as much as some professional handlers. Amateur handlers tend to write more about training and field trials, as a rule, and professional handlers conduct clinics and seminars as another source of income.

In *The American Field* more than anywhere else, we can read glowing accounts of amateur handlers and their reputations with near reverence. The American Field Publishing Company has helped make its championship trials the elite of field trials for both its amateur and professional handlers. Its Field Trial Hall of Fame has further strengthened and enhanced this feeling for its dogs, owners and handlers. It is true that there are no restrictions to the great dogs in other breeds, but the weight is shifted too much to be voted in without some subtle conspiracy or fraud.

The book *Jones*, by James E. Myers, is a novel which enhances the sport and championship field trials under the American Field. The principal character is an amateur handler and his close associations with the professional handler is not unusual in the real world. Those familiar with handlers in real life American Field trials will recognize the references to them with names changed by transposing a few letters.

What is said about Dr. Alvin Nitchman? Here is a sample from page 532, 1981, *The American Field*:

"Dr. Nitchman's field trial accomplishments are legendary. He goes to a trial to compete and this he does fiercely, yet he is honest, always straightforward and helpful to his brace mate. The man is of strong convictions and one who does not hesitate to express them. He shoots straight from the shoulder and says what he thinks. If you don't want to hear it like it is, don't ask Doc."

Obviously, the Field Trial Hall of Fame for people will find many writers euologizing men and women in the sport and all surely deserve the accolades.

The work, sweat and sometimes tears of working and supporting field trials for the opportunity to occasionally run one's own dog for the sake of dog ownership and the breeds leaves many by the wayside early in their life. What the owners who stick with it all their lives learn is that they have acclimated themselves to the jealousy, hatred, selfishness and bitterness of some owners and handlers and the vagaries of the terrain and weather. The beauty is found in enjoying working with people and everything about field trials, dogs and horses. There are some of these great men and women in the sport called amateur handlers who brighten the sport as the early morning sun at breakaway.

PROFESSIONAL HANDLERS

How credible are self-employed professional handlers? How does a dog handler become one? For some it is easy--they just start charging money to handle dogs.

It would be ideal if every professional trainer/handler met some established criteria of training and experience that uniquely qualified him or her to train dogs for the public.

There are dog owners who never broke a dog and know nothing about field training who accept money for "dog training." It is strictly a case of owner beware!

New owners need professional trainers from time to time. Unfortunately they have no way to evaluate the competent professional trainers.

A dog is sold to someone as a hunting dog. He is then taken to a professional trainer at the beginning of a week and is back before the end of the week because the dog will not hunt. This is just one example of many which the dog owner encounters.

What is wrong? That "professional handler" says that the dog has no ability. He may have been correct, but no trainer, no matter how great his reputation, can evaluate a dog in a few days or weeks. A dog transferred to another person must have time to acclimate to its new environment and trainer, and that time may not be reliable in determining the dog's potential. Seldom do dogs make this transition in less than three weeks. Some unattach and reattach slowly. A dog seeking some form of security after being removed from its old environment and owner needs time to establish new human bonds.

Those in the sport for sometime learn who the better professional trainers are, but the average dog owner does not have enough knowledge, association or experience to know. His solution is trial and error which can be expensive with sometimes poor results.

Should an amateur train his own dog? Sure. It is a good idea and can be done. But, every first dog owner should go to the library and read every book available on pointing dogs, field trials and observe competent handlers at field trials. It is a waste of money to buy a dog and put it in the hands of a professional trainer who only trains the dog. Who trains the owners? There is no advantage in having a dog trained and returned to an inexperienced owner. The dog will not work for him and he has no idea what to expect or how to work his dog properly. All he knows is that his money was wasted and the professional handler was no good. That may not be true, and as a consequence the good name of a professional trainer can be tainted--maybe ruined. Some owners use a professional trainer to solve a particular problem, but even that is not always successful.

There are poor professional trainers and handlers. The problem is to learn which ones do the best job with a particular breed. Some professional trainers are good with some breeds and not with others. Why would an owner send a dog to a major circuit professional trainer to be used in shoot-to-retrieve trials or vice versa? The dog should be sent to someone who specializes in that training.

Before a dog goes to a professional trainer, the owner should learn how he works, what he charges, what results to expect in a given time period, and how long he expects to keep the dog. If the dog is to be field trialed, he will want to keep it in his string for a long time. If the owner expects to handle his dog in trials, the professional should know that and be willing to spend time with him. A professional should not enter a client's dog in field trials unless it is part of the contract. Some owners are talked into it after he has had the dog for a few months. Owners should be wary, and be certain they want to become involved in large expenditures of money. Memories dull with time, and some are poor for some things. Owners should insist on a written contract for time and specific services rendered with provisions for renewal.

The professional handler is entitled to all prizes and money he wins with a clients' dog.

Dogs change from one professional handler to others oftentimes before they become competitive. These are usually problem dogs and it is a good practice for some dogs, because they normally do not carry over training resentments to a new handler.

The professional field trialer who makes his living exclusively from training and handling dogs is a versatile businessman having many and varied expenses. He spends much of his time on the road away from his home base. Some may never know what or where home is from one month to the next. They must be a jack of all trades and master of many to become top professionals.

Doyess Boyett in January 7, 1984, *The American Field* page 8, wrote:

". . . not enough kudos are bestowed upon the dedicated professional trainer-handlers of field trial bird dogs. A successful professional bird dog trainer for contemporary field trial competition requires ingenious qualities in a vast and varied field. Over and beyond having an exceptional love for an honest bird dog and sincere sports people, he manifests a code of ethics and bond of of mutual integrity unequalled in any other professional sport. Of necessity, he must be a shrewd business man, cowboy, agile athlete, and possess an extrasensory perception of a bird dog's mental and physical behavior. Too often his talents are taken for granted. He is the unsung hero of our beloved field trial sport."

Albert F. Hochwalt said:

"The successful professional trainer must be peculiarly fitted for his work. He must understand his canine pupils, their individual eccentricities, the queer quirks of temperament. He must win their confidence--a famous trainer once said, 'You can't train a dog if he doesn't like you' and the professional must be gifted with those talents that enable him to develop the inherited and potential qualities in the dog. Not everyone can do it. An apprenticeship must be served by even the best of them."

It is unfortunate that some few professional trainer/handlers put more emphasis on winning by using unfair tactics which are many and varied. It is difficult for the average field trialer to catch one in the act of dropping a quail (alive or dead) for their dog to point, sacrifice one or more of their dogs to take out the competition, or use simulated shock collar prongs in collars as just a few examples.

Albert F. Hochwalt wrote:

"Professional bird dog trainers constitute an integral part of field trials. Veteran votaries recognize their importance by attributing to them much of the popularity the

265

game enjoys. It is unfortunate that occasionally some take
up the training of pointers and setters and fail to live up
to the ethics of the profession. But the entire fraternity
should not be condemned for the defection of a few of its
members. Undesirables are found at one time or another in
every profession or walk of life, and it would be expecting
too much to believe that bird dog training would never
attract such as these."

Some people claim that the professional
trainer/handler is the backbone of the field trial
sport and it is true for some of the major circuit
trials, which is just a small segment of the sport.
Most trials are amateur handled and they would not
exist except for them.

Whereas, the professional handler is important, he
must depend exclusively on the work, time and money of
amateur owners. They pay for his services and
generally do all the work of setting up and running the
trials. Professional handlers better serve the wealthy
who do not have the time to train or handle their own
dogs and who make many other worthy contributions to
the sport with their money and status.

David Grubb wrote on "Professional Handlers" in *The
American Field*, 1981, page 763:

"First of all, we do appreciate all the work, time, and effor
that is put into major trials throughout the United States. Th
Club officials spend long hours in preparation and in running
the trials. It is fully realized that this is a labor of lov
and they get no monetary compensation for such, and many time
don't even get thanks. And, without these people we would hav
no major trials as we know them today. Some fail to conside
the expenditures made through the years to assure grounds i
satisfactory condition with an ample crop of native birds."

Pointers on a chain gang type stake out.

This is typical of a professional handler's way of staking out his mixed string of dogs for emptying out, feeding and watering at trials.

267

The biggest gripe of professional handlers is the small amount of money offered in prizes and clients delay or failure to pay for their services. Clients gripe when their dogs do not win enough times or the important stakes to suit them, or about the high costs of the professional. If an owner gripes about the cost, he is in the wrong sport and really should forget it.

Keep in mind that in major circuit (pointer and setter) trials there are more than enough championship trials to keep a professional handler field trialing with the same dogs all year long, except for a short summer break for training in Canada, North Dakota or a few other select states. A top winning contender can make a professional handler much money, but if that happened it would be a deserving accomplishment. Most professional handlers keep up their daily routines of training and handling because of their love and dedication to the dogs and sport and live a sometimes lonely and difficult life. Credit must be given to the professional handlers' helpers who do most of the training and scouting and may have better rapport with the dogs.

No other professional in any sport has to know more, work harder under difficult circumstances and in bad weather to receive low pay for his services. Professional handlers probably stay in their profession longer than all others--some are born doing it. Daniel Burjan, New Jersey, is just one of those who recently stepped into his father's footsteps as a partner when just beginning high school. Many sons who stepped into their father's professional footsteps in American Field big circuit trials became famous.

WOMEN HANDLERS

Women have probably been more active in retriever
trials than pointing dog trials for a longer time. For
many years, they have been treated as though they were
not welcome in pointing dog field trials. They were
not. Men did not want to compete with them anymore
than they would expect to invite them to a stag party
or a night on the town. Women have had their
detractors by men who believed their "place" was
somewhere else.

A woman won the Vizsla National Amateur Championship
in 1983 (with a professionally trained dog), and they
are becoming a force in that breed to be reckoned with.
They are generally welcome and are encouraged to
participate in trials under the American Kennel Club.
Field trials are a family sport. These women are not
relegated to doing the paper or kitchen work, and are
also active as field trial officials.

I have worked with several young women in helping
train their own dogs--my wife worked and helped me for
many years. Some women have been more successful than
others, but they love dogs, horses and the outdoors as
much as any man.

Women do not always get fair and honest judging by
men. They tolerate women because they have no choice.
These men will not place women any quicker than they
would a handler from another breed at their breed
trials. With several women now judging local and
championship stakes they can play the same game.

With proper training, many women can handle as well

A successful woman handler taking her dog to the starting line at a National Championship Stake.

A woman handler attempting to flush a bird in a bird field stake.

as most men. Some cannot shoot, run, holler or
mistreat dogs as well as men do. The biggest problem
is that their voices are usually inadequate for
training and handling and they should use whistles.
Most women love horses and a few are fearless riders.

Herm David wrote in *Hunting Dog* magazine, December
1967:

**"Men who can't bear the thought of being beaten by a woman
best stay away from bird dog, spaniel and retriever trials.
At the National Shooting Dog Championship over the Maytag
Plantation last spring I saw two ladies do capable jobs of
handling their dogs into the finals."**

SCOUTS

A scout in a major circuit trial is most always in
the employment of his handler--and boss. He may remind
you of a cowboy bringing an errant stray back into the
herd, for he has the most work to do in finding dogs on
point, keeping them to the front, and insuring they
win. He must have a well trained horse to do the job
and be a fearless accomplished rider.

These particular scouts probably do more training
than the handlers. They are trained (or learn) never
to take their eyes off their dogs.

For an interesting account of scouting I recommend
Bird Dogs and Field Trials by Jack Harper.

In *Hunting Dog* magazine, October 1968, Herm David
wrote:

**". . . These are the fellows who ride off like the wind
(with the permission of the judges) when a bird dog is
missing during a field trial. They work amazing feats of
discovery and can usually, and within a few minutes, show**

some errant competitor (that has been casting to the rear) a way out in front. With a little luck and a knowledge of dog and grounds, they can even manage to put their dog into birds."

There are complaints about handlers and scouts riding too fast and too far out pushing their dog on the guise they must keep them in sight. If the judges try to keep up, they are risking life and limb over strange terrain and are usually somewhat less skillful horseback riders.

In American Kennel Club trials the handler's scout, who is a friend or acquaintance, must ride behind the judges and in front of the lead marshal. They can only go out on permission of judges who normally are too lax. Judges should ask a gun dog handler to "show" his dog first, but they seldom do. A gun dog should not need scouting except under unusual circumstances or if suspected of being on point.

In the *German Shorthaired Pointer News*, November 1981, Diane Schumacher wrote:

"For those of you who don't field trial regularly, and don't know the rules, and for those of you who do trial and choose to ignore, bend, break or refuse to learn the rules....AKC states that a dog may be absent (OUT OF SIGHT) for up to 5 minutes or 1/6 total course time at any one time. Think about that! Not seeing your dog for 2, 3, 4 or 5 minutes is a LONG, LONG time in a gun dog stake. Because of that the implication in the AKC rules was that if a dog was absent beyond that point of time, he was disqualified unless found on point. In the 'good old days'...like several years ago...you used to see handlers get a little nervous if their dog was gone several minutes...they had to make a big decision..."Do I call my dog on point or not?" Now they panic if more than 10-15 seconds pass without someone raising hue and cry."

272

All judges mark the start of dogs being timed differently. When a judge informs a handler that his dog has been gone too long, the handler may send his scout out, call for his dog to show, or call point and go to look with his scout. There is no grace period beyond the stake time unless a dog is making game or is found on point.

A gun dog should not ordinarily need a scout often for his range should be limited so that the last place he was seen would be the ideal place to send a scout to look for him on point. Scouts must not handle the dog or it can be disqualified. If the handler continues on and the dog is on point he would normally be found to the rear and the left or right side of the line of travel. If the dog is a renegade, or out of control, he will not be found and will not be in the placements.

Diane Schumaker further wrote that the rules should be stated as follows to erase the ambiguity:

"The scout shall be sent out only with the permission of the judge, to LOCATE A DOG STANDING ON POINT."

It is best never to make a rule that will not and cannot be enforced. We all want to find and reward the best dog in the stake so we can train to beat him, but may not always want the judge to put that dog up. Dogs do get out away from their handlers who become uneasy after a few minutes of not seeing them. If they are hunting, they will start searching in areas where the dog might be found. In field trials the handler must follow the course and either call his dog in or send someone out to look for him. It is just that simple. Judges want to find and see a dog on point, but they too must follow the course until a point by the dog is verified. There is a need for **one** scout for each dog and handler.

273

A recent rule change by AKC now permits the scout to take a handler's dog and hold it by the collar while the handler mounts his horse and then casts his dog on to hunt. This is for dogs which can be collared.

One Association now requires designated scouts to do the scouting for the entire stake in an effort to insure fairness to every handler. Another has eliminated scouts.

Some require scouting on foot. This rule can really work a hardship when the handler continues on course, and the dog shows up forward in front of the judges where the foot scout would have problems in catching up. Some scouts could easily become "lost" and never catch up. In every instance where I have watched scouting on foot, I thought it was an impractical requirement. The AKC does not have a requirement that scouts work from horseback, so it is an unwritten option clubs can use.

Chapter 4

Birds For Training

GAME

We expect pointing dogs in field trials to point game birds, but they can also point other game and should not be faulted. What is game? Some of us are stereotyped into thinking that game is only game birds (gallinaceous). Pointing dogs are not game bird purists. It is true that one dog may point one type game when another will not. It all depends on their background and experience. Most pointing dogs are taught to ignore certain birds and animals, and some learn to ignore them without being trained. The owner must show some enthusiasm for a particular species of game if he wants his dog to point it. If the trainer continues to ignore and show no interest in game the

275

dog may also which could be costly in trials.

Dogs frequently caution up and point into multiflora rose hedges where there are concentrations of song bird droppings. If the handler then makes a mistake, and calls point, he will likely be charged with an unproductive or a false point. It is a mistake to train dogs to stay on command instead of letting them learn how to work out the scent and go on.

Pointing dogs will point turtles. In one trial a handler wanted to be given credit for a turtle find. The judge told him to pick it up, throw it, and if it flew to shoot it. The dog broke and was ordered up.

Webster indicates that game is used as an **adjective** designating wild birds hunted for food or sport, and as a **noun** for wild birds, fish or animals hunted for sport or used for food. And, it is a fact that pointing dogs point fish, flies, shadows, flashlight beams, etc.

Dogs have been known to have a point on a rabbit and win the stake. To meet **all** the requirements, the judges should have called the dog back on a bird to see if the dog was steady to **wing and shot**.

The American Kennel Club standard states:

"The dog must locate game, must point staunchly, and must be steady to wing and shot."

I have spent many hours studying the rules. They are grammatically correct, exact in meaning and skillfully prepared. If we took the above quotation in itself, we could assume that the **game** mentioned would be able to fly. Otherwise, how would the dog prove that he was steady to wing and shot? The Ohio Division of Wildlife's definition of game includes game birds, game quadrepeds and fur bearing animals. Most of the pointing dogs are **versatile**, but the American Kennel

Club uses the term "pointing breeds," not **bird** pointing breeds.

At an American Field trial, the winning dog came to his handler carrying a freshly killed skunk, was not observed pointing game and won the stake. In an American Kennel Club trial the skunk would have to be stone cold for the dog to remain in contention, and the dog would also have had to point game, and show steadiness to wing and shot to be judged properly.

Ohio's definition of game birds include pheasant, quail, ruffed grouse, sharp tailed grouse, pinnated grouse, wild turkey, Hungarian partridge, chukar partridge, woodcock, black breasted plover, Wilson's snipe or jacksnipe, greater and lesser yellowlegs (shore birds), rail, coots, gallinules, ducks, geese and brant. Non-game birds are defined as other wild birds not included as game birds. Wild animals include snakes and turtles.

Quadrepeds are defined as including hares or rabbits, gray squirrels, black squirrels, fox squirrels, red squirrels, groundhogs, deer and bears.

Fur bearing animals include minks, weasels, raccoons, skunks, opossums, muskrats, foxes and beavers.

A dog must give a finished performance over his point. Sometimes a dog's handler would prefer to take his dog by the collar and lead him off certain points, instead of heeling him away by voice. Rattlesnakes, skunks and porcupines are just three examples where **flushing** is difficult or ill advised, and a dog should be collared and taken out, except for the breeds that do not allow this. We need to have Australia's rules where dogs flush on command, but in these examples it might be harmful to our dog's physical well being.

Experienced handlers make their dogs look good in

abnormal situations without having to consider
semantics. Yet, it is important to learn the exact
meaning of every rule. Verbs used range from
conditional to absolute. We must understand the
difference. **May** and **shall** are verbs used with
conditional and absolute meaning. Remember the verb
used in the Ten Commandments?

Summing up, a dog is never to be faulted for pointing
game or non-game. He must be faulted if his manners
are not acceptable. For game that does not fly, the
judge can call the dog back to work a bird, if he is
considering him for a placement. A judge may overlook
a dog pointing a dicky bird, or non-game, once but not
twice. He cannot know that the dog was not pointing a
game bird, or game, and it ran off, while the non-game
stayed the first time.

GAME BIRDS

Facilities and availability of grounds vary for each
dog trainer. As a minimum, he needs more than one or
two places where he can kill birds over his dogs'
points all year round. It is better to kill birds at
several training locations and when hunting.

Birds are essential for bringing the natural
instincts and ability out of pointing dogs. Wild birds
are best, but should not be used to the exclusion of
pen raised birds. Wild birds do not always lend
themselves to controlled situations for staunching and
breaking. Wildlife areas managed by the state with
year round dog training areas are not always
convenient.

A serious dog trainer is forced to own, or lease,
land, and raise birds. Each type bird requires
somewhat different facilities and care.

Pigeons are not considered game birds but dogs do not know that, and they are the easiest to care for all year. They stay healthy under most any living condition and are suprisingly clean. A small enclosure with an opening for them to leave and return through bobs is adequate. There are several variations of the return door (bobs). Pigeons will breed just about anywhere.

Pigeons are caught and killed by dogs which break point so homing birds need to be kept above some minimum level. Pigeons used for killing to break dogs can be bought locally and are much cheaper than game birds.

The more times homing type pigeons are used in dog training the more difficult it is to keep them down until the dog finds and points them. With these birds, methods of restraint must then be used. Bird releasers, folded wings, brailled wings and other methods can be used.

Coturnix quail are easy to raise, are prolific breeders and mature sooner than other birds. They eat much more than bob white quail and the droppings need to be removed oftener. Coturnix quail hatch in 16 days. Once they are flight conditioned, they have excellent flight qualities, but are short lived when released or they migrate elsewhere. They normally do not develop strong wings unless forced to fly in the pens, but when they are released they remain in the area for a few weeks and become excellent training birds.

These quail are excellent birds to promote staunchness and seem to have strong scent even when they bury under the grass. But, they are a problem in some kinds of enclosure. They have high acceleration from a combination of legs and wings. They beat the skin off their heads and oftentimes kill themselves. A pen having a low height will result in a high mortality. They do not recall well and seem dumb, yet they make excellent house pets and can be "house broke," so they cannot be too dumb.

Bob-white quail are the best birds for dog training and are easy to recall or to establish in a suitable area. There are many schemes for calling them back into an enclosure, or putting out call birds in cages to hold them in an area. Feed should always be placed at call bird locations. Quail taught to recall are not contaminated with man scent when released. Dogs point these birds stylishly similar to the way they do with wild birds.

Some states prohibit the use of quail recall pens, but some have provisions for licensed or designated private dog training area where birds can be shot the year round, or shooting preserves where birds can be shot except during the nesting season.

Strong flight conditioned quail really build desire in dogs and are essential in breaking them. Quail can be made to walk near and under dogs to teach them not to grab birds. Dogs can be trained to hold point and not creep using this method which is a necessary training condition for field trials. It is not unusual to find a dog standing on point on top of a quail. Dogs must handle these situations without making the slightest attempt to catch or grab at the bird. Otherwise they are out of contention in the stake. I have seen a cock pheasant walk up to my dog on point, peck it on the nose and then casually walk off with the dog still holding point.

Pen raised quail usually lack survival capability in bad weather, do not hold well and walk under and around a dog on point like barnyard chickens.

Quail kept in recall pens and released for dogs to work become more wild-like in behavior. Dogs work them much like wild quail. Some trainers effectively use recall quail without ever handling them for training, but it is wise to use them with man scent from time to time.

Quail and chukars are not as bad about pecking each other in pens, but pheasants are bad and special methods must be used to control it. These problems are minimized by having adequate space for the birds to escape from each other.

Chukars are ideal for training dogs to retrieve for field trials. Dogs must become accustomed to retrieving them since the feathers seem to be sticky to their mouths the first time they pick them up. Once they learn to retrieve this bird, they will have no difficulty with the other birds except in learning to carry the weight of heavier birds.

Chukars have a bad habit of running instead of flying and handlers must chase them a good distance to flush. But, it is good for a dog's training and they are excellent to teach dogs how to road and point them again.

Some trainers recall chukars, but they usually do not stay around long after being used. Where chukars propagate naturally in the wild, their survival is probable.

Chukars are easy to keep, need little space, but must be kept on wire the same as quail.

Pheasants are the most difficult to keep when young, although they may be easier to feed, the pens to hold them are expensive and much more elaborate, but after several weeks young birds can finish growing on the ground. Pheasants kill themselves by pecking, flying into obstacles, and other ways. Blinders are used to help control pecking and flying into obstacles. Brailled birds can be kept in open pens and when the brail is removed the birds will soon recover the ability to fly.

Dog trainers may prefer to buy their birds as chicks or at a few weeks or age to finish them out. It is more practical for trainers with less than a half dozen dogs to buy birds as they are needed and have holding pens sized to meet their needs. Time spent on raising birds is time not available for dog training.

It takes hundreds of birds to train each dog and in spite of ingenious trainers who invent gadgets and gimmicks, they use just about as many birds. It is important to discover several different ways to save on birds.

Birds can be bought from local breeders who usually belong to the North American Gamebird Association, Inc. which publishes a membership directory.

PIGEONS

It may be assumed that during the training lifetimes of Er M. Shelley and Ernest W. Wunderlich, pigeons were not as essential to bird dog training as they are for today's trainers. Both of these men are given credit for first using dizzied pigeons in training. Shelley was in pointers and Wunderlich in spaniels. It is possible that other trainers used the same or similar training techniques even before they did, but if so it was not documented. It seems a natural thing for a smart trainer to do where there are not enough wild birds to properly train and use in breaking his dogs, and it is a great convenience for yard training. People in those days had chickens and would have observed them sleeping with their heads under their wings.

Pigeons are universal training birds for all pointing, flushing and retrieving breeds, and are highly recommended for any age dog. Dogs must be accustomed to human scent on birds that are set out for training purposes, and pigeons are best. But, there are problems too. Dogs learn to associate human scent on birds with punishment and discipline and react sometimes in strange ways--but it is not strange that they learn to avoid unpleasant experiences.

Dogs learn to blink birds with human scent on them. It does not matter what type bird either, and the more a dog is worked on wild game the more difficult it is to get him to point birds put out for training that retain human scent. There are different scents sold that supposedly smell like pheasant, quail, etc., but they do not mask human scent even though sometimes they may improve a dog's interest.

The use of gloves when handling birds has questionable value, for a bird planter leaves most of the scent from his feet and pants that brush the cover. It does not seem to matter whether that person rides something to the place he puts down birds or walks. The acute sense of smell of dogs can distinguish every scent they have learned no matter what precautions are used to mask or diminish it. Bird dogs may not ever learn to pick up scent several days old as do hounds, but their noses are adequate.

Pigeons can be found in just about every city, most barns and under interstate bridges all over the world. City officials and residents detest their filth as do farmers and are delighted to have dog trainers trap them.

Pigeons are the cheapest of all birds used in training and are easy to catch at night in barns, on roofs, under bridges and in building attics, and with some extra effort can be trapped. There are many pigeon fanciers who cull birds of no further use to them.

Pigeon traps can be purchased or be home made. A location should be used where there are many pigeons roosting or feeding such as a grain elevator, barn, bridge or city building. Traps must be tended for long periods of time where birds learn that food and water are available.

Success is not instant as it takes time for pigeons to get used to something new and may avoid traps for several weeks. Bait the area first with the traps in place, but with no food inside and the bobs tied open. Once birds begin eating the corn, then it can be put inside the traps so they learn to go in and out to feed. When the bobs are closed pigeons are easily caught but many get out. Newer traps developed and marketed by Tom Scott help prevent this. Traps should be visited every other day unless they fill up sooner. Too much visiting might lessen the catch. Corn should be placed in feeders or containers inside the traps, and water should be changed each time the trap is emptied. Traps should be moved off the pigeon droppings frequently. One or two traps on the same building should catch several hundred pigeons a year where there is a good supply.

Homing pigeons readily enter traps as they are accustomed to the bobs. Doves are also caught in these traps. Homing pigeons can be released, or kept, and a

Dogs must learn to not catch birds that walk under and around them, or hide under them as so often happens in stakes using pen raised birds for either shade or security.

(Photo by Jeannie Wagner)

This is one effective pigeon house design for recalling birds thus cutting training costs. Such bird houses should be designed and built to prevent entry of birds or animals that prey on them such as hawks, weasels, mink, opossum, raccoon, cats and rats.

local pigeon fancier contacted to learn the owner by the number on the band which also has the year the bird was hatched.

Older common pigeons taught to return to the loft are quick to start laying eggs and hatching young birds. These young birds adapt the best, but all birds should be taught to return from short distances first. They should be started in sight of the loft and moved farther and farther away in training. I do not know just how far common pigeons will return from training, but there will be losses from dogs catching and killing birds.

Homing pigeons will return from a longer distance, but homing pigeons must be raised in their loft for the best success. Older homing pigeons do not home back to a new place as well as common pigeons from my experience.

Common pigeons trained to the loft soon begin pairing off and nesting. With reasonable care the young birds will even be better than those used for starting.

Pigeons are long lived and the biggest problem to keeping them for a long time are predators. They are lost to hawks, oppossums, raccoons, weasels, minks and rats. One weasel will destroy all the birds in one visit.

My own problem has been solved for several years now with what I built to be a varmint-proof loft. Squirrels get in, but so far nothing else has. The structure is eight feet square with a chicken wire (galvanized after weaving) floor, and is eight feet high, set two and one half feet off the ground. It has a roof overhang and deck closed in with chicken wire with a long board for pigeons to land on and an opening into the deck where they enter the building through recessed bobs. The studs are covered with chipboard

A pigeon with head tucked, not slept, head first in a heavy clump of grass. All game birds can be put down without dizzying using proper techniques.

A banded pheasant required by the state of Ohio for field trials. AKC requires that gloves be used when handling birds in trials.

and the north wall has studs covered on the inside and feeding stations are between the studs. Feed is loaded from the outside. It easily houses thirty birds.

Pigeons, or any bird, can be mesmerized in many different ways, but dizzying them by swinging in circles when holding them in one or both hands, putting them in a feed sack and swinging it around, or causing their head to rotate quickly in a small circle has inconsistent results.

Best results come from doing nothing more than placing the bird's head under its wing and placing it head first in a clump of grass or weeds with its tail up. Another method that gives consistent results is folding the birds wings over until they lock. This works best on pigeons. I use these two methods in combination with bird releasers all the time. Once in awhile I will tuck the bird's head under the wing and hold it until it relaxes and place it down on its back. Another method that works is by putting the bird's head under its wing, putting it down on its side, with head on the ground side, and pumping its legs when alternately pushing the air out of its lungs several times after which the legs are held extended until the bird relaxes and does not pull them into its body.

Birds are often killed by too much dizzying and this procedure may give a different scent for dogs. They seem to know that the bird cannot fly and often break point and pick it up. Identical methods of putting birds out for training should not be used, and the methods and procedures should be varied as much as possible. The best success is obtained by **not** using the same method all the time.

Every dog should be started on pigeons with a gradual introduction to the other game birds. A flushed pigeon

eldom ever lights where the dog can re-point or catch
t. No other bird does this so consistently. Young
ogs develop their lungs chasing pigeons which adds
urther value to using them.

Most field trials are for the entire family. How can we
tell this youngster with gloves much too large that he is
not needed to plant birds?

Chapter 5

Training Psychology

DISCUSSION

The use of animal psychology by the skilled dog trainer may be nothing more than making an effort to understand the cause and effect (stimuli and reaction) related to behavior exhibited in the combined genetic and environmentally learned characteristics of individual dogs.

An in depth understanding of genetic behavior in dogs is made even more difficult to learn when it is modified by stress from training. At the time of a mating, the male and female are equal contributors to the genetic makeup of the offspring, but the female influences how environment affects their outcome. Experienced owners are able to observe different behavior patterns caused from the variances in

nheritance. Weak ones (phenotype) are more prone to
he environmental effects. In terms we best understand
n the field trial sport, it means that what we see is
hat we have to work with. If those required inherited
raits (genotype), so important to a class field dog,
re not strong, it is best not to waste time with the
og. This is not intended to infer that a pointing dog
ith only a slight interest in pointing birds when
oung cannot be taught to point when mature and can
lso be broke to wing and shot. It can be done, but
ften with considerable more effort and frustration.
et, some trainers and writers swear by stopping dogs
rom chasing early and breaking them. As I said
efore, there are all kinds of ways to train pointing
ogs, and the question of which method is best remains
nanswered.

It seems foolish to pay good money, or waste time,
rying to train a dog with poor potential and even more
o use it in a breeding program. Trainers working with
ogs having poor genetics become frustrated in trying
o piece together and understand certain behavior and
erformance patterns. When carried to the maximum in
sing these dogs in a breeding program, it results in
he complete loss of inherited characteristics
ssential to a pointing dog.

Dogs bought for hunting or field trials should be
btained from proven parents for better prediction of
eritability for conformation, temperament, pointing,
etrieving, nose, intelligence, trainability, size and
he capacity to withstand the stress of training.
tress may be considered in the same category as
emperament by many trainers. I consider these
eparate but related qualities.

Environmental stress can be detected in many ways:

blinking, biting, barking, whining, panting, excessiv
urination, excessive bowel movements often followed b
an irritated anal gland, running somewhere to hide
different appearance in the eyes, laying down, comin
to heel, jumping or holding onto the trainer
nervousness, low tucked tail, grinning expression an
others.

A dog where its **big** experience in life comes fro
laying by the fireplace at the feet of his master, wit
an occasional quick trip outside to evacuate, neve
experiences the stresses of a trained pointing dog
That dog simply is not ever trained to serve any usefu
function for its owner. A pattern is set or develope
over a period of time and the dog learns to accept suc
situations, and becomes incapable of learning in tha
environment. Yet, trained dogs are capable of learnin
new things every day of their lives.

There are hundreds, maybe thousands, of successfu
dog training methods. The use of psychology ranks hig
in the best ones. The trainer or handler must as
himself many times, over and over, when training eac
new dog why did this response occur under exactly th
same circumstances. And how can I improve my methods
techniques or manipulations of this dog, to avoid o
improve the repsonse I want. This is an importan
secret of dog training.

Rote is an effective training method and require
patience and consistency, but it takes experience an
knowledge of dog behavior to train effectively.

I have read articles on the great amount of knowledg
a puppy accumulates in its first few months of life
and I find it difficult to relate uninhibited play
chewing and mouthing or eating everything exposed to i
as learned behavior. These activities are essentia

292

o normal development and puppies do use different enses as a substitute for feeling and touching. A uppy's knowledge and sense of touch is learned through ts nose and mouth. An older dog's tool is primarily ts nose. Imagine how a dog points a bird when arrying a freshly killed skunk in its mouth. It is an mazing feat. A dog's nose works along with its brain n ways we cannot understand, and it requires the rainer to use intuitive reasoning, or some form of dog sychology to unravel many of its behavior patterns.

We have been given many concrete examples by esearchers to prove that dogs **cannot** reason. What oes a dog do when its source of heat and comfort are emoved? Curl up tighter? Does it search out a warmer lace, or accept the discomfort of the colder emperature? True, it does not know how to turn up the hermostat, put another log on the fire or use the elephone to make a service call to fix the heat, and s not capable of learning these tasks. Dogs are iologically unsuited to learn them.

Yet, dogs reason in many other ways. What about a og which points birds and waits just so long for his andler to find him, then leaves to find the handler nd by body language or barking signals him to follow ack where he re-points the bird? Or, the dog which as been in too many bird field stakes and goes in arly, finds and points all the birds briefly, and then eaves to hunt elsewhere until seeing the handler pproach before going back in to point the birds. Or, urries to the bird field to watch the bird planters ut down the birds, returns to the course and when ntering the bird field promptly goes to each bird to oint. Conditioned reponse? There are other examples f how dogs appear to reason, survive and adapt in many

ways better than we do with less ill effects unde
extremely difficult circumstances.

Many pet dogs are human imprinted so deeply tha
their owners assign to them human-like thought an
behavior patterns. Some dogs make convincin
demonstrations, but we bolster our ego by maintainin
that we are superior, more intelligent and capable o
reasoning when they are not. Aside from all the eg
serving claims we make, the dog remains unconcerne
about its status compared to ours and puts us to th
test and tries our patience in its training.

Not every trainer can develop the maximum potentia
from a dog for competition. A college degree is not a
indicator of the intelligence or ability required. Th
worst mistake a trainer can make is that of assuming
dog training is a simple task.

Animal behaviorist Leslie Van Hull of Green Bay
Wisconsin, wrote in Dog World, November 1982:

**". . . owners also have many characteristics that interact
with their animal's behavior in such a way to make problem
solving impossible unless they change their ways. . ."**

The owner is a **slave** to his dog. He must provide
food, water, general care and housing as a minimum.
Proper care includes many other things and if ownership
justification is for hunting or field trials, the
supportive tasks never seem to end. After a few months
or years, many owners tire of this servitude and find
other outlets for their ego, pride and time. Both the
pointing dog and its owner must enjoy their work. When
they work well together there must be rapport between
them which is a necessary relationship.

A good owner and trainer must be able to recognize
unfavorable reaction in a dog's attitude or behavior

294

before or as quickly as it develops undesirable stress behavior. The eyes, tail and body movement tell nearly everything we need to know most of the time. When training, we must know when to continue or stop activities, or control the degree of correction, discipline or punishment.

Some things asked of a dog are not supported by its history or breed purpose. The trainer must do such training by rote and the dog learns only after many repetitions, if at all. Pointing, for example, is supported by pointing dog breed history and a basic inherited characteristic, and in most pointing dogs it need not be taught—it happens naturally. A trainer can contribute to style, staunchness and desire. Where breeding for other qualities is paramount and carried on for too long without consideration for the pointing instinct it is modified or lessened. The red setter breed was developed from the Irish Setter and English Setter in an effort to recover certain desirable hunting qualities no longer dominant in the Irish Setter breed.

Many dogs lose their pointing desire from unpleasant experiences in early training where there is a lack of intrinsic motivation and the trainer unintentionally destroys it. A trainer may be too eager to get to his dog when on point or to prevent him from catching a bird off point or catching and eating it. Depending on what the dog is thinking or how he interprets his trainer's action, serious problems develop from just one experience. The dog reacts unfavorably to negative feedback. The desire to repeat the pointing process is thereby decreased. The trainer is then placed in a position of trying to analyze the cause of his problem. If he does not become involved in a similar feedback

process of his own and is unable to "read" the dog'
reaction, he will fail in training the dog.

His failure is no different in effect than that o
his dog failing any given task. Both lose some desir
to continue. The primary difference is that a novic
trainer may give up field trialing altogether and ge
rid of the dog. A dog may just lose style or intensit
on the first interacting experience with his trainer b
not understanding that there is supposed to be
relationship--a team effort. When trainers fail t
correct their methods with these dogs, they blink bird
and usually the blinking will be limited to just th
one type bird which was used to develop the unfavorabl
reaction. This is not to say that the dog and traine
cannot have problems on other birds, but dogs lear
from incorrect training and may later reason out wha
the handler wanted of him earlier. When a dog does no
have fun at a task, he has no motivation to repeat i
even when he instinctively loves to do it.

Beginning trainers are too eager and overwork thei
dogs, which can also cause serious consequences. To
much talk to dogs can have a paralyzing effect o
learning. It breaks a dog's concentration. Beginner
forget to reward dogs for good performance, or consider
rewards out of the question. A kind word, a pleasin
tone to the voice, or a pat on the back may be the onl
reward necessary. Too little or too much praise or
reinforcement may cause dogs to resist further work.
Too much work at the same task for too long a time
results in diminished interest with most dogs. There
are exceptions where a dog will keep his owner or
trainer playing **its** game until one or the other gives
up from exhaustion. Dogs normally do best at
self-invented (instinctively learned) tasks as they

ave a basic stimuli to please themselves or to do what
akes them feel most comfortable, or that which is most
uited to their heritage. Trainers should be wary. It
ay be their way of showing dominance.

Without having devotion and respect for their owners
nd trainers, pointing dogs may refuse to learn or will
ot behave properly. This is often indicated early in
uppies that when forced to play they will refuse.
hey are not yet ready to work with people, but if
llowed to mature, most will make that transition.
uch behavior is indicated by the dog being unsure,
oing to the house, car, barn, hiding, running off with
he bird, running off to self-hunt, or going to another
erson for a feeling of security. The dog plainly just
oes not want to conform. Trainers should try to
nderstand the training limitations of a breed, or an
ndividual dog at every age of development. Many
rainers justify their disciplining or punishing dogs
y an honest belief that their dog "knew better" when
ailing or refusing a task.

Man is supposedly capable of unlimited knowledge, or
he capacity to learn with varied ability. He can make
ssociations and learn from many different ways. Dogs
earn regimented training in a limited way. They are
iologically and genetically incapable of learning some
asks no matter how easy they seem for us. Yet, we
ust never underestimate the basic intelligence of dogs
r their thought processes. They have the capacity to
hink, react, dream, be jealous and angry and to adjust
nd modify their behavior. They have excellent
emories of both pleasant and unpleasant associations
nd experiences. They survived without us down through
he centuries, but if they ever made a mistake it was
electing companionship with humans. Then again, many

297

dogs fared well by this association, because many have
made slaves out of their masters.

Dogs under high stress do not learn well and develo
defenses against learning. Yet, some stress i
necessary to their learning. Biting or rapid pantin
(hyperpnea) are just two examples of this stress
Trainers may resort to forceful methods to teach a tasl
and in many dogs it only reinforces the negative. Mos
often trainers fail to see the telltale signs o
undesirable stress in time to stop training, and wai
to resume it at a later time or at a different place.

Sometimes it may be difficult to identify high stres
levels by just observing the dog panting rapidly
Panting serves the function that sweating does fo
people to cool-down. If two dogs are panting there i
a strong possibility it comes from exertion. Blinkin;
indicates stress or confusion. Some stress effects ar
not relieved by giving the dog vitamins, food, water o
rest. Abstinence from work may be the only solution.

Trainers should vary their tasks and modify thei
methods and techniques and look for different trainin;
approaches. Often an iterative process is helpful i
finding solutions. If at first you do not succeed,
try, try again. Sometimes the mere presence of the
trainer causes stress, and that problem can be avoide
which is as simple as making the work tasks fun for the
dog. What other signal is needed for success?

There are trainers who are never successful in
trials. The fault generally is reflected by their
temperament, ego and lack of self-control. They are
bent on teaching through totally negative physical
punishment. Dogs learn to bolt, escape and refuse to
return or come when called, or pretend to be making
game. If it is no fun for the dog to be associated

298

ith that trainer, he will avoid him when a choice is vailable. Nervous or high strung trainers also get oor results and never completely gain a dog's onfidence.

The threat of punishment, or the punishment itself, ecreases intrinsic and trained motivation. Punishment n other than young puppies, should be used only as the ast resort, if at all. In some remote cases, dogs hrive on punishment, for the effect does vary with the ifferent pointing breeds, and a dog could become just s dependent on punishment as some do for verbal raise.

Discipline, verbal or physical, should not be used in ost training situations until a certain rote has been stablished with demonstrated progress toward some oal. In a well trained dog, it can reinforce an arlier established, fixed, relationship. Regression ay be overcome by force or by removing the source ausing lost rapport. Force can reinforce the egative, but temporarily ignoring the condition might e a wise choice. It can usually be corrected merely y separation and reattachment.

Repetition of commands will often result in the dog ecoming dependent on them. A command should be used nly once and if it is not obeyed, the trainer should orrect the dog. This is done by returning the dog to ts original position and repeating the task. It is ot unusual to observe handlers at trials repeat a ommand over and over when their dogs are on point with o visible effect on them. Repeated commands do not revent dogs from doing what they have a mind to do. f anything this repetition forms dependence and is a orm of intimidation which shows that the handlers have o confidence in their dogs. It represents a **training**

.

situation as opposed to a learned one.

Vizslas are probably the most submissive, an
socially oriented of the pointing dog breeds. Ther
are a few dogs in other pointing breeds that ar
dominant, active and less social which are trainable
but require a strong hand and even physical punishmen
for a time. Since so many of the traits which defin
pointing dogs vary, it brings into focus that no tw
pointing dogs can be trained identically.

Looking at a list of these traits with strong an
weak inherited genetic levels, we expect all pointin
breeds to be strong at **pointing**. Some must be high i
retrieving, but may not be expected to be strong a
backing. Dogs weak in one which is essential t
winning, must have the difference made up throug
training and environmental association or change. W
could have a near perfect dog in all heritable traits
except pointing, and that one instinct could be so lo
to make it impossible to improve upon. There is n
need to train that dog for field trials or use it in
breeding program. Most trainers are willing to accept
the work of molding weaker traits while appreciating
the lack of work needed to intensify the strong ones.
A professional trainer cannot be expected to spend muc
time with a dog lacking the pointing instinct or one
with a poor nose. It is a fact that for traits of
lesser importance to performance in competition, that
different trainers are able to make better progress
with the same dog. They know this and oftentimes will
inform the owners and suggest they use a different
trainer.

American Kennel Club requirements do not discourage
the natural traits of pointing breeds as some people
believe. Trainers must develop these to high levels

first before spending too much time on obedience, control and manners. An undisciplined dog that has developed its natural hunting ability to the maximum may become a renegade with the wrong trainer, or an outstanding competitor with the right one.

The trait of laying down on point or at flush in this country is undesirable. We like to see dogs stand high and rigid on point. At one time in history, and in Europe today, laying down on point was important and they required the dog to lay down when the gun was raised. Training to discourage and stop this behavior is sometimes difficult and rote at picking the dog up is the most effective solution, but it takes **time**. On a comparative scale of values there are worse problems.

Looking at a different side of performance in comparing field trial competition to hunting, we may have a **perfect** hunting dog, but it might lack speed and range which are required for competitive field trial dogs. Under hunting conditions, it is possible for dogs to learn to pace themselves from prior experiences of having hunted all day long. Field trial competition demands that dogs show all the important traits in a short period of time where they run full out for the stake time set. This is desired, but not all do it consistently.

The training required to develop manners and obedience are unnatural for dogs, but necessary for a happy and enduring relationship. Pointing dogs with traits for checking to the handler frequently may be disturbing, but these dogs are seldom lost or lose contact with their handlers as do pointers. Field trialers who find a noble challenge in hunting for their dogs, instead of having dogs work for them are on the decrease. Hound owners, such as coon hunters, must

301

accept hunting for their strayed dogs as a basic fact
of life to be endured to enjoy their sport. Pointer
and setter owners do also.

Professional trainers are seldom permitted to develop
all the heritable traits to the maximum. Amateur
trainers can do that if they have the know-how and
tenactiy to work long and hard.

DOMINANCE

Dogs are pack animals and usually submit only to one
leader. If that leader is lost for whatever reason,
another takes over as top dog. They are social animals
and learn to work together as a team for their common
good.

Every dog which associates with others regularly,
must find its rung on the "pecking order" ladder. The
top rung is the top dog and he could be the smallest!
All others must follow and fit in some order of
descending submissiveness.

A dog kept with the family must learn where he fits
in. The smart owner will not permit his dog to become
top dog with any member of his family. In practice
this may be difficult.

Every dog bides his time and makes his move toward
dominance when an opportunity is presented. Allow him
too much freedom, lax supervision and control, and
improper discipline and he will become boss.

The least problems are experienced when owners use
metal crates for the dog's home inside the house where
he is usually safe from discipline or punishment. But,
he should not be allowed to bark uncontrolled when
confined.

A dog must learn that when he is in the house that all four feet must remain on the floor always, and no food stealing from counter tops or tables and he must stay off furniture and beds.

Dogs are happiest when they live in an environment of responsible supervision and control. They expect and want supervision and are happier as a result, and learn where they fit and are comfortable.

Some breeds develop loyalty and a close attachment to each family member. Others know only one master and never ascend to the second spot in the pecking order. These dogs are better off in an outside kennel. There are owners who insist that nobody else in the family will attend to their needs or training no matter what. I know one man who would get up from his death bed to feed his dogs.

Dogs are like children. They will test owners in many ways and times trying to find a weak place in their armor. Owners who give in are losers every time their dogs test them.

Certain dogs need a strong hand. What may appear as cruel treatment with one dog may be necessary to maintain dominance and control. Yet, it is a fact that more can be accomplished with kindness and patience which is true when taming most wild animals. Dogs must learn to respect their owners.

Owners must be leaders who provide the proper introduction to their dogs' progressive training, and minimize their lack of understanding of what is expected. Dog training cannot be hurried to meet an artificial deadline such as an important trial.

Physical punishment must not be used in the introduction of any training.

The advantages of keeping a dog in the house are that

the owner and dog have more time and opportunity for active and passive training and supervision more than if kept in an outside kennel. Kennel dogs remain strangers by comparison to their owners and trainers, but kenneling is a necessity for many owners. The problem of dominance between the owner and his dog may be simplified.

Some dogs kept in the house can become **too** submissive which is devastating to their field development. These dogs always seem to be in a distressed condition, and it is difficult to make them bold. They will escape work by turning into a jellyfish at the trainer's feet or run off.

The dominance syndrome obviously varies with each dog and his environment. A dog may refuse to work for his owner, but work happily for someone else. This may be a situation where the dog instinctively refuses to give up dominance to one but will willingly to another person.

Dogs which refuse to retrieve birds to their trainer may be highly dominant where it signifies an act of surrendering (food) to a lesser member of the pack. He may retrieve inanimate objects without considering it a submissive act.

It is difficult to separate jealousy and dominant behavior when a dog's owner brings in a new dog. Dogs not only get jealous, they get angry. Owners should make an effort to understand what causes the change in a dog's behavior and temperament. Punishment may just be the worst thing they can do in their efforts to correct the problem.

MOTIVATION

A good dog is self-motivating, but training may alter or destroy this trait. He should want to do things naturally and the training should intensify the desire with the trainer being integrated gradually. Any training may stifle natural desire. A trainer should not have to become involved in the art of teaching motivation, but must develop it to the fullest. A lazy, lack-luster, dog cannot be easily motivated and working him may be challenging but not productive. Unless it is a personal (only dog) used for giving the trainer experience and to learn from his mistakes in training, his time is wasted.

Havilah Babcock wrote in *Tales of Quail'N Such* , page 152:

"Too much butting in befuddles a dog, especially when he gets instructions which run counter to his nose and judgment. He loses his spirit and initiative, just piddles around to give the appearance of hunting. Leaf-raking we called it in the WPA days. A dog's instincts are refined out of him. He quits thinking and soon forgets how to think. He becomes man-conscious instead of bird-conscious, and pleasing his master is more important than finding birds. Now, if a dog has a nose, let him use it. If he hasn't, trade him off for a wheelbarrow or something useful."

LEARNING

We often hear the statement that, "You can't teach an old dog new tricks." The inference is that an old dog cannot learn. This is **not** true. Yet, there are some tasks dogs of any age cannot learn to do no matter how

305

often it is repeated. The dog fails to learn. It is true that some dogs can learn more easily and quickly than others and some breeds may learn a given task where others cannot.

A pointing dog instinctively learns to point more readily than one having a different instinctive ability. Therefore, he is already prepared to learn that task. Genetics plays an important part in learning. Some dogs learn a difficult task the first time because they are instinctively **prepared** for it.

The enemy of a dog's teacher is his inability to control all the training parameters which often results in negative stimulation. A dog must like and be happy in whatever task is being taught for the teacher (trainer) to be effective.

Negative stimulation can disappear or last a long time depending on whether it is reinforced accidentally or otherwise. Punishment can cause either negative or positive stimulation depending on the individual dog or breed, the situation and how it is done. Praise is usually positive and must be included in every phase and aspect of training. Too much praise can be as bad as none, or ineffective praise. A dog wants to please his master, teacher or trainer, whether he is in a learning situation or in other forms of contact.

Instinctive performance altered by stress situations can be modified but is nearly impossible to completely destroy. A dog that blinks a bird is a good example. The dog blinks because of situation stress caused from negative reactions to previous training, but will point staunchly if not in that stress situation. I have watched several dogs leave point when approached by their handler, but they would point every bird they found. Whenever the cause of their stress enters the picture they blink. When it is gone they will point again.

A puppy begins learning from its mother soon after gaining sight and hearing. It reacts to motion and sound. It learns from its littermates although not always what is needed for human association which has proven to be necessary no later than forty nine days of age.

The next few months are extremely important to learning. I expose puppies to live and dead birds before seven weeks of age to give them that experience and to see what each individual's reaction is. They should be aggressive and try to eat or carry the bird off to safety from littermates and have no desire to share. This is not to mean that a puppy which ignores birds at this age will when older. I would hesitate to pick one that did not show interest at seven weeks of age. I have had puppies point a wing at three weeks of age, but this may not be typical.

A lack of intrinsic motivation will cause dogs not to point. The longer a puppy or dog is delayed in exposure to birds the lower its motivation or desire is to point. Therefore, it is best to expose them early in life and give intermittent exposure until serious training can begin. Punishing a dog on point further decreases motivation.

Make it fun and interesting and as a rule give no food as a reward. Praise by touching or by saying, "You are a **good** boy, or you are a **good** girl." Food does have value as a reward, but how and when it is used is important. A dog which is uncomfortable in his surroundings, or in any situation must be put at ease and his mind changed to more pleasant things. Food may just do the trick in one situation and in another the dog's behavior should be ignored.

I strongly believe that trainers must be able to **read** dogs to train them effectively. Too many trainers are late in recognizing the need to make corrections or changes, or analyze the situation wrong.

It reminds me of a joke about a research biologist who proceeded to cut off each leg of a frog and commanded the frog to jump, which he did each time, until the last leg was cut off. The frog would not jump when ordered to do so several times, and the researcher wrote in his project book: "The frog cannot hear."

Trainers are sometimes like that. Dogs have limits which can be caused by sickness, environment or evolution. Rote must be used to teach dogs not genetically prepared to learn. It may take weeks and even months before a dog will learn a task, but persistence and patience will win out when it is a task that he can learn. Some dogs need re-broke to wing and shot after several months layoff. Therefore, it is better to continually reinforce training with some dogs, but others need little additional training to reach previous peaks in control, manners and range.

Learning is the process of molding a dog's instinctive behavior into something useful to his owner or trainer. We cannot honestly say that evolution, or man's selection of desirable characteristics causes a dog to want to work with him as a partner more. The pack instinct is foremost and must be modified. Some dogs may only work for themselves. The Vizsla is a good example of breeding for a close association with man and for centuries were always kept in the homes of royalty. There are dog breeds which identify with sheep and even resemble them, but how the breeding of such dogs was done is unknown.

Dogs learn to work with man through a system of reward and punishment as they are taught certain tasks which they have the natural ability to learn. Dogs punished without knowing what they are being punished for, or when sick, modifies their behavior and learning ability at the wrong time and place in a negative manner.

When I whipped my first pointing dog for chasing other dogs away after he returned, it never occurred to me that I was making a mistake. My only previous experience was with coon hounds and they are different from pointing dogs in several ways, but they would probably react the same way. We usually caught them by intercepting them on a trail without punishment. Too many trainers try to use temper or anger to teach their dogs, but it always has undesirable consequences.

I often see similar behavior when judges call time. Handlers must have help to catch their dogs and get off the course so another brace can start, and it is not because these dogs have that much desire to continue hunting.

TRAINABILITY

What sires and dams do and learn will also be found in their get. If a breeder does not like some particular thing about a dog, or bitch, he should not breed it. These traits are not one hundred percent positive--nothing is in breeding. Inbreeding can intensify certain qualities and can improve trainability. Sons or daughters will have similar characteristics and idiosynchrosies of their parents, but good inbreeding and line breeding of well trained dogs does seem to improve trainability of the get.

Trainers who have worked with several generations of planned inbreeding--mother, daughter, granddaughter, great granddaughter, etc. have the experience to overcome problems successfully and because of this are able to train each succeeding generation easier.

I define **trainability** as that quality a good field trial dog must possess to handle and learn under the stress and rigors of training to be successful, obedient and love working with his trainer. The living and working environment of dogs in these succeeding generations is important to trainability too.

Jerome B. Robinson wrote on that subject in *Sports Afield*, November 1981, about picking the most promising pups in a litter when they are only two or three days old.

"According to Dr. Michael Fox, Director of the Institute for Study of Animal Problems in Washington, D.C., simple tests will indicate which are the best learners and the least timid individuals. Research has also proved that it is possible to increase a puppy's trainability at a young age and make it a better learner, a more willing performer and, generally, a more stable animal."

"The most promising pups are those that, from birth, have the highest heartbeat rate, says Dr. Fox. In a typical litter, a third of the newborn pups will have resting heartbeat rates that measure 170 beats per minute or faster, a third will measure 160 to 170 beats per minute, and a third will be less than 160. The medium and high rate pups will be quickest learners, the least timid, the most able to accept new things and, therefore, they are the most promising. The U.S.Army now accepts only puppies with medium or high resting heartbeat rates for its K-9 Corps Super Dog program."

Pedigrees are important to buyers only if they have knowledge of every dog's behavior and success. Titles may be indicators, but should not be given much credence unless the owner or handler has seen them work. Sure there are other things that can be learned from pedigrees, but are not important and have little value. All training for competition helps future generations. Breeders and trainers do not believe in environmental changes in a dog's genes, but there is much yet to be learned. Identification of the best genotypes comes from training, and competition followed with selective inbreeding and line breeding continued into successive generations.

COMMUNICATION

A dog must love and respect its owner before real communication is realized. Fear is also important to this process as with a parent-child relationship. They must ask themselves: What punishment will I get for doing this? Love and respect may not necessarily go together.

The medium of communication is by voice, inflection, tone, whistle, hand and body signals and by touching. Dogs learn to love their masters no matter what their social status, color, race, skinny or fat, ugly or pretty, short or tall, mean or kind or how their voice sounds. Dogs easily adapt to whatever is their lot.

Dogs also tell us things in many ways. They bark, growl, use eye expression, body movement, tail movement, ear position, facial expression, position of body, tail, ears and other movement.

Dogs learn to understand us quicker than we do them. They have more time and less to distract them in their endless hours of what we would call boredom. They learn better whenever they share much of their time with their owners, and can be more of a problem or nuisance when kenneled outside.

Touching is universally understood between man and his dog. Dogs touch with their noses, tongues, feet and bodies. They love to be touched, and will often want it done to excess. They become spoiled with too much, but they can sense the difference in the touch from that of love to punishment.

Too much punishment makes a dog hand, foot or body shy which can cause it to take a defensive posture. Too much touching causes the dog to want nothing else and this inhibits learning.

Staunchness usually involves touching by the handler in the beginning of training. The trainer may stroke the dog's head, back and tail to improve style and intensity. After breaking, if too much punishment has been used to do it, a dog may learn to fear touching. It may cause him to break point, sit or lay down.

Dogs can sense unintended forms of unspoken communication. It borders on extrasensory perception. Trainers have demonstrated this form of communication by looking at their dog and thinking the command, and their dog readily responds.

It has been my own experience that dogs can instantly sense anger, nervousness, fear or lack of confidence of an owner, trainer or handler.

Trainers and handlers must work at trusting their dogs more and allow them the opportunity to make mistakes. They learn from their mistakes if corrected properly in a timely manner. It makes no sense for a dog to be perfect in training and be incorrigible in competition. They know the difference. I maintain that training time has been wasted, if no corrections are needed. Punishment should not be part of correction.

We often overlook the importance of a dog's hearing to its environment and learning. It is acute and has a greater range than humans. I see dogs when hunting stop to listen for something moving or making a noise before moving on to continue hunting. They recognize sounds which cause pleasure and displeasure. They seem to learn every decibel and tonal change in their master's voice. Therefore, a harsh voice is enough to let dogs know they have done wrong when given at the **exact** time of the infraction which is punishment to dogs.

Timing is **critical** in communicating with a dog. A fraction of a second too soon or too late and he fails to learn the correction intended. Trainers must avoid making corrections too long after a dog has done something wrong or incorrect. They should start over and work on timing and avoid being distracted. Too late is a blink of the eye.

Feedback is like an echo. In everything done in dog training there is an echo. It cannot be heard, so it has to be "heard" with the trainers' eyes. When I use the term "reading a dog" it is done by never taking my eyes off a dog in training or competition, or important signals needed for correction will be missed. In simple terms, it means that every action and reaction of a dog must be seen all the time.

Before a dog thinks of it, trainers must know when he

will try to escape correction, soften, blink, feign deafness, be jealous, bark, growl or refuse a command. Who can work with a neurotic dog? With practice, trainers will know when a dog is inclined to break and chase or refuse to back and be able to do something before it happens.

Trainers must become good at reading their dogs' reactions and behavior correctly so adjustments and commands can be started without loss of natural desire and ability. The signals are **always** telegraphed by the dog--he is normally not smart enough to feign them.

By working at it, trainers can predict what a dog will do next, how he will point and when, if he will be staunch or break.

Dogs should not be confused by trainers repeating commands or signals where unnecessary. When in doubt, do nothing. Be firm, gentle, fair, earn his respect, but do not beat him. Use praise and affection.

Barbara Woodhouse says when punishing,

"Look the dog straight in the eyes, scold him with a thunderous tone and give him a few shakes. This will make the dog feel slightly silly, and he won't want it repeated."

That works and it is usually safe to look pointing breeds in the eye without fear of attack, but not all dog breeds are safe. Dogs do not normally like direct eye contact if not taught at an early age.

The lack of discipline sows seeds of disrespect and makes training difficult if not impossible.

Any owner or trainer having a dog with no respect for him can turn it over to someone else who may be capable of commanding the dog's respect and may do well in competition. It happens all the time.

A trainer who cannot control his own emotions, cannot

314

expect to be a successful trainer. There are exceptions and certain dogs can make the exception. Usually these dogs are not **really** trained, but are intimidated into acceptable performances a few times in competition to win. Read how Jack Harper worked his dog over before the brace heat. I have known several handlers who took their dogs off somewhere and beat the hell out of them just before they ran, or took them to another part of the grounds and ran them for a half hour or more. That was "required" for the dog to "handle."

Dogs have a special way--at least to our understanding--of communicating among themselves. I have observed what seem to be strange happenings. I do not understand how a trained dog can instantly detect one that will break and chase in gun dog stakes by looking at it at the starting line.

The chain gang is a common method professionals use to train dogs. They are put on the chain to watch other dogs being trained. Dogs can and do learn by working with and watching other dogs work. Many trainers use older dogs no longer in competition to put dogs in training on the straight and narrow without always creating jealousy or adverse effects.

Successful dog trainers must practice dog psychology. An example is to never give a command when in no position to enforce it, or allow a dog to anticipate a command.

PRAISE

Praise is the most important reward a dog ever needs in training. It helps establish a healthy relationship

315

and develops a social relationship with the trainer in achieving a team effort in competition.

Yet if praise is offered too frequently, or in large doses, it is detrimental to that relationship. Dogs can become dependent on it to the exclusion of everything else. They have ways to achieve self satisfaction for a job well done and sense the satisfaction of their trainer.

It may come as a surprise but many trainers feel embarrassed or humiliated when told by an instructor to "praise your dogs." Some people just will not stoop so low to praise them. They probably never tell their wives, husbands or children that they experience the common emotion called love.

FOOD AS A REWARD

Food has no place in competition as a reward stimuli. The reward a good working dog needs is to smell a wild bird and point it.

I have seen handlers use food at trials as a reward to get a retrieve. It was not impressive. Once a dog becomes dependent on food as a reward, it is hard for him to become a **real** competitor for his mind is not where it should be-to win.

There is no harm in using food in the house or yard to **start** a task such as retrieving. Dogs can be worked at retrieving a tid bit and forbid their eating it until retrieved. Food as an occasional reward will not be harmful if no habit pattern is formed.

The best use of food is to provide dogs an energy boost after hard work under adverse conditions, or before competition to help maintain strength, stamina and endurance. It is interesting to learn many of the methods handlers use in trials to give their dogs "peak" energy for trials. Some even **withhold** food two or three days before a trial which is based on the "theory" that a hungry dog will **hunt.**

PUNISHMENT

Punishment should act as a positive stimulant when used in training. It must be done when the dog is in the act of doing something wrong, but only after he has been taught repeatedly the correct way or proper method. Once punishment is started it is necessary for several repetitions with some dogs until they learn by rote punishment.

Correction is best used without physical punishment. A dog should not be allowed to get away with any improper response to instructions or commands without an immediate correction. A couple seconds after a dog does something wrong is often too late. The act must still be fresh in his mind for correction to be effective.

Defiant behavior indicates poor training techniques, confusion and no rapport. All work must be directed at becoming a team between the trainer and dog. Neither can do the work properly alone.

It is my belief that any trainer who loses his temper because a dog fails a task should find some other work. Punishing a dog because of the trainer being unable to control his temper insures continued erratic learning behavior.

Most dogs do certain tasks from intimidation or fear of punishment, and in the absence of a trainer or handler will not do them. A properly trained dog will work for any knowledgeable handler when he is not mistreated or mishandled.

Some dogs are trained exclusively with shock collars around their neck or loin and will not work properly without one. These trainers lack knowledge, patience or the ability to train using progressive persuasive methods that brings to peak perfection the natural ability of dogs. John Gardner says:

"a dog that does not have the brains to know it has a shock collar on does not have the brains or mental balance to work."

But, they are smart enough to learn how to escape punishment.

Trainers should never punish unless they are **absolutely** certain their dogs can and have learned how to do the tasks. When a trained dog absolutely refuses to do something asked and no amount of enticing can cause him to do it, he is either sick, jealous or angry. There is no logical choice other than to force him to comply, except it might be best to ignore his behavior temporarily if sick. The trainer must use his best dog psychology before taking any action that would prove to be negative.

Havilah Babcock in *Tales of Quail'N Such*, pages 148-9, 1957, wrote:

". . . Certainly he should have been disciplined, but not overdisciplined. Dogs differ greatly in the amount of punishment they need, or can take. A word of disapproval here may have as much effect as a whacking there. Never give a dog more than that particular dog needs. It's the inevitability of punishment, rather than the severity, that counts anyway. When too harsh, it may backfire and overreach itself. Through temper or inexperience, a dog owner may overcorrect one fault and replace it with a worse one. A cure sometimes cures too much."

Smart professinal trainers have their scouts or helpers whip their dogs so they can always be the "good" guy when handling them. Amateurs are always trying to be friend, master, trainer, handler and disciplinarian.

Oftentimes it is important to stop a dog's training for a short or long period of time and let him lay in his crate, or kennel, or watch other dogs work. It is an amazingly effective settling technique for training problems.

According to Konrad Lorenz in his studies at the Max Planck Institute as reported in the *New York Times Magazine Section*, July 5, 1970, a dog is incapable of ceasing to love his master.

"If you kick your dog, he thinks it's his fault. . . .the more pain you cause a dog the more submissive he becomes and the more he asks your pardon."

Ivan Pavlov who discovered the conditioned reflex in dogs was upset to learn that conditioned reflex was not the only element of behavior. He failed to really understand all the psychological behavior during his experiments of which the famous bell ringing salivation response was one.

Many trainers to this day believe that dogs must be punished to learn. Punishment is the absolute worst tool at their disposal.

Herm David quoted Clyde Morton in *Hunting Dog*, October 1966:

"If there is one area where more dog trainers, both professional and amateur, fail more than in any other, it is in punishing dogs. They don't do enough of it, too much, at the wrong time, in the wrong way, for the wrong reasons—out of anger. These errors are often irreversible and many excellent prospects are ruined."

319

JEALOUSY

Dogs instinctively want to guard and protect their masters. They do not want their affections replaced or shared with another dog, or person sometimes, and act in predictable ways.

Jealousy is normally not recognized soon enough in training and competitive situations and can destroy the dog's desire to work for his handler the same way as with one severely distressed.

I had a bitch that I **swore** would never get jealous until I used her to teach backing to her litter sister. It was slow in evolving, but eventually affected her competitive ability such that it required some psychology before finishing her two field titles. The solution was to quit working with the other dog and wait her out.

Jealousy is especially common in dogs that become overly attached to their owners. These dogs are difficult to work with and train. We want just enough attachment to effect constructive and enjoyable work together in training and competition.

Dogs like attention. Care must be taken that they are not given too much. Jealousy is demonstrated in subtle and unsubtle ways. Simply changing the conditions that a dog learns under can create jealousy. Dog owners like to use the word temperamental because they lack a better definition of what they experience.

Dogs have ways to get back at owners, trainers and handlers at field trials. The first thing they will do is quit hunting and show no interest whatever. They may eat horse, owl, bird, or animal droppings, dig for mice, point them, or seemingly go into a trance over some delectable odor--something they never ever did before a jealous or distressed condition existed. Dogs freak out. I see these problems in bitches more than in males. Males generally restrict themselves to smelling and covering everything with a squirt of urine, or quit working altogether.

Something inside the dog serves as a trigger mechanism that causes jealousy to surface. The dog becomes stubborn, defies the handler and refuses to heed commands. Maybe its pleasure center in the brain is out of kilter.

They may be selectively jealous of their kennel mates. It has been proven that dogs do learn by working with and watching other dogs. The question is then when and how, in these cases, do dogs still get jealous of each other or just with one or two?

I have had dogs fully trained and highly competitive suddenly turn into a renegade, and deliberately bust every bird they pointed and then chased them with reckless abandon. Punishment only exacerbated the problem. Once the source of jealousy was uncovered and corrected the dogs returned to normal almost overnight.

Sometimes a trainer can force a dog to work under jealous demeanor, but being patient, looking for the problem, or waiting it out if it cannot be found usually works.

Jealousy in field trials is not restricted to dogs. The first thing we realize is that we have a spoil-sport in our midst who suddenly attacks a handler and his dog as being more putrid than sewer scum. The people who are attacked are aghast at what they did to provoke such senseless attacks only to suddenly realize that they have won and have become a worthy adversary. Ever hear someone at a trial say, "His dog looks like hell and runs like shit?" That dog just won! Somehow an adjustment in previous relationships becomes necessary and handlers learn once again they are back to the philosophy of "dog eat dog." Probably that behavior caused the phrase to be coined.

STRESS

Men and their dogs live together, work together and many even sleep together. They form close bonds that are long lasting. Pointing dog field trials are just one activity where this relationship is at its apex. The best competitors--man and dog--comprise a perfect team.

In spite of this closeness, many things required in competition are foreign to a dog's instinctive nature even after hundreds and thousands of years of close association. If there is a perfect animal, perfect love, dogs qualify first.

Perfect teamwork is not easily accomplished and requires considerable work and experience between man and his dog. To this, or any number of other levels of development, the dog must learn to handle daily training and working stresses.

Dogs are stressed in some manner in everything trainers attempt to have them do. It manifests itself in many ways and when carried to the extreme causes hyperpnea, distress, psychosis, neurosis or a complete breakdown. Stress is devastating to a dog when it gets out of control. Trainers must learn to recognize the danger signals and not let them reach critical levels.

A good rule to remember is that if a dog is not happy in a given task, he is under heavy stress and immediate efforts should be made to relieve it. The more difficult a task and the more repetitions under a stressed state of mind, the more harm is done. Stress is cumulative.

Beatrice Lydecker, a dog psychic, says,

"You have to be consistent when training dogs. They want desperately to please, but they get confused and neurotic if you don't give them clear signals."

Let them know where they stand by praising them often and stop training, not on a sour note, but on a happy one.

Since stress is not always obvious to the untrained eye, it is easy for a trainer to destroy a dog's ability to be trained. Sometimes a single unpleasant experience can be devastating and permanent in nature. For that reason it is essential that every trainer learn to READ his dog quickly and correctly.

Both experienced and inexperienced trainers must learn what stress is? No need to look in a dictionary because the word stress is a misnomer. Strain is a more appropriate word. Both are engineering terms and both mean the same in literary works. Fortunately or unfortunately, stress is the more common word used. Wrong words do take on new usage such as this one which deals with the emotional responses.

The ALPO Center For Advanced Pet Study's pamphlet states that the stress response is the way a dog's body reacts to anything that puts a demand on him. It signals his internal systems to go on "alert." Nerves tingle and hormones pump into the bloodstream causing heartbeat and breathing rates to increase and muscles to tense. Extra energy is needed. Protein is mobilized from tissue reserves and protein elements are used to produce antibodies and new blood cells. The same thing happens with humans when confronted with a charge of a grizzly bear.

Dr. David Kronfeld, February 1983, *Pure-Bred Dogs/ American Kennel Gazette*, wrote that :

". . . stress is the general response of the body to any extra demand, physical or emotional. It is a series of adaptations, some regulator, others effector in nature. Primary regulatory responses occur in the nervous and hormonal systems. Major effector responses occur in the nervous and hormonal systems. Major effector responses occur in metabolism, i.e. energetic and chemical transactions in the body. The capacity of these metabolic responses is influenced by the availability of energy and nutrients supplied directly from the digestive tract or retrieved from body stores. So intakes of food energy and certain nutrients are just as important before stress as during or following stress. Nutrients that may influence our ability to cope with stress include protein, riboflavin, niacin, ascorbic acid, vitamin A, potassium, calcium, magnesium, iron, copper and zinc."

Field trial dogs should be fed food containing at least 30 percent protein, so it is important to feed properly and train only healthy dogs. It is important to remember that some dogs are allergic to some kinds of food. Stress increases some of the blood constituents and decreases others. The chemical reaction is complex and originates in the brain. How dogs are returned to normal is equally as complex.

324

H. Seley, in his book *The Stress of Life*, divides the stress of everyday life into eustress and distress. Eustress is pleasurable and distress is not and eventually debilitates. Eustress, he says, helps prevent distress. It follows that a dog must be happy to avoid distress.

How do dogs escape the effects of stress--distress? They escape by showing no further interest in the game or task, biting the trainer when forced to do a task further, running off, refusing to leave their immediate surroundings, returning to the field trial assembly area or staying at heel.

Stress mobilizes a dog's response system to run or fight. Yet, a limited amount of stress helps keep dogs healthy.

A healthy dog will handle stressful situations better. Diet and vitamins are also important in helping alleviate its effects. Therefore, a sick dog, or one behaving temporarily out of character, should not be trained until it is feeling better.

Bitches are notorious for having hormone imbalance between their seasons when not bred. Sometimes problems develop because of their lack of tolerance to stress at these times.

Most trainers are slow to correct or adapt their methods to individual dogs or such problems might never develop. The usual solution for field trainers is to get rid of their "problem" dogs and keep at it until they find one with a strong enough constitution to handle the stress from their training methods. These dogs do exist and carry inept trainers to success at least for a short time.

Particular pointing dog breeds and individual dogs in all breeds are distressed by the tone of one's voice, while others are only from physical punishment. Harrassment, teasing and intimidation are also damaging. It is a good policy not to tease or stare.

It is obvious then that stress and distress are by-products of training. Whenever it appears severe enough to interfere with a dog's progress, his training should be stopped for a few weeks or months. The astute trainer will keep it within bounds. I have seldom seen severe stress occur when dogs are exposed to actual hunting situations where they are free to hunt and explore on their own with little, if any, interference or direction from their handlers.

Progressive training helps keep stressful situations within bounds, and is the only way a dog should be trained and then only for one thing at a time, and not when fatigued, sick or during severe weather.

After working and observing my own dogs under stress for many years, I have decided that they all experience what I call **situation stress.** This occurs where a dog was severely stressed and later is placed back in the exact same situation. One example, of many, comes when a dog has a poor experience in a field trial situation with another dog on breakaway. Put him back there at a later time and he will refuse to leave. Blinking is another form of situation stress as is refusing to retrieve, eating and chewing birds. I have seen many dogs run away or go back to "his" vehicle at trials which is another form of situation stress. The best advice is never do anything that produces these situations as they are difficult to overcome.

How does one identify stress? By body language, ear position, facial expression, tail position, eating horse droppings, eyes, hyperventilating, urinating, etc.

Dogs required to retrieve in competition are exposed to the most severe stress situations. Outstanding dogs are ruined by too forceful training for retrieving when being broke. That's why training for **one thing at a time** makes sense. I have known many dogs that did well in non-retrieving stakes, but failed when asked to retrieve. This should be kept in mind when comparing great dogs. Those dogs that retrieved and were good at other performances learned to handle greater stress.

DELAYED STRESS

Stress is delayed when starting to break a dog for wing and shot as one example. A dog which sits on the approach of its handler, or at flush of the bird are two excellent examples. The dog stands tall for a period of the breaking process without sitting, but it slowly accumulates. It is apparent for the experienced trainer to see it coming if he stays alert. Every dog suffers stress in the training process to one degree or other and each one shows it in slightly different ways. Dogs with stable temperaments will be less noticeably affected and will bounce back with no serious lasting effects. Trainers must learn when to back off and delay further training from time to time. Males usually show different stress signs than bitches. Bitches sit or lay down and males tend to lift legs, soften on point or blink. The worst example for males is to lift their legs and urinate on the birds. These are all precursors for situation stress.

EFFECTS OF EXCESSIVE COMPETITION

Too much competition can have an adverse effect on dogs. There is no set formula for calculating what is too much, because every dog is different as well as every trainer and handler. A dog can become over saturated with too much of the same exposure, become bored, distressed and fail to sparkle, or will develop serious habits that are detrimental to good performance.

A well bred dog should like the field trial experience more each time he is put down in puppy and derby stakes, but this is never assured because of brace mates, weather conditions and birds used. Owners of dogs that behave positively become infected with their progress and enjoy the opportunity to compete. Scintillating performances are not forever, and we must keep reminding ourselves that dogs are frail animals and not machines. How much is too much competition?

If a dog is always taken up when thirsting for more, has a whetted appetite to run, the desire intensifies and everything is plus. Under these circumstances, a dog never seems to get too much work.

Dog clubs tally points toward Top Ten in puppy and derby, gun dog and all-age stakes. Many owners' goal is to put their dogs in the number one position. It means entering every stake the dog is eligible for every weekend. Every dog entered in a stake adds one more number, and the better each dog performs, the more respectable is the win. Many field trialers' goal is to win rosettes and are happy to win over inferior competition. After all, once the win is posted the status is never questioned. It is assumed that all dogs in the stake were good. Who would ever know that all other dogs in the stake but those placed were ordered up or had submarginal performances?

We should exercise care in our statements about somebody else's goal, because it is usually counterproductive. It is their money, time and dog.

There are many owners who insist that their dogs continue to run in all stakes after winning championship titles. This requires all trainers and handlers to work to beat them or to breed better dogs. This practice is better in some respects than winning titles over mediocre dogs. Every dog has his day. Handlers who keep working and entering learn that it averages out.

Show champions are not entered in regular classes once the title is won. Peer pressure would soon stop an owner from entering a Champion in open bitch or open dog classes. There is some peer pressure in field trials, but most owners feel no compulsion not to enter any or all stakes with their champion dogs. Field trials are a different sport than dog shows.

PATRONIZING DOGS

When training and in competition, handlers should never cater to a dog's idiosyncrasies. They should never stop and watch dogs potter, urinate, defecate, or anything else. It is best that handlers go on and ignore some behavior. They should command dogs to move on that potter, but honest elimination should be totally ignored. It is a bad training habit to stop and watch dogs smell some strange odor, track horse droppings, potter, urinate or whatever which is not constructive to hunting. Once a dog urinates he should be forced to stop other attempts in competition if it appears stress induced.

HYPERPNEA

Training stresses cause hyperpnea. This is rapid panting caused from stress, not from the temperature being hot or from over-exertion. Panting is the basic mechanism for dogs to remove excess body heat. When caused by heat or exertion, there is a loss of body fluids evidenced by dripping water or saliva. Hyperpnea is not caused from physical exertion but is mentally induced. It can be triggered **off** as quickly as it can be triggered **on.**

How is hyperpnea recognized? Sometimes it is not so easy, since it can occur from some physical exertion or high ambient temperature. The stressed dog usually cannot exert itself enough to collapse from heat exhaustion except when the temperature is hot. Hyperpnea occurs even in below freezing temperatures.

A chemical change occurs in the blood from an abnormal breathing rhythm involving carbon dioxide, and it renders a dog incapable of physical exertion. There is a **lack** of oxygen in the blood and an excess of carbon dioxide.

Dogs will be extremely excited, pant as if very hot and pull on the lead when going to their training or competition, and they can hardly be restrained in their anticipation to start work. When released, they will not hunt.

A dog can run, hunt and breathe normally when running the back course, but as he enters the bird field, his handler will say "find birds," and the dog will shorten its range and loop around the handler closely and pant so hard that he is no longer capable of smelling a bird at any distance.

Dogs do not have to be in training or competition to get this condition. It can happen at any time, any place. They can get the condition by trying to get out the door before the owners. Dogs with hyperpnea must be given stern correction. Usually a strong "NO" used each time they develop this condition will eventually get some control. Sometimes taking the collar and shaking the dog with a strong "NO" will snap them out of it. Eventually dogs learn not to bring the condition on. Every working dog must learn to establish a balance between anticipation, stress, excitement and control. Hyperpnea is a complicated condition, but if not controlled it renders dogs practically useless for field trial competition.

MAN-DOG RELATIONSHIP

Dogs work better for trainers and handlers they like. They are like children. They can spot a phoney a mile away. Dogs and children are attracted to and like certain people at first sight or contact. Strange as it may be, they are usually correct. Some people are born natural dog trainers and handlers.

Properly trained dogs become more confident and have more consistent performances as time goes on. They develop the best relationships with their trainers and handlers under proper training regimes. But, there are few relationships of this kind observed on the field trial circuit. The better bird dogs always work for

331

their handlers, but not like they are robots. They are permitted to think and make decisions themselves and are not diverted from their instinctive and learned hunting patterns by excess vocalization.

Field trial dogs are often brought along with limited exposure to wild birds, or none. Some never learn the pleasures of hunting without the pressure of knowing that their handlers are expecting certain behavior under strict control and no freedom of choice. Many dogs never learn that birds come without human scent on them. Too many are driven around the course or learn to follow horse tracks for security or a way back to the starting point.

Trainers and handlers who put too much stress on a well trained dog with which they have had a previous healthy relationship find out they will rebel. Dogs that are punished too much unfairly learn how to punish their trainers and handlers.

Knowledgeable trainers can read their dogs and change according to what best benefits the man-dog relationship as a working team. Sometimes a dog has an off day, may be sick or feel poorly. These handlers do not force their dogs to work. They put the leash on, praise them, and return another day.

Dogs must learn to hunt and handle both retrieving and non-retrieving situations in the same weekend and in the same stake, yet it does not confuse well trained dogs. They know what and when they are expected to do things in certain ways differently. But, sometimes they get confused for a short time.

I often hear trainers lament about how their dog "hates" something which makes me wonder if they believe dogs are incapable of using their intelligence. An owner might say, "My dog **hates** the taste of a pigeon."

That dog has plainly been confused by his trainer and what he is observing is an adverse reaction to training, and repeated **situation stress** effects. Dogs cannot develop intelligence when their brains are kept tuned waiting for a signal, command or punishment.

Self-hunting dogs are free to develop on their own when not under a training regimen and learn to develop a wide variety of interests on game birds and fur bearing animals. Put man in the loop and the dog develops stress. The amount is related to the trainer he has. Dogs tend to avoid situations they do not understand.

A dog may learn to enjoy pointing or chasing birds better without the trainer, and the object of the trainer is to become a partner to that. It is possible for a beginner to do everything wrong and cause no permanent damage to his dog. Some dogs are born that way, and these owners tend to believe that there is nothing difficult about dog training.

Dogs which make game should be left alone to point and the handler should go on in most situations until he does. There are situations which naturally lend themselves to the handler helping his dog. Normally, handlers should encourage their dogs to work faster when they keep moving forward. Stopping does not improve quickness, nose, pointing, intelligence or style.

Dogs must learn to be quick and decisive!

Dogs will turn sour all at once for no apparent reason. Stress accumulates the same as radiation, and eventually will break down any dog when carried too far. The man-dog relationship is at low ebb then for a long time.

Chapter 6

Puppy Development

THE NEW PUPPY

House breaking is the most important part of a new
puppy's training--that is if it is to be kept in the
house. I will not write about kennel housing.

There is already enough written on puppies and their
early training and socialization, but the first three
or four months are extremely important to their
development.

Delmar Smith recommends putting a short length of
nylon (braided) rope on the puppy's collar. It should
be about three feet long without any knots or loops,
and is left on the collar for a few months. This
extends the owner's arms and legs. When the puppy is

in some devilment, and they will be in plenty, or starts to piddle, the owner can step on it and correct the puppy with a stern "NO" and put it in a crate or take it outside to relieve itself. The rope is a handy way to teach the puppy to lead and accept it as part of its environment. With the use of the rope, the new puppy will not become hand shy or afraid of its owner.

Puppies must be supervised, controlled, and disciplined when they are loose in the house. They want to play constantly, except when eating and sleeping, and toys should be given them that are theirs always. An old pair of heavy socks tied in a knot is cheap and fun for them. Some of the plastic or rubber toys are supposed to be indestructible, but I have never seen one stand up with my dogs yet. Puppies should not be left loose without supervision. In a few months they will learn their limits and can be left alone for short time periods.

Using the rope, they should be taught to wait until told to go out a door. It is important to watch the level, frequency and kinds of discipline for it is real easy to cause puppies to become too submissive. This is seen when puppies urinate when they see or are touched by their owners or lay down at their feet, but there are other indicators. They should be watched for and owners should lean more toward less discipline than too much for the first few months.

WORKING ON GAME

The first game contact can be given puppies at three or four weeks. Within a short time they learn to play the game of pointing a wing (tied with monofilament

335

These seven week old puppies are playing with a dead pigeon bringing out their latent instincts.

These puppies are displaying their natural instincts and boldness in tackling a large pigeon their own size.

line to a fishing pole). At about seven weeks of age a litter should be allowed to play with a dead bird to their heart's content. The behavior of each puppy varies. It ranges from feral like possessiveness, eating, plucking feathers, hiding it, proudly carrying the bird or running off with it.

At three months of age, I give each puppy the opportunity to point a released quail or pigeon, or let individual puppies into a pigeon flight pen. Their early experience gives me a reasonable picture of the pointing style and instinct they will have after being broke.

Putting puppies on game at this early age may not be so important, but it should not be delayed past six months. The important thing of value is the association and reaction. There is no reason to become upset when a seven week old puppy chews birds, tries to eat them, or does not share with littermates. These are normal behavior patterns and are not a precursor of a grown dog's behavior. Some puppies completely ignore a dead bird when others will pounce on it and are feral-like in behavior. A puppy which is placid and uninterested can grow up to have the best natural ability. The ones which ate birds or refused to give them up, may turn out to retrieve tenderly when the timid ones may eat the birds.

Puppy intelligence tests are sometimes used in an effort to classify them from best to worst. These tests are most valuable to the person who conducts the study. Most tests are just guesses. The important point to consider is that someone is handling and working with puppies being tested which if continued has high value in early development and attachment. This effects environmental change. I believe that natural ability can be measured, but the varied imprinting, or bonding, of the human association is apparent early. Some human relationships enhance natural ability and intelligence for some puppies and retards development in others. It does not require testing to see these effects. Some puppies, for example, fear nothing or nobody. They readily accept any and every living thing, and are not discouraged from trying to make friends even after being hurt or put down by older dogs or other animals.

Puppies will indicate submissiveness when wagging their tails, crouching, urinating and laying down exposing the underside of their bellies. Of course, if a puppy is barely touched by an older dog, its only defense is to scream as though being tortured, or killed, and that defense mechanism usually works.

Fear and insecurity will show up in some tests, but if the tester waits a week or a month the results will probably be different or inconclusive.

In the so-called practice of picking the best puppy in a litter there is insufficient development for the first few months to make an accurate or reliable assessment. It seems an impossible task to pick the puppy that when grown will have the best appearance (conformation), temperament and trainability. I know several breeders who **believe** they can, and breeders who work with their litters every day can make important observations which fixes their likes and dislikes. These breeders learn many things about the individual puppies at **that** stage of their growth. It is also possible by proper selection of sires and dams through scientific breeding practices to fix certain important desirable characteristics. I think selecting the "pick of the litter" or the most perfect one in a litter at seven weeks, is a farce. Environment enhances, modifies and changes puppies until they are fully grown.

If the litter is healthy and active, a good way to pick is for the buyer to shut his eyes and pick one, or take the one that comes to him first. Some people are better gamblers than others.

The most important consideration in any litter is that several people be allowed to handle the puppies from the day they are born.

There are good owners and bad ones and when some bring out the natural ability, others seem to retard or destroy it.

Experienced trainers develop instinctive methods to evaluate bird dog potential--they have an **eye** for good dogs. Some develop and use their own written test, as I have done, but they are no more effective than the person using them, as a rule. Inexperienced owners cannot properly evaluate a puppy from a written set of test conditions. My method involves food, commands, stress, retrieves, shot, pointing, searching, distractions, check cord, loud noise and commands, bracing, water retrieving and backing at six to twelve months of age. It works for me, but probably would not for anyone else.

Well planned breeding programs are essential to outstanding field trial puppies--dogs. J. P. Scott learned that heredity can limit functional abilities and affect behavior directly. Heredity may modulate instead of create or abolish specific behavior. It affects the growth of motor, sensory and coordinating systems and organs, modifies hormone enzyme and neurotransmitter synthesis processes.

Some people claim that the best gun dogs come from

all-age dogs. No matter. The best dogs come from field trial dogs where their lines have demonstrated continued desirable hereditary characteristics which are unknown in ordinary hunting dogs. Puppies should be bought from breeders with a history of good field trial dogs. Nothing is ever one hundred percent certain.

HANDLING PUPPIES ON BIRDS

Puppies often catch poor flying birds and will refuse to give them up. It is no big deal, for the first instinct of a puppy is to play and enjoy carrying something in its mouth, and sometimes tossing it in the air and catching it.

My philosophy is to prevent puppies from catching birds off point. We want them to point, flush and chase all the birds they can find.

Many teaching methods cannot stop puppies from catching birds and they can compound training progress. Novice trainers react improperly, become excited, start hollering for their dogs to come to them, holler "NO," shout "FETCH," chase after them, or punish them. The best practice is to leave the puppy alone, walk away, or continue the direction started and ignore it.

Puppies like to play and have fun with their freshly caught prizes doing what is natural from instinct. They are not prepared to understand that the owner expects a master-slave relationship or a cooperative work relationship.

I owned a male dog which during his puppy, derby--and later--years would outrun every bird he or I flushed. He might have had to flush and chase it several times

Most all puppies love to retrieve at a very tender young age.

This is an example of a trainer trying to restrain a puppy and flush a slept bird by himself. Some personal dogs do not accept helpers at first.

before catching it at distances which sometimes appeared to be a mile away, but he always raced directly back with his catch to give it to me. He once retrieved both a live pheasant and quail at the same time after chasing each one down in turn.

Handlers may have problems with their young puppy (or derby) which refuses to quit hunting when the brace time is over. There are tricks that work a few times such as tossing a dead bird in the air, tossing a cap, or bending down pretending to dig or kick something out of the cover. Their natural curiosity can be used to advantage. There is no reason to panic. Some dogs can never be caught by a handler chasing after them. No embarrassment should be associated with this type puppy or derby behavior. Each dog behaves differently, requires slightly different training techniques, and takes different time periods to accept the handler as a full partner in its work.

A dog will learn to eat birds because the trainer, or another dog, forces the issue. Left alone, a young dog will seldom eat birds. They like to chew, play and carry birds, and will soon start looking for another bird, even when carrying one in their mouths. Some just like the feel and taste of dead or live game. It must give them a sense of pride or satisfaction, instills confidence and a feeling of accomplishment. We need that, they need that to grow. Puppies must be praised more often than scolded. It takes time to make the transition.

PUPPY TRAINING AND DEVELOPMENT

There are several mechanical versions on puppy

training for field trials with an essential ingredient missing that the novice trainer may not realize. **Telling** someone how to "train" a puppy is difficult, if not impossible. Knowledge and experience are extremely important to successful puppy training.

Puppies must be allowed freedom to develop their natural instincts to the fullest and retain all the natural inquisitiveness, play and spirit to become great field trial dogs, or hunting dogs.

A few years ago, I took two nine month old puppies to the back acreage, interrupting their play at the large pond in front of the house, and sat down to watch them play at a smaller pond there. As at the larger pond, they continued to chase dragonflies with absolute reckless abandon. They were running around the pond, into it, and at times seemed to take flight in mid-air across it. They chased far out into the corn field before returning to find another dragonfly. They picked out their own to chase each time. As I watched them, I thought about the difference in attitude of these two puppies as compared to those I usually see in training, or at field trials, where the trainers or handlers are all too serious and competitive with the hope of similar enthusiasm.

Handlers expect puppies to be mature before they ever approach readiness. I have seen enthusiastic performances at one field trial, and those puppies, in chasing the quail, were plunging through snow and into ice cold water completely oblivious of discomfort.

I believe that puppies are mentally incapable of being **trained** for field trials from lack of maturity, and the better ones in trials will do their own thing or ignore their handlers. If they needed help from their handlers to show them the way around the course

343

A puppy turned loose in a flight pen with just a few birds in it can create a strong interest in birds.

Many trainers want young dogs to chase (but not catch) birds after they are flushed to create interest and build desire--to become birdy.

and out from under foot, they would never be any good.

Puppies should be allowed to develop their own natural abilities, under the supervision of their owners or trainers. Yet, they have to learn to adapt to stress early. They should never be coddled or patronized when they experience something unpleasant or strange.

A judge in the 60's, back when I was a beginner said:

"The desire, sparkle and bounce cannot be built in and if it is taken out, you don't hardly ever get it back. It is much better to have too much hunt and drive with the training coming later." Another said: "A puppy and derby age dog should be happy in everything he does."

Clyde Morton told Herm David in *Hunting Dog*, October 1966:

"A puppy must have a <u>determination</u> to hunt—and to do the things <u>you</u> want him to do. Then—and this is the most important—you have to study each dog's personality, abilities, and qualities—you have to fit each dog's training to the individual."

"I don't think anyone should ever shoot over a puppy the first time he points—or that you ever ought to walk up there and shoot over him unless he's chasing a bird."

"I always try to get my puppies chasing birds before I shoot over them—and then after they get used to it, when a dog points you can walk up there and shoot over him and he'll know what it's all about. The gun will become a part of the pleasure the dog gets out of hunting."

After reading several books on dog training and watching trainers and handlers at field trials, I have learned that puppies should be left alone, and trainers and handlers should not expect perfection in their performance, behavior and manners. Sometimes in the heat of competition it is difficult for us to remember what we know. I am still looking for different and better ways to bring out the natural ability and build desire in puppies. Praise helps them think its fun. This is the time trainers put the "foundation" on future champions. They must be allowed to learn to self-hunt until they show the necessary intelligence to solve scenting and hunting problems. There is no problem in puppies wanting to hunt for themselves, but there is if they continue into old age. I suspect, there is an **ideal** time to start each individual puppy.

Puppies, under the trainers' supervision, must have opportunities to develop experience which makes them bold, stable and unafraid to work with them. Puppies must be thoroughly socialized with their environment: strangers, other dogs, barnyard animals, horses, automobiles, trucks, thunder, lightning, loud noises, airplanes, insects and whatever else there is which can cause a reaction. They should not be forced to accept things before they are mentally or physically able.

Young dogs must learn about horses early and a special effort should be made to get them socialized with horses. Horses are their beacon of the future, and a partner in a team effort with their owners. They will one day learn to get their bearings and the direction to go from the horses in trials. They will learn to stay to the front headed in the direction of the horses.

Too many owners are preoccupied with getting a pointing dog used to the gun and cause unnecessary problems. Not every puppy can withstand the rigors of early training. It is wrong to fire a gun over a puppy before feeding or when it is eating, expecting the puppy to become accustomed to the noise. This is another way to abuse a puppy. Yes, I know, some of the writers say do it and many trainers do follow that advice. There are better and less destructive ways to expose puppies to noise. They need much exposure to noise, but a puppy's association with the gun **should be on game** to develop a love for the gun. A gun and shot should mean only one thing to a dog—game, and a pleasant meaning it must be for the maturing puppy.

When going to retrieve, it should know that the gun rendered the game immobile and hunt for it until found. When using simulated game, it might just be a dummy, but the same enthusiasm should be apparent. When accustoming a puppy to a gun, the owner should avoid entering it in field trials until he is sure there is no potential problem. Puppies sensitive to shot can be made gun shy, but they need not be which is why most clubs do not permit firing over them.

Some puppy stakes do require a shot on game contact, and that in itself might not cause the puppies problems, but when combined with other situations over which the handler has no control, serious problems do develop. It is better to wait a few months if there is the slightest doubt. There is no reason to be in a hurry to cause unnecessary and avoidable problems.

Established learning patterns can be stopped and started again without much loss. Therefore, when reactions to situations develop in early training, trainers lose little by waiting for more growth and maturity.

Trainers should never stop, pet, or play with puppies in the field, or allow them to play with each other or

Some trainers take all the dogs in their kennels out for a fun romp together. This helps them accept each other better and can alleviate stresses.

At a very young age, puppies should be given fresh killed birds to carry around and play with to create desire and their retrieving instinct.

a brace mate in trials. Many will check back too much which can be a difficult problem to correct, but trainers must be patient and systematically and progressively work at their correction over a period of time.

Field trial puppies should be exposed to game under training and hunting conditions enough to have learned independence and desire to hunt. They should be checked at casting off with a brace mate before ever entering a trial and be immediately commanded "NO" and scolded for playing. It only takes two or three corrections for most puppies that are prepared.

Excessive bracing and running puppies, or older dogs, together develops **dependence** and most early learning should be with the puppy running alone.

We must never forget puppies and older dogs benefit from playing. Letting two play together is good, and letting an entire kennel out together for a fun run is also an excellent practice. Playing is important to the physical and mental development and well being of any age dog. Fortunately, this is the best form of exercise, or conditioning, available to the trainer. Even so, puppies and older dogs do injure themselves playing, but the benefits outweigh the risks. Playing helps relieve stress.

Acceptable field trial dogs come from an infinite number of puppy environments. The average puppy owner makes one of two mistakes: Overtraining and undertraining in that order. The early novelty just wears off. With every successful puppy, it takes work and dedication that must continue for its lifetime.

Overtrained puppies show less desire, less sparkle and more faults than those having had a less demanding schedule. For that reason, some owners **need** more than one dog to train so as to ameliorate the stress.

Training patterns should be varied as well as conditions when maintaining some visible rate of progress. Training grounds should be changed frequently. A puppy should not be worked more than three or four days a week at any one thing and it should be done in different sequences: Every day, every other day, every two days then skip one or two, and every third day. Different people should be around when the puppy is being trained on occasion as should horses and other dogs. Field trials are dogs, horses and people, so too much field work without these should be avoided, except for what I have written about working puppies alone.

Age is a factor, but no puppy should be overworked in the quest for a high class field trial dog. Puppy training should be stopped before they tire, or when they lose interest. Trainers can put forth their best efforts and still have poor or mediocre puppies.

There are pitfalls all along the way, and most trainers, **in spite of what they read,** must learn from their own experiences although reading and studying training books is very important to learning.

A few years ago, I watched an immature puppy in a field trial under the guidance of a professional handler. He never got excited, did not over-react or issue any commands when the puppy was performing poorly. He smiled some and seemingly enjoyed the puppy. He was patient to a fault. He obviously saw **future promise** and was willing to **allow the puppy to adjust to field trials** and develop properly. That puppy later developed into an exciting gun dog.

Whenever a puppy stays too close to its handler, becomes distracted easily, comes back frequently to see if the handler is safe, it has not been developed properly and is insecure.

PUPPY POINTS

Many dog owners experience a tremendous thrill when first seeing their new puppies point or back. But, they get a terribly deflated ego when the opportunity is given to them and their puppy fails.

Even veteran trainers may have palpitations of the heart, flushing of the face, fast breathing, slight tremors of the hands, tightening of the skin, tingles up and down the spine, hair standing up on their necks or weak knees when seeing a new puppy point. Their hearts skip a beat or two and their minds may go blank for a few seconds.

Puppies must be able to discriminate many different scents and learn to separate out only bonafide game bird scent for which it is genetically programmed to point. Without any previous experience puppies will instinctively point certain kinds of game and ignore other kinds. They often sight point and chase just about anything that moves or flies.

There are puppies which will not point until first introduced to the smell of game birds or pigeons and tutored at pointing.

It is a simple task to teach a young dog to point after a single exposure to a bird. Some may take a few more times. It helps if the puppy already knows the smell, but it is not essential. I do this on a simple obedience type exercise. It involves see-smell first followed by no-see and smell in cover. The puppy is put on a lead and led to a planted pigeon or quail

351

in the open on the grass from downwind. The puppy may smell the bird, but it will sometimes have no meaning and ignore it except the trainer stops the puppy short and styles it up when a helper rousts the bird and causes it to fly. Most pointing dogs will point the instant they smell the bird, but not all, and this type training is important. The second bird is placed in cover and the puppy led up the same way, and most will point the first time even if they did not point the one laid out on the grass. If a puppy fails this test the trainer should wait a day or two and repeat the exercise. Usually no puppy fails to point after a few repetitions.

The helper can also cause the bird to fly by holding it in front the puppy and tossing it in the air to fly whereby the puppy is allowed and encouraged to chase. No verbal interference should be used when the puppy is on point or chasing, except for words of encouragement and praise.

Puppies with the right genes progress rapidly and will soon establish point without being on lead or check cord/strap, but care should be taken to keep them from breaking point and catching birds.

The purpose of chasing is to catch birds, but when dogs realize that the birds which fly always escape, they will in time break off the chase. If they do not catch birds off point, they will staunch up quicker and never try to catch them, and allow their handlers to do the flushing. This comes with experience and age and is not expected of puppies. It is good exercise for puppies to chase.

Kicking around in front of a puppy in attempts to flush birds engages the springing and breaking desire. It offers a few advantages in training at a young age,

352

but can also cause the puppy to lay down, crouch down or sit. This is evidence of too much stress and can be difficult to correct later.

Puppies should never be disciplined so much that it creates too much submissiveness when working game.

A remote release of the bird by string or electronic control can be helpful, but trainers must not cause puppies to blink releasers. Some releasers give a nasty wallop and a loud noise when puppies jump in and cause premature release.

Birds should be placed at landmarks and objectives which the puppy will remember and learn to go to such as a clump of bushes, tree or fence line, or taller grass which stands out. Where possible, puppies should be worked more on wild birds than planted birds.

Anytime the trainer notices a slight drop in concentration, intensity or interest, the training session should be stopped. The puppy is signaling potential problems justifying backing off. If these signals are not seen, problems can be created that were preventable.

One distinct advantage to leading a puppy (or older dog) on a check cord/strap to a planted bird is that it can be directed away from the bird planter's tracks. Puppies learn to track the bird planter to the bird and either do not point, pick up the bird or point too close. Another advantage is that the trainer can detect the first indication of the puppy picking up scent and stop it until point is established.

Some puppies have a strong desire to chase which eclipses their desire to point and lasts for two or three years. They may establish point for a short time but their main desire is to run hard and try to flush something to chase.

Unfortunately, some trainers do not understand, or do not have the patience to work with them and wait for them to mature. I have had several dogs that chased so hard and so far that it seemed a waste of time to teach them to point staunchly and break them. When they were ready it was not too difficult.

One dog was almost four years of age and I was ready to believe that it was a waste of time to stop the chasing. One day she decided it would be fun to chase a young colt and the two older horses. I chased her down, caught and scolded her on no more than two different occasions. The next time she chased a bird I scolded her and she stopped at once. The horse incident was what turned the trick and she quit chasing altogether. Within three months she was finding and pointing more birds than other dogs and was almost competitive in trials.

INTRODUCTION TO SHOT

There are several pet methods used in getting a puppy accustomed to shot such as shooting a gun when it is fed or by taking it to a gun club. These methods probably cause more gun shy dogs than those caused accidentally. One owner used the "shoot before feeding method" and his dog learned never to eat until a shot was fired.

Well bred puppies will not normally react unfavorably to shot at three to six months of age. After a time dogs naturally accept the gun as a partner to their hunt much the same as they do with their handler and horse. Puppies must learn the purpose of the gun and it not necessary to hasten it just to show that they are **not** gun shy. It should not be delayed too long in their early development either.

I pretend to be the clumsiest person alive when my puppies open their eyes and begin to hear. Doors seem to slam and feed pans are fumbled and dropped. Every action has more noise than normal such that **noise** is part of their early environment.

If a puppy reacts unfavorably to noise, it can be reassured, but the best practice is to **ignore** the noise and its reaction.

Puppies should never be shot over unless they have chased several birds first. Then shot over only when they chase and there will never be a problem. This is one subject all knowledgeable trainers agree on. The puppy soon learns to love the sound and sight of the gun.

A standoff.   Which will make the first move?

A pigeon being shot over a dummy pointing dog with a real
dog backing.   (Photo by Jim McCord)

Chapter 7

Field Trial Training

GENERAL DISCUSSION

Training of pointing dogs on birds can be frustrating--so much so that many trainers resort to physical punishment as their best, or only, training tool. They justify its use with many time worn phrases. The truth is that their training methods are not adaptable and they are not in control of their emotions. Progressive techniques, patience and repetition over a long period of time are not used. They are unable to see progress whenever it is slow. Each dog in a given breed responds to training differently and some breeds respond to punishment better than others. Nevertheless, it is better to use none if it is at all possible. Many dogs win field champion titles not because of their steadiness and apparent manners on birds, but due to their fear of punishment and correction, and/or intimidation. They may not have accepted or retained prior training.

The basic nature of many trainers is such that they will start a training exercise using persuasive techniques only to resort to physical punishment, if the dog's progress is too slow. "I showed him once, and he knows better," is enough justification for physical punishment.

The electronic shock collar may infer severe punishment in some people's minds. Maybe they associate it with the electric chair. Wrongly used the shock collar will not be effective in solving a problem, but compared to some physical punishment inflicted on dogs by trainers, it is mild and humane by comparison.

I was training a bitch that was difficult to stop from breaking and chasing at flush, and later began sitting during the transition period. She either chased or sat down. I told her owners that she did not even know she was sitting at flush and indicated it was nothing to be overly concerned about that it would pass when she understood and gained confidence. She almost won the national championship title, but lost it by sitting on the flush of a pheasant. She went on to win both her field titles with superiority in every category of performance. Winning is fine, but the memories of superior performances last forever.

In an effort to prove to that dog's owners that their bitch was completely oblivious to sitting at flush, I took a cactus leaf and put it on a stick and when she pointed I placed it where she would have to sit on it. I then flushed the bird, she sat, and after the bird was well out she stood up with the cactus leaf firmly attached to her rear. Not once did she indicate pain or any awareness that she had painful needles imbedded in her rear end. I never repeated that again, and it showed me that concentration makes great dogs.

Some dogs may resist yelping, or showing signs of being shocked from the shock collar the first time, but they cannot ignore it for long. The correction needed is transmitted, received, and more effective with less repetition than any other method of correction. It is so effective when properly done that its use should be left only to experienced trainers.

The sound burst, in one model of electronic trainer, followed by an electrical shock signals the dog to cease and desist before the big jolt comes. After that the sound button can be used without shock and has about the same effect as being shocked, and dogs then learn to avoid the shock by stopping their bad habit. A firm "NO" command when a dog is aware that his trainer will enforce the command should get the same results. Dogs learn the effective range of both when used too often or improperly.

The first basic rule in dog training is that trainers should never give a command unless they can enforce it. If always done timely and successfully, the training and control procedures are greatly simplified. Then and only then is dog training a simple undertaking—by comparison.

There are no set formulas or techniques in successful bird dog training. There were once enough wild birds in most areas of the United States whereby a dog could be trained exclusively on them. A dog pointed. He chased. He repeated this enough times that coupled with some correction and scolding learned that it was futile to chase birds and that he could not catch them. The gun quickly taught him that there was help. He pointed and his handler shot. This process of pointing and shooting continued until the dog became smart or was conditioned to the gun, with or without commands from his handler, to hold position until the bird was shot out of the air and he marked the fall exactly. Times have changed and most trainers now use pen raised birds that are more domestic than wild in a completely artificial training environment and try to vary their methods to suit the individual dog's talent and ability. It is an entirely different sport, yet a bird dog trained that way can be used effectively on wild birds with little additional training.

It has been my observation that a dog can be trained steady to wing and shot by almost any method when repeated enough, even when wrong, providing the dog holds together for the time it takes. Some methods are more efficient, more effective and more enduring than others. Each dog is different and as training progresses variations are essential to a dog's development providing they do not confuse it. Some intelligent dogs recognize the "game we play" early, appear to always remain honest, or dumb, and seldom develop bad habits such as tracking bird planters, horses, running to the guns stationed at the bird fields, or going directly around the course to the bird field. Field trials are a game to some dogs. Some learn to enjoy them more than training or hunting. Others will play the part and fake performance or behavior so that the handler thinks it is natural, or foils everything when it then takes a genius to out think them.

These bad habits do not have to start from field

trial training experiences. Competition requires such meticulous and dedicated training, but dogs trained on wild game exclusively and then placed in field trial situations often become problem dogs.

A trainer's voice can be self-defeating and sometimes the use of a whistle is a godsend. I never have used a whistle except where I handled a professional trainer's dog in an amateur stake. I quit that. Professional handler's who use strangers to handle their dogs at field trials in amateur stakes should realize how much damage they can do to their dog and its training.

Properly trained dogs do not need whistle or voice signals to take the course apart. Few pointing dogs are trained well enough under field conditions to stop on a whistle command if they are in danger where stopping them would prevent a problem. In an emergency, they **should** be trained to stop on command.

A voice command to whoa is necessary to keep a dog from going in on another dog's point if it does not back. Some dogs when whoaed establish point because they are trained that way.

The primary objective of all pointing dog training is to make a team of the handler and his dog. The dog must learn to obey and willingly stay under the handler's control when exercising its own independence and intelligence in hunting the course to the front. It is difficult for some trainers to do this under a regimented program using physical enforcement and reinforcement. They are **satisfied** with mechanical performance. Most never have anything else simply because they insist their dogs do only what they are trained to do and are never allowed to make unilateral decisions.

It is easy to establish a proper relationship with a

dog to the gun. He soon learns that the gun helps solve a problem by stopping the bird in flight, and becomes excited everytime it is brought out--it gives him a good feeling just like seeing his owner put on a hunting coat or anything else he associates with hunting. Maybe this is the only thing that holds many dogs to their natural desire to hunt when force trained.

The mistake of many trainers lies in the fact they refuse to accept the necessity for a dog to mature before undergoing severe training stresses. My own program requires a dog to be past three years of age before I start breaking or start certain obedience associated with breaking. Most owners will not wait that long. My prerequisite for breaking dogs is that they must be staunch on point, allow me to approach from a long distance without jumping in and will not break point until the bird flushes. These dogs are simple to break and although a select few may take ten birds before understanding what is expected, none will take a hundred.

The owner pressure on professional handlers requires the most progress in the least amount of time. They fail to recognize, or accept, that dogs need to mature after derby age and want them broke too soon. Dogs are sometimes put in gun dog competition as young as six months of age, but most are almost two, or past two, and the trainers do not even have them broke and hope to luck through. Sometimes they do.

In competition, some owners find puppy and derby winning an opiate and will not wait until their dog is more than "green broke" before continuing. The usual result is that it takes longer to break these dogs at greater cost and they finish with poor style and performances, and only a fragment of the dog's real capability is left.

By allowing dogs to continue playing and maturing, but still giving them the basic hunting experience to develop natural skills and conditioning, when the time comes breaking should require no more than three months to complete. Pushing dogs forced into training before maturity creates problems in which a skillful trainer may require three months or more to solve a **single** one.

The early broke dogs in competition are not completely trained, but often win their titles and are seldom seem again. They get the right breaks and are lucky. The effect on these dogs mental well being from premature stress is that they burn out quicker than dogs allowed to mature first. Mature dogs are competitive until old age sets in and then dislike being taken out of competition.

TRAINING

Training means something different for every person who engages in this sport and each one may believe that his training methods are the best. Many are poor, and they will never improve.

The average trainer must be aware sometime early in his career of just what he is training for, other than winning. The beginner always starts at the bottom and learns how to work his way progressively to bigger and better competition. Each step along the way requires slightly more knowledge, training and effort. Almost every trainer and handler begins the sport by walking and later advances to horseback handling. The hunter may become a field trialer of gun dogs and advance to all-age dogs.

Most of the mechanics of dog training are not field trial oriented. Nearly all the basic training is considered unnatural for dogs and requires extensive work. Field trial dogs do not have to **hunt** to win, but dogs trained to hunt wild game when undergoing all the other basic training are always the more honest dogs.

Inexperienced field trial dogs may stay on the upwind side of a fence row, for example, when an experienced one always take the downwind side to use the wind to advantage. Field trials do not always allow dogs to learn the correct use of the wind, for they must learn to follow courses to the front without regard to wind direction.

Hunters follow singles after a covey flushes. But trainers for the American Kennel Club trials must train their dogs to **never** follow in the direction of flight. If they do, they are charged with a delayed chase and are usually out of competition. Trainers must understand the different rules and ambiguities between organizations. Dog breeds in the American Field umbrella have different requirements. Heeling from flush and collaring from flush are examples, so it is better to train dogs to heel away and when in competition where the breeds allow collaring, handlers can collar their dogs and cast them on in another direction.

There is a practical reason for not allowing dogs to work birds again after they flush. They are air washed and even in good scenting conditions, dogs sometimes overrun or cause birds to flush prematurely. This practice can confuse dogs and help destroy confidence in pointing.

Teaching dogs not to follow birds may initially cause

stress, but they much prefer to hunt and point and the stress dissipates quickly. Therefore, handlers must learn to deal with the stress that does not go away. Dog learn permanently what we do not want or intend for them.

There are good books on training pointing dogs, but they do not provide all the information needed. The most important topic **not covered** is the psychology between trainers and their dogs for successful training and competition. This is what I believe is essential to success.

Clinics and seminars are held by professional trainers, but maybe the best way to learn is to follow every brace at field trials and know the placed dogs and why they were, if possible. This is not always practical.

Praise and "sweet talk" are most important to success. Delmar Smith says:

"Always get their mind right first before training."

A dog must want to work. And, some need more work than others to reach the same level of performance. This is important to remember and easy to forget.

People claim WHOA sounds like NO to pointing dogs. I still use both and have no problem. A dog's hearing is superior to ours, so we need not stop using words because one sounds like the other to us. Dogs are capable of learning the same command in many different languages. Trainers are more comfortable using commands which are easy for them or seem natural.

I like to believe that trainers do not intend to break a dog's spirit as is done with elephants to tame and train them, but we must remember that dogs do not need tamed--just trained.

ACCUSTOMING TO DIFFERENT THINGS

Dogs learn from experience. The first time they may run into a fence or get cut on barb wire, but not the second. Once dogs get accustomed to where the fences are, don't change them or they have to learn the hard way.

It is important to introduce dogs to horses, train with several other people and in groups and never encourage strange behavior when experiencing something new.

Trainers and handlers should not wait until something is to be used in field trials for the first time. I have seen dogs react to visibility collars being put on at the starting line and refuse to run until removed. Bells and check cords are two important training aids which should be used early. A bell should be put on a dog first in training before taking it hunting. Check cords/straps should be put on young dogs when they are running and having fun before being trained with one.

Everything in a dog's natural and unnatural environment must be accepted without fear or unfavorable reaction. It the only way they can work and concentrate on the job of hunting.

FIELD TRAINING SCHEDULE

6 - 12 WEEKS

Attach short braided nylon rope on collar.
Buy crate for indoor kennel or setup outdoor kennel.
Name puppy.

Housebreak.
Teach COME.
Teach NO.
Teach KENNEL (to enter crate, outside kennel or vehicle).
Socialize.
Play with fishing pole and wing.
Work at sight pointing objects.
Teach to lead.
Buy or make play toys.
Give puppy dead birds.
Slams doors, bang pans.

3 - 6 MONTHS

Give puppy live birds.
Take swimming.
Teach use of whistle (optional).
Play water retrieving.
Take out with check cord/strap.
Take for car rides.
Make loud noises.
Take to shopping centers.
Test for pointing and backing on birds.
Play with puppy using ball, frisbee, fishing pole, etc.
Let puppy chase birds in field.
Take to fun field trials.

6 - 12 MONTHS

Start yardwork or obedience training.
Put out quail and pigeons for puppy to hunt.
Water retrieve on dead pigeons with wings wrapped.
Land retrieve dead birds.

Put check cord/strap on dog when working birds.
Accustom to gun.
Put on roading harness and check cord/strap.
Accustom to horses and livestock.
Accustom to strange dogs.
Accustom to bell.
Introduce to chukars in field.
Take hunting.
Work from horseback.
Take to fun field trials.
Enter puppy stakes and Junior Hunter tests.
Shoot birds.
Chase birds.
Play.
Use hand signals.
Work on planted birds.
Brace with other dogs on limited basis.
Continue Socializing.

12 - 15 MONTHS

Continue accustoming to shot.
Take hunting.
Work at water retrieving.
Teach Go Out; Go Right; Go Left; or any voice command,
whistle, hand or voice signals.
Enter puppy/derby stakes and Junior Hunter tests.
Work on field commands.
Set up and teach to wait at starting line.
Teach hand tap to head to release.
Chase birds.
Work on planted birds at objectives.
Work at staunch pointing.
Brace with other dogs.

Work at limited force control.
Work at independence in hunting.
Continue socializing.
Continue shooting birds.
Work from horseback.
Enter shoot-to-retrieve stakes.

15 - 18 MONTHS

Continue 12 -15 month work.
Work on pheasants.
Teach roading of birds.
Work in roading harness.
Work at staunching and flushing.
Enter derby stakes and Junior/Senior Hunter tests.
Begin using dummy launcher.

18 - 24 MONTHS

Continue 12 - 15 month work.
Shoot and miss birds with helper holding dog by collar and hand in flank.
Teach WHOA close, then at distance.
Set up to stay at starting line without holding.
Enter walking hunting dog stakes judged on not being steady.
Holler at dog for chasing, bring back to place of flush and stand and praise.
Extensive exposure to wild birds.

24 - 30 MONTHS

Continue 18 - 24 month work, but eliminate derby stakes.

Stay on starting line from foot or horseback.
First breeding of bitches.
Use of wire releaser on planted birds.
Kill birds and holler at dog when breaking. Return to
flush and stand and make stay until released.
Throw out dead bird, shoot and make dog stay, then
fetch on command.

30 – 36 MONTHS
Continue pertinent previous work.
Steady dog to flush.
Train with other dogs.
Train from horseback and chase down dog when it chases.

36 – 40 MONTHS

Start breaking to shot.
After dog is well broke require retrieve to hand.
After dog is broke on killed birds teach backing.
Perfect the retrieve.
Enter gun dog or all-age stakes for training and
competition and enter Senior/Master Hunter tests.

30 – 48 MONTHS

Improve retrieves as necessary.
Improve backing.
Improve manners on game.
Work on manners with brace mate.
Have brace mate steal point.
Brace with dog which interferes.
Condition for peak field trial performance.
Win field trial stakes and pass Senior/Master
Hunter tests.

NOTE: This schedule is intended **only** as a guide. It can be adjusted for faster or slower learners either way. I do not encourage any beginner to shorten it unless his dog has had training with a professional or experienced amateur trainer. Problem dogs will develop with inexperienced trainers who hurry or skip important training exercises.

GIVING COMMANDS

Practice and experience are required to correctly read a dog. Many trainers never seem to consider this important.

Telling a beginner he or she should learn to read dogs is usually just so much Greek. They usually have an inadequate experience to measure or understand what is really meant or its importance.

In working with beginners, aside from instructing them: "Never take your eyes off your dog; Give a command only once and then make the necessary correction; and, Learn to trust your dog." They must work at these things before they understand why it is so important.

A dog is on point and his handler starts to flush the bird and keeps him from breaking by intimidation when flushing. Later, the dog may creep and the handler remembers, "Trust your dog, don't look." I also said, "Never take your eyes off your dog." Contradiction? Not really. When flushing game the handler must be aware of what his dog is doing, or will do at different levels of training, and a quick glance is enough to see a need for correction. The statement "never take your eyes off your dog" is extremely important when he is working his way around the course, but also applies to training.

A dog can be trusted to stay when the bird is flushed and shot, only after many flushes and kills. Once a dog is trained, the handler should take a quick look at his dog as he flushes and raises his gun to shoot. He or his helper should holler "WHOA" if he moves. How far would he have moved if the trainer had not stopped him? The dog's moving might have been to mark the bird, but it is better to expect, or assume, that he was breaking than to be late in the correction.

Yet, trainers and handlers must eventually learn to trust their dogs. The above example usually helps the training if wrong, but too many mistaken commands will cause dogs not to trust trainers and handlers and react improperly. Then there is a problem!

Handlers who keep their eyes on dogs all the time are better able to determine when a correction or command is best made and given at the **exact** instant the dogs make a wrong move. Then again, it is important if the dogs need help from them.

HEELING

A dog heeled to the starting line must be well trained and willing to obey his handler. Many handlers train their dogs to ride on their horse with them, so that when picked up at the end of a brace it is easier than forcing their dogs to heel to the horse or using a check cord. When the dog is nearly exhausted, it is the most humane way. All three methods are used and vary with the ability and preference of the handler.

Yet, forcing an excited dog eager to hunt to walk at heel should not be done too soon.

Dogs, excited to get started, will pull and strain on the lead in getting to the cast off point at field trials. It can be aggravating and irritating, even hazardous, but care should be taken in stopping it too soon in order not to dampen the dog's enthusiasm.

Forced heeling of an overly excited dog, wanting to satisfy his natural desire to hunt, is too stressful and can damage his ability to accept training.

Some dogs are extra strong and can cause injury, especially to women. There are times that dogs must be **controlled** regardless of what it might do to their enthusiasm.

Keep in mind that dogs trained to heel in basic obedience must also be trained to heel to the start of hunting. The trainer should put him on a leash and lead him to the place he is to be released. The dog should be allowed to pull to its utmost desire and the handler should say nothing to discourage him. Later, after the dog understands the process and is eager to begin training, he can be heeled, or trained to heel. Control is important and necessary, but dogs off lead are normally not under control and too much yelling and hollering are needed to keep them in line which produces unnecessary stress. They should be kept on lead. Some dogs may be three years old before then can be heeled to the starting point without being stressed such that it affects their performance.

The primary objective is to have the dog restrained without using any form of correction, coercion, intimidation or physical punishment which would detract from its desire to train or hunt. We must build and maintain desire and enthusiasm, for once lost it is nearly impossible to regain in any given activity. A trailing check cord/strap is also effective in gaining control at important times as the dog hunts or is being trained. It usually eliminates the need for strong voice commands, and makes the dog easier to run down and catch. It is much easier to run and step on the check cord/strap to gain control rather than trying to tackle a dog at a fast run. This is extremely important for dogs must have some freedom of choice, otherwise they will be unable to think for themselves, or to maintain the natural desire to hunt. This maneuver should be handled in such a way that the dogs do not interpret it as punishment.

Eventually a finished dog should be obedient and heel to the starting line, on or off lead, but there is no requirement that it be done. A mature, trained, dog will have become used to the undesirable stress experienced in training and will have learned to slough most of it off. It takes time, but good dogs get used to it after all aspects of their training is completed.

In trials where dogs cannot be collared away from the flush, they must be taught to heel away using the command to HEEL. Some handlers use a hand signal first and other variations. Smart dogs learn to anticipate the trainers' command and release themselves on a wild flush before the handlers get to the place they can control them. This can become a bad habit and should be stopped, but this is different from a dog out on the limb that has a bird flush and releases itself to continue hunting. When done properly, a dog can really look good when released by its handler.

Dogs are quicker to learn to heel away from a flushed bird with less stress than most other training requirements. Heeling is an integral part of breaking to wing. Dogs quickly learn to forget about chasing or following the bird just flushed and are anxious to hunt for another bird to point.

Whatever the reasons are that different breeds allow handlers to collar dogs away from flushes, some trainers and handlers use it to intimidate their dogs as they are choked, dragged away and thrown forward at great speed, or led several hundred feet away and then cast on.

Since the German Shorthaired and German Wirehaired pointer clubs do not permit collaring of dogs at flush, the other breeds are at a distinct disadvantage when entering their trials. Trainers of the breeds which permit collaring may not want to enter these trials. But, it behooves every trainer to teach his dog to heel away from flush by voice even if it is not a requirement.

The handlers who must heel their dogs away in their breed competition can easily compete in the other trials with their "green broke" dogs when collared from flushes and be competitive.

STYLE

Training stresses tend to destroy style. The destruction can be seen by tail position, creeping, crouching, sitting, lying down, circling, changing position, softening on point, turning to look, failure to hunt, panting, running off, running back to the vehicle, going to the other handler or blinking. Inexperienced trainers may believe that dogs with these behaviors are ruined for field trials. Not true. The style seen at the start of training should eventually return and usually reappears early in field trials when no training stress syndromes are present. The stress is removed temporarily by new environment, but it can be caused again by using wrong methods of control and correction.

We often hear people say that their dog is broke at home but is a renegade at field trials, which only means that the dog needs trained under field trial conditions too. It is difficult to do in some trials. Dogs developing training syndromes at home are also candidates in field trials when similar corrective methods or punishment are used. Not all dogs having training stress syndromes react to correction as stressful in field trials which is logical. Once a dog is trained to accept training commands which did once produce stress, they will not normally accumulate much more at field trials. Handlers who have no control problems in training will normally not have them in field trials.

The most interesting situation facing handlers is knowing how their dogs will handle in field trial competition after being broke. They will handle birds differently in training, usually better, sometimes worse. It may be necessary to adjust the way the dogs have been **read** in training to be correct in field trial situations. These dogs have usually competed in puppy and derby stakes, and if they had primarily developed a "love-for-hunting" in field trials, it will be retained. If this is the case, the transition to a stylish broke dog for field trials is easier and the faults brought about in training will soon be gone. It is also possible for dogs to fail miserably in training and do well in trials.

CHECK CORD/STRAP

Check cord or strap restraint in dog training is important, although not essential, and I never recommend inexperienced trainers use it for one important reason: They risk ruining their dog as they would using a shock collar incorrectly. When I started bird dog training, there was nobody closeby with experience. When the time seemed ripe for me to break my first dog, I followed instructions given in a pointer book on using the check cord. As my dog chased the bird, I waited, then when he got to the end, and with perfect timing, I stopped him with all my strength. I did not read the dog, probably would have ignored it anyway, and continued this process with increasingly poorer results. It was not long before my dog came to me when a bird flushed. He blinked pigeons and would **never** work with a check cord.

I failed. Also, I failed to realize, and the book did not give that secret, that my dog had to be pre-conditioned to the check cord, although it did mention yard training. I had no idea what that entailed. Had I known the need and how to prepare this dog to check cord corrections, that problem would not have developed.

A bitch I was training at the same time accepted my ignorance, impatience, and was so stubborn and resilient she carried me as I learned. The male would not.

The use of a check cord is not recommended for beginners for another reason, and this one requires alertness and skill to avoid being injured. Severe hand, wrist, ankle and leg burns can result when a strong dog chases after a bird. Invariably the dog manages to circle the handler before chasing at full speed. Gloves may help, but are usually ineffective since it is not always possible to hold onto the cord and a good rope jumper might escape having it wrap around an ankle. The most severe rope burn occurs when the cord is trailing and the dog wraps it around the trainers leg and changes directions to chase. It takes experience and care to avoid getting caught up in it. Most everyone invariably suffers burns. Although I am against using a check cord, there are times when its use is necessary. Handlers must work alone at times even if they prefer to work with another person.

I recommend the 25 foot nylon or cotton web check strap at least one inch wide. The frequency and severity of burns are lessened with the strap. It seems easier to stop dogs by stepping on the strap as opposed to a rope. It has more friction. Trainers should avoid picking it up when a dog is moving and be prepared to get out of its way when the dog circles. I never pick up the strap on a moving dog but run after him and try to step on it with my weight to stop or slow the dog down when hollering at him to "WHOA."

The check strap is a useful training tool and an inexperienced trainer can learn to use it well. Rope dodging and jumping are useful skills, but the realization that the check cord or strap are dangerous is important to remember.

As mentioned in the puppy chapter, a short rope is attached from about seven weeks until four months of age. This is the first step in pre-conditioning dogs for check cords. It is not without danger to the puppy, and it does get filthy when dragged through its urine and stools and must be changed frequently.

A three month old puppy can run with a regular check cord/strap and ignore it completely. Trainers who wait until dogs are much older may have problems getting them to accept it.

I quit using the check cord/strap for dog breaking for several years when I had help. I stayed with the dog and stroked, sweet talked and praised it, and my helper flushed. I kept one hand in the flank and a tight hold on the collar, or blocked the dog depending on its progress. I continued to use it on the puppies so I could gain control when correction or discipline was required, and this conditioned them to the check cord/strap when I had to break dogs by myself. I oftentimes break dogs without help, but more problems can develop which require more work later to overcome.

DOG CARE

Dogs have it rough when cooped up in close quarters when traveling all day long, or longer, to trials and between trials. It is either too hot, too cold or not enough ventilation, and no water. They must learn to travel the long hours without relieving themselves or foul their confined space. Some even die under these conditions. Care among professional handlers varies, but it is a problem that must be worked on under less than desirable conditions. Feeding and watering must be regulated to time, distance and opportunity.

Once the professional, or amateur, handler with several dogs, arrives at the trial grounds, he must first be concerned with getting his dogs staked out for them to urinate and/or defecate.

Professional handlers all use individual stakes and chains, or a long chain staked down at both ends with dropper chains along the length spaced far enough apart so adjacent dogs cannot get to each other to tangle, fight or breed similar to a trot line used in fishing.

Dogs are all put out in shifts at least twice a day. They usually waste no time in elimination.

The professional handler who takes the best care of his dogs and keeps the traveling crates clean may not be the one who wins most.

There are advantages and disadvantages to the chain

gang methods and it also relegates the dog to the status of other domesticated animals.

It is a small wonder that they run and hunt hard and are slow to come in and return to the cramped kennel or stake out chain. Field trial braces and training are the only time they have freedom to do something. They receive the most attention when fed, watered, trained and trialed.

When staked out, dogs are exposed to all the elements, insects, snakes, ground fungal diseases, loose dogs and loose horses just to name a few. They are often inadequately supervised. Their barking is annoying and few handlers make an effort to keep them quiet. Dogs slip their collars or break their chains and run off. Once a dog is spooked, or distressed, he may not allow anyone to come near.

Dogs running loose, intentionally or by accident, are exposed to hazards which the handlers have no control over. It does not matter whether the owners or handlers are stopped at an Interstate rest stop or some other place, for dogs that are loose are often killed by moving vehicles. It is also possible for dogs to eat or drink toxic substances, and be cut on broken glass or jagged cans. A dog can be injured enroute to a trial or test and the trip ruined.

Owners and handlers seldom lose control of their dogs when on leash and can control what they do. All other methods are faulty. Dogs off lead can spook and run off and be almost impossible to catch.

Amateur owners and handlers have a closer relationship and most walk their dogs on leashes for them to eliminate. It is time consuming and the dogs must learn to do it quickly which may take a few long trips. They have more personal attention and may not always run with gusto in field trials and may check back to their handlers more frequently, and be less competitive.

Field trial grounds with dog kennels are a tremendous help to professional and amateur handlers. The better private and state grounds have them.

EXERCISING DOGS OFF LEAD

We do not normally think about being injured by our own dogs when taking them out off lead to eliminate. Younger dogs tend to run hard from place to place and do run into their owners. Consider a collision with a forty to eighty pound dog hitting its owner from behind when unexpected. The result can be torn ligaments, torn muscles, sprains and broken bones. These injuries are caused by feeling sorry for a dog that would not eliminate on lead.

I never trust any dog that approaches me from the rear no matter what we are doing. It is safer to work them from horseback, but then the horse can cause injuries to the rider when a dog comes in too close from behind and surprises the horse.

HORSE CARE

Field trial grounds having horse barns are a godsend in bad weather which is common at weekend trials. Several private and state field trial areas have barns available at a reasonable fee to clubs. Handlers also keep their horses in their horse trailers, or they stake them out for the night to eat grass and rest.

Water at field trial grounds is an important consideration. It is difficult to haul enough water for one horse and several dogs. Owners and handlers prefer to haul water that dogs are used to drinking, but it is nearly impossible to do this for horses. Water is often available somewhere on course where horses will normally drink during the day's running.

Horse tie-outs are made up with a nylon rope of fifteen to twenty five feet long threaded through a rubber garden hose. A snap is tied on one end and a ring on the other to drive a large metal stake through. Some stakes are scrapped car axles. The horse can feed in a radius the length of the rope and lay down to rest. It can be moved as needed for new grass.

Horses must be trained to a stake out under close supervision first because they will wrap the hose around a leg and may fight and be injured. The stake should be pulled first before unwrapping a leg or getting too close to the horse. Horses are smart enough to quit fighting after awhile, but may still fight hard enough to get a severe leg burn. If the horse pulls the stake out, he will normally not go far. Horses are social animals, barn animals, and they seldom go beyond the first farm with horses.

A lost horse is easier to find than a lost dog. Motorists are not too anxious to run them down.

At the end of a warm day, horses can be washed down if too sweaty as the salt will dry, stiffen the hair, and make them uncomfortable. They should be completely dried and if too cool a horse blanket put on them.

Horses should be walked and cooled down, then brushed, before putting them up for the night with grain and hay. It is a good practice to feed and water horses at mid-day and let them have all the water they will drink on course when convenient to their riders. The decision to put shoes on horses depends on what the horse is being used for other than field trials. Some horses are never shod. The mud at field trials will suck shoes off and blacksmiths are usually only at the large trials.

A wool saddle blanket absorbs sweat and will not usually contribute to saddle sores. Horses backs should be checked frequently and the girth strap loosened when the horse is not being used for awhile. The bridle should be removed too and not used to tie the horse.

BRACED DOGS

Every competitive field trial runs dogs in braces. It is time saving and tests their independence at hunting. At one time a dog had to beat his brace mate and the brace winners were braced together until only two were left. It is no longer done as it can be time consuming in picking a winner and the dog has to beat itself several times in the process. Still dogs must beat their brace mates, but some that do not may be in the placements. Frequently both dogs in a brace are placed. One good dog often brings out the best in another one.

Running two dogs together in field trials seems as reasonable as hunting two dogs, but it does cause problems which do not happen when running one dog.

The most serious problem is fighting as the dogs are cast off to start competition. They quickly learn that they are indeed in competition in more ways than one.

Another problem is in chasing and tagging their brace

384

mates. Most dogs break this off after a short run, but some learn to love it as a fun game--better than hunting. There are other forms of interference as busting the brace mate's birds and stealing point. But, dogs must be braced together and trainers must solve these problems.

Dogs regularly braced together in training may assume dependence roles--one the leader and the other the follower. They develop a habit pattern where when braced in field trials they do nothing else. The follower type will go everywhere the brace mate goes and is a continuous invitation to disaster for both dogs.

It has been repeated over and over by all knowledgeable trainers that each dog is an individual. If for no other reason **two or more dogs should never be trained by the same trainer at the same time.**

The correcting, scolding or disciplining of one **adversely** affects the other. Many trainers, by necessity, work two dogs together at times for various reasons. Backing is only one. Trainers should make an effort to get help to handle one dog when they work the other. Handlers do work two dogs together with limited success, and if one dog is no longer in competition, the damage done to it is of less importance. But, the danger of causing bad habits and jealousy with the one being trained is ever present.

Amateur trainers with only one dog to work may not even know another field trial trainer with a dog they can work with. A dog silhouette is used by some to teach the dog backing. It is amazing, but this method has merit. Necessity is always the mother of invention. It was only recently that I checked this method out with dogs **already** trained to back.

It is important that **two** trainers work together from time to time, but the training is selectively directed to each trainer's dog. Important reasons are to improve backing and cast off, to stop playing, to stop fighting and interference, extend range or correct some other undesirable habit. The bracing of two dogs together to save training time is a poor reason, and should not be done, but we all do it.

Older dogs are often used to extend puppy range, but there are problems with this method, and is not the best way to develop range and does nothing in developing independence. When dogs are trained as individuals, they often resent being used in a training role for another dog, or a puppy.

Bracing puppies with older dogs that will not tolerate play helps them learn to stay to themselves. It is as natural for puppies to want to play as it is for them to breathe. But, it must never be tolerated in field trial training.

More good dogs are ruined by bracing them together without control or discipline than any other reason. Role assumption, fighting, intimidation, playing, and interference of any kind must be prevented when dogs are braced together.

It is usually simple to correct. But these dogs must know what "NO" and "WHOA" means in order for the handler to solve it quickly. The dog should be run down if he does not respond to commands, caught and scolded. If he fails to respond after a few times, discipline is warranted. Dogs learn to put down their brace mate and have the course and birds to themselves.

If all else fails, the shock collar will usually solve most of these problems. It adversely affects the range of some dogs for a time but it stops the bad

An example of controlled pointing and flushing with a pigeon on the pigeon pole. The dog is prevented from jumping in and catching the bird with a check strap.

Anytime a handler deliberately leads his dog over to become acquainted with his brace mate it is a sure indication that that dog has problems on cast-off and just may create another one for its brace mate.

habits. Dogs with affected range should not be stressed any further in training and put up for awhile.

There are dogs on the circuit, trained and handled by professionals who ruin many of the dogs (and bitches) they are braced with. Beginning handlers can be excused if they do not have the experience or knowledge to recognize it as a problem.

When a dog is entered in a field trial, the owners are saying that their dog is trained to the stake standards. The dog's handler has a responsibility to control his dog under all circumstances that arise in a brace. When dogs are entered in a stake they are entitled to run the full brace time, but the judges should not have to watch a training session.

There is no such thing as a "perfect" brace mate but some are preferred over others. Trainers must train to compensate for those dogs which interfere, tag, fight, trail, one which hunts to exactly the same places, those which steal point, bitches near or in season, in false pregnancy and running alone when the brace mate is picked up or when run as a bye. It is unfortunate that trainers must increase the stresses of training to compensate for poor trainers and dogs, but it must be done until all trainers are educated and proficient at their work.

INDEPENDENCE ON CAST OFF

A pointing dog must be competitive for field trials. He should throw dirt back as he casts off at top speed and upon smelling a bird screech to a halt and point it like a marble statue. Performances such as that seldom happen, for something always gets in the way. Usually it is the brace mate.

Handlers can set up conditions in training to get the speedy cast off by putting birds out in places the dog knows so that he will cast immediately to them in their training. Birds can be set out in electronic bird releasers a hundred yards or so on cast off and released just before the dog gets there. Intelligent use of objectives in putting out birds helps immensely. The dog's direction can be manipulated so he goes to the likely looking tree lines, fence rows, weed clumps, and copses.

Training more than one dog this way almost guarantees an independent cast off with no interference. Both should drive to the front in trying to get to the birds first. Trained dogs can be adversely affected by too much correction on cast off and it should be avoided. Hyperpnea (panting) is a stress indicator and it can be detected by comparing him to the brace mate working under the same conditions.

Conditions set up to correct a problem dog should be done by at least one experienced trainer who knows instinctively when to stop working, and if the correction is working as planned. But, artificial conditions never seem to work the way trainers want. Something usually goes wrong and quick adjustments are necessary to keep from creating a different or worse problem. It is important to vary the conditions and routine.

For example, if the cast off is unsatisfactory, both dogs can be stopped, set up and cast off again.

It is important that the problem dog be fitted with a long check cord/strap to aid the trainer in catching him if necessary. Different dogs should be used to avoid using the same one all the time.

Dogs which are taught to hunt independently ignore

brace mates and go hunting. Judges wrongly seem to like dogs to cast off in a straight line to the horizon without first using their noses along the way. This may be true whether it is a gun dog or all-age stake.

A serious problem with dogs first starting out is that they usually need to urinate and defecate which detracts from their cast off. Some dogs do so from stress, and judges seem to be lenient with them. Handlers can do all kinds of things before the brace to get their dogs cleaned out to no avail. But, when they are cast off it comes quickly. Dogs which are honest in this when finished will go on and do no more, but many keep at it all around the course. They do the same thing in training and are not corrected, but they should be forced to stop it and go on.

RANGE

A dog's range depends on many things such as the type of cover and terrain among many others. Good gun dogs should instinctively quarter in heavy grass and when able to see an identifiable objective should reach out to it.

The love to run and the desire to hunt are extremely important in a dog's development and range, but these should be supported by the dog's ability to find birds and point staunchly. The greater the range the longer the dog must stay on point.

What is considered "extended range" for one breed may be short for another. There is considerable disagreement on ideal range for the all-age or gun dog. A half mile may seem proper for an all-age dog and a hundred yards for a gun dog.

The so-called American Kennel Club "restricted breeds" have increased their range by selective breeding. Many now range out with pointers and setters. Some undoubtedly acquired the heritable traits for greater range by being crossbred to pointers.

The newer associations which stress walking handlers and retrieving stakes may be more interested in decreasing range but not hunting desire. Trainers in the National Shoot-To-Retrieve Association stakes do effectively train pointers and setters to stay and hunt within a small area—20 acres.

I believe that a given range is important, but not nearly as important as how dogs apply themselves and use their intelligence in hunting the course. Running to great range to hear the sound of the wind pass by their ears is not hunting. Like race horses, some dogs just naturally love to run fast. Sometimes they will accidentally run head on into bird scent and point. To some judges that looks impressive.

Training affects a dog's range. Many dogs, upon being freshly broke shorten their range. Many regain it after the stress is reduced and develop renewed confidence and greater range. Those that have been allowed to learn to self-hunt will usually hold their range better from breaking stresses.

In the 1960's, handlers would make a special point of finding out what range a judge wanted. In those days, dogs were entered in both all-age and gun dog stakes on the same weekend. They could and did win in both stakes and some were handled from horseback in all-age and on foot in gun dog stakes. Some dogs won both stakes from horseback because the judges put up the dog they liked best without considering the type stake they were judging. The problem then was in knowing the judge so the handlers could attempt to adjust the range of their dogs. Since that time, the margin in range is no longer in doubt.

Some of the all-age German Shorthaired Pointers can run as far and as fast as any pointer and get lost just as often, but sometimes cannot be honestly placed in either a gun dog or all-age stake.

Many clubs are having gun dog walking stakes as they once were in the American Kennel Club trials. There is also more emphasis on scouting now with the increased range and attendant poor handling qualities of the dogs.

Alvin H. Nitchman wrote:

"It has been my observation, in the last fifty years, that the consistent winners have been dogs with moderate range that hunt hard and point the most birds."

It should be the same now. My experience is that a well mannered broke dog will win and place regularly with medium range, but will win most all the time, all other things done properly, with a range of two hundred yards when he hunts to the front, runs hard and handles effortlessly to objectives. A few years ago, I watched the American Field Amateur Championship at Killdeer Plains Wildlife Area and the winner was never out of sight.

BIRDINESS

When bird scent is evident, dogs indicate its presence by their animation, movements, being more excited, or quickening their search.

This behavior should be encouraged in young dogs as

392

they build interest and develop toward becoming bird finders. The scent of a bird is exciting to the dog, and brings out animation exuding anticipation of finding something soon.

Dog trainers should beware of using only wild birds in a dog's early development and training. They should never interfere with a young dog making game or investigating natural odors. If it turns out that the scent is of no interest, or is not game of interest to the dog, he must learn this mostly through his own experience. He must learn to reject most scents in his environment and develop the scent of birds used in field trials to the fullest.

He may at first become confused when smelling human scent on birds. Some dogs will completely ignore birds having human scent when hunted too long on wild birds. They have no opportunity to be warned that a bird is closeby since planted birds do not walk to the place they are placed. They are taken to that place by a person and it is unnatural for human scent to be on birds much less having no preliminary scent of the bird's presence as in the wild. For that reason, dogs should be exposed to birds having human scent early. Dogs cannot get excited in making game on planted birds unless they track the bird planter which must be prevented. I have watched dogs in field trials pick up the bird planter's scent where the bird field was in the middle of the course and take it to the bird, soften up on point because of human scent, and win over a dog having a dug up find in the middle of the course with a fantastic mark in high weeds and retrieve directly to hand. Both dogs ran similar courses, but the judges did not fault the dog for tracking the bird planter to the bird and then softening on point.

Dogs should be animated in anticipation of finding birds when hunting.

SCENTING

I have hauled pigeons, chukars, quail and pheasants in closed vehicles, and believe me, there is nothing exciting about how they smell and dogs have to be odd to get excited when they smell them.

Paul M. Jamerson in *The American Field*, December 1, 1979 wrote:

"Like a soft summer breeze, 'scent' can be felt but not seen. We can detect the good from the bad, one scent from another, just as a hunting dog can detect one game species from another. But we don't know how it is done. It is at once the most sublime, the most misunderstood, the most frustrating of all senses."

"True enough, there are other highly important elements that a good bird dog must possess. But to observe and follow one as he sifts the air currents and drools at the mouth as he tastes the sweet elixir of game can section anyone's heart like a pie. To follow a bird dog that doesn't have a keen sense of smell can be as painful as trying to play a violin with a butcher's cleaver. Without that so-called 'nose' you have nothing."

The amazing scenting ability of dogs has been the key to their survival. We have taken the dog and used those powers for our personal enjoyment without really caring about a scientific explanation of the mechanism for scent.

There are days (and nights) when the combination of

air movement, temperature of the ground and air and humidity make a dog's nose just about useless. These conditions in combination, or sometimes singly, with ground type and moisture content make these gaseous scent molecules **not** release from the game, tracks, or grass and brush enough for dogs to smell. Game birds seem to have an uncanny way of "turning off" scent, and **tired** dogs have difficulty learning to find birds when their tongues are fully extended.

The scent molecules cause a chemical reaction that are dissolved as a watery secretion in a dog's olefactory organs. These are transmitted to the brain and dogs learn to discriminate between different chemical reactions which results in the release of adrenalin into the blood stream. Smells can create excitement, caution and fear, and dogs learn through smell and experience what to do with different ones.

I try various schemes when putting out pen raised birds so that my dogs will not track me up to the place the birds are placed. A person could "walk" on air and still leave enough scent for the dog to track. Whatever the chemical is **we** release, it is tenacious and long lasting.

Kim Heller in the December 1972 *Hunting Dog* magazine wrote:

"A bird's body scent is probably given off in about the same way as perspiration in people. When it comes to the skin it evaporates and floats off into the air. The foot scent of other animals is given off in much the same way from between the pads or hoofs of trailed animals. As he walks around this oil or skin lubricant brushes off on the ground vegetation."

"The scent starts to evaporate from the vegetation in much the same way it did from the bird's body. Therefore

anything that affects the way evaporation takes place will alter scenting conditions."

Paul M. Jamerson further wrote in his article:

"We know that the scent of deer is secreted from a gland. Likewise the skunk, fox, coon, cottontail and various other wild animals. But where does the scent of wild birds come from? Many convincing testimonials have led us to believe it comes from the oil gland. Others say the skin, when another knowledgeable editorial appeared in the FIELD some years back insisting that it definitely comes from the bird's breath."

Further on in his article Jamerson told of making a bet that his old Pete could find two dead quail shot by two friends when hunting rabbits. During the night snow fell and old Pete found both birds the next day and,

". . . if old Pete were alive today, and could talk, he would tell us that those two birds had the damndest case of halitosis he'd ever smelled."

Field trial dogs are always finding dead pen raised birds that are soaking wet, dead or frozen stiff. We can of course discount scent coming from the breath as the source dogs follow on a frozen bird as silly as that opinion seems.

We hear about, and experience, air washed birds having little scent left for a dog when marked and followed again to point. Maybe some aerodynamics are involved which help keep the feathers closer to the body and also washes away scent on feathers already there before they flushed.

Smart hunters soon learn this and wait several minutes before following up to look for singles, and maybe somewhere back in history this led to the practice of heeling dogs away from the direction of flight. This is a good practice for it helps prevent dogs from pottering around on scent.

Dogs learn by the strength of a bird's scent cone, which varies according to air currents, wind, bird's movements, nearness and other conditions. They learn how close they can get without flushing by the strength and source of the scent.

Take a dog that has learned under ideal scenting conditions, and put him in the desert, and he will quickly learn to point much the same way as on **poor** scent cones. Dogs can discriminate body scent below a certain threshold level. Some dogs dilate their nostrils and suck in air to better appreciate the sensation of smell. They must also learn how to sample the air properly when running full out with their tongues dragging the ground. Some never seem to master it and it can be called "losing his nose."

Jack Harper wrote:

". . . vets told me that when a dog is overheated, tiny blood vessels in the nose burst, and in about six months little polyps form which interfere with the scent reaching the scent buds and the dog's nose goes off."

The physical condition of a dog alters its ability to smell. Sick dogs have difficulty. Certain pollen from weeds and grasses irritate the membranes and dulls the scenting ability. I do not know of any area of the country that does not have plants which do not affect a dog's ability to smell.

Rapid changes in temperature of the air and ground cuts down on scenting as does a warm sunny day having low humidity around three or four PM when the ground and grasses are dry. Scenting conditions change from

397

daylight to dark (and dark to daylight), so the luck of the draw in field trials is extremely important, except nobody knows which braces will be fortunate to have poor, good or the best scenting conditions. For that reason it pays to have dogs with sharp eyesight and taught to sight point birds. The problem with this is they sometimes try to "manufacture" birds and point corn shucks, clumps of grass or bunches of leaves for guaranteed unproductives.

The studies of scent conditions were made by H. Budgett "Hunting by Scent," 1933, according to an article in *Poplar Dogs*, March 1973 by Bashkim Dibra. He wrote:

"Good scenting conditions exist when the earth is warmer than the air (this is usually the case at night or early morning), when there is a sudden fall in the temperature of the air, and when snow has fallen before a frost."

"Bad scenting conditions exist when there is any rise in the temperature of the air, when the sun is shining brightly, and when snow has fallen after frost has entered the ground, and when there is a heavy rain to obliterate the track."

"In addition, a high wind causes eddy currents of air and makes scenting uncertain. Barometric pressure is not known to have any perceptible influence on scent."

I kept temperature and humidity records on several dogs I broke and found that on days of high humidity they could find birds better at the same temperature. That was my observation and there was nothing scientific about it. I listened to the local TV station for humidity and temperature.

Dogs develop scent filters in their brains and learn to ignore scent. For that reason, I always let dogs

398

see--smell--carry birds before I ever expect them to point.

How far can dogs identify the scent of a bird? I have seen and heard about amazing feats, but these were not ordinary field trial dogs.

Weather affects the feeding, watering and movement of birds, so there is not much use to hunt when quail are under a brushpile, under snow or in a hole. Yet, field trials must go on regardless of the weather and scenting conditions--especially weekend trials. It is true that birds released for stake braces lack the ability to find suitable shelter and hump up near where they are released, but finding them can be difficult when conditions are poor.

ACCURACY OF NOSE

One time when braced with a German Shorthaired Pointer which was running at near all-age range, he slowed, and rooted around until my dog caught up. He went on and my dog immediately established point on a chukar that could not fly. The chukar had apparently walked around in a small area, hid, and the dog was lucky the bird did not fly and be charged with a bump. He continued on, had a stop to flush and two finds and won the stake. At the time he failed to point, but pottered around, I had written him off as a loser. He failed in more than one area, but he **ran**.

Under most any other circumstance that dog would have bumped or pushed out the chukar which would be cause for the judges to order it up according to current judging methods. I am not relating this story to criticize the judging, although it was not good, but to show that if my dog had avoided that area nobody would have known he had worked a bird improperly.

My dog blinked birds in one trial, and I was positive that I was the only one who saw it, and the setter brace mate pointed both to my embarrassment.

Nose is what makes a top bird dog, but it must be combined with brains and experience. Some dogs never are introduced to game properly and fail to learn how to use their noses to full potential.

With an accurate nose, it is almost impossible to misjudge where a bird is located. The handlers and dogs must get experience together, and the handlers must do a good job of finding and flushing the birds, otherwise the dogs will not develop confidence in their ability and will break point.

We all know that a dog will have a bird pointed with pinpoint accuracy, yet hunt for it as we may, we feel the time constraint burdening us, and we then make the decision to have our dog move up and put his nose **on** the bird. If we are lucky the bird will not flush and the dog will not grab it. Even a bob white quail can be buried under grass and invisible and coturnix seem to always bury under but none to my knowledge are used except in Shoot-To-Retrieve trials. A handler should be reluctant to send his dog to relocate unless he is trained to show the bird with his nose almost touching it, but recognizing the occasional need, I train my dogs to do that. Handlers lose many stakes by sending their dogs to relocate birds that have been pointed precisely and when relocating move in and pick up the bird, or it flushes.

Dogs **can** learn or be trained to locate game with pinpoint accuracy, or stand (point) the first bit of scent they smell and have many unproductives. The choice is up to the trainer. Yet, some trainers are not aware their training methods caused the problem.

DIVIDED FINDS

A divided find occurs when both dogs in a brace establish point at the same time on the same bird. Sometimes one dog does not see the brace mate when establishing point. It is usually impossible for judges to know which dog pointed first and it is not important since each dog is normally credited with a find. The judges will direct one handler to flush and shoot. It is important that handlers not move to flush until the judges have made a decision.

When both dogs in a brace are hunting independently this situation rarely ever happens. Trainers who brace their dogs in training can expect it to happen frequently, for these dogs when braced with a strange dog know nothing else but to go where it goes. One may take a backing role or a point stealing--divided find type--role. Sometimes judges are where they can see this happen and order up the dog stealing point.

In deep or heavy cover, it is possible for both dogs in a brace to be hunting without either one knowing where the other is exactly. Sometimes I doubt that these situations occur with complete innocence, for the acute sense of hearing and smelling can pinpoint the location of the brace mate without too much conscious effort.

In field trials, we prefer that dogs hunt freely in braces without concern for where or what their brace mates are doing.

Judges riding up on this situation might assume that one dog is backing, but both are pointing the same bird. Could this be a divided find? Or, did the backing dog move up until it could smell the bird?

A crude dog silhouette can be used when a good pointing dog is not available. This crude three dimension cut-out looks like a pointing dog to the backing dog, but a cardboard cut-out will suffice.

402

APPROACHING DOGS ON POINT

There is a certain courtesy and good manners due the other handler and brace mate when seeing a dog on point. The one handler should do nothing that will cause stress on the pointing brace mate, or interfere with it in any way. Whenever a dog is on point, the fact should be made known to a judge, and if appropriate the other handler too, so he can make whatever adjustment or decision needed to handle his dog.

Once a handler has called point, he should walk or ride at a normal walk and refrain from repeating WHOA or STAY commands. If a dog needs controlled when coming in on a backing situation, that dog's handler should do nothing intentionally to cause the brace mate to break or soften on point. That handler should get his dog under control with a minimum of effort if he knows, or it appears, that he will not back naturally.

It is best never to create an unnecessary backing situation, or one in which one handler cannot control his dog. Given the choice, handlers should continue hunting their dogs if their dogs do not see their brace mates on point. If they do, and go on they can be charged with failure to back.

Handlers should **never** run or ride fast to their dogs on point, especially in competition, for it is a form of intimidation. It further signals those judging and watching that the dog cannot be trusted, and the dog experiences the same feeling and responds poorly. It is true that some judges do not know enough to mark dogs down when this is done, but handlers should be warned and if done again, eliminated from the stake.

Handlers should approach their dogs from one side and

This is a good approach by the handler to flush birds helping to keep the dog from shifting its attention to the handler.

This shows a handler trying to flush birds under more difficult conditions. The dog should remain motionless until after the bird is flushed and until its handler takes it by the collar or commands it to HEEL away in another direction.

under no circumstance walk from behind and close to the backing dog on the way to their dog.

On horseback, they should approach within about fifty to seventy five feet and dismount, and judges should approach no further with their horses. If they want to see a bird on the ground in heavy cover, they should dismount and proceed cautiously on foot.

FINDING POINTED BIRDS

Not all handlers can find pointed birds when their dogs are looking right down their noses at them. A few never seem to learn this skill.

The worst of many problems in training, or competition, is caused when the planted bird leaves before the dog can find and point it. The dog points though and the handler, assuming the bird is there **forces** his dog to stay on point when he attempts to flush. As a result, the dog never learns to use his natural ability and is forced into unproductives. Dogs trained on wild birds should make fewer mistakes.

The inability to accurately locate and pin (hold) birds is detrimental to the dog, wastes valuable time in competition, and is also stressful on a backing dog which must wait through unsuccessful flushing attempts.

A properly educated dog will accurately locate the bird and the handler can produce it with a minimum of effort. A dog will often hold point after the bird has left and will not relocate on its own. But his intensity should indicate to his handler that the bird has left. That dog has usually been trained never to release itself after establishing point. Handlers who make a mistake of training this way usually have many unproductives. Releasing these dogs to relocate assures non-productives.

Dogs should know precisely where the bird is and look and point their noses directly at it. Handlers should look at their dogs nose and eyes and walk straight to the bird.

There are times when the best dogs cannot "tell" their handlers where the bird is no matter how hard their handlers try, but the bird is **there**. Dogs which freeze on first scent can be on top of a bird, or have it behind them, where the bird for whatever reason should have flown but did not.

The time a handler uses to produce a bird is oftentimes critical for the backing dog where time is not called in the bird field. The handler of the backing dog should handle his dog without intentionally avoiding a backing situation. And, avoid it he must if possible. Some dogs are so poorly trained, along with their handlers, such that backing situations cannot be avoided. When forced into backing situations, the pointing dog and his handler may be poorly trained and spend an eternity trying to flush. Some handlers do this deliberately, but they are the minority.

After a reasonable time for the pointing dog's handler to flush without success, the backing dog's handler should ask to take his dog off the back and continue hunting if time is not called on point in the bird field, or when on course.

Once a bird is located, there is always difficulty in flushing pen raised birds. They are unpredictable. No matter how skillful the handler is at flushing, the bird invariably runs back to the dog, or flushes and flies back over the dog's head or in his face, and causes him to fault. The handler tries to flush to avoid such problems, and to prevent his dog from shifting position to mark. Oftentimes changing position causes a dog to sit because he cannot turn and keep all four legs in place. Judges should not penalize dogs for this, but many wrongly order them picked up.

Handlers must try to produce the birds for gunners with full safety to judges, dogs, handlers, the other gunner, marshal, gallery and away from backing dogs. Birds must not be picked up and thrown unless instructed by the judges. Often the elements are so bad that pen raised birds cannot fly. Handlers who go ahead and pick up birds instead of flushing should be warned and penalized depending on the situation. Handlers will do this intentionally when they have "green broke" dogs.

CONDITIONING

Competitive field trial dogs must be healthy, without internal parasites and in top physical and mental condition. To have a winning run each time, their physical and mental condition must also be balanced. I have known dogs which did not need conditioning to put out their maximum effort when exercised sparingly for thirty minute heats. Their desire was not dulled by mental overwork and stress. Normal work should build desire in dogs.

Conditioning should not be done only in the field. Dogs get tired of working the same area all the time. They need diversion. Working all the time **without** finding birds fails to maintain a keen interest or sense of excitement. Dogs need to find many birds!

There are many ways to road dogs with mechanized vehicles. The author is shown using his riding lawn mower for that purpose which is safer than from horseback.

Dogs can be conditioned many different ways. Most dogs delight in chasing, catching and retrieving Frisbees. This activity can be done by city dwellers in back yards, parks or in almost any space.

When working unfamiliar trashy areas, dogs can injure a foot or pad. There is probably a good name for people who dump their trash along roadsides and discard bottles and tin cans in the woods. Dogs are injured on them. Nature is not so kind either as it prunes and drops thorns, but those areas can be avoided when training and conditioning dogs by knowing the location of such places.

The work of conditioning is wasted if a dog becomes lame. Therefore, it is essential that he be conditioned at the least risk. He will have difficulty winning if he has been overworked, or is in poor physical and mental condition.

Consider the amount of energy used in running a hundred yard dash at different speeds. If a person could possibly run it in nine seconds, he would be so exhausted it would be difficult to stand up or breathe. It would not exhaust anyone to run this distance several times a day at a moderate speed. Dogs are much the same way. Whenever they are run for too long a time without rest, or when conditions are too hot or miserable, they break down and learn to pace themselves thereafter. A dog suffering from heat exhaustion may never regain the drive he once had.

It is wise to condition dogs with methods that they do not associate with hunting or training. Water retrieving, ball or frisbee chasing and retrieving are excellent methods.

I want dogs to run at top speed in trials for the allotted thirty minutes without the need to stop and pour water on them regardless of the temperature. If there is natural water on course, they should want to continue hunting if properly motivated and conditioned. A stake of an hour or longer duration would not always be sensible to expect that, but can be done without adverse effects. The point I want to make is that I do not <u>train</u> my dogs to **expect** water or stop for it during the brace. This may not always be possible or sensible but is a training goal.

When dogs are expected to run at top speed under all conditions, they should learn by experience their limitation under all kinds of terrain and weather conditions. Dogs learn to avoid obstacles by experience. After one or two crashes, they no longer run full speed into woven or barbed wire fences. Dogs learn how to handle the heat in much the same way without heat exhaustion when it gets hot.

As Herm David wrote:

"It's a pitiful sight to watch a hunting dog, loaded with game-finding desire, press on and on long after his heart, lungs and muscles have been screaming at him to stop and rest. We have to admire the guts of a dog that'll keep right on hunting after his pads are worn out and bleeding. But, we have to wonder about his owner who didn't condition the dog for the work that was to be asked of him."

Professional trainers learn that the best method for conditioning their dogs is to use the roading harness and work them for progressively longer times until they reach top physical condition. There are several ways to do this, and it is advantageous to road more than one dog at a time. Weights may also be added and dogs are encouraged to pull on the lead rope.

Motor vehicles are used with the trainer holding onto a leash with an arm out the window. Accidents can and do happen using this method. Some professional trainers use the motorized "horse type" exerciser, or a special fixture attached to the front bumper of their vehicles, and also use the motorized moving belt exerciser.

The important thing to remember about roading whether it is done from bicycle, horseback, riding lawn mower, vehicle or other means is that the dog is not learning bad habits or making mistakes on game. He might get bored or have his muscles so overdeveloped he cannot run properly, or pads worn down, but it pays dividends when done sensibly.

Dogs should be roaded one day and run in the field the next time with a day or more of rest minimum each week. How much exercise is needed depends on the trainer's short or long term goal, and time available. They should be worked up to the maximum gradually. Trainers should not work dogs the same length of time each session whether roading or running, so they will not develop a sense of timing and decreasing enthusiasm with time.

Everyone has different ideas about working pregnant bitches. I have won in field trials a few days before they whelped. The worst thing an owner can do is to **stop** exercising a pregnant bitch. Once they make milk it is best to put them up and prepare them for whelping, but under no circumstance force them to work too much or for too long. A week or two before whelping is the time to quit. Some bitches probably will not work that late in their pregnancy and should not be forced.

Dogs should not be overworked. It takes a long time for pads to heal or build up a tough cover when damaged by overwork on the wrong type surface. A dog too muscled up runs like a plow horse.

The most important consideration in a thoroughly conditioned dog is proper diet and amount of food.

411

Handler is styling up and sweet talking the backing dog to keep it intense and less stressed.

Some pregnant bitches are capable of winning trials as late as two weeks before whelping. This depends on the dogs development, condition and desire.

412

Working dogs are under more stress and need more high protein food than dogs on a maintenance diet. The higher the protein content the better dogs can handle stress.

A few handlers still practice starving their dogs a few days before competition. The theory they have is that a hungry dog will want to hunt harder (for itself). The best performing dog works for his handler, and has no thought of finding something to stay his hunger pangs. Frankly, this seems like a dumb and antiquidated practice. Those dogs probably will not have to defecate during the brace time and that is a plus. Some dogs just love to run whether they have a full or empty stomach. It is better to have a dog that loves to run and hunt for his handler always, and when properly conditioned, to run better than other dogs in competition on that day. We all want winners!

Hard running excites the bowels, so it is advisable not to feed dogs several hours before they run. If fed twice a day, skip the morning meal, although I never worry about it and let the chips fall where they may. It is too difficult sometimes to predict when a dog will run the best. He might just need that energy from his last feeding.

Once a dog is well trained, polished, and has finished performances, he is not in need of further training. He has graduated. What does the trainer do with him now? If he is to remain competitive he must be kept in top running condition by working him under actual hunting conditions or field trial working conditions. There are hazards involved. The old trash dumps made by individual families and illegal trash dumpers from towns and cities are being slowly replaced with garbage collection. But, on any field trial grounds the careless, sloppy, lazy, unthinking, uncaring slobs are throwing away their beer and pop cans and bottles. Cut pads are usually disabling injuries to dogs. Old crabapple trees and honey locust trees drop woody thorns which will completely penetrate a dog's foot. There are the usual other hazards and farmyard animals that injure the **good** dogs. The poor ones never get hurt.

Dogs in a professional's string are hauled long distances and may be allowed to relieve themselves only once or twice a day. They get sore and stiff and need worked out and exercised at field trial grounds before they run in competition. Some clubs provide places that dogs can be trained before, during, and after trials. The roading harness can be a great asset where it is difficult to exercise the dogs in open fields.

Amateur handlers are faced with the same problems to a lesser extent, but are less likely to use the roading harness. They prefer to run them unrestrained and intimidate them when doing it to reinforce their control for what is to come.

It is to everyone's advantage to have their dogs at full potential and exercise grounds help. The American Kennel Club rules did not permit training on the grounds. That seemed all inclusive and restrictive and was confusing. The rule now states:
"There will be no training of dogs anywhere on the course until the trial has been concluded." This is further qualified:
"For the purposes of this Procedure, roading a dog behind the gallery is considered to be training."
American Field handlers have always roaded dogs in the gallery, and sometimes do it to be at the starting point of the next brace.

Clubs must have some control and handlers cannot be

414

allowed to train without regard to the conduct of trials. Handlers should always check with the field trial chairman, or stake manager, about a place they can work their dogs.

Laws vary in different states on dog training. Some permit out of state field trialers to shoot birds without a state license under restricted conditions and other officials turn their heads for the good of the sport. Many states have reciprocity agreements. Handlers should always check with the field trial chairman or stake manager if there is any question.

Dogs in top physical condition enjoy running and are better able to handle the varied weather and ground conditions. Yet, there are dogs which can lay up in bed from one week to the next and still get out and scorch the ground they run on with drive and enthusiasm.

BIRD FIELD TRAINING

Bird field timing starts the instant the first dog crosses an imaginary line which designates the bird field, unless he has cut the course to get there.

Dogs must be trained to work bird field stakes properly to become consistent winners. One dog can clean it out to the detriment of its brace mate even though that dog might not have had a winning back course and the birdless dog did. A good back course performance is what it takes to win, and the bird field only serves to confirm it. Handlers and dogs must learn to make the most effective use of bird field time and work as a team.

Some dogs point or check out bird field markers and

in time learn that these mark the boundaries.

Exposed gunners draw dogs from down course like flies to dead birds. Some dogs never learn to run to them or will shy away. Gunners should stay hidden from sight until one or both dogs have entered the bird field.

Trial-wise dogs learn to run to the bird field and do not waste time on the back course searching sterile ground. Judges can no longer appoint bird field observers to report dogs which enter early and have unacceptable game contact.

There is no doubt that experienced field trial handlers do the best job of working bird fields, but many do not because they hack in their dogs. They will not permit their dogs to hunt freely and use a heavy hand on them all the time. They are hacked or intimidated to **hunt close.** Judges should penalize those dogs or handlers, but seldom do.

And, of course I must mention the clever handler or confederate who watches where birds are planted for previous braces. Someone in the gallery with pre-arranged signals tells the handler where to take his dog in the bird field. It is almost impossible for judges to know this goes on as they keep their eyes on the dogs.

If all else fails, and their dog does not find a bird shortly before time is to expire, desperate handlers may cause their dogs to stop "on point." (Some dogs are easily trained to do this.) The handler then searches over a large area in the hopes of flushing a bird. Once in awhile it works. A few cheats even carry birds to fake finds in much the same way. This is usually done with quail. Honest handlers make a point of demonstrating good sportsmanship and take whatever happens in stride.

My dogs are allowed complete freedom in the bird field when they are where they cannot interfere with another dog working game. They learn to work to the front whenever I change directions, or I call them to "come around," if they leave the bird field.

My plan is to enter the last third of the bird field, with the wind at my right side or in my face. Sometimes this is not possible because the other handler has the same plan, and I will work the near side into the wind and follow this same pattern when avoiding the brace mate. I walk two thirds of the length, take a diagonal to the opposite corner, cross the upper third with the wind again to my right side, or in my face, for two thirds of the length and take a diagonal to the opposite corner near where I entered. That path represents two triangles with apexes joined at the center. Then I work the other two sides and the middle.

Handlers should stay as far away from the other handler and the brace mate as possible so that there is no likelyhood of interference, busted birds or stolen points.

It is possible to train dogs so that when handlers stop in the center their dogs will work in a circular pattern around them with ever widening circles.

Some handlers work one bird and then try to avoid any other bird contact. This practice is obvious and should be penalized, but some judges may encourage it if they like the dog for a placement. Other handlers will try to find every bird to skunk the brace mates which makes for tough and interesting competition. Either handler is entitled to all the birds if his dog can find them, but some view this as not being fair.

It is interesting to watch pointers move out at top

417

speed and then swing around to stay within the limits of the twenty acre bird fields in Shoot-To-Retrieve trials. These dogs learn where birds are and where birds are not normally found and conduct their searches as if programmed that way.

It is important to train dogs for bird field work to win consistently. By the same token, they must have enough variety to keep from becoming bird field-wise dogs which prevents them from winning.

Stake requirements where time is called in bird fields requires that the dog not on point must be stopped, or be on a back, if he is close enough and sees the other dog on point. There is normally no great concern for how long it takes the handler to find and flush his bird, for both dogs will get their full eight minutes at hunting the bird field. It does concern handlers of backing dogs if their dogs get bored, restless or move which often happens. The best solution is for the handler to avoid backs in bird fields.

When time is **not** called, handlers should keep hunting their dogs, under control, all the time when the other handler is flushing and retrieving. There are dangers here, for the bird may be shot near or fly over and cause their dogs to chase or retrieve it.

Deliberately putting dogs on backing situations in a bird field is dumb. Handlers have been known to deliberately spend most of the bird field time looking for a bird when they knew where it was all the time. The brace mate went birdless standing behind the pointing dog most of the eight minutes. Handler's should not wait for the judge to send them on, they should request permission after a reasonable length of time for flush, or heel their dogs on and let the judge

418

make decisions as he sees fit. It is the lesser of the two evils. Handlers must help their dogs and avoid situations where their opportunity to hunt for birds is penalized.

Training dogs for bird fields is done the same way as in field trials so that the dogs know how and when to hunt in an imaginary confined space. It is just about that simple, but they can eventually learn it in bird fields at trials. I know dogs that hardly ever see training except in field trials and eventually do well enough to win championship titles.

Some field trialers are vets and their "free" services are of great benefit to the sport. David Heinold, DVM is caring for a dog with all four pads gone from competing on the Mojave Desert at a National Championship trial.

Chapter 8

Breaking

WING AND SHOT

Breaking dogs and horses to our will and domination is contrary to the nature of both animals. But break them we must, if we are to enjoy our sport. The longer we wait to start discipline and control, the more difficult training is later, so we usually begin the first day we get a new puppy, but not to wing and shot just yet.

There is a tremendous motivating force for dogs to find and chase, or catch, game, and serious training to break dogs should not start until their desire is allowed to peak at the highest possible level. Breaking before this peak, or maturity, is reached can cause trainers to misjudge their dogs or apply too much

420

force and cause bad situations, create undue stress and other problems.

Too many handlers want to be **first** or **create** a first. They want to prove something to themselves, so the psychological needs of the trainer/handler are important to them.

I know a professional handler who won a fun gun dog retrieving stake with a six month old puppy, but was never able to do anymore with it in competition as the puppy became confused and was incapable of handling the stress and was ruined. This same owner used a handler some years later and won puppy, derby and all-age stakes in American Field trials with a dog while still puppy/derby age.

Finishing the **youngest** field champion in a breed is a foolish goal. It also gives one's ego a big boost to brag that he has the youngest champion. Unfortunately, most of these dogs are never seen in competition at the age a dog normally matures and is competitive not to mention all those ruined trying to be a FIRST.

It is true that dogs can be broke steady to wing and shot with less time and effort and less problems when they are not required to be steady to shot or retrieve and it is done successfully at a young age. But, there is no reason to hurry the breaking. It is done mostly because of ignorance or impatience.

Dogs in each breed, and within breeds, mature at different ages. The two sexes mature at different rates and that too must be given consideration.

Even though I have had dogs that really could have been broken when young, I would not. I wait until they are fully mature at between three and four years of age. Waiting until that age allows the dogs to mature, simplifies the breaking process, speeds progress and gives fewer problems in their training for competition. It is true that just about anyone can break a dog even when using inconsistent and all wrong methods by persisting over an extended period of time. It is one redeeming quality of dogs--they can adapt and learn from inept trainers.

It has been stated that a dog must give his trainer both his confidence and respect and vice versa. Confidence is earned mostly through progressive training with fairness, gentleness and respect using well timed correction and discipline.

It requires a child a long time to learn the alphabet, even longer to spell, several years before it can read, and many more before it can think and act responsibly. Yet, there are trainers who expect a puppy to learn from one or two training exposures and corrections. Some people should be prevented from marrying, bearing children and owning dogs, but our society allows it for everyone, with few minor exceptions.

One fallacy in dog training is in comparing the age of dogs to humans--seven years to one or a graduated formula. It is true that children can be made to work at a young age and have been made slaves to their elders for centuries. How difficult is it for most people to memorize a simple written paragraph of one hundred words? At what age can humans reason and show simple intelligence in play, social behavior or work?

Dog trainers fail to understand the repetition necessary before and during the breaking process. Although some readers may scoff at this, obedience training is of great value in preparing dogs for breaking. Yard work and field work is **obedience** training, although the purposes may be different, and every experienced trainer knows that yard work must **precede** breaking.

Obedience training accustoms dogs to obey commands without punishment or fear of it, and they learn that it can be fun and rewarding.

Many dog owners, turned field trainers, fail simply because they are usually impatient and unable to see the **minute** improvement in their dogs from one session to the next--if and when there is any. They show their ignorance by resorting to improper and untimely physical punishment.

How much faster do people learn where the parents and teachers beat them to force learning, or because they learn slowly? My fifth grade teacher was a "preacher" and would finish a morning prayer and take his belt and beat the hell out of several of us kids. It did not make learning easy for me, and destroyed my desire to learn under him. Many kids rebelled, fought back, quit or ran away from home to escape.

Dogs and children are alike in many ways. What they do must be fun for them in all of their training and learning.

Using the ratio of one to seven for discussion, maybe we can understand better why dogs at two years of age are not mature enough to be broken. First, it is contrary to their nature, and nothing in their background has prepared them for this event. It goes against the grain. It is different from "obedience" training where they had no predetermination to do something else--like chasing and catching birds when being trained.

Teach a child at fourteen to be socially responsible as an adult, make intelligent decisions in competition with elders and be accepted by peers and that child is an exception--a genius, but even they need experience. The "new" adult at twenty one years of age has had most of his education and learning for functioning as a member of society--he or she has not had the education or experience necessary to compete with or without stress or jealousy. People fold up under stress (nervous breakdown) just as quickly, if not more so, than dogs.

A dog at three years of age, similarly educated or trained is at the same approximate level in its "place" in the breaking process.

This simplistic comparison should be adequate for the example intended. But training for field work should be accomplished within a certain time span. If any part of the training is delayed too long, tasks become difficult and the dog is more stubborn to work with. This same situation is apparent when trained dogs are put in retirement and then brought back into training.

Dogs at the proper age, for the various training levels, will respond quickly and want to please their trainers. Older dogs, when started in field training, are more difficult to train for given tasks.

As breaking begins, not many dogs, if any, are capable of **understanding** their being cussed out, thrown about, kicked, beaten and physically abused in other ways for having chased a bird. **All previous training allowed chasing.** Some dogs have such a strong desire to chase that they can learn to resist all punishment.

Too many trainers make the transition to breaking too abruptly and use a check cord wrong, or when it should not be used. Dogs in every breed will not tolerate inept discipline and will seek an escape mechanism.

Teaching steadiness to wing, shot, backing and

retrieving are the apex of a dog's training. But, dogs must also show a certain level of **natural** ability and experience before being broken for field trials and hunting. Dogs which cannot be made to staunch up on point and stay for flush cannot be broken well enough for competition. Many dogs are broken before they learn to hunt and range to objectives naturally. These dogs are hacked around the course.

Dogs can be broke to flush and break at shot, or be broke to flush and shot, but break when birds are killed. It may be necessary to combine the first three phases at the same time with some dogs. It really depends on the individual dog and his development up to that time. Obviously, if a dog has difficulty learning to hold point at flush, the trainer might as well combine all three to minimize the stress induced by having to work too many planted birds for the three phases separately.

Breaking should be pleasant and fun for the dogs—not brutal treatment for slow learning. Somehow a gradual transition must be made from chasing to where dogs will stop at the flush of birds. Some learn this on their own. Once a dog understands what he is supposed to do, he will take pleasure in doing it.

Breaking for shot implies that the dog already has been broken to flush. In breaking to wing, a shot can be fired or trainers can wait until their dogs are steady to wing first. A blank pistol shot does not teach dogs the real purpose of the gun. This relationship is learned only when birds are killed for the dog, and should be done before they are broke.

At one stage in training for flush, dogs expect to chase at shot and have not learned the proper relationship of the **shot** and **gun** which kills birds as opposed to a blank gun. A strong relationship to the gun must be developed and is an integral part of the trainer and dog developing into a team.

This training can be broken down into breaking to wing, breaking to shot, breaking to kill and breaking to retrieve. Backing can be held off and kept separate for awhile. The retrieve is the most difficult to perfect, for most dogs use this to defy the trainer. For that reason, when breaking dogs, trainers should only train for **one thing at a time**. Retrieves should not be forced until steadiness to wing, shot and kill are perfected first.

If we look at the dog's point of view this might be understood. We encourage dogs to chase for two to three years and then suddenly require them to stop chasing. All too quickly we ask them to "chase" again to dead birds. We further compound their mental faculties by **requiring** retrieves back to hand. Many dogs become confused. Trainers get angry. Dogs are stressed more when trainers **force** them to retrieve when not fully understanding what is expected. Trainers have told me time and again, "My dog knows what he is supposed to do." Hogwash! That belief has ruined dogs by causing problems they could never solve.

Not all dogs can be broke easily or effectively using the same methods. Breaking should be done with a trainer and helper when possible. Experienced trainers can do a good job of breaking by themselves if they are free from emotion and anger when training. Sometimes we need someone else to caution and warn us when we are not up to our usual training disposition.

A dog broke with a helper, must also be broke by the trainer shooting and killing birds over the dog himself. This is important, for dogs condition their

426

Professional trainer Jim Basham (Ohio) facing a dog while releasing a pigeon behind his back. This allows him to control the dog by position and intimidation which is an excellent technique.
(Photo by Jeannie Wagner)

Jim is also doing an excellent job of kicking a pigeon into the air for the shot. Making a bird fly in the best direction for the dog is no easy task.
(Photo by Jeannie Wagner)

responses as they are taught in rote training. They must be worked around several people, horses and different grounds when being broke. Obedience and control with two people working a dog does not equate automatically to one person or several people.

How do trainers tell when they are making progress? The signs are elusive. It often may take several weeks before any progress is noted. Before that time, an inexperienced trainer may have given up, or abandoned one method for another which results in confusing his dog. Adjustments should be made based on how dogs react, behave and progress. If there is any doubt, dogs should be put up for a few days or weeks and started again at the point training stopped. Their progress from being laid up will surprise handlers. Dogs apparently continue to think about what they were doing.

Dogs must be stopped by voice command and have a good working relationship with their trainers to be broke.

Breaking is started by flushing over a staunch point, and by hollering "WHOA" as the dog breaks at the flush of a bird. The trainer stands in place and waits for his dog to return which most will do. He then stands his dog up at the place he pointed for a minute or so, praises him, and then casts him on to hunt for another bird where the process is again repeated. From time to time, a bird should be planted at the same place while the dog is out chasing, so that whenever he returns, he will find it and point again. He will learn to return quicker and with less hesitation, and will hesitate to chase if he thinks more than one bird will flush. Dogs like to point better than to chase, and given a choice, they will stop chasing.

Once a dog's enthusiasm for chasing has been dulled,

The method used for fastening a pigeon to the pigeon pole.

At an Iams Seminar and Clinic by Roy Pelton he is shown demonstrating the proper way to restrain a pointing dog while a helper flushes a pigeon using the pigeon pole technique. He claims that dogs can be broke just using this method which lends itself to city yards or small areas.

and we must discourage barking and panting when being held from chasing, and he shows good response to commands, the serious job of breaking can be done. Not before.

One method is to have a helper flush the bird when the trainer holds the dog by the collar with the open hand held in his flank. This method is repeated until the dog will stay with only a hand in his flank. There is no hurry because repetition, patience, kindness and consistency are essential here. It may take three or four sessions each week using three to five birds each time (pigeons) for two or three weeks. Some dogs require more time. The trainer should gradually work toward taking both hands off the dog and stroking his back and back stroking his tail and frequently pushing him at the shoulders toward the bird. He must slowly work the dog to a hands off condition to stay. If he continues to hold the dog by the collar, the dog becomes conditioned to this and will pull against the collar as long as he is held by it.

Once the dog learns to stay, the trainer should work him by himself for a few sessions. When he breaks, he should be run down and brought back by carrying him or walking him back by the collar while being scolded mildly then set up and sweet talked at the place he broke. If the dog is difficult to catch, a check cord/strap can be used to help.

The dog learns a little bit of what is wanted each time he is chased down and returned to the point of flush. Eventually force may be necessary. This is administered by twisting the collar and lifting up on it when walking him back to the point of flush. The first few times the twisting is light and is increased as necessary on other breaks until the air is shut off

This method is effective when breaking a dog for the dummy launcher by a trainer working alone.

After the dummy is on the ground, the trainer lifts one leg over the dog while holding its collar, or places his open hand in the flank and praises the dog before releasing it for the retrieve. A few sessions of this should teach the dog what is expected and the trainer can begin blocking by voice and hand signal followed later only by voice command.

and released just before the dog becomes wobbly legged. Trainers should holler WHOA when chasing the dog. After a time the trainer should not chase but command the dog to return.

This method of breaking is not recommended for trainers in poor physical condition. Dogs may need to be chased for a half mile or more before they will allow the trainer to catch them. A horse should be used later, if available, but the first chasing down should be done on foot. Helpers can also be spotted out and hidden along the bird's flight path to waylay a dog. All-age dogs can be impossible to catch after flush or from pushing a bird out at the trainer's approach. They will tax the ability and ingenuity of the best trainers and helpers.

I first break dogs on pigeons, quail, chukars and pheasants in that order so they learn that they will not be allowed to break and chase these birds. Each one in turn will likely cause dogs to break a few times and need correction. I always say that when dogs are worked and corrections are not necessary that it was a waste of time, but it sure is a good feeling. That's part of it.

Another breaking method is with the check cord/strap for restraint. The dog is first held at flush with no slack. Three to six pigeons are put out in releasers in a small area about an acre in size. Birds should be arranged so that the dog will work into the wind and the flight of each bird is in the opposite direction to the line of or circular placement of the releasers. This plan does not always work, for we want to have the bird fly in the opposite direction of the next releaser, so the dog can be heeled on to another bird and opposite the flight path of the last one.

432

The dog is led into the first bird. He should be allowed to establish point, styled up and then praised. If the dog has good natural style he may be touched less and "Good boy" or "Good girl" may suffice before flushing. When the bird is flushed, the dog is held tightly by the check cord/strap, and once the bird has disappeared from sight, a HEEL command is given and the dog guided toward the next bird by the collar. The trainer holds and leads the dog by the collar until he forgets the previous bird and feels that he can control the dog by voice (or whistle) before releasing. This may be six feet or a hundred feet. Under no circumstance should the dog be allowed to go back to the place he pointed last. He must be stopped.

A blank pistol is normally fired at each flush, but for some dogs it may be better to delay shooting until the dog is steady to flush. While it is usually best to train for only one thing at a time, flush and shot may be combined.

It helps to remove the check cord/strap after a few sessions to see if the dog can be controlled by voice commands to stay put at flush. The check cord/strap must be abandoned when progress is made. Dogs will learn to stay when it is attached, but not when it is off.

This work is trial and error mostly. Artificial conditions are set up which result in good learning experiences with luck, and are difficult to get right every time. No two trainers will make the same progress with the same dog under the same conditions. One will do a better job than the other.

Dogs must be chased down when the check cord/strap is removed and they break. When dogs ignore the trainers' commands they need more training under restraint, or more pressure must be used when twisting the collar and then taken back to where the bird flushed.

Collar twisting should be done only to the extent necessary to obtain the proper response. Unfortunately, some dogs will need all the air shut off until they nearly pass out. This should not be done unless as a last resort and somewhere those dogs will have to receive praise for something. Most dogs will not fight or bite, but some will struggle to free themselves. I have never seen a dog where this method did not work, but as I say nothing is one hundred percent. Trainers must use their head and search for acceptable solutions.

When he was still living, I trained with Collis (Bill) Mitchell and his German Shorthaired Pointers. I am not sure if he developed this method or borrowed it from another trainer—but it is extemely effective, and is the one I described. This is an excerpt from an article he wrote in *Hunting Dog* magazine, September 1968:

"Listening to other handlers, I have abused my bird dog to the whip, ear twisting, and subjective degradation of the dog's ego. After all this, the best method which has worked for me is that of chasing the dog from the point where it broke, grabbing it back-handed by the collar, twisting the collar and cutting off the dog's wind and physically carrying the dog back to the point from which it broke. This method boils down to simple formula for the further the dog breaks, the less wind it will have when returning to the point of breaking."

"This method does not call for cries of wailing from the gallery or field trial committees as the dog physically has no ability to cry out in pain nor to bark in disapproval."

"This is a universal method of training steadiness to point whether it be in field trials or in practice."

434

Roy Pelton at Iams Seminar demonstrating how to teach the WHOA command using a pinch collar. Used with a check cord it can help in chasing down a dog and correcting it.

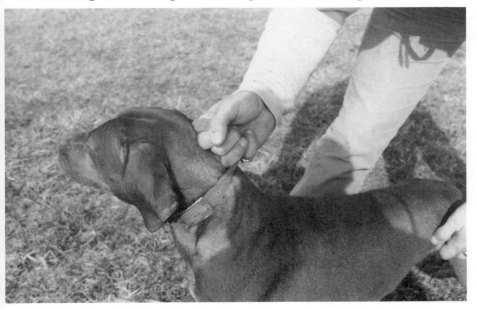

The collar twisting method of discipline shown with a light twist. This method is not practical to use if the collar is too tight. Chain collars for obedience should never be used.

A word of caution to trainers. This method should never be used with a choke chain. It is too easy to lose a finger or two. Dogs should wear leather or nylon collars at least one inch wide.

Another method Bill used in breaking was by using a fenced in area about an acre or less in size. This eliminated the need for a long chase and excessive punishment.

Both the methods just described can be used, or with variations as necessary, to break dogs to wing, shot and kill. Some dogs need to retrieve birds immediately. Others must not be allowed to retrieve since they require more control and discipline before they will submit to working as a team with the trainer and his gun.

Trainers working alone can use a check cord/strap around a stake placed behind the pointing dog. I prefer putting the dog between my legs and holding him across the loins with slight pressure, and I use this method successfully when working young dogs on the dummy launcher, and when starting to break older dogs. Then the bird is released remotely from a releaser with a string, electric or electronic device and the shot is fired. The dog should be held until he settles down before taking him by the collar and stepping back to the side. It will usually take several flushes before he will begin to settle down.

The next step is to get in front and make him stay until the bird is released. Again the shot may be optional. This method is by blocking and intimidation. Eventually the dog will stay on the command "STAY." The command should always be used **only** once, then correction as needed without punishment. The dog should be made to stand and stay for varying times and taught to wait for the release command or be given a tap on the head for release, or both, or be taken by the collar and heeled away from the bird's flight.

Dogs trained this way will need to be chased down several times, because they invariably escape when the handlers are flushing the birds. Correction should follow along the lines previously described.

Dogs anticipating commands must learn that the trainer decides if he will allow the retrieve and only when commanded to or when released. Dogs must be taught not to break position without a voice command, or a tap on the head.

Sometimes in competition it is not practical to walk back to the dog and release him for a retrieve, so it is important that he be taught both ways.

Most dogs will continue to break from time to time after they are well broke. They should be ordered back, or chased down and returned to the place of the flush. They should be set up and commanded to STAY only once. If they creep, they should be set back and again commanded to STAY only once. This may have to be repeated several times and in time they will want to handle correctly.

When breaking dogs they should not be **forced** to retrieve as an additional requirement. They may retrieve if they will, but if they do not, no harsh words or punishment should be used. The trainer should walk away in the opposite direction. It is natural for dogs to chase, or follow, and they will usually come toward the trainer with birds. By watching and turning at the right instant, the trainer can take the bird or hold the dog and praise him. Dogs should be praised before taking birds from them. It is natural for them not to want to give up their birds in training. It takes time and patience.

Dogs develop methods of handling, relieving and escaping stress from training situations at the expense of style, intensity, staunchness, manners and control. Style can be lost on a trainer's grounds, or just on birds handled by man, and the behavior will not be carried over to other grounds or on wild birds. A dropped tail, crouched pointing, sitting, or blinking action are visible expressions of distress, and the dog's training should be suspended for awhile. Trainers should remember that there are no hard and fast rules for breaking to wing and shot. Rote, repetition, patience and time usually works.

It is important that pigeons be used for the **complete** breaking process first before using quail, chukars and pheasants for breaking, although dogs must be worked on them before breaking commences.

Most dogs can be green broke within a few months and will beg their handlers to take them out time after time. It is a sure sign that the training has gone well, and the dogs like working for the trainer.

Once dogs are broke, it will take about one year of further work and experience before they will become polished workers. They must still be corrected from breaking, catching birds, stopping to flush and pushing birds out when sent to relocate.

One owner I worked with kept track of the time it took to break the dog which was a total of fourteen hours over a period of several months since the dog could only be worked a couple times a month. The best dog I ever had for breaking took only nine pigeons within a week's time and was truly competitive in trials without being worked on any other species of birds before competition. Usually the best performance in training is not matched in trials. The brace mates create higher competitive spirit in some dogs.

When dogs are first entered in field trials and break, the handlers should not just sit on horseback and watch or stand and gape. They should run the dogs down and put them on lead. Punishment is not necessary, but scolding helps. If the judges feel that the handlers corrected to the disadvantage of the brace mates they can do whatever they feel necessary. Dogs that break are not going to win or place and correction is warranted.

Once a dog breaks in a trial, many judges turn deaf ears and backs to the dogs and handlers. Rules require that handlers be disqualified from the stake and reported to the field trial committee for striking or severly punishing their dogs.

Many dogs are only broke to a given situation with one trainer/handler. Professional trainers/handlers can do outstanding work with dogs, but their owners still can do little with them in competition unless they work in close association with the professional trainers in breaking and learn to handle their dogs.

TEACHING DOGS TO POINT

There are pointing dogs, for whatever reasons, that will not point and must be taught. Sometimes they will point only certain birds. Dogs worked too much on just one type bird for too long a time may ignore other game bird scent. They must be taught that other scents represent birds which must be pointed for the trainer.

Picking up a pointing dog and spinning him around and around to improve staunchness can cause problems. Most dogs will become staunch on point once they understand what is expected and develop enough desire.

One method of teaching pointing, whether the bird is planted or put out in a releaser, is to flush the bird and place another there before the dog returns. With releasers, if the dog does not point, the bird is released anyway and when the dog is chasing another bird is placed in it. After the dog returns, he will usually point. Initially, one bird can be placed in the releaser and one planted next to it with either one being flushed the first time.

In the puppy Chapter a discussion was given of teaching puppies to point and this method can also be used on older dogs.

Sometimes it helps to shoot birds after leading the dog onto point on leash. Giving a dog the bird's head to eat may help some dogs, but not all. Habits are hard to break later. Some dogs should be given the birds to do whatever they will with them. Most dogs only eat an entire bird feathers and all once.

When putting birds down for a dog in training, the heads should always face into the wind. This helps when flushing so that the birds do not flush in the dog's face tempting him to jump up and try to catch them. This is a serious fault and must be prevented. Breaking dogs of this habit will usually create other problems equally as hard to solve.

GETTING TO DOGS ON POINT

In early training, dogs have a tendency to break point at the approach of their trainers and jump in on the birds. It is essential that the trainers get to the dogs and flush the birds. Most important is the need to get to the dog, pet, talk to it, stroke it and then flush the bird when restraining the dog long enough for the bird to escape.

Each trainer works out his own pet way of getting to his dogs on point and to keep them from pushing out the birds until flushed.

A bird can be placed inside a wire circle of ten foot diameter, or larger, which delays the dog on point long enough usually for the handler to get there and style him up and flush the bird. This can be made from three or four foot field fence wire. This method must be used sparingly. A friend who lived in the city worked his dog on the wire enclosure and when taken home he immediately started pointing the trees having chicken wire encircling them for protection from the rabbits. Another method is to put a check cord/strap on the dog which is in effect an extension of the trainer's arms. When the dog points, the trainer must go where he can quickly step on the check cord/strap to restrain him. The trainer should **walk** up the check cord/strap and not pick it up in his hands.

The practice of running to a dog on point can cause problems. It may be done in a dog's early training to intimidate him to stay on point, but should not be overdone as it will result in softening on point or blinking. It is better to practice slow approaches in full sight of the dog.

A good method is to have a helper stationed near the birds so that he can quickly get to the dog on point before he breaks and jumps in.

Then there are bird dogs which point so staunchly when young that approaching them on point is no problem.

441

Professional trainer Jim Basham shown styling and staunching up his young dog by touch and praise.
(Photo by Jeannie Wagner)

A large circle of farm fencing with a bird placed inside in a releaser or slept to keep a dog from flushing and catching the bird. This gives the trainer adequate time usually to get to his dog to control it, stroke and staunch it up.

BIRD PLANTING

Trainers must use pen raised birds and put them out in the field for dogs to point. The human scent on birds causes problems in the dogs tracking the planter to the birds and developing bad habits pointing.

There is no **good** way to mask human scent. Rubber boots do not help and putting birds out from a motorcycle, tractor or horse does not fool many dogs. Pointing dogs **must** get used to working birds with human scent.

It helps for trainers to first walk through the field where birds are to be put out and make many tracks. The dogs then should be run over the same area before putting down birds. This helps keep the dogs from tracking the trainer's scent to the birds.

Manufactured scents may help, but my experience indicates that the human scent is still on birds and dogs smell it along with the manufactured scent and the scent of the bird itself. Dogs learn to associate human scent with finding birds. Most dogs quickly learn to play the "game" of hunting for human scent on birds or a combination of scents.

It is interesting to note that poor style on birds with human scent is not retained when the human scent has left or has never been on the birds.

Dogs should be allowed to hunt free to the birds without leading them onto the birds but this is not always possible. They should learn to hunt to find the birds and trainers hope they will be in the general vicinity where put out. There are methods which keep

Roy Pelton is placing a pigeon down in cover by putting its head under a wing and pulling the legs back until it relaxes. This technique can be used on any bird and dizzying is not necessary.

Water work is excellent exercise and training for performance dogs. It encourages dogs to pick-up and bring back dummies tossed out by hand or by a dummy launcher. They eagerly retrieve dead pigeons with locked wings.

birds in place, but these methods should not be used in every training session. Methods and birds must be varied.

Birds can be dizzied and their heads tucked under the wings, put in a bird releaser, a baby sock put over their heads, placed in a mesh bag, put in a wire enclosure, their wings wrapped around each other, Velcro around body and wings and any number of other methods. I prefer putting out birds with the head under a wing and then tuck the bird head first in a clump of grass without dizzying, wrapping their wings until they lock or using game bird releasers. The birds should always be wiped in a circle on surrounding cover at or near the area they are placed.

Chukars have a bad habit of running. A rubber band wrapped around the legs will keep them in place and when handlers try to flush they will struggle and free themselves. Sometimes the rubber band must be pulled loose by the trainer.

Weights and pieces of cardboard tied to the feet prevents birds from flying far after flushing.

There are fifty different animal species subject to a form of hypnosis. It is believed to be an innate fear response that freezes an animal or bird. Eye contact alone may do it and it increases immobility time. The phenomenon of **tonic immobility** is a highly adaptable fear response. This is why birds will stay put when their head is placed under a wing and put down on their side or back.

Some trainers recommend pulling a few feathers and sprinkling them around the planted bird. This could lead to feather sight pointing and unproductives the same as putting a bird down and **assuming** it is still there when a dog points. The tendency is for trainers

445

to force their dogs to stand and stay causing dependency and unproductives.

In trials, gloves must be worn when putting out birds and they should not touch the planter's body. My experience causes me to believe this practice is unnecessary because it is impossible to get rid of human scent from the gloves, or pants and shoes as the bird planter walks out to put down the birds.

DELAYED CHASE

A delayed chase will occur at either flush or shot, or after a dog has been heeled away. The dog intentionally follows the flight of a bird after having stood steady on point and the bird is gone.

In training, the dog should be brought under control and returned to the spot of the infraction and made to stand and stay before being heeled away again. A scolding or mild punishment may also be required before or when the dog is being returned.

In field trials, the delayed chase is a major infraction and dogs are usually ordered up. Handlers should not allow their dogs to continue even if the judge does not order the dogs up. But, it just might be that the judges did not see it happen, or did not consider the dog had a delayed chase and place it. If the dog is picked up by the handler, he should be put on lead and scolded. Dogs quickly learn to take advantage of inconsistent handling. They learn when and where discipline will be given, so dogs **must** be corrected in field trials as in training.

STOP TO FLUSH

Stop to flushes are sometimes difficult to evaluate properly and when in doubt they should not be called by judges in field trials. There can be too much subjectivity involved.

The simplest method of training dogs to stop at flush is with wild flushed, or by using electric or electronic releasers and releasing the bird when the dog first smells it. The dog is run down when it chases and is brought back to the same spot. This training is done when first breaking dogs to a flush.

A stop to flush happens when birds flush close to a dog that were not pointed and the dog does not chase. Dogs can be running full speed and overrun birds without smelling them and cause the birds to fly before the dog acknowledges their flight by stopping and showing no interest in following them.

Birds being roaded by dogs often fly for reasons other than knowing a dog is following their tracks and the dogs are charged with pushing birds out when they did not. The nearness of the handler, judges and gallery cause ground vibrations which makes them nervous and precipitates their flight.

A shot is fired by the trainer/handler if within shotgun range of his dog at flush. Then the trainer/handler should go to his dog and release him if he has trained him to stay and wait for the release. It is foolish to require dogs to stand and stay when a hundred yards or more away or for the handler to fire a shot. Dogs having stop to flushes at these distances, or when the handler is out of sight, should not be expected to stand until the handler arrives or is found by a scout and then be charged with an unproductive.

447

Smart dogs will release themselves, ignore the direction the bird flew and continue hunting. Dogs do stop and stay when birds flush and most do it because they are trained that way, sometimes unintentionally. A quick look at the dog's non-verbal communication should indicate the situation to his handler.

To charge a dog with faulting on a flush, he must deliberately cause the bird's flight and be intent on catching it. It must be a deliberate act by the dog! Dogs must "point" flushed birds the same as sight pointing birds on the ground and not appear whipped in the process. Some dogs feel badly and it shows. This should be enough indication that the act was not deliberate.

Dogs are usually excused when running **with** the wind when a bird flushes and the dogs stop. When running into the wind most judges cannot understand why dogs fail to smell birds other than believing they have a **bad** nose. There are many situations when a dog is running into the wind where he fails to catch scent in time to point. What about dogs running into the wind and pass birds up before pointing. Only by the grace of God the birds failed to flush, but in this situation the dogs are credited with a find and may later be declared the winner.

Dogs should be given the benefit of doubt, for if they were at fault on one bird where there is some doubt it will usually be removed on the next find. Dogs with nothing but a stop to flush will not win if it was their only bird contact in most stakes.

A few dogs ignore birds flushing wild and it may be a form of blinking, but we have no way of knowing the dogs did see the birds.

448

COLLARING

A pointing dog is required to leave a flushed bird when not shot, never follow its flight, and continue on hunting. This may be done in two ways--by voice command or by taking a dog by the collar and turn it without voice command to continue hunting when birds are not shot for retrieving.

The majority of AKC pointing breeds may be collared, and it is the handler's option if he chooses to heel his dog away by voice command. The breeds which are not collared can only be heeled away from a flush by voice command.

I do not know why collaring is preferred. I have heard many arguments relating to training, manners and style between the two methods.

I have observed a multitude of different methods for physically collaring dogs. Many were offensive to me and bordered on training in trials, intimidation and unnecessary hands on control. If there are correct methods for collaring, they have escaped my observation and nothing in AKC rules gives any directions on a proper method.

By contrast, I have seen many dogs which were sent on by voice command that would thrill an experienced handler or judge. These dogs demonstrated excellent biddability, training, manners, extreme style and happiness or animation.

Trainers and handlers argue that it provides an opportunity to touch, pet and sweet talk their dogs which improves style and enthusiasm. This is important in early training. The best example I watched was with handlers at the National Championship at Ames Plantation, but a few when touched let down their style as if they expected punishment which may have been

449

coincidental. The dog felt it might have done wrong.

Heeling a dog from flush by voice command is quick, clean and efficient. It is easy to teach a dog to do, and many trainers/handlers with breeds which allow collaring send their dogs away from the flush by voice command.

Different procedures may be necessary for horseback handlers and foot handlers. The horseback handler must exercise greater control over his dog in order to remount and continue on. The foot handler is in better control as a rule. Both must have absolute control in these situations, if they expect to demonstrate winning performances. A dog returning to the location of the flush or which follows the flight of the bird after being taken on will be charged with an error. The severity will vary with individual judges and many will order dogs taken up for returning to the area of the flush.

Trainers must develop their own methods which always begins with physical collaring and leading their dogs away from flush until they forget it and continue on hunting. Handlers who compete in other breed trials where collaring is not permitted must train both ways in order to win.

Handlers in trials under the American Field umbrella may be requested by judges to send their dogs after a flush to point singles. Meat hunters would never consider the practice of not allowing their dogs to follow the flight of birds. Field trialers who use their dogs for meat hunting can make a circuitous route to effect the same thing without undoing previous training for field trial competition.

RELOCATION

We want to train and develop field trial dogs so that their birds are always pinned directly in front of them. But, different pointing breeds work and point somewhat differently. Some dogs will stop at the first scent contact and point rigidly. Often this pointing behavior can be attributed to trainers who take short cuts to winning and **teach** their dogs to point **scent** instead of birds. Pointing dogs having short tails look less stylish than those with long tails held at twelve o'clock looking as though they are pointing the sky with them.

Birds run off from a dog's point and dogs must learn to relocate automatically once they realize that birds have moved out. But, trainers interfere with their natural intelligence and make them stay until released or heeled (collared) away in a different direction.

The best trainers/handlers can read their dogs correctly, and will often take them on without attempting a relocation. This is good if the birds have flown which otherwise makes it a waste of time looking, and does nothing positive for the dog's mental attitude. It may also be better to take a nonproductive than send the dog to relocate and have a bump. Handlers may often choose to do this on the first nonproductive, but will not take a second one willingly.

When the dog is released for a relocation, he should not potter and poke along on ground tracks, but move quickly and cautiously along the scent trail until the body scent becomes strong and then caution up and point to keep from flushing the bird. Judges often credit dogs with bumps when a bird flies when being trailed by dogs. These birds fly from fear of the handler, judges and gallery moreso than because they are being pursued by a dog. Pheasants will put a good distance between themselves and the dogs before flying--it is just part of their survival and feeling of safety.

Wild birds, especially pheasants, run off or fly when they hear human voices. The loud noise of handlers and gallery in field trials never helps a dog's situation.

Handlers must realize that they can lose out because of subjective judgment by the judges when birds flush on relocation. Sometimes it is better to accept an unproductive and continue, but if the relocation means the difference in winning the stake outright, the risk should be worth it just like it is to send a dog on a long retrieve. Dogs which cannot handle running birds are poor candidates for winning championship stakes. The best field trial dogs can and do handle running birds.

ROADING BIRDS

Roading is used as a term when a dog follows along the path of a moving bird and when also being exercised in a "roading" harness. There may be some ambiguity, but for the lack of a better explanation it remains in the field trial lexicon as does "whoa" and "no" which may sound alike.

It is best to wait until dogs are steady to wing and shot to put too much effort into roading work. Less time is involved and there is less stress put on the dogs since they already have learned to obey well. It is easier to teach when done after dogs are broke. It can be done earlier, but it should wait until the dog is prepared.

Roading is teaching dogs not to overrun or try to catch game they are tracking and point when the bird stops. It is natural for dogs of any age to learn to track.

Training can be done by cutting the flight feathers of a bird and plant it in the usual way. Allow the dog to point and cause the bird to run since it cannot fly. After pretending to search for it, allowing time for the bird to move off, the trainer taps his dog on the head or releases it by a voice command and as the dog moves along tracking the bird he is restrained by a check cord/strap as the trainer says "e-e-e-easy" and follows. When the trainer sees the bird out front, he stops the dog and praises him. He may then "flush" the bird by picking it up and throwing it, or continue to close in until the dog points. The trainer then picks up the bird and carries it back to the dog and allows him to smell it and praises him. A few repetitions and most dogs work like experts.

The final test then is to leave the check cord/strap off and use birds that run off and are capable of flying where the dogs can learn to stop to flush, then wait to be released or taught to release themselves in a direction away from the bird's flight.

Trials other than the American Kennel Club will allow dogs to follow marked birds. The Shoot-To-Retrieve Association has a time limit after which the marked bird can be hunted again. Judges in some of the American Field trials will have dogs follow flushed covies to work singles. It all depends on the standards of performance.

BACKING

Backing or honoring is the act of one or more dogs **pointing** a dog **on point.** It is instinctive or a trained behavior which is essential if two dogs are to be worked or hunted together as is done in field trials.

Pointing dogs must learn to have confidence in brace mates otherwise they will learn to push out birds, or steal point if they are supposed to back. Backing dogs also must learn to have confidence in the pointing dogs. Jealousy between either dog will result in problems that may take considerable work to overcome.

The requirement for pointing dogs to back is utilitarian as well as esthetic--a part of class.

Good dogs will back instinctively and be as stylish as when on point themselves. Not all dogs have the same instinctive inclination to back and must be trained. The style of a dog trained to point may not always be as pretty as one which backs instinctively. Training is still required for dogs with the natural ability to back, but much less and in different ways.

When teaching dogs to back, the dog used on point should have great style with a high head and tail so there is no question to the backing dog that he is on **point.**

Trainers should avoid bringing backing dogs up behind the pointing dog where they can smell either the birds or the dog. They should be kept far back and off to the side and should be stopped whenever the backing dog is seen. Dogs learn to pretend not to see pointing dogs, or only back when smelling birds the other dog is pointing.

The trainer is check cording his dog on a walking pigeon
to teach it to point when the bird stops and not try to rush
in and catch it.

The trainer who has no access to a different breed can
take the silhouette and paint it to represent any other
breed. The lone trainer is preparing to flush for the
"pointing dog."   (Photo by Jim McCord)

It takes a good stylish pointing dog to teach backing, otherwise it is difficult to teach it. Look again--this is a dummy dog guaranteed always to be stylish and rigid on point.

Field Champion Cider Mill Prairie Schooner and Prairie Cotton Mo pointing and backing. Owned by Regis Cantini (Ohio). It is possible to finish a field champion title without a back in AKC trials, but all must be trained to honor another dog's point, and back when the opportunity is presented.

456

My policy is never teach backing intentionally until after the dogs are fully broke. It is much easier and takes less time with fewer problems. This is not to say it cannot be done earlier, for many trainers believe this is as important as breaking.

Trainers should alternate the position of their backing dogs from directly behind to the side and front until their dogs will back from any position on sight.

I have seen dogs start to back pointing dogs head on and come around behind and move up close before backing. Then some dogs smell the pointing dog in a stationary position and point him. Others may do nothing else but follow the brace mate around the course and back everytime he piddles or stops for any reason.

A few handlers delight in demonstrating backing at every opportunity. Too much backing is bad and handlers should never purposely put their dogs in backing situations because the effects of dependence, jealousy and stress are harmful.

The American Kennel Club has varied from no requirement, to one in which the first two placed dogs **must have demonstrated a back,** to the present requirement which is like the American Field where a dog is expected to back when encountering his brace mate on point and must be penalized if he does not, but a back is **not** required to win a regular or a championship stake. All of the newer associations now under the American Field umbrella require backs for placement. The Shoot-To-Retrieve Association scores only **one** back, and the handler is required to hold the backing dog by the collar to prevent any interference with the pointing dog's retrieve.

Requiring backing for placement once caused all kinds

Professional trainer Jim Basham (Ohio) working at backing dogs by himself. Amateur trainers should avoid working two dogs at a time. The bottom photo shows Jim teaching an English Setter to back which is pointing the pointing dog as it should be done. Bringing dogs in behind all the time does not teach backing.

of problems and grief from the handlers to the club officials, and was often a costly requirement. A bird is needed for each dog called back to point for the backing dog, and pointing dogs when called back on planted birds do not always show their best style or manners. In a retrieving stake, the pointed bird must be shot and gunners have been known to miss a dozen or more birds in succession. The better dogs in the stake usually failed because of the artificial situation and sickly style of some pointing dogs and poor gunners. Under no circumstance should judges have a dead bird thrown out for a retrieve.

Judges on course would have handlers call back their dogs from an out front cast and bring them in on a backing dog hidden in cover. It always seemed to work to the detriment of one or both dogs. More often than not the birds would run or fly off before the brace mate could be called in because of the loud hollering, long wait, or both.

Field trial situations are artificial, and there is no reason to exhort them. Any interference with a dog's natural ability or normal training creates stress, and artificial situations must be handled to mollify but not to exacerbate it.

In field trials, there are really just two situations which call for a brace mate to back. The first is on course where he sees his brace mate on point. The key is **see,** and has nothing to do with distance. The handler of the pointing dog approaches his dog and waits until the backing dog's handler is in a suitable position to handle his dog before flushing the bird. He fires his gun and once steadiness to wing and shot is demonstrated, he heels (or collars) him away from the flight of the bird and sends him on hunting. At that time the handler of the backing dog is free to take his dog on.

The second situation is in retrieving stakes when time is called on point, either on course or in a designated bird field. The requirement is the same as before, but here the backing dog must wait until the pointing dog completes his retrieve and is ordered on. Then the backing dog can be released and taken on hunting. Judges can release the backing dog if the pointing dog is slow at the retrieve or when the handler takes time to clean the feathers out of his dog's mouth, or water him. When this is done, the backing handler need not wait and should heel his dog on hunting.

Whenever the pointing dog's handler spends too much time searching it is stressful for the backing dog. If time is not called the handler should ask to take his dog on. If the pointing dog's handler cannot locate the bird and sends him to relocate, the backing handler can release his dog, but he should not go and hunt where the bird was pointed.

Trainers should train only as much as needed to fix backing and no more, and handlers should not try to get into backing situations.

TRAINING TO RETRIEVE

There are **two** kinds of pointing dogs--those that retrieve and those that do not. Training to retrieve takes much desire and enthusiasm out of dogs and is a measure of how easy or difficult dogs are to train. Stress affects pointing dogs made to retrieve more than those not required to retrieve, and can negatively affect range, style, desire, intensity, application and independence.

Young puppy and derby dogs are encouraged, taught and allowed to chase birds with reckless abandon. As they mature, they are then forced to quit chasing. **That** they can handle. But, then the birds are shot, and they must stay until **given** the command to "chase" out to the bird and bring it back. Confusing? Trainers must try to think like dogs.

The severest stresses occur in teaching dogs to retrieve. When first training on retrieving, the dogs usually run out with enthusiasm to the birds, pick them up, then look to their trainers as if unsure what to do next and drop the birds. A perfectly natural reaction. By this time the dogs have learned to obey and try to please, but now they may refuse to return to their handlers for fear of having done something wrong by chasing out to the bird and want to avoid punishment. This is the **critical** phase of retrieving. Trainers must then avoid the mistake of **forcing** dogs to retrieve. The trainers should turn around as the dog reaches the bird and walk in the opposite direction which resurrects the dogs natural instinct to chase or follow back to the trainer. As the dog passes with the bird the handler steps on the check cord/strap, catches the dog and praises him **without** trying to take the bird.

Birds should never be taken without first praising the dogs, and many dogs will readily give the birds to the handlers which is the first step toward understanding what is expected. Dogs must be happy and proud of this accomplishment, and the trainers should work at making them that way.

Punishing dogs when they do not retrieve properly in

461

the breaking process is wrong and counterproductive. This only confuses and causes dogs to eat birds, pick feathers, chew birds to shreds, bury them, run off with them and **not** retrieve.

Dogs must understand what is expected in retrieving. One method that helps is to have a helper hold the dog when the bird is flushed and shot, and the trainer walks out, picks up the bird, brings it to the dog, and praises him. He may then elect to throw out the bird, fire his blank pistol, and send the dog, but not require a retrieve to hand just yet. If the dog does retrieve, this indicates a quicker and better chance of success. After doing this a few times dogs learn what is expected. Then they can be released to retrieve by a voice command and a tap on the head at the same time. Depending on the dog's behavior, the trainer and helper can walk in the other direction or wait for the dog.

Trainers must remember that teaching retrieving for most dogs must wait until they are steady to wing and shot. Dogs will still break after being broke. When they do, the trainers should run them down and the first few times just lead them back to the place the bird flushed and offer praise. What for? Well, they can think of some reason. If dogs fail to stay after a few repetitions, the twisted collar method should be used. Dogs should never be whipped for not retrieving, and when the dogs break, the trainers should stop or catch their dogs, set them up at the place they pointed and retrieve the birds back to them. They may elect to throw out the bird, shoot, and send the dog for a retrieve.

Patience is important in this teaching. Trainers must remember that even after they have taught dogs to retrieve perfectly with the dummy launcher, balls,

462

sticks, Frisbees, water retrieving, etc., that it still takes work to perfect their retrieves on birds.

No two dogs respond or work alike in retrieving training and it is important for trainers to recognize this fact. Retrieving makes or breaks potentially good dogs.

Fresh killed birds shed an unusual amount of feathers in a dog's mouth which may be a bird's escape mechanism, but after some experience dogs become better at picking up fresh killed birds.

I always give my dogs the last bird killed to carry in when field trialing which boosts their ego and pride. This is not always without problems for some dogs will want to stop hunting after the first bird and carry it. One of my dogs insisted on carrying something when we quit and it didn't matter what it was and was happy with a glove or a paper towel.

Dogs sent to retrieve must first learn to **mark** the fall of birds and any distraction or distress will cause them not to mark. Some dogs learn to mark at incredible distances and others are under too much stress and forget. When sent, dogs should go out quickly, pick up the marked birds and without hesitation, turn and run back and give them to their handlers. Not all dogs are ever this proficient but do manage "acceptable" retrieves.

It may take some dogs up to a year before they will make these quick retrieves to hand and a bird shot to pieces should not alter this ideal, but usually does which reflects on their training.

Once dogs have been given every bit of progressive work at retrieving without force and do not work satisfactorily, force retrieving training must be done.

My method does not involve punishment. I force them

Some dogs are very hard mouthed and must be stopped from clamping down on birds and ruining them. Giving them birds when young helps solve this problem. But this dummy is constructed of a round section of a tree limb with small finishing nails driven around the circumference for its length and covered with several pheasant wings.

When a dog returns part way and drops the dummy short, the trainer should go out and force its mouth open, insert the dummy, and give a HOLD command before taking the collar and leading him back to the place the dummy was launched. He then takes the dummy on a GIVE or DROP command.

to hold and carry birds first and then force them to deliver birds to me. And, this usually begins with the dummy launcher and then when required for retrieving birds it takes little time and effort. Dogs must be forced to hold birds until commanded to drop them and learn it is fun without fear of punishment.

Training dogs to retrieve teaches us the most about dog behavior. It shortens range temporarily and some permanently no matter how good a job the trainers do. Some dogs of course are ruined by impatience and wrong methods which would not have happened with a better trainer.

Trainers should not worry too much about the loss in range and help encourage their dogs to have fun and regain confidence. Too many trainers put winning ahead of proper dog development and basic training, but sometimes do luck through with a champion title with poorly trained dogs.

How many misses can a retrieving dog stand before he decides to break and chase the missed bird? That too is part of his training. How many birds can fly over his head without him trying to catch them? That too is another part of his training. How many times can he stand for his backing brace mate to break for his retrieve? That too is part of his training. In time, he will learn to maintain his composure, trust his handler, and be steady and mannerly in all these situations.

When a dog moves to **mark** a bird he should **not** be faulted and judges often order them up unfairly. **A reasonable move to mark** is permitted whenever the dog waits to be released. How far is reasonable? It should not make any difference if the **only** purpose was to mark. If his handler hollers WHOA as he moves, this

465

is proof that he thought his dog was breaking. That may be wrong. He may have become nervous and acted spontaneously as if in training. The dog may have had no intention of breaking. Good dogs will eventually overcome poor handling, poor conditions and poor judging. That is a fact.

Water retrieving training is excellent for teaching retrieving later on land. Dogs have little or no freedom to escape coming back to the trainer. The Continental breeds in my area used to have outstanding water trial competition. Even setters made difficult marks and multiple retrieves.

The dummy launcher shoots special dummies out one hundred yards or less depending on the type blank shell used. Regular .22 blanks shells can be used, but unfortunately Remington quit manufacturing the smokeless blanks and those using black powder are messy. The manufacturer of this device sells shells of varying power and Ram Set shells for masonry work can also be used. This tool is recommended for **every** dog trainer. It helps make breaking and retrieving an easier task and can be used with dogs of any age. They love it!

When my dogs develop problems chewing dummies or birds, I put sharp objects in them or wrap a row or two of carpet tacks around them with Velcro. Frozen birds also help. I also take pheasant wings and wrap them on a round piece of wood with small finishing nails pounded in it in rows about an inch apart.

If dogs have difficulty holding onto pheasants, and many do where they try to hold them tenderly, weights can be put in a dummy, or heavy objects can be used in retrieving training. Dogs will eventually learn the correct grip for each object and bird.

Chapter 9

Problems

BAD HABITS

Dogs form bad habits and obnoxious behavior patterns that should be corrected. But many things they do which we consider bad habits are for them natural behavior patterns. The urine marking of male dogs served a useful function in the past, but it detracts from their performance in field trials.

Rolling in other animal's manure and dead animals is a disgusting act, and nearly impossible to stop. It is difficult to prevent dogs from eating animal droppings. After a long hard winter and the spring melt, it is preserved for dogs to smell and eat. Cat manure is particularly attractive to all dogs probably because of animal protein which never seems to bother them, but is potentially dangerous.

Most dogs learn to ignore horse droppings at field trials, but a few delight in eating it to the chagrin of their handlers. It becomes an obsession with some dogs to quell some inner burning, nervousness or stress as some do by eating grass. All these behavior patterns are distressing to handlers at field trials and detracts from the dogs' performances. It is a sure sign that their minds are not on hunting.

Much of this behavior is stress induced. It is a carryover behavior from past experience where stress was a factor and the dogs developed **situation stress.**

Most dogs roll on the remains of dead animals. Maybe it is to make them smell like their quarry. Whatever the reason, it too is a disgusting habit since we must live in close proximity and be with the dogs.

Many of a dog's bad habits are caused by the lack of training, improper training or too much training. This is seen when a dog points a bird, then urinates on it, changes directions and urinates on it again.

Dogs may do nothing else in trials but follow their brace mates for no other reason than to back, and back even when their brace mates stop to urinate. They are followers and have (temporarily) lost the desire to hunt for themselves.

Self hunting can become as bad a habit as blinking birds. One results from the lack of supervision and control--too much freedom for too long a time, and the other from too much discipline and control.

Dogs that run away instead of coming when called are really **blinking** their handlers for fear of punishment. Dogs are like children. They will accept punishment only if it is timely and fair. Too much can result in misplaced blame where the dog blames the trainer for something another dog, person or thing does to them.

Handlers who wet down dogs too much when training, and at field trials, destroy their initiative and desire and develop a bad habit where the dog expects to be watered every ten or fifteen minutes even in cold temperatures. It becomes a learned behavior pattern.

Dogs which chase stink birds and four footed animals can learn to love it and develop bad habits. Yet, it is expected and desirable in young dogs.

Not every trainer, handler, or judge, learns to recognize when dogs follow horse tracks in trials. That is a bad habit. Some dogs classed as true all-age may win regularly only when they are not run in the first brace. In the first brace, they do not run well and seem confused. They learn to use "crutches" and follow the dog and horse tracks from previous braces. They are confident and appear to do a super job to the untrained eye in later braces. This is the best reason to use continuous course stakes where dogs will show all their trained and natural abilities.

In bird field stakes, as in training, dogs learn to track the bird planters and may point where every bird was put down. These dogs find birds, but not in an impressive manner.

Blinking, bolting, pottering and every other bad habit detracts from a dog's performance and style. These dogs seldom impress judges.

It is important to correct undesirable behavior at the first opportunity regardless of age or place. Trainers must train to avoid, prevent and correct bad habits without creating new ones.

TERRITORIAL MARKING

Dogs are not totally unaware of their marking behavior. I had a female that when braced with a male quickly learned how to outrun and out maneuver him in finding birds first. Just about the time the male would pull even, she would stop, urinate, and when he stopped to smell and cover she would find and point game leaving him in the secondary roll of backing.

Females normally do not mark territory and seldom urinate when running in stakes.

Male dogs are helpful at home in covering the places females urinate which apparently neutralizes the odor and helps keeps stray males from coming around. Other than that it is a nuisance.

Most male urination in trials is the result of training stress and it can be lessened or stopped in some dogs.

Dogs that are fed twice a day on top quality dog food will usually defecate a maximum of four times a day when being trained or run in field trials. The problem is that when taken out of their crates at field trials, they are excited and refuse to eliminate until they are put down in a brace. They probably do not need to urinate as often as some do either.

Heredity, in some breeds, may be a factor which from impression statistics has the male dogs doing nothing else but going from one fence line to the next to piddle, but more than likely it comes from improper training and correction. Situation stress does not fit this problem, but it is stress related. Generally, dogs permitted to hunt freely, seldom show this piddle syndrome.

How can we train to avoid this problem? It must be stopped early before serious training begins and must never be patronized or condoned. A shock collar is effective and might be more effective if taken from the neck and strapped around the loin and penis, but I do not recommend this practice.

Shouting a firm NO is the way to start, but allowing dogs to learn self-hunting under reasonable control of the handler will help in avoiding it.

In some males it is a strong dominant characteristic and eventually causes them to fight their brace mates for real or imagined territorial claims. Or, they learn that by growling and bullying the brace mates at the starting line it causes them to hesitate in leaving and they have the first opportunity to find all the birds. This happens too often for there not to be a method in their intimidation tactics.

SICK DOGS

Sick dogs cannot, and should not, be trained. Furthermore, no effort should be made to train or compete with them. We always expect our dogs to be in good health and whenever they do not respond we blame it on other reasons. Not all trainers can tell when their dogs are sick until they collapse or fail to leave their crates or kennels.

When dogs appear lack luster and the trainers push too hard, there can be negative reactions that would never occur if the trainers could have read their dogs or if the dogs were healthy.

Most dogs are healthy when given comfortable living conditions and are kept free of internal parasites. Tapeworm infestation must be bad, I am told, to prevent dogs from performing satisfactorily. I have doubts.

471

Tapeworms cannot be detected in stool samples by veterinarians unless they happen to see the ivory colored segments. The owners who walk their dogs on leash will often see the segments that are about one half inch long shorten up and move.

Dogs should be checked regularly to rid them of internal parasites, ear mites, ticks, fleas and skin irritations, cockleburrs, stick tights, sores and hot spots. Matter which accumulates in a dog's eyes overnight can be a clue for internal parasites. Lack of weight gain when on extra rations could indicate a tapeworm problem or when they always act starved no matter how much food they are given.

False pregnancies in bitches are traumatic and some should not be trained when acting weird or goofy. It is better to wait until their entire mood and personality returns to normal.

ANAL GLANDS

The anal glands are located just inside the anus under the tail. They are often a source of irritation which can be started by excitement or stress. Symptoms are attempting a bowel movement time after time with diminishing results each time, scooting on the ground and a crooked or "broken" tail.

An infected anal gland is uncomfortable and will cause dogs to run slower and have difficulty keeping their minds on hunting.

It seems that male dogs are affected more often than females, and once the problem begins, it recurs frequently. Preparation H is effective in relieving itching, pain and swelling. It can control the onset

472

when used after the gland is expressed and before the dog is run in competition.

The tail position is affected and is the first visible sign of a sore or infected anal gland. It is sometimes called "broken or limber tail." It is more noticeable on dogs having long tails.

Dogs affected with this problem should have their anal glands expressed periodically as a precautionary measure before competition. The best method is to straddle the dog facing backwards and with the thumb and index finger reach over the tail and force the liquid out. It is a simple task with experience and the dog will soon cooperate, although he will initially resist. The anal glands can be removed surgically when the problem persists.

DOG PADS

Dogs depend on their pads to stay tough and trouble free to hunt at top speed. Professional handlers who compete all over the United States, Canada and Mexico are aware of the various hazards to the feet and pads and know how to minimize the problem of sore feet.

Championship stakes are often held on grounds where dogs can tear pads off in a short time period. Many stakes are run where there is crusted snow or frozen ground and water which quickly cuts dog feet.

Both professional and amateur handlers travel long distances to trials and need to condition their dogs' feet for varying climatic conditions and abrasive grounds.

Several commercial chemical products are available to help toughen pads and rubber or leather boots can be put on a dog's feet for protection. The feet can also be wrapped with elastic bandage and adhesive tape providing the feet remain dry or are wet only for short periods of time and then removed.

The older type bicycle balloon inner tube cut in short sections and placed on a dog's feet and taped to the leg with adhesive tape works well and gives good ventilation. The front is usually left open which may pick up sand and small stones, but causes no problems.

When weeds are mowed late in the summer for field trials or hunters the stubbles are hard on their feet. Some dogs will quit running on grounds where there are mowed stubbles. The feet can be protected but the bellies can be worn raw in a short time. Most handlers never give this much consideration until after the dog runs.

The western states have rocky, granular or sandy soils which support little or no vegetation where foot protection is essential.

Pad tougheners are of no value to stop thorns, cactus needles, broken glass or sand burrs from cutting or injuring pads. Old discarded broken beer and soft drink bottles and cans are unnatural hazards that should never be found on field trial grounds.

Trainers generally never consider wrapping or protecting their dogs feet until after the problem occurs. Even on ordinary hard clay soil or grass, dogs can tear pads off. The front pads usually are the first to go and put dogs out of commission for a couple of weeks. The front feet act as shock absorbers and the pads take a high shearing force. Cut pads are slow to heal and must be protected and a dog may not be willing to work until healed.

I have seen dogs run and hunt hard in the grouse

woods a half day with a large wooden thorn completely through a front foot. The dog stopped to lick the injured foot, it was checked, but nothing was found until much later. Dogs are tough which is why we compete and run them when they are hurting before wising up to their pain.

DOG STOOLS

Stools are an early indication of potential health problems. Normal stools indicate the quality and digestibility of the dog food. With some commercial dog foods, firm, solid, stools are never formed. Stools should not have a foul odor.

Loose stools can indicate an overly excited dog and some are prone to this condition in competition, but usually grow out of it. A potential winning performance can be lost by dogs with loose stools, or sore anal glands.

Kennels are easier to keep clean where the stools are firm and solid which makes for easier pickup and cleaner runs. The extra cost of dog food which makes firm, solid, stools may be worth the difference.

Stool samples should be taken to the veterinarian periodically to check for internal parasites and the dogs given the medication prescribed. Dogs should not be wormed indiscriminately although some heartworm tablets contain worm medicine.

WETTING DOGS DOWN IN COMPETITION

There are field trial handlers who put out more

An example of a special dog wetting down tank so that
handlers will not use the horse watering tank which is
thoughtless of handlers and makes the water unfit for horses
to drink.

Some field trial facilities have water under pressure
which is used to cool dogs down prior to or after being run.

effort in having an ample supply of water, carried by a friend in the gallery, than in handling. Horse watering troughs are often turned into dog dunking tanks. Some dogs do not ever run fast enough to get any cooling effect from evaporation.

A few handlers are faking when wetting down their dogs. It becomes a ritual and they concentrate more on that than allowing their dogs to hunt. The act is often designed to rest their dogs and delay the brace if they can get the other handler to wet his dog too.

I have experimented with several dogs which could run in the hottest temperature and never take water when available on course, and never slow down when some got so hot running they were ready to collapse. None of the watering down experiments convinced me that it was beneficial, physically or mentally. Stopping dogs to wet them down may be the worst thing a handler can do.

I have seen dogs which needed first aid for heat prostration in high temperatures when most in the stake showed no affect of the heat. Lack of conditioning probably was a factor, but not all dogs have the same metabolism and are more affected by heat than others.

Part of the problem is with trainers who only work their dogs in the early morning and late evening hours during hot weather, and the dogs never learn how to cope with mid-day hot weather conditions in trials. That may be their first exposure to the really hot conditions. They are accustomed to running all out, because they were not bothered in early morning and late evenings and never learned the need to pace themselves. Trainers might serve their dogs better by running them for short time periods during the heat of the day and gradually build them up to a little more than the brace time. Dogs should not be forced to continue running once they are hot by wetting them down. They should be rested until their body fluids are replaced and then taken out for another training session if it is needed. It is a slow process. The dogs learn to recognize their capacity for the heat and will slow down the same as they learn to pace themselves when hunted all day long. But we do not want that in field trials. They have to learn the consequences of too much heat without suffering brain damage from heat prostration. Those dogs may not run or range to the same level they did before they suffered that condition.

Dogs watered every ten or fifteen minutes will learn to expect it as a condition of running or hunting and will slow up and wait to be wet down. They learn to love having water poured all over their bellies.

Dogs not accustomed to being watered in training or competition should not be watered and then continued on in competition. It is too much of a shock to their systems and upsets their concentration. They may even consider the watering as punishment!

Trainers and handlers should carry water in training and competition if the dogs become thirsty. A container from which they can drink should be carried along instead of pouring water into their mouths which can go into their lungs. Water is also essential when dogs become over-heated. Then ice should be used to help lower the body temperature, if available.

The truth of the matter is that handlers who wet their dogs down on the back course are hurting their chances of winning--unless all do it. In the bird field, it does no particular harm to wet a dog's mouth and give it some drinking water from a container, or hand, after its first retrieve.

When one handler is watering his dog down, the brace mate is possibly finding birds. I have seen no evidence that watering dogs down improved their scenting ability in hot weather. Dogs have to learn to smell with their tongues dragging.

It is difficult to do, but I believe that if a dog stops half way around and is unable to run or breathe, the handler should pick him up and hope for a better day. He may not win on that day, but in the long run he will be the **winner**. It is easy to give advice, but sometimes harder to take it. We all like to win, but it is better not to expect that when our dogs are not in condition to run in hot weather.

POISONOUS SNAKES

Pointing dogs will learn to fight and kill snakes when encouraged, or allowed. It is a natural instinct and it is a question of which one can make the quickest move. Smart, experienced, dogs can kill most snakes.

Dogs should be taught to respect and fear snakes. There is no advantage in doing anything else, and they should be "snake proofed" which may save their lives since some trials are held on grounds having poisonous snakes. More hunting dogs die from snake bites than are killed in traffic accidents according to *Gun Dog* magazine.

Non-poisonous snakes can be used for snake proofing where poisonous snakes are not readily available, but may not be as effective. Different snakes probably have slightly different odors. A water snake or pit viper can be meaner and nastier and strike as quick as a rattlesnake. The difference is they have no fangs but do have holding teeth which can be painful to a tender nose.

One way is to place the snake under a bucket or place it in a wire enclosure in an open area where the snake will not escape, then bring the dog in on a lead and release the snake. Let him get close and be struck and at the same time the trainer should shout a loud NO and jerk the dog back as he acts afraid and excited. After several encounters over a period of a few days, the dog can have the shock collar put on for further reinforcement.

The shock collar training method is used with defanged rattlesnakes by Bill Gibbons, a professional trainer in Arizona.

Most dogs bitten by poisonous snakes at field trials were not moving at top speed, but stopped to urinate, defecate, potter, or point at the wrong place at the wrong time. Pointing dogs also point snakes which is a big problem for their handlers.

Horses are seldom bitten. I saw a horse step on a massasauga rattlesnake at Killdeer Plains Wildlife Area and he only tried to escape, but when I got off my horse to capture him, he was ready to fight. It was interesting to observe the snake's behavior later. We used him on dogs in the parking lot and the snake made no move when people walked close, but when a dog came near he was ready to strike--probably because dogs have higher body temperatures.

Poisonous snakes never seem to stop field trial activities even in the Mojave desert which has Mojave green and western diamondback rattlesnakes.

Snakes do not like hot temperature and cannot survive for long so early morning and late evening are when they are likely to be out in hotter climates, but during field trial seasons when temperatures are cooler they will come out to sun during the middle of the day. The severity of a bite depends on many variables. Dogs can and do survive some snake bites without treatment, but some will die too. A new method using electrical shock of high voltage, low amperage, such as from a lawn mower, car spark plug, stun gun and perhaps a shock collar administered to the bite area appears to have merit.

The dog should be taken promptly to the veterinarian and given proper treatment. If possible, the dead snake should be taken along for positive identification.

DISORIENTED OR LOST DOGS

Not all dogs panic when they realize they have been separated from their owners, trainers and handlers for awhile. Some dogs are perfectly content to keep right on hunting until **they** are found or tire and find a place to rest. All-age dog owners lose contact with their dogs frequently because of their extended range and must be hunted to be recovered.

It is not unusual to find a "lost" all-age dog many, many miles from the field trial grounds and their handlers expend considerable effort in hunting and tracking them down. Only too often they are found along the roadway dead or are never found. Residents living near all-age field trial grounds are accustomed to owners and handlers looking for their "lost" dogs. Most of these dogs are not the least bit concerned about their owners or handlers being lost from them.

Self-hunting gun dogs, renegades, bolters, or dogs blinking their handlers because of too much rough treatment in training also become lost.

Judging sentiment is so strong for big running dogs that the only reason some do not win is that they are out of judgment too long or lost. Many of these dogs win every time they are kept on course and seen when or shortly after time is up.

All-age dogs may hunt for days, or go from place to place when tired of hunting, until they are recovered eventually by their owners. Some are never found and are adopted by someone with no knowledge of their background.

Dogs do become genuinely disoriented and panic as a result of being in strange surroundings. These dogs often avoid all human contact, including their owners if they find them and are difficult to capture.

I had a wide ranging self-hunting male dog that became disoriented in the grouse woods. He had been in the habit of making a wide circle behind to pick up my tracks and re-establish contact, but this time he failed. He paniced and my calling for him and shooting the shotgun got no response. I later saw him at the top of the next hill in a power line coming in my general direction. But, when I called him, he reversed direction and ran away. I followed in the general direction he went without any plan. He was apparently hiding somewhere in the woods near the power line and must have smelled me before he came close enough for me to see him and was wary in making a positive identification before he recognized me and became happy.

Dogs are often "lost" in braces which are merely hunting closeby, know where the handler and trial entourage are, but have no interest in making contact until after the brace time. They learn to avoid handlers for a half hour or hour, depending on the heat time they are accustomed to staying down. Some dogs hunt in a wide circle a mile or so in diameter, and like a rabbit run by hounds, will eventually circle back and catch up. They know full well how to find their handlers, the horse gallery or the field trial headquarters or their kennel vehicle, but enjoy being **free.** Dogs use the Doppler Effect to tell whether the field trial party is getting close or going away.

It is no great pleasure for handlers to have to stay over after trials to look for their lost dogs. But they accept this as a necessary part of their sport.

A quotation from a Gordon Setter Newsletter involved a setter that had a **habit** of getting lost.

"The dog may have had many owners--if you let him loose he runs into the wind until he is tired, then goes to the nearest house and waits to be adopted."

What is the best way to find a lost dog? Establish contact with game protectors, area managers, local humane societies, sheriffs, highway patrols, radio and TV stations and local newspapers. Then go door to door or drive all the side roads in the surrounding area for miles around looking and asking people along the way. A picture of the dog helps and should be carried for dogs in the habit of getting lost when contacting the various people and organizations. Most important is that the dogs wear a collar and name tag with the owner's and handler's address and telephone number--call collect.

DISTRACTIONS

Field trial dogs cannot be trained and hunted in

isolation. They must become accustomed to every kind of distraction.

Handlers and dogs must tolerate boistrous noise from the gallery, loud hollering from handlers, whistles blown indiscriminately and without purpose, unruly horses, irresponsible handlers and horses, bells, gunners who empty repeating shotguns and miss, hunters wandering on the course with and without dogs, off the road vehicles, snowmobiles and other strange things.

Dogs must truly turn into statues when on point as the other handler runs his horse at him pretending it is out of control.

The smart dogs learn to stay away from the horse gallery and not come from behind through them. But there are ignorant dogs that like to dodge the hoofs.

Many dogs love field trials because they can easily find horse piles to eat. It causes no harm, but it looks disgustingly bad and aggravates their handlers.

Frequently someone in the gallery becomes dismounted, for many varied reasons, and the horse runs away with a few riders from the gallery becoming cowboys trying to catch it. It is not difficult to imagine how difficult it is to train dogs to ignore these shennagins when on point. These things serve to keep field trials so interesting and challenging, but a little more consideration for the dogs and handlers would be welcomed.

CHECKING BACK OR IGNORING HANDLERS

The tendency for dogs to check back to their handlers for reassurance or to maintain close contact varies among the different pointing breeds. Vizslas are well known for checking back and it is one of their greatest assets as a personal hunting dog. With work, they grow out of it.

Coming back in is a disgusting habit and is a sign of broken concentration, dependency and is bad for competition but it can be corrected. Checking to handlers without coming back can be bad too when done at the expense of performance such as stopping, looking back, standing as if to wait for encouragement and reassurance. Handlers fall into the trap of giving voice, hand and whistle signals to send them on.

Dogs should be trained to stay out front all the time. Ten o'clock to two o'clock is ideal. Anything past three and before nine o'clock (behind the handlers and judges) is an indication the dogs are not working for their handlers.

Sometimes a young puppy will begin checking back to see what his trainer wants when given commands or hollered at. If a puppy stays in front, the handler should keep his mouth shut. If not, he should do whatever is necessary to encourage him to stay out front in training when at the proper stage of development. It may take time and work, but eventually these dogs will come to realize that where they go their trainers and handlers will follow and eventually learn to expect it.

Hand signals given to a young puppy may be confusing and cause him to come in to see what is the matter. Each one responds differently. This is never a problem with self-hunting dogs. Those dogs require more work to keep in contact than training one to get out and stay out front.

I have observed some brutal methods used by pointer trainers to keep their dogs from ranging out too far

485

and fast. Extreme methods are also used to make dogs stay out in front and they learn to run and stay away from their trainers.

Success cannot be achieved by using a shock collar indiscriminately to drive dogs out or to force them in. They have no idea what the trainer wants or his reason. Dogs are chased down with horses to bring them under control and must cope having to drag heavy chains. Some have chains fastened to the collars so they strike their front legs as they run. A new gadget has two balls on cords which hits the front legs and upsets a dog's rhythm as he runs.

The saying goes that it is easier to get dogs to work in closer but more difficult to get them to range out farther. The usual problem is to force them to range out farther for the Continental breeds.

After puppy age, trainers can holler and run at their dogs to force them out. This can be done on every workout for a few weeks. If the dogs begin to respond favorably, it should be continued for awhile. Then trainers should work the dogs and say nothing. The dogs should be allowed to do whatever they will so the trainer can observe progress to see if they have developed a dependency syndrome.

With some dogs it works to WHOA them when they start back, and the trainers should go and give praise before casting them off again to hunt.

Other dogs will stop cutting back when the trainers change directions abruptly to the right or left.

It may be necessary for trainers to throw gravel, shelled corn, or shoot the dogs with a sling shot. There are a few trainers who shoot dogs with bird shot for checking back or shock them. A long switch across their legs will make them think twice about coming close in to the trainers and this creates a healthy respect for staying away.

Once a dog is cast off, he must learn to begin hunting freely in a forward searching pattern and that the trainer or handler will follow him wherever he goes. He eventually learns to check the direction of the handler and adjusts his direction accordingly. This instills confidence and results in good performance.

In many ways it is easier to train from horseback, as the dogs can see the trainer and handler better when farther away. The pace of the horse can be increased such that the dogs hardly know they are being **pushed**. Training should be done both ways—from foot and horseback. A few stakes are walking stakes and dogs must learn to adapt.

Dogs are not dumb. If trainers are too harsh in forcing their will and set difficult goals too quickly, dogs have ways to compensate and combat their efforts. They range from coming in at heel, running off, hiding, feigning deafness, crawling under vehicles, etc. Many of the big running dogs are only running off to escape their handlers. They find some safe spot to watch for them and do whatever they please from urinating on every bush and weed to laying in a mud puddle or digging a cool place in the ground to lay.

The methods some trainers and handlers use are cruel. They range from running the dogs down from horseback and shooting them with bird shot to putting a shock collar on and holding the button down until the dogs scream out their location—that is if the trainers or handlers are within hearing range.

The better dog trainers reach their goals of achieving longer range and independence, or to hold their dogs in close for bird fields or grouse hunting without inflicting corporal punishment or abuse.

SHIPPING DOGS

The only form of commercial transportation available to dog owners, trainers, handlers and breeders is by air. They can travel as excess baggage or freight. Dogs traveling as excess baggage must have advance reservation space on the airplane. They are taken on with the travelers luggage in the terminal building and are picked up at the large parcel baggage claim areas in airport terminals. Dogs shipped by air freight must also have reservations a day ahead for cargo space since the number of dogs allowed each flight is limited.

The cost is based on dimensional weight which means that if a puppy is shipped in a 400 size crate (the largest available) the cost is based on a minimum weight of 100 pounds. Field trial handlers may find shipping as excess baggage the least expensive method to attend trials. Every effort should be made to schedule direct flights, or flights which do not involve a change in planes at stops along the route. The cost of shipping dogs by excess baggage is cheap when compared to freight charges.

The traveler, or shipper, must have an "airline" approved crate (a molded type crate which is made with tough copolymer plastic material). It may be purchased from dog specialty firms such as Dogs Unlimited or the airlines. This crate can serve as a kennel crate at home or when traveling to trials and Hunting Tests.

A Federal law requires airlines to ship animals only when the temperature is above certain minimum and

488

maximum set values at the intended destination.

In the past, airline personnel have lied about the conditions in cargo compartments. They have been reported to get a high as 131 degrees Fahrenheit, or as low as 60-70 degrees below zero with no air circulation. The only air available for the dogs is between the cargo spaces.

Advertisements should not always be believed. Animals die even before airplanes take off with heated, pressurized, air conditioned cargo compartments.

I once tried to ship a puppy and the freight attendant told me that the airplane on that flight was not safe to ship animals.

During bad weather conditions flights are often cancelled or are late, and dogs can become distressed without the owners ever having to consider such problems as too much or too little heat and ventilation, or that they are receiving proper care.

The treatment of animals on the ground at terminals is not always what is claimed. They are really just another item of cargo even though they are the last to load and the first to unload. Airlines are making improvements and the workers are generally courteous and helpful to travelers with dogs.

Airlines do lose dogs and dogs do get out of the crates. One I know of made several flights cross country before found hiding in the cargo compartment. It took persistence and determination by the owner to find the dog.

Nothing is without risk, and owners and handlers traveling with dogs as excess baggage are generally satisfied with the services given. Proper attention to details can make travel easier and trouble free.

Chapter 10

Judging

RULES AND STANDARDS

The American Kennel Club has only one performance standard each for puppy, derby, gun dog and all-age for its licensed or member field trials. It has separate standards for its walking Hunting Tests for Pointing Breeds which has three categories: Junior, Senior and Master.

Sometimes it is difficult for trainers and handlers to know where standards begin or end and when **rules** govern. Too often the two are interchangeable. Some rules are not written, but are derived by individual judges based on what they believe, or interpret, the standards and rules mean, or have been judged in the past. Many judges are extremely negative and order

dogs up for minor infractions, real or imagined.
Albert Hochwalt said:

**"There is so much bitter dissension about field trial rules
and field trial judging that I will give my views. The fact
is, rules are not required when you get judges who know
their business, but unfortunately you cannot get them to
think alike. The main cause of this is the different
opinions held by different judges of what constitutes field
trial ability and a field trial dog. Some judges want dogs
to get out of sight and stay out of sight, and place more on
"leg work" than "brain work." If their kind of dog gets
away and stays away, but is eventually found on point, he is
glorified as a "class" dog. Then there are judges who want
a dog to work out his ground intelligently, to keep busy,
and if he keeps on the course and finds birds twice while
the crowd is hunting for the class dog they give him more
credit than they would a straight liner that got lost and
was found pointing."**

The Shoot-To-Retrieve Association trials are judged
on a point basis. No dog can be thrown out of
competition and if the handler insists on removing his
dog during the heat, the club must put another dog in
the brace for the remainder of the heat time. The dog
scoring highest on the most points and retrieves wins.

The American Kennel Club rules and standards are not
too unlike those accepted and used by the American
Field over the years—at least they resemble them
closely with minor changes. After all a **pointing dog
field trial** for class work by its nature will
resemble all others.

Individuals who break off from these trials, for
whatever reasons, and start new clubs and associations

make the rules and standards to suit their own personal ideals.

The National Bird Hunters Association, according to its founder Dan Smith, was formed by ordinary hunters with its prime motivation to **improve hunting dogs** and to bring "the bottom to the top." Its standards are directed toward a walking handler with a big running dog with birds shot on course with four basic levels: Local, State, National and Invitational. Local clubs are loose, and state competitions are fifty percent bird dog and fifty percent field trial with the national being a pure field trial dog run for two hours. According to Dan Smith, its formation had nothing to do with discontent with big running major circuit trials or local pointer and setter trials.

The American Bird Hunters Association is apparently an offshoot of the National Bird Hunters Association with the inclusion of an amateur stake and the desire for **shorter** running dogs.

The American Field, the National Bird Hunters Association, the American Bird Hunters Association, the United States Complete Shooting Dog Association and the American Kennel Club trials are judged by the spotting system which picks the best performing dogs using subjective opinions. Any trainer or handler who participates exclusively in a different organization's trials when asked to judge another one's, should study the rules and standards of performance and understand what is expected. If in doubt, they should ask before judging.

These different organizations offer something for every pointing dog owner to help enjoy his dog more whether he chooses to run in hunting type stakes or the major circuit trials.

Judging varies with locality and individuals. Some judges order up dogs for moving slightly on point, yet allow handlers to ruin brace mates by excessive hollering and whistling. Once a **warning** is given to a handler, if he does not obey, the judges should eject him and his dog. But, it is seldom done although dogs are ejected every weekend for minor infractions which never appear in any of the standards or rules.

The American Kennel Club gun dog and all-age standards are designed to serve usefully for all game birds and they may be revised in the future if the need arises. The principal differences in the gun dog and all-age requirements are in range, handling, checking to the handler and independence.

AMERICAN KENNEL CLUB GUN DOG STANDARD

"A gun dog must give a finished performance and must be under its handler's control at all times. It must handle kindly, with a minimum of noise and hacking by the handler. A Gun Dog must show a keen desire to hunt, must have a bold and attractive style of running, and must demonstrate not only intelligence in quartering and in seeking objectives but also the ability to find game. The dog must hunt for its handler at all times at a range suitable for a handler on foot, and should show or check in front of its handler frequently. It must cover adequate ground but never range out of sight for a length of time that would detract from its usefulness as a practical hunting dog. A dog must locate game, must point staunchly, and must be steady to wing and shot. Intelligent use of the wind and terrain in locating game, accurate nose, and style and intensity on point, are essential. At least 30 minutes shall be allowed for each heat."

AMERICAN KENNEL CLUB ALL-AGE STANDARD

"An All-Age Dog must give a finished performance and must be under reasonable control of its handler. It must show a keen desire to hunt, must have a bold and attractive style of running, and must show independence in hunting. It must range well out in a forward moving pattern, seeking the most promising objectives, so as to locate any game on the course. Excessive line-casting and avoiding cover must be penalized. The dog must respond to handling but must demonstrate its independent judgment in hunting the course, and should not look to its handler for directions as to where to go. The dog must find game, must point staunchly, and must be steady to wing and shot. Intelligent use of the wind and terrain in locating game, accurate nose, and style and intensity on point, are essential. At least 30 minutes shall be allowed for each heat."

The Amesian Standard perfectly fits the two three hour courses on the Ames Plantation, and no matter how poorly all the dogs might do, a champion **must** be named. Yet, the judges there do order dogs up and allow handlers to pick them up too. The assumption is made, rightly or wrongly, that the remainder of the field is better and it most always is because the

494

judges already have a prospective winner in mind when looking for another dog to change their collective minds.

AMESIAN STANDARD

"The dog under consideration must have and display great bird sense. He must show perfect work on both coveys and singles. He must be able quickly to determine between foot and body scent. He must use his brain, eyes, and nose to the fullest advantage and hunt the likely places on the course. He must possess speed, range, style, character, courage and stamina—and good manners, always. He must hunt the birds, and not the handler hunt the dog. No line or path runner is acceptable. He must be well broken, and the better his manners the more clearly he proves his sound training. Should he lose a little in class, as expressed in extreme speed and range, he can make up for this, under fair judgment, in a single piece of superior bird work, or in sustained demonstration of general behavior. He must be bold, snappy, and spirited. His range must be to the front or to either side, but never behind. He must be regularly and habitually pleasing (tractable) and must know when to turn and keep his handler's course in view, and at all times keep uppermost in his mind the finding and pointing of birds for his handler."

NATIONAL PHEASANT STANDARD

"With the passing of years, there gradually arose among sportsmen the opinion that the ideal pheasant dog was necessarily different in his methods from the quail or ruffed grouse dog. This is granted to be so, but it is not to be concluded that per se the high-class quail or prairie chicken dog will not prove a performer of merit and worth on pheasants. It is in the manner of negotiating the terrain and hunting the country wherein the difference lies, for where the quail dog may quickly and thoroughly wind the likely cover and thus cover a wealth of territory, the pheasant lurks in practically every kind of cover, even the sparse meadows, and the sagacious bird dog needs to adapt himself accordingly and hunt the fields with precision. There are no particularly birdy places, for the pheasants are everywhere in some situations. It follows therefore that the pheasant dog cannot race past unlikely fields like the quail dog, nor is it to be desired that the pheasant dog be restricted in range and quarter his ground after the manner of the grouse dog."

"Sportsmen have been evolving a desirable type, a class pheasant dog which has rapidly gained in popularity. These sportsmen want a class performer, withal a bird dog. They demand style, speed, snap and decision, intelligence and precision, a finished performance. The slow potterer and grass prowler of former days that creepingly nosed about on foot scent has been consigned to the discard. The fast, dashing, positive bird-finder is being glorified, for such a dog has the seemingly magical faculty of wielding a hypnotic influence over these sprinters of the stubble and compels them to lay."

NATIONAL GROUSE DOG STANDARD

"A high-class grouse dog is one whose very action denotes great interest in his work, which is full of animation and which is at all times searching for birds, in an independent and intelligent manner. He should be under such control that he will do his work with the minimum amount of handling, by either voice or whistle. He should keep the course and hunt to the gun and within reasonable distance; in a fast, snappy manner work out all the likely cover in front of his handler. He should not cut back, but should consume his speed by working out his ground on each side of the course taken by his handler. When the cover is heavy and the course full of briers, he should not hunt the easy footing and pass up the likely objectives. He must pay little attention to the scent of fur; occasionally pointing a rabbit could be overlooked, but under no condition should he chase one. He should accurately locate and point his birds and be perfectly staunch on point until the birds are flushed, when he must be steady to wing and shot. He must back at sight of a pointing dog and not approach close enough to interfere with the dog on point or to disturb the bird. After the bird has been killed over a point, and the dog has been steady to shot, he must, on being ordered, go for and retrieve the bird in a prompt manner and without dropping it deliver it to his handler in an unruffled and undamaged condition. A dog is classable according to the manner in which he performs these requirements."

The Amateur Field Trial Clubs of America revised the "Standards of Judicial Practice and Field Trial Procedure" which is now "Guidelines To Field Trial Procedure And Judicial Practice" to include a description of the all-age dog. This description was written by John S. O'Neall, Jr. and Collier F. Smith. It is important that an exacting standared be met when a Champion title is awarded for a single heat as opposed to those which must accumulate wins and points to become one. Also, such wins qualify these dogs for more prestigious stakes and various other awards. Therefore, it is important that these all-age dogs perform flawlessly and better than all others in the stake while meeting this standard.

THE ALL-AGE FIELD TRIAL DOG IN AMERICA

The familiar capsule description of the all-age dog, attributed to old-time trainer Jim Avent, declares that he (or she) is a dedicated hunter of upland game birds which "runs off--but not quite." The all-age dog is a free spirit and fills up all the available country (plus a little more) in a bold and even reckless manner, yet ultimately acknowledges the control exerted by his handler and courses to the front in such a pattern as to maintain periodic, suitable contact with the handler. The really intelligent and accomplished all-age dog exhibits the knack of "showing" at strategic, distant, forward points on the course during the progress of his heat. He may frequently pass from view, only to show again after a lapse of time, or to be discovered by handler or scout pointing game.

The all-age dog should incorporate the direction of the wind and the lay of land in his hunting effort, enabling him to range to the fringe of contact with his handler. He must possess a superior nose, allowing him to hunt from objective to objective at a very fast pace. In an ideal all-age performance there is little or no time for extended probing or rechecking of coverts.

498

A successful all-age dog is not a straight line runner. Despite his speed, power and extended range, he must be hunting as he goes. He must take the edges and apply his superior olfactory powers to pick up vagrant scents that might lead to discovery of game.

The all-age should exude animation and happiness with the task at hand. He should display loftiness of head and tail in his gait, maintaining this appearance in cover and on bare ground, despite traveling with the utmost speed and drive. He must not be deterred by punishment meted out by cover and weather.

No matter how far flung and well executed the casts--no matter how beautiful and powerful the stride--no matter how lofty and animated the carriage--no matter how strong and indefatigable the heart--this running machine must have foremost in mind the discovery and near-perfect handling of game. He should stand proud, rigid and intense on his birds, showing confidence that he has them pegged exactly, and in front. Quite often he must maintain this posture for many minutes, and remember his training, before handler or scout discovers him on point. He should be fearless at approach of his handler and the field trial party, and he should maintain keen interest, intensity, upright posture and good style while the handler flushes and the shot is fired. If birds cannot be flushed and relocation is required, he should proceed when released with dash and determination to search out and pin running birds, exhibiting powers of nose that take him straight to the quarry.

The all-age dog must voluntarily and cheerfully back on sight a bracemate on rigid point. However, the judges should attempt to see the backing situation through the eyes of the moving dog, taking into account the less acute eyesight of the dog and the possible interference of cover, terrain and background as he approaches the scene. The approaching dog should get the benefit of any doubt about his ability to see clearly the pointing dog. In an all-age performance a back should be accomplished if the opportunity presents itself and the bracemate is in the vicinity, but a race should not be interrupted and a dog returned from a distant cast in order to achieve a back.

In the all-age dog stamina is a watchword. Regardless of whether the heat is a half hour or three hours, prime consideration should be given the competitor which can convincingly finish the allotted time with range and speed undiminished. Emphasis should also be placed on the dog's ability to find and handle game in all parts of the heat, but particularly in the latter stages when fatigue may take its toll on olfactory powers.

NORTH AMERICAN WOODCOCK STANDARD

1. "First and foremost the dog must be a bird-finder."

2. "Dog must show intelligence in his ground pattern--be a quartering dog and not a line runner."

3. "Dog must not potter on scent and must not run with low head and root for scent."

4. "Dog must prove that his nose is equal to his stride."

5. "Dog must be merry in character, enjoy what he is doing and do it with style and boldness."

6. "Dog must hunt to the gun not waste time in non-birdy places, and go unerringly to tight birdy corners, with range adaptable to cover."

7. "Excessive close range will detract. However, excessive long range that makes handling and location of the dog extremely difficult will also distract and detract. It is also most important that a fast, hard-driving dog with style and class is desired."

8. "Dogs will be expected to show stamina and endurance and finish the hour with some to spare."

9. "When given the opportunity, a dog must back his bracemate."

There are other standards of performance for the different organizations and game birds, but these should suffice to give the readers an idea of the differences which can be expected. Judges should know and be familiar with all the different standards even if they never judge outside their own breed or organization. Education is important to knowledge and the two instill confidence not gained any other way.

In Albert Hochwalt's biography its authors wrote:

"During the first decade of 1900 class cranks placed a premium on speed and range, de-emphasizing bird work. However, Hochwalt held fast to the standard that finding and handling game was of paramount importance; the work had to be intelligently accomplished, be of high quality to win his approval, but he never subscribed to the view that mere heels were sufficient justification for placement."

"Judges, or at least a great many of them, were carried away with straight-line runners and crazy sprinters, and handlers were able to get by on pace and range. No attempt was made to steady All-Age dogs, much less Derbies, by a certain class of handlers, for under these class judges they could win without showing bird work, so what was the use?"

Well, history is noted for repeating itself each time a new organization is formed, and nothing much has really changed except those trials were not single course trials on planted pen raised birds where dogs ran horse tracks. Now the same type judges put up these dogs that do nothing much else but follow horse and dog tracks.

I suggest that each reader having more than a passing

interest in a good dog and field trials, study each of these standards, and if ever asked to judge one of these trials remember what a pointing dog is expected to do in **different** kinds of trials. Withhold placements when there are no worthy dogs if the standard permits, but do not help the continual degradation of field trial judging with inept decisions. Judges should ask themselves **why** a dog is out of sight. What is the real reason for his absence. When we cannot judge what we cannot see, we should be alerted, our suspicions aroused, and give no additional credit to dogs that cannot be seen. Too often these dogs are hiding from their handlers, are in the bird field early, are pottering on ground scent of birds **they** flushed, are chasing birds, rabbits, deer or playing in the water or are back at the kennel vehicle.

Authors of *National Field Trial Champions* wrote that Hobert Ames

"would not permit the wild riding so common to many trials. The dog was supposed to be broken; therefore he could (and must) hold his game while he awaited the not-too-hurried arrival of the judges. The so-called 'out on a limb' find of a wild running dog was not impressive to Mr. Ames. . . he expected the dog to serve his handler by intelligent application on the course."

JUDGING QUALIFICATIONS

Many experts declare that judges are **born**. Maybe. But they need to be "born" to different judging standards with so many different kinds of pointing dog trials. Judging is much like training and handling--they are all an art.

503

In American Field prestigious championship stakes oftentimes the same men judge year in and year out. Once they reach that **select** circle they have learned what **good** bird dogs do and are saddled for life. Hobert Ames judged the National Championship at Grand Junction, Tennessee for thirty years. He had **class** according to many who knew him and worked with him.

As William F. Brown wrote in the book *Albert Frederick Hochwalt--A Biography* :

". . . the judge must have class if he expects to judge class. Class in this sense means that he should be able to form quick and prompt conclusions; that he should be able to concentrate his mind on the work before him; that he should possess the personal dignity which appeals to those who run dogs under him; that he inspires confidence in his decisions and ruling on the field, and lastly, that he possess a good memory so that he may be able to carry the work of the dogs that have run early in the stake constantly in his mind and thus make mental comparisons with those that follow, for it is a psychological fact that the last impressions will frequently carry weight, to the detriment of the earlier ones."

Judges always rise from the ranks of owners, trainers and handlers. Not every one makes a good judge and strange as it seems, poor handlers do often make good judges.

Judges must be honest, conscientious and have unquestioned integrity. He, or she, must be kind, courteous, impartial, fair and firm in making decisions. A good reputation is important. He, or she, should have a thorough knowledge of the rules for the particular type trial being judged and possess the experience and ability to recognize the best dogs in the stakes. It is important that such men and women have recently campaigned dogs in the particular type of trial they are asked to judge unless they are veterans of long standing.

Local trial judges are ordinary people often found in competition from one week to the next with their peers who also have their own selected friends as well as preferred strain or line of dogs within their own breeds. Whenever their decisions are not accepted, and oftentimes they are not, these judges risk not being asked to judge again by that club. Sometimes they are verbally and physically abused.

It seems prudent then that beginning, as well as experienced, handlers display their best behavior and manners at trials. They should make every effort to maintain good relations with every other handler and judge. This is not to say that they cannot nor should not express disagreement about poor judging decisions or the conduct of trials. What they learn and how they behave as handlers is viewed by their peers as how qualified **they** are to ride the judicial saddle.

Humans are never perfect and their bias and prejudice is bound to creep into and affect results. It is not what is done, but **who** does something. Politics also casts its ugly shadow. Professional handlers, all things equal, receive more placements and wins. The "foreign" breed is often looked upon as being inferior. The evidence can be found in the history of the setters and pointers as the first example in trials. The setter was once the best, but he has long since been replaced by the pointer. Preferences have changed and there are years at the National Championship when **no** setters are entered; whereas, it began with no pointer entries.

Handlers can experience the feeling of "not belonging" by entering trials put on by other breed clubs. Judges are solely responsible when they refuse to put up a different breed that did a better job. It still happens. Such men and women lack the necessary qualifications to judge. Token placements are equally bad. Yet, we hear many owners declare that a dog which cannot win against other breeds is not worthy.

Another example of this bias is found in the slow acceptance of women in the sport as trainers, handlers and judges. They have always been praised by the men handlers for servant type duties and record keeping chores, but we still find male judges who absolutely will not give women placements.

I know of one situation where the judges in a breed trial placed another breed first and were never asked to judge that breed again. They were blackballed! The entire club had a sickness.

It takes a special type person to accept judging assignments when he knows his honesty will get him into trouble with handlers and owners. Or, the pattern of judging is so sloven and inept that poor judging becomes the accepted standard, and he tries to buck the pattern.

We might never know what the qualifications of a judge are from one day to the next, one trial to the next, or one breed to another breed. It is somewhat like asking what are the qualifications for being a Christian. It requires much more than merely going to church. Judging requires more than being asked.

I hear people ask why the American Kennel Club does not educate and approve men and women for judging assignments. Just being over twenty one years of age to judge, if asked, is inadequate criteria. First time

506

judges signed a statement that they read the rules and standards. The AKC is now working on methods to educate pointing dog judges which will require them to attend seminars and perhaps take tests.

The American Kennel Club pamphlet "The Status of a Judge of Licensed Field Trials & Hunting Tests," describes what a judge is, what he is expected to do and how he is to behave. A copy is sent to each field trial and Hunting Test secretary.

Some quotes:

"The judges on the day of a licensed trial do not merely represent themselves as individuals. They represent the entire sport of field trialing, and particularly The American Kennel Club."

"They and they alone decide what shall be entered in the permanent records of The American Kennel Club. And the entries made there form the basis for the breeding plans of other field trialers in the years ahead. Thus, it might be said that a judge, by his decisions, influences breeding trends and the course of the breed's development in future years."

". . . The future of the sport is going to depend on the extent to which its judges really know good work in the field; know the rules and procedures, and judge strictly in accord with them; demonstrate complete impartiality in their decisions; and act in a manner fitting to the dignity of their position."

The only published guidebook for judges was first prepared by the Amateur Field Trial Clubs of America in 1947. It has been replaced with the "Guidelines To Field Trial Procedure and Judicial Practice." It is an excellent guideline for handlers and judges. There are no educational programs for teaching proper judging for American Kennel Club and American Field trials, and this booklet can give one insight to judging. Individuals, clubs and dog food manufacturers offer training and judging seminars infrequently.

The American Kennel Club has a formal training program and gives leadership and direction for Beagle field trialers. It is just a matter of time before it will apply to other breeds since all Parent Club presidents have agreed to accept the use of seminars and testing.

Judging is usually subjective whether the spotting system or a point system is used. Few people are perfect in this work but their decisions are final and binding. Some are better liked, and the best ones are aware of the import of what they do and the effect of their decisions on future breeding and training, but may not be well liked. Entirely too many handlers want to **win** and have little regard for other aspects of the sport, but many do learn to give more than they take from it.

We all at one time or other try to "reinvent the wheel" in many things we become involved in. It is the only way some of us know how to make ourselves feel important or that we are contributing something as individuals. This has no place in judging.

Fun and informal trials should help provide the opportunities for judging apprenticeships. Future judges should marshal extensively and compare placements of the judges with their opinions privately. Unfortunately, too many beginners are asked to judge the juvenile stakes--puppy and derby. These are the **most** difficult to judge because potential is an elusive form to recognize. Potential is paramount for deserving juvenile placements as well as a certain level of demonstrated performance. Who among us dares to withhold puppy or derby placements? It happens and although it might not speak well for the current crop of young pupils, judging decisions should reflect the truth on that day. These same young dogs on the next weekend might burn up the course.

Professional handlers are sometimes idolized to a fault. Some people claim they are the **backbone** of the sport. They should have the best qualifications to judge the important stakes also, but they cannot be expected to volunteer their services whenever they should be handling dogs in competition for clients. Some do make that sacrifice, but they are used mostly for amateur stakes when both amateur and open stakes are offered at the same trial.

Judges who believe dogs must have a **perfect** performance are wrong since that performance level is not possible. Dogs are not mind readers anymore than their handlers. They are not preprogrammed machines and should be judged according to standards used in their training.

The spotting system of judging has faults, but not nearly as many as any other scoring system if we consider that a judge can recognize dogs which please him most and also meet the minimum requirements of the stake. A knowledgeable bird dog man, or woman, has no difficulty whatever in spotting the best dog in a stake, but might need to make notes to pick the other placements. They recognize a **winner** and any other winner that beats their first one and are decisive. Those with less bird dog experience may suffer and agonize over which dog should be placed where. Sometimes they guess correctly.

JUDGES CONDUCT

An "unknown" person becomes visible once he, or she, takes up the judicial saddle. We never really know our friends or acquaintances until we observe or experience them in stressful positions of authority, or in situations from which they must make sound decisive judgments quickly and with fairness to all competitors.

I lost my naivete in World War II upon graduating from aviation cadet training. Upon becoming an officer, I observed a strange transformation among many of my fellow classmates. Their Jekyll and Hyde nature was suddenly revealed. The enlisted men called them "pricks." Their having to listen to the continuous rubble that officers were a cut above the rest, the cream of the crop, affected their brains. They changed personalities overnight. It is a small wonder that feudalism and slavery lasted so long. Strangely enough, I witness this same behavior in some of those who judge at field trials. The sense of power corrupts their thinking and behavior.

We must not forget that those of us who judge come from the ranks of handlers who we all know or will know someday. Many are friends who train, travel and socialize together. I have seen first places awarded to the "worst" dog in stakes more than once to the handler who rode to the trial with a judge.

It is difficult to quit normal associations with our friends and acquaintances when we judge, but our contacts should be modified temporarily for the good of the trial. Judges, for example, must **never** discuss their impressions and evaluation of dogs when the stake is in progress, or indicate the best dog up to that time even to their best friends.

Field trials are family affairs and at one time or other we will judge each other. Many different people judge, but few continue doing it for a long time. Some realize they are not suited to the task and a few use their assignments to get back at others for past wrongs, real or imaginary.

Rules must be administered in fairness to all participants. Order must be maintained. The judges word is law with whatever transpires during the stake and what goes into the record books. They have broad authority and it should never be abused. Their position is highly respected and deserves respect.

Field trial chairmen should know where their judges are staying and maintain positive communication so there are no foul-ups with being on the starting line on time. Motels may be far away from the grounds and the weather plays a big factor in their being able to drive to the grounds. Ice storms and blizzards sometimes make traveling impossible the morning of a trial. Judges should try to be on time, and if for some reason they cannot make the stake starting time, they should try to get a message to a club official. This allows the field trial committee or chairman to select someone else to judge the stake without much loss of time.

It helps if the judges know the course being used, but it is the marshal's responsibility to get judges and handlers around the course with a minimum of direction and confusion. Judges should keep to the course and not ride all over the place trying to keep the dogs in sight. A scout who is designated before the brace leaves the starting line should be available to look for his handler's dog when necessary. It is a fact that handlers and galleryites expect judges to see

511

Judges marking books at end of a brace at Sandhill Game
Management Area, Hoffman, North Carolina.

Winners should be warmly congratulated. Judging can be
tough and miserable under all kinds of weather conditions.
If they make mistakes, those who place are not responsible.

every infraction, but hope they do not see mistakes of their own dogs. Judges should give their undivided attention to all dogs in a stake as they are run and hope they see everything the dogs do that affects the placements.

Judges are expected to be helpful and courteous to novice handlers particularly, and to all handlers where no advantage is given. Handlers should be told when their dogs make mistakes and are no longer in contention, but not order them up.

Every dog is entitled to and should have a brace mate whenever there is no interference. Some dogs run better without one, some with, but their faults or polished manners can only be observed when running with a brace mate.

Nothing irritates me more than having two judges come to the line and spend five minutes or longer fumbling with their judging books causing dogs and handlers a delay in starting off. Once judges leave the end of a brace and ride to the starting line for the next, the marshal should identify the dogs, and then they should be cast off. I fail to understand the problem and am intolerant of it.

Clubs should furnish a qualified marshal thoroughly familiar with the course in order that judges be allowed to concentrate fully on the performance of the dogs.

Judges may suggest to their partners the way they see a given situation to influence them. The psychological sciences have proven just how faulty man's perceptions and memory can be without any effort or suggestion from anyone. A good judge must have self-confidence and positive self-evaluation capability to see everything in proper perspective and then defend it when required.

513

A study was made by a group of researchers in an effort to determine why hunters were mistakenly shot for deer and the conclusion was that the hunter looked so long and hard for a deer that somehow he created a condition with his eyes and brain which caused him to see a hunter as a deer. This same situation can be created in judging field trials when the judges get too much sun or too much wind and cold temperatures, or at least I would like to attribute some of their decisions to this phenomena.

When the total quality of the stake is poor, both judges may still be looking for a first placement when the last brace is run, and may be looking for other placements too. If at any time they honestly disagree on the two dogs which they are considering for first place, a second series using just those two dogs is appropriate and fair to all contestants.

It happens that the finer points which make one dog slightly better than another are not seen by one judge and further evaluation may be proper. Nobody wants the second best dog to win except the owner. Everyone eventually develops similar philosophies about their winning when undeserved--it only partially makes up for all the times their dogs "lost" stakes they won from other episodes of poor judging. It supposedly averages out.

When judging, I prefer to compare notes as the running progresses with my judging partner and keep dogs placed as any become deserving. Some judges like to keep their judging partners in the dark and then sort out the placements after the stake. I have seen judges take an hour or more after a stake trying to make placements and then flip a coin, or one giving up and telling his judging partner to place the dogs as he damn well pleases. This behavior is unfair to the participants and is damning to the sport.

Judges should be prepared to hand over their placements to the field trial secretary, or chairman, as they dismount unless they have call backs or another series to determine winners.

It is always prudent to have another series when judges become separated on course and believe the dog they each watched when alone was superior, or the first place dog. Who do I trust? I was separated when judging another breed trial, but was fortunate to be able to watch the brace mate all the time. When I rejoined my judging partner he told me that his dog was first place. We had separated the derby dogs because one was trailing and the other might have been glad. The dog he watched quit working, and I made him aware that I had watched the dog and would not consider placing it. He backed off. How often does this happen and the "easy going judge" accepts his partner's selection? And that judge who tried to put his friend up when judging with me most likely told him that he had his dog in first, but the bastard he was judging with would not agree.

The Shoot-To-Retrieve Association judges are required to judge each dog one half the time. This is done by a few judges in other trials and in championship stakes having only two judges. It is the fairest way to judge. In most weekend trials both judges are able to see both dogs in a brace anyway and there is no reason to formally change over.

Unsportsmanlike behavior toward a judge or dog occurs frequently and ranks high as the biggest problem judges face except for unfavorable weather.

Judges who accept assignments because they like the

515

challenge or believe they owe their time to the sport because of all the men and women who have judged their dogs in the past should give their best effort. It is difficult or impossible to judge with fairness to the contestants when talking all the time to the judging partner, listening to a football game on a portable radio, judging in a tornado, hailstorm, icestorm, thunderstorm, blizzard or severe cold or wet conditions. Human senses cease to function when miserable for too long a time. Experienced judges know better than accept an assignment requiring that they ride two full days in weekend trials. Those who judge the prestigious championships for up to two weeks for six to eight hours each day truly love the sport and are physically tough.

Weekend trials often require judging from daylight to dark, and a day can be over twelve hours without a break. Many of the dogs are entered in as many as four stakes and judges impressions, good or bad, are unfair to other handlers and their dogs. Judging assignments should be split up such that no person judges both puppy and derby stakes or more than two gun dog stakes on a given weekend. There have been times when I was so cold and weary that my brain worked in slow motion and there are no supermen under similar circumstances.

Judges should make notes even when their fingers are too cold to write, or when it is raining so hard the paper disintegrates, or the ink dilutes with the paper as they write. The more miserable and fatigued judges are, the harder it is for them to remember subtle or even important differences in dogs.

Field trial dog owners, trainers and handlers should remember this when they are being asked to judge. They should let the club official know if they will be running dogs in the trial. Some people want to, and even insist, on judging all stakes. It reduces club expenses for the trial but it is not fair to the competitors.

I do not understand the rationale for eliminating bird field observers appointed by judges, but there are times when the first place dog will have pointed and chased a bird and be seen by those in the gallery, and not seen by a judge. This leaves a bad taste, but nobody can judge what they cannot see. From my point of view this was a useful, necessary, option.

Another situation could occur where the potential first place dog made a long cast ending up pointing in the bird field, the bird flushed without the dog being at fault, eventually the dog released himself, and continued hunting. This was the only find and was not observed by a judge, so the dog is not placed: whereas, had there been an official bird field observer this could have been a first place dog.

Judges should be experienced riders and use their own horse for convenience and safety. Wranglers always try to provide their best horses for judges, but a strange horse is an unknown and causes problems for judges on occasion. A judge is more proficient on a horse he knows and trusts.

Invariably judges are asked to comment on the dogs they watched at weekend trial banquets which are held for judges, but really are an excuse to socialize. They should be careful, and if comments are made none should be critical of the dogs. Judges should say how much they appreciate the opportunity to judge the dogs and are trying their best to please the club officials and handlers in finding the best dog from stakes having several good dogs. They may think the handlers are ignorant, inept, clumsy, nervous and all the dogs they watched were potterers, but discretion here is the better part of valor. The judges should never mention that they spent most of their time counting how many times the male dogs lifted their legs to piddle, and mark, and stopped counting when a pattern of once a minute was determined, or how many times they looped back which again gave enough statistical data to formulate an empirical equation. And, if anyone does this they should give up judging. Something is wrong!

Many people who judge have, for one reason or many, quit going to judges' banquets, or whatever the clubs call them. They leave the grounds at the end of the day's judging and are not seen until the next morning.

Judges must recognize that owners paid an entry fee for them to watch their dogs for the time of the stake. Yet, it is not a training session and judges should not allow it, nor is it a place for dogs not trained to meet standards of conduct and behavior. Should a judge tell a handler his dog is doing poorly, but nothing wrong, and will not be placed leaving the handler the choice of making a decision to pick up or continue? No handler wants to hear judges tell him at cast off that better dogs have already run and if theirs does not cut the mustard, they will be picked up. But it is done.

Situations like these cause promulgation of new rules, angry handlers, or splits in a club or association. This is why new bird dog associations come into being. Something was wrong in the current one that could not be tolerated or changed, so it became easier to form another with new rules to overcome the problems.

Judges should never shorten the minimum brace time of thirty minutes even when there is a bird field of eight

518

minutes. And the eight minute bird field should not be shortened to protect dogs the judges want to place. Dogs should be judged the **full** time. No judge can predict which minute of the stake will prove more fruitful for the dogs in finding game or in making mistakes. Eight minute bird fields should be **eight minutes.**

It is the duty of marshals to direct the handlers such that they arrive at the bird field in thirty minute stakes in twenty two minutes. It does not make any difference what type thirty minute stake is being run, all dogs in contention must be kept down the full time in fairness to every dog and handler. Some dogs in bird field stakes may not get the full eight minutes, but when delayed on the course, they should get a total time of thirty minutes. Any delay in getting to the bird field does not entitle them to the full bird field time or additional time.

Judges must not protect their best dogs or preferred winners. Dogs should never be picked up in bird field stakes after they have had a find and successful retrieve to protect them. This is unfair to every dog and handler entered.

Dogs must establish their superiority on the back course and then confirm that standing in a bird field on birds still heavy with man scent from the bird planters.

Good judges readily refer to the rule book or ask some other knowledgeable official in the club when they have a question. False pride has no place in judging when used to cover up a lack of understanding about a rule or plain ignorance. Judges should ask the chairman if his club has any special requirements to follow in judging, but they cannot tell judges how to judge the dogs. Once the first brace is released the judges are on their own. Judges should carry the club's premium list as well as the appropriate standard and rules for the trial.

It is no secret that many breed clubs do not hold retrieving stakes and their handlers are not qualified to judge them. These handlers have a lesser appreciation of how much additional obedience training is involved, the difficulty, or the stresses the dogs experience in retrieving stakes as opposed to non-retrieving stakes.

Many who judge never read the rules or the premium for the trial. They already know it all. Why some judges persist in giving wrong, undeserving dogs first place, or placements is difficult to fathom. Handlers and owners are often humiliated. Some are honest mistakes sometimes corrected in time by the judges themselves. Others are not, but are so obvious to anyone watching the stake that the judges should never be asked back. We must always be careful in blaming the handlers and dogs for they are usually innocent victims of the gratuities.

The search for good men and women willing to serve the necessary apprenticeship of self-learning and self-experience goes on and on. Some do dedicate themselves to the sport and channel their egos to advance dog breeding, judging and field trials. Field trials are on the honor system and must be self-policing. Having good qualified men and women in the saddle makes most rules unnecessary or redundant. This is the way field trials should be, but the rules must be ready when needed.

Socializing with handlers or owners when judging is not in the best interest of the sport. Nor, should it be done with the gallery, yet many judges do just that and are not attentive to the dogs being judged. It is no surprise that many owners and handlers subtly, or openly, try to influence the judges by fraternizing when running which is often started by the judges. Handlers will give some cute girl money to entertain judges at bars to get on the "good" side of them. They are also extremely generous with them at trials with free food and drink.

TALKING TO JUDGES ABOUT DOGS

Since judges come from the ranks of owners, trainers or handlers, we are in effect talking to each other but from a different perspective. It is true that some of us do not like or accept the way others see and judge many situations in trials. We cannot find perfect judges who satisfy everyone. It usually happens that the winners are satisfied, but this is not always true.

Most judges are willing to discuss a dog's merits or problems in a stake. It is best to wait until they are finished with their judging assignments before handlers talk to them about their performances. It is difficult for judges to find time when judging another stake that follows the one of interest to handlers. Handlers should refrain from asking judges about their dogs when entered in other stakes yet to be run. Handlers should only discuss things of importance with judges through the field trial chairman or stake manager if necessary during a stake.

After the trial, questions should be limited to a learning process in order that the handler can clarify questions in his mind about his dog's performance which he did not understand. Such discussions should not be used to belittle, intimidate, harass, embarrass, or abuse judges unless the handler plans on quitting the sport. Such scars may be long lasting and some handlers may know more about judging their dogs on that particular day, but they do not have the judging assignment.

Judges do make mistakes in placements and when informed through a club official before the records are signed, they will gladly correct them. Once the placements are made official the decisions are final.

We must always try to remember that the judges are in a better position than anybody else in a stake to see the dogs and have a better mental outlook when making objective and subjective decisions on the dogs' performances.

It is generally useless for handlers to start a conversation with judges about their dogs. Smart judges will tell them how well they like their dogs regardless of whether they placed the dogs or not. Judges will lie to handlers to avoid confrontation.

My experience leads me to believe that the best policy is to accept the judging without talking to the judges about dogs. Experienced handlers with judging experience are able to tell whether they got a fair shake and talking to judges if they did not is a waste of time. Handlers who need an ego boost are dreamers, unless their dog was a winner and the result is a re-hash of what should be obvious.

Handlers do often have legitimate complaints about judging decisions. They are also members of a club and have a voice in its affairs and selection of future judges. Their complaints at trials should be directed to the field trial chairman who may or may not do anything about the complaint, but he should take it under advisement and discuss it with all other members of the field trial committee and act. They may not offer relief at the trial, but the seed of discontent with the judging was sown.

Handlers should be courteous enough to thank the judges for looking at their dogs even when they disagree with the decisions. Judging is really a thankless job.

JUDGING BOOKS

Every judge needs something on which to write down what he observes during the running. Oftentimes the JUDGING BOOKS are blank in the small space available, except for the names of the dogs in each brace.

Some judges prefer this method, and some want the names of handlers included. Others work up and provide their own judging books with rating factors and space to make notes. Some dog food companies furnish judging notebooks which fit in a shirt pocket, and field trial secretaries should write and ask for them.

The JUDGING FORM in my book *The Vizsla* is repeated. It is not perfect, but can easily be improved upon and modified to suit individual needs for the spotting system of judging. Ratings can be in any manner desired by numbers, letters or words. I use numbers from five to zero which relate to outstanding, excellent, good, poor, fair and awful or disqualified. A high percentage of the dogs in a stake do not merit ratings as they are picked up or make fatal mistakes and are picked up by handlers before the page can be marked. This judging form has been used in many breed trials.

A second JUDGING FORM was developed for a stake for field champions which is an hour, or longer, with handlers shooting birds on course for retrieves. The points represent only the relative value between rating factors and could be factored to represent a relative index of importance from one to five. The spotting system of judging was still used, and the relative values could be anything a judge wanted. Abbreviations cause problems if someone who does not know the judge's personal code happens to see what he puts in his judging book. PU might mean PICKED UP to the judge. It is necessary and helpful to use a form of shorthand when judging. A judge's notes are his own personal property and cannnot be correctly translated or interpreted by anyone else.

JUDGING FORM

DOG'S NAME _____

BRACE _____ DOG NO._____ HANDLER _____

RATING FACTORS	RATING	REMARKS
CAST OFF		
RANGE		
APPLICATION		
INDEPENDENCE IN HUNTING		
OBJECTIVES WORKED		
OVERALL BACK COURSE		
MANNERS WITH BRACE MATE		
RESPONSE TO HANDLER		
STYLE		
BACKING		NO._____
BACK COURSE BIRD WORK		NO._____
BIRD FIELD BIRD WORK		NO._____
MANNERS ON GAME		
QUALITY OF RETRIEVES		

REMARKS:

(From *The Vizsla*)

JUDGING FORM

DOG'S NAME _____

BRACE _____ DOG NO. _____ HANDLER _____

RATING FACTORS	RATING GUIDE	RATING
Cast-Off	5	
Application/Hunting	25	
Desire	10	
Intelligence		
In Hunting	10	
In Handling Birds	20	
In Use Of Wind	5	
In Picking Objectives	5	
Range	5	
Manners		
With Brace Mate	5	
On Flush	15	
On Shot	15	
On Backing	5	
Stamina	15	
Speed	15	
Style	15	
Accuracy Of Nose	10	
Quality Of Retrieves	25	
Number Of Finds: _____		
PLACEMENT: _____		
REMARKS:		

Judging would be more uniform if the American Kennel Club could get agreement from the pointing breeds and prepared Judges Books and sold them to field trial clubs. Most people who judge appreciate rating factors as reminders when they judge. These judging forms are not intended to have values added for placement as with the Shoot-To-Retrieve Association's judging form. It is a heavy card which must be used on a clip board with one dog in the brace listed on each side. The individual scores on each dog are added up by the field trial chairman from both judges' forms where each dog is judged for approximately fifteen minutes by each one. The scores are posted on a chalk board or hardboard for everyone to see as the stake progresses.

It is possible, and happens occasionally that judges mark the wrong dog in a brace, which may or may not always be detected before placements are made. This is why every judge should check his ratings after each brace to help avoid such mistakes. This form has greater value and advantage than requiring memory recall at the end of a stake. There are not many Howard Cosell's among us in spite the pride we have in our memory recall.

A serious problem in judging is with breeds of uniform color like Weimaraners and Vizslas, and those marked similary such as Brittanys. The trend is to use visibility collars. Red on the odd dog and yellow on the even dog in a stake. It is easy to be watching and marking mentally, or on paper, the wrong dog. Handlers can handle the wrong dogs in braces.

CARE OF JUDGES

Field trial judges do not charge a fee. Show judges charge a fixed amount plus expenses. Field trial judges may even furnish their own horses, and if they accept money they never get all their expenses. They are entitled to all expenses they incur for travel, food and lodging. Judges should be paid the same amount for their horses as the wrangler charges the club.

Many dog clubs maintain a list of acceptable judges. Those on the list are removed from time to time for unacceptable judging or behavior. Just because a club has a list of names of people who can judge does not make them qualified.

After being burned a few times with lousy judging partners, some judges want to know who they will be judging with when asked to judge. It is a poor practice to pair two men or women who have widely divergent views and expect fair treatment be given to all handlers and their dogs. When asked to judge, they should indicate any physical disabilities which a club might want to know before accepting an assignment. Some people cannot judge twelve straight hours two days in a row.

Judges should inform the field trial chairman or stake manager if they will bring their wives, if they will use their own horse and if they will need a motel room. Some clubs make their motel reservations, but never do anything special for them. Others may place a bottle of champagne with cheese and crackers in their rooms before they arrive and a flower for their wives.

I once judged for a now defunct club which hung special treats along the course for its judges. Each brace held a different surprise which was fun and gave us a sense of being important and appreciated. It had the added advantage of not having to stop for food or drink which speeded up the trial. There may have been method to their madness.

Most clubs hold a judges banquet where they are presented judging gifts. It is customary to buy a small gift for judges. The judges and their wives are given a complimentary meal too.

Clubs may claim to be have no money in their treasury, but they should not try to make up their expenses by expecting their judges to accept no money. It is easy to cut expenses by using a club's own members or someone who lives closeby.

The field trial secretary should write or call the judges before the trial to arrange for their needs during the trial and make motel reservations early. After the trial, the secretary should write a letter of appreciation.

Judges should not be forced to ride all day in all kinds of inclement weather without getting off their horses. I have seen judges so cold and miserable they wet their pants and did not even know it. Someone in the club should be appointed to furnish food and drink periodically with the kind and frequency suited to weather conditions. Club chairmen should insist their judges take periodic breaks in extremely cold weather to avoid frostbite and restore circulation. They can become so cold they lose any sensation of cold or pain. Probably the most important consideration is that clubs take no more entries than they can effectively run in the time allotted.

Any verbal or physical abuse of judges should be quickly stopped and immediate disciplinary action taken against the offender with the intention of barring him from future trials and he should be asked to leave the grounds. Any situation which gets out of hand should involve a call to the local police or sheriff to obtain whatever help is required.

Chairmen should be aware of the nearest emergency clinic, hospital or veterinarian if people, dogs or horses are injured.

It always helps a judge to know that his work was appreciated by handlers and club officials. He always knows when they are not satisfied.

A quote from John Rex Gates who knew Cecil S. Proctor as among the best who ever judged:

"(Cecil S. Proctor). . . was not concerned whether he would be asked back, whether someone was griping, or what anyone other than his judging partner thought about a dog's performance. He was confident with his own judgment."

When a judging assignment is completed for each stake, the judges should write the name of the stake, dogs placed, number of dogs judged and sign their names on a slip of paper and give it to the field trial secretary. Upon completion of the trial, judges should go to the field trial secretary and sign the official American Kennel Club stake results that they judged. It is sometimes easy to forget in the rush to get started home.

JUDGING SITUATIONS

Judging is both objective and subjective based on an individual judge's experience and interpretation of established rules and standards. There are a few people who judge by the seat of their pants. But, differing opinions can be genuine, honest and conscientiously arrived at. Two or more people can watch the **exact** same thing and come away with different versions of what happened. It is a psychological fact. Judging pointing dogs is no different, but the people having the most experience and knowledge make more accurate observations.

Rules and standards vary for different organizations. Sometimes the differences are major such as requiring backing be demonstrated for placement or dogs not required to be steady to wing and shot.

This list gives things dogs do when competing in pointing dog field trials in American Kennel Club licensed and member trials, and is intended as a guide for judges. They are in no particular order of importance and represent my own opinions. A dog with a penalty may be placed first if he is **the** best dog in the stake and is otherwise worthy. A dog or handler who is disqualified must not be placed, and placements should be withheld when dogs do not meet the standard at an acceptable level.

1.   Gun dogs should not be placed in all-age stakes because of inadequate range and strong dependence on their handlers.

2.   All-age dogs should not be placed in gun dog stakes if they have extended range and are not under the handlers' control.

3.   More weight should be given for good ground work in both gun dog and all-age stakes as opposed to bird work, although it is required to place.

4.   Derby Dogs **must** find and point game to be placed.

5.   An all-age or gun dog **must** find, point and handle game birds to be placed.

531

6. Flagging on point indicates training stress and is a minor fault.

7. Softening on point as a handler approaches is a major fault.

8. Dogs turning their head at approach of handler is a minor fault.

9. Dropping birds on retrieves is a minor fault.

10. Dogs which repeatedly drop and pick up birds when retrieving is a major fault.

11. Chewing birds before picking them up or picking feathers is a major fault.

12. Excessive commands to make a dog retrieve is a major fault.

13. A dog sent to retrieve and points the dead bird is a minor fault, but he must retrieve even though the handler has to "flush" and shoot again.

14. A dog sent to retrieve that points a different bird is not to be faulted. The bird should be shot and retrieved, and the other bird picked up.

15. A dog sent to retrieve that points a different bird and is commanded to retrieve off point by his handler and fails to catch it on the ground, but chases will be disqualified. The dog must stop to flush.

16. A dog sent to retrieve must return with a bird to his handler.

17. A dog sent to retrieve that failed to mark should not be placed if the handler locates the bird for him.

18. Failure to properly mark a fall and retrieve is a major fault, unless the dog's vision was blocked by handler or gunner and then he should be directed by voice or hand signals to retrieve.

19. A gun dog or all-age dog must be picked up for chasing game.

20. A dog should not be given credit for pointing a stink bird, but must be mannerly at flush and shot. A minor fault might be appropriate. Two points on stink birds should result in non-placement.

21. Dogs must be picked up for chasing stink birds.

22. Dogs should be faulted for pointing non-game and reptiles.

23. Dogs must be given credit for properly handled rabbits or any **game** worked properly.

24. Dogs chasing rabbits or any game must be disqualified.

25. Dogs deliberately flushing game and/or chasing must be disqualified.

26. Dogs stopping to flush after causing unintentional flushes should not be faulted.

27. Extra credit should be given dogs for properly handling stop to flushes where the dogs could not be guilty of causing them.

28. A dog that breaks and is stopped on command by his handler at flush should be charged with a major fault.

29. An unreasonable move to mark a bird after the flush is a fault, the seriousness is a minor or major fault.

30. Dogs moving after flush to release themselves to continue hunting when their handlers are close by can be charged with a minor fault.

31. A dog seen moving at a wild flush that stops on his own and waits for his handler to release him should not be faulted.

32. Dogs stopping to a wild flush without command and ignoring the flight to return hunting should be given extra credit.

33. A dog deliberately following and repointing a bird, or if after a short delay it follows in the

direction of flight after being cast forward, should not be placed and in many cases should be ordered up.

34. A dog that points a bird, holds it, and the bird flies for no apparent reason, and then releases himself, forgets the bird, and continues on hunting should be given extra credit.

35. A dog running under a bird in full flight should be picked up.

36. A dog having one unproductive point should not be penalized except under unusual circumstances.

37. Dogs having two or more unproductive points may not be placed depending on the scenting conditions and running birds. When it is obvious that pheasants or rabbits have run off as indicated on relocation efforts dogs should be given the benefit of doubt.

38. Dogs should be penalized for false pointing.

39. Dogs which have several unproductive points should not be placed.

40. Man-made unproductive points should not be charged against dogs.

41. Dogs which sit down when a bird flies closely over its head where the sit is caused by turning to mark should not be faulted unless it is repeated on subsequent flushes.

42. When dogs sit upon the approach of handlers they should be given a major fault.

43. When dogs sit at flush, they should be given a minor fault. If repeated they should be charged with a major fault.

44. A dog that lays down to hide from a bird on point should be put on another bird, if possible, before considering non-placement.

45. Dogs lying down on the approach of a handler should be charged with a major fault.

46. Dogs lying down at shot should be faulted.
47. Dogs working or running horse tracks for more than a short distance and not seeking likely objectives should not be placed.
48. A dog that breaks point after a bird has run off and relocates and points it again in a stylish manner should be given extra credit.
49. A dog observed trailing his brace mate after cast off should be charged according to the severity and if it unduly affects the brace mate he should be disqualified.
50. Scouts or anyone in the gallery giving commands to dogs should result in the dog being disqualified.
51. Judges should start timing dogs out of sight only after asking the handlers to show them, or after reaching the place on course they were last seen by the judges.
52. Dogs timed out should be found on point to prevent disqualification.
53. Handlers who cannot flush a bird and do not allow their dogs to relocate are charged with an unproductive.
54. Dogs working too methodically and slowly should be penalized.
55. Dogs running continually with their noses to the ground should be faulted.
56. Dogs blinking birds should not be placed.
57. Dogs habitually marking around the course with urine should be given a major fault.
58. Dogs breaking point when handlers are attempting to flush should be given a major fault.
59. Backing dogs that take steps at shot should be penalized.
60. Backing dogs breaking at shot to retrieve are

considered to have interfered with brace mates and should be picked up.

61. Backing dogs lacking style should be penalized.

62. Handlers who instruct gunners to shoot birds on the ground after shooting them from flight should be disqualified.

63. Dogs trying to breed dogs on point or licking their rear ends must be picked up. It may be run in the last brace if a veterinarian determines the female was in season.

64. Dogs pointing their brace mates' birds or moving in too close in backing situations should be penalized and depending on the seriousness may be picked up.

65. Dogs that come in from upwind toward pointing dogs and then circle to the rear before backing, instead of backing at first sight, should be penalized.

66. A WHOAED back should be a major fault.

67. Dogs reported fighting two times by judges at AKC trials are permanently eliminated. The dog picking a fight should be ordered up on the spot.

68. Handlers who cause their brace mates to lose style from loud commands to either their pointing or backing dogs should be penalized.

69. A handler who gets into an argument when handling should be disqualifed depending on the nature and severity.

70. Handlers who argue with judges should be disqualified and reported to club officials.

71. Handlers who block or intimidate pointing or backing dogs should be charged with a major fault. If the dog is considered for placement the dog should be put on a bird and the handler warned. Then if he blocks or intimidates the dog he should not be placed.

72. Pointing or backing dogs that are collared, or heeled away, should be penalized for later going to the place the bird flushed. Depending on the situation, it could be cause for disqualification.

73. Disguised double handling should be a disqualification where one dog is on point and its handler hollers WHOA as the brace mate is coming in for a back.

74. Dogs refusing to retrieve wounded birds should not be placed.

75. Breed trials requiring dogs to be heeled away from flushed birds should not be taken by the collar for any reason. This can be considered by judges as picking the dog up. Therefore, it is important to request permission from judges to water dogs, etc.

76. Handlers not calling point in derby stakes may be given no credit for a find.

77. Handlers who delay shot beyond normal shotgun range should be penalized.

78. Handlers forcing their dogs to hunt close is a form of intimidation and should be penalized.

79. Dogs backing every time the brace mate stops without it being on point should be penalized.

80. Dogs back casting excessively should be penalized.

81. Dogs cutting the course to the bird field should not be placed.

82. Dogs that have not run the full brace time, for any reason, should not be placed.

83. Dogs returning with a live bird or a warm bird should not be placed.

84. Dogs returning with a cold stiff bird should not be penalized, but suspect.

85. A dog should be credited with a find when a judge

sees birds on the ground even though they cannot be made to fly.

86. Handlers who arrive late for a brace cannot run that dog in the stake.

87. Handlers shooting over their backing dogs at flush should be penalized.

88. In fairness to all handlers and dogs, no dog should be run without a brace mate, but is not a requirement.

89. Handlers should not pick up birds and throw them into the air except on direction of the judges.

90. Continuous and excessive noise by handlers should result in disqualification after being warned by judges.

91. Blocking of dogs must be severely penalized.

92. Severe methods of correcting and disciplining of dogs by handlers is cause for expulsion and must be reported by judges to club officials.

93. Handlers who fail to dismount before firing should be penalized, warned and disqualified if repeated.

94. Dogs stealing point must not be placed and must be ordered up.

95. Dogs not obeying their handlers should not be placed.

96. Dogs interfering with brace mates should be picked up.

97. Handlers who run or ride fast to their dogs on point should be penalized. Refusing to quit undesirable behavior when warned by judges should result in disqualification.

98. There should be a minimum of interplay between judges and handlers. It is best if judges judge, and handlers handle their dogs. Too often judges in trying to be helpful are not.

Too many people who are asked to judge do not actually know the reasons why dogs should be ordered up. They order dogs up on minor faults. Actually, only two reasons are listed in the AKC rule book. One is for a dog which picks a fight and the other is for stealing point. But, there are a few others which should not be tolerated.

In a broke gun dog stake, a dog should be ordered up for chasing a bird, pushing out a bird, jumping in and catching a bird off point, jumping up to catch one which has flown over its head, intentionally causing a bird to flush with or without stopping, crowding in too close to a backing dog (interference), interfering with a brace mate, double handling, breaking at shot, refusing to retrieve, handler interference and for handlers who ignore a judge's warnings. That makes a total of fourteen which are acceptable, yet there is nothing in the rules stating that dogs may not be placed for any of the other twelve faults listed.

A dog which becomes lost or exceeds the allowable grace time of being gone in all AKC stakes cannot be placed.

Most handlers do not object to judges who use these reasons for disqualifying their dogs. Unfortunately, it continues to be done for imagined offenses where the dog is **never** given the benefit of a doubt.

Conclusion

This book has focused much attention on American Kennel Club trials, hunting tests, rules, procedures, standards, training and handling of pointing bird dogs. AKC has begun to take on new leadership and a new face. It's new Hunting Tests spawned *The Hunter's Whistle* in 1986 with a newspaper type format. But, just as important are the references to those trials and stakes held under the umbrella of the American Field Associations which should be an indication that we cannot separate one from the other.

Field trials are dynamic. They are growing, as are the hunting tests, and are constantly changing to suit the needs of pointing bird dog owners, trainers and handlers. They provide a healthy sport and outlet which can consume all of their hobby time, and they can be enjoyed for a lifetime.

There are hundreds of different pointing dog field trials and hunting tests every year and there are over two hundred championship stakes under the American Field umbrella alone. Each organization has rules and standards which suit each individual depending on his level of interest.

Some clubs and associations enjoy large entries while others in the same area struggle to get enough entries for a weekend. Most breed owners, trainers and handlers become locked into their own breed trials and stakes and seldom participate in other breed trials even when closeby.

Most participants experience emotional highs when seeing their dogs establish point way out front--out on a limb. A few see this as something expected of their dogs without much emotional sensation or thrill, but are pleased to see their training progress.

In fact, anyone who has a dog trained for the American Kennel Club gun dog or all-age standards (that is one of the top competitors) can cross over into many of the other associations' stakes and do well.

While it is not possible for everyone to do this because of being locked into their breed's field trial activities, or even compete in more than one or two different AKC breed trials, it is interesting to know that this training is almost universally suitable.

A field trial or hunting test can be found somewhere every weekend of the year by traveling outside of one's immediate area. It is a healthy exercise that forces owners into the field which they would never do just using their dogs for hunting. If field trialers are also hunters, their dogs are much better trained and they provide much more pleasure than do dogs with little or no training.

Long standing friendships result from field trial activities, especially in the same breeds. This is not to say that everyone will become friends. There are many factors regarding dog ownership within breeds and between breeds which create jealousy and adversary relations. Jealousy is as natural as breathing for some dog people.

There are no perfect dog owners, trainers or handlers and they all make mistakes just as their dogs do in training and competition. It takes great skill and patience to bring out the best in dogs, and the truly great ones are few and far between.

The beginning trainer must learn by his mistakes and by the dogs he ruins. Some owners should use professional trainers for the early phases of a dog's development with the owner taking over at some later time. Other owners cannot find the time to train and they advance their breed and the sport by using professionals trainers and handlers. There are no shortcuts to learning the sport. While on the surface it appears simple, it is not.

There are thousands of ways to train dogs, but few will ever achieve the kind of perfection we want. Correction and discipline in training create stresses which cannot be prevented. The dogs are being taught to do things unnatural to their make-up and against their will.

Each trainer must learn how to use a progressive, systematic way of training which suits him with whatever variations are needed for each individual dog. However, before any serious training begins each dog must be comfortable with its surroundings without being distracted easily. The trainer must be a practicing dog psychologist who can read his dog well.

And how are the best dogs found in field trials? It is through people selected from the ranks who act as judges. Judging will never be a science and it is the weakest link in the sport. The best qualified people will be competing with several dogs every weekend. They have broken a number of dogs and finished their field titles. But, even though they are not always available, they are not in great demand or have had bad experiences from insulting handlers and decline the invitations. Therefore, the more inexperienced owners and trainers get the nod and make mistakes that are damaging and are not corrected. Their interpretation of rules and standards are often wrong. The only recourse is for owners to join a club, attend the meetings, and prevent these poor judges from being asked again, or withhold their entries if due to poor judging. Unfortunately, some judges do not put up the best dog, if it is of a different breed than what they own. Too many honest judges have been blackballed. Requiring judges to be licensed will not solve this problem. Somehow a system must be found which rewards dogs with the best overall performances even when they make errors. Too much emphasis is placed on head and tail carriage when running and pointing, as opposed to a dog's bird hunting and finding ability. If a dog is capable of having a perfect performance, it is seldom repeated.

There are still problems in the sport that should be corrected such as keeping birds healthy during trials, releasing or planting them under conditions which will help them fly like wild birds. Add the poor, sometimes unsafe shooting, loud handlers, loud galleries and inexperienced judges which hurt many handlers. The rules are usually being changed every few years which usually require different training methods. The weather conditions cannot be overcome easily.

There are seminars and clinics offered across the United States which help instruct and give answers, but never seem to be effective in making dog owners into dog trainers. The same can be said of most books because many do not do the job adequately. Frankly, there are no step by step books written on training which substitute for experience. Hands on work, along with written material is required for learning. That means mistakes and corrections several times over. Much of this is difficult to separate from a person's personality and emotions which oftentimes negates positive progress.

Education of owners, trainers and/or handlers for judging has been sorely neglected or overlooked. The problems of inept judging reflects on everyone in the sport, but there is no apparent solution. A few organizations have seen the need and have been able to educate the members who meet the necessary qualifications. The sentiment is changing toward this in many of the other associations, but no matter what is done an individual's subjectiveness will not change.

These are some of the things that need solutions to improve the sport and make it fairer and more enjoyable for everyone. It is not an easy task.

I have covered almost every aspect of the sport, its training and handling, but this is not to say that everyone who reads or studies this book will become a good trainer or handler. Even if it were presented in a formal course structure, all students would not succeed. It is on the surface a very simple activity, but only experience reveals its compexity.

Field Trial Terminology

Aaah, aaah--Used for getting dog's attention and to caution it not to continue whatever it was doing.

AF (American Field)--An organization established for registering dogs, recording wins of sporting dogs and for governing field trial activities.

AKC (American Kennel Club). A registering and supervising organization for shows, obedience trials, field trials and hunting tests.

All-age--A dog of any age. A dog which runs to the front with intense hunting desire with great speed and range for horseback handling trials.

Animation--A dog that exhibits excitement and movement in search of game. A merry tail movement side to side. Happy.

Back--A command meaning to move backwards. The act of one dog sight pointing another dog which has established an intense point.

Bark--A vocal sound made by a dog. Also the command for a dog to make a vocal sound. Tongue.

Bevy--A flock of birds. Most commonly used to mean quail.

Bird bottle/cage--Holds a call quail which is placed up in a tree to keep released quail near it where feed is also placed.

Bird dog--A dog of the sporting breed used to flush, point and/or retrieve game birds. Also used to mean only dogs which point (exludes spaniels and retrievers).

Bird field--A designated area (5 acres or more) where birds are placed for each brace in a field trial stake.

Bird harness--A restraining device to prevent a bird from flying or running off from where it was placed.

Bird releaser--A mechanical device used to hold a bird in it until released by a mechanical, electric or electronic method.

Bitch--A female dog.

Birds--Game birds or pigeons used in field trials or in training.

Blind retrieve--The act of directing a dog to a bird it did not see fall either on land on in the water.

Blinker--A dog that smells game and avoids it or leaves on the approach of its handler.

Blinking--Avoiding game after scenting it.

Board--Keeping a dog (food and shelter) for a fee.

Bolter--A dog that will not hunt for its trainer or handler and is difficult to catch.

Bolting--Running away from a handler or trainer to hunt alone.

Brace--Two dogs which are run together.

Brace mate--(Bracemate) One of the two dogs in a brace.

Breakaway--A designated location where dogs are released in braces at the beginning of the course.

Breed--A kind of dog. The act of bringing two dogs together at the proper time to produce a litter of pups. Pure-bred ancestry over many generations.

Breeder--The person responsible for producing pups--the owner of the bitch which has whelped pups.

Brood bitch--A female dog used primarily for having litters of pups.

Brush--Bristle looking hair at some point on the tail or back raised by excitement or fear.

Bumping--A dog that smells or sees a bird and rushes in deliberately causing it to fly.

Bye--The odd dog which is left over after all dogs in the stake have been drawn.

Carded--A dog given credit for a find--point.

Cast--The pattern of a dog moving to cover or objectives. Direction of movement.

Cast-off--The beginning of a brace. The place a brace begins.

Castrate--Removing the testicles of a dog surgically to neuter it.

546

Catwalking on point--A dog that established point and then moves stealthly toward the game in a cat-like movement.

Champion (Ch.)--A show title in AKC. A field title in American Field and other associations.

Chasing--The act of following a bird in the direction of its flight by sight or where the dog thought it flew.

Check cord--A rope or strap of a given length (variable) to restrain, guide, correct or stop a dog.

Choke collar--A neck collar which tightens as it is restrained on a leash or check cord causing choking of the dog.

Check cord--A rope or strap of a given length (variable) to restrain, guide, correct or stop a dog.

Close (Hunt Close)--A command to make a dog stay near its handler to hunt.

Collar--A length of material with a buckle and place to attach a lead on a dog's neck. The act of taking a dog by its collar and turning it 180 degrees and leading it away from the flush.

Come--A command for the dog to return to its handler.

Come around--A command used mostly in bird fields to bring a dog back into the boundaries or to search for a bird closer to the handler.

Conformation--The physical looks, type, of a dog according to its written standard.

Continental--Meaning dogs from the European Continent.

Course--A specified pattern of travel by the handler and judges over suitable terrain over which each brace in a field trial stake runs.

Covey--Several birds grouped together--usually refers to quail.

Covering ground--The way in which a dog runs and hunts the terrain in front of its handler.

Dam--A female dog.

Dead bird--A command given for a dog to find a shot bird.

Derby--A dog not over two years of age in AKC trials. In AF derby dogs may be slightly older than 2 years of age depending on when born relative to spring and fall field trial stakes.

Discipline--A method used in training and correcting dogs. The assertion of authority in dog training.

Disqualification--A dog or handler declared unfit to continue in competition by the judges for rule infractions or unsportsmanlike conduct.

Divided find--Both dogs in a brace point close together and it is not possible to determine which pointed first. (A possible stolen point.)

Dock--Shortening the length of a dog's tail (usually done about four days after birth).

Dog--A male or female animal of the dog species. Also used to mean a male dog.

Dog wagon--A vehicle used to transport dogs in a continuous course stake with boxes or crates to hold the braces which will run that day.

Downwind--The lee side of objectives. When a dog runs with the wind at its back.

Down--A command for a dog to lie on the ground in a prone position.

Drawing--The selection of dogs for braces and the order which they are to run prior to the stake (trial).

Drive--The force with which a dog runs.

Dropping birds--A dog which when retrieving birds lets the bird fall to the ground for a new hold or drops it because of training stresses.

Dropping on point--A custom of making dogs lie down on point or when the gun is raised in European and other countries for hunting and field trials.

Dual Champion--A dog in AKC which has both field and show titles.

Dug in--A dog that has gone into heavy cover, found, and has pointed birds. Hidden from view.

Dummy--A round oblong object made of canvas filled with some material for bulk used for retrieving from land or water. Also made of plastic of different colors. Boat bumpers.

548

Eating birds--A dog which has not learned the team relationship, or from wrong training refuses to retrieve and eats the bird.

Easy, E-E-E-asy--A command to cause a dog to move slow while roading birds or which is about to point.

Exercise--A task in training. Letting dogs run to stimulate muscles or for conditioning for stamina and endurance.

Faking--A dog which feigns or pretends to hunt or point.

False point--Faking, or pretending to point where no game is present. A training fault caused by not allowing dog to use its own senses.

False stand--A point that produces no game. Faking.

Fetch--A command used when sending a dog to retrieve.

Field Champion (Field Ch.)--In AKC, a dog which has met its prescribed requirements in competition to earn the title.

Field trial--A competition of pointing dogs with established rules and standards of performance for awards and prizes. A test.

Find birds--Words used to encourage a dog to hunt.

Flag--A dog which moves its tail from side to side while pointing. Caused by enthusiasm, excitement or anticipation. Probably derives from the action of a setter's tail movement. Can also be caused by man scent on a bird.

Flagging on point--A lack of style, composure or intensity with the tail moving while on point. Flagging can also be caused by man scent on a bird. It may also be a dog with a happy tail.

Flush--Startling or frightening birds from cover causing them to fly.

Futurity stake--A stake for derby age dogs for which nominations or dams and pups precede the running. Nominations are after breeding and after whelping.

Gait--The manner in which a dog moves such as pace, trot or run.

Game--Wild birds or animals.

549

Gallery--Spectators who follow dog braces in a field trial stake to observe how the dogs perform and who are in no way part of the official operation. A gallery may follow on foot or horseback behind the judges and marshal, and must not participate in the handling of dogs in AKC trials.

Game birds--Birds approved for use in field trials. Pheasant, quail, chukar, grouse, woodcock and prairie chickens primarily.

Git out, Git out of here--A command for the dog to move on.

Go, Go on--Encouraging words for a dog to go out.

Give--A command, or request, for a dog to release an object or game being held in its mouth.

Gun dog--In AKC, a dog that hunts to the gun for its handler at a suitable range for a foot hunter.

Guns--Official field trial gunners.

Gun-shy--A dog made afraid of the sound of a gun being fired. A product of improper early exposure to gun fire.

Gun-shyness--A condition where the dog fears the sound of a gun being fired.

Handler--A person who follows after and works a dog in field trials.

Hand signals--The movement of a handler's hands and arms to direct a dog to go out, go left, go right, stop or come in.

Hard-mouthed--A dog that destroys birds it is sent to retrieve or refuses to release a bird it has retrieved.

Harness--The combination of straps in front of a dogs legs and which attach around its rib cage for pulling.

Heat--The time of a brace. Air temperature.

Heel--A command for a dog to walk on the left side of its handler as in obedience. A command for a dog to turn 180 degrees and leave the flight of a flushed bird.

Here--A command to come in.

Hey you--Attention getting words to get a dog to listen.

Hie-on--Words to encourage a dog to range out.

Ho--A command used by some handlers to whoa a dog, but can mean other things.

Holding onto bird--A dog which refuses to give its handler a bird freely.

Honor--A dog which stops at the sight of another dog on point.

Hunt close--Words used to encourage a dog to restrict its range.

Hunting--A dog that is purposefully and actually engaged in searching cover for game.

Hurry up--Words to encourage a dog to get on, move faster.

Hush up--Command to stop a dog from whining or barking.

Inbreeding--The breeding of closely related dogs such as mother to son.

Judge--A person with field trial experience who accepts an invitation from a club to follow all the braces in a stake to evaluate dogs and pick winners.

Jumping in--A dog which cannot resist the temptation to catch game off point. This is normal in young dogs as its handler approaches to flush.

Juvenile--Young dogs. Puppy and derby age.

Kennel--A command for a dog to enter an enclosure or vehicle. An enclosure for a dog. Generally used as "kennels" (plural) as most have more than one dog or breed.

Launcher--A mechanical device which restrains a bird until released mechanically, electrically or by an electronic switch.

Lead--A strap of four to six foot length used to restrain or lead a dog.

Leaving point--A dog points and then breaks point which he does for a number of different reasons. Usually denotes a training problem.

Liberated birds--Pen raised game birds which are set free for use in field trials.

551

License--An approval by AKC to hold a field trial for points toward a field champion title.

Line breeding--Breeding of dogs not so closely related such as aunts, uncles and cousins, or distantly related.

Litter--A number of pups whelped by a female dog. A litter can have more than one sire.

Losing point--Usually caused by wind shifts. Scent disappears and dog continues hunting.

Mate--The breeding of a dog and bitch.

Manners--The way a dog conducts itself on game when flushed, shot, retrieved or when heeled away. Its behavior around game, other dogs, horses and people.

Marshal--A person designated in field trials to help judges and handlers follow a prescribed course and also maintain control of the gallery.

Mechanical dog--A dog that does everything correct, but has no character, desire, speed or enthusiasm for its work.

Moving close--A dog that points and then continues to move up before holding point.

No--One of the most essential commands to control the action of a dog. Means to stop that now!

Nonproductive--A point where no game is produced by the handler.

Nose--The ability of a dog to detect and discriminate different scents and different intensities of scent.

OK--Used to release a dog at cast off, retrieve or to reassure the dog.

Organized competition--Sanctioned or licensed events authorized by different field trial organizations.

Pace--The movement, progress, manner of speed and action of a dog as it hunts.

Pattern--The way a dog searches in its hunting application, a style of hunting a course.

Pedigree--A dog's ancestry.

Planted bird--A bird used in training of field trials which is placed at a specific location and immobilized temporarily by various means.

Placement--One of four winners in AKC trials. One of three winners in most trials under the AF umbrella.

Plodder--A slow, deliberately moving dog. Not exciting to watch.

Point--A dog stops at the scent of a bird which is stationary, not moving, and holds that position until the bird leaves or is flushed.

Pointing dead--A dog which when sent to retrieve points the dead bird.

Pointing non-game--Pointing trash birds. Dinky birds. Most dogs learn to point only game or game birds. No fault, no credit in field trials when mannerly unless done to excess or if it detracts from normal hunting behavior.

Pottering--A dog which wastes time in one place too long and is indecisive in its actions. Wastes too much time and is ineffective in finding birds.

Praise--A verbal reward for a dog doing a satisfactory or better job.

Premium (list)--An advance notice mailed to dog owners which gives details of a forthcoming field trial or hunting test.

Professional handler--A person who accepts money for his work in training and/handling dogs.

Put down--Euthanasia of a dog. Belittle one's accomplishments.

Puppy--A dog less than 15 months of age in AKC. In AF a dog born from January 1 to December 31 after June 1 of preceding year.

Pure-bred--Dogs of known lineage which are closely bred (inbred) for many generations.

Quartering--A dog taught to move right to left, left to right on a hunting pattern in front of the handler as the action of a windshield wiper.

Race--The movement of a dog on the course. Quick, swift, movement for the duration of the heat on the course.

Range--The distance a dog maintains in front of its handler.

553

Rapport--The way a trainer/handler and his dog relate and work together in harmony.

Register--An official record of the dog's name, birth date, sex, sire, dam, breeder and owner by a registering organization.

Retrieve--A requirement for some pointing breeds to complete a field champion title. The bringing of game to a trainer/handler and giving it up.

Release--The setting free of game birds for field trials, hunting or training.

Released bird--A pen raised bird which has been turned loose on a course for field trials.

Relocation--Allowing a dog on point to move and hunt for the game by its handler after he has been unable to locate and flush it.

Renegade--A dog that refuses to hunt for or to return to its handler or trainer. A dog out of control.

Ringer--A dog run in place of the drawn dog which closely resembles that dog.

Roading--Exercising a dog in a harness while it pulls a load. The art of a dog following the scent trail of a moving bird without flushing it intentionally until it stops, hides and can be pointed.

Ruff--A collar of hair raised by excitement on a dog's tail, neck or a line down its back.

Run--Similar to race.

Running horse tracks--A dog in a field trial which follows horse tracks around the course without hunting for game.

Saddle--Used on a horse's back and fastened with a strap around its chest for a person to ride upon while following dogs.

Sanction--A competitve activity approved by AKC as a step in giving a club approval for licensed events. Confirmation for holding a field trial or hunting test by some organizations.

Scent--The release of odor, perfume (effluvium),by game which can be detected and followed by pointing dogs.

Scents--Those odors from game which excite the sense of smell of dogs. Artificial scents made for different game used in training.

Scent cone--The envelope of scent emitted by game which is influenced by various environmental conditions and moves with air currents.

Scout--A helper for a handler in field trials who walks or rides out to look for a dog that is out of contact with handler and judges to determine if he is on point. Also, a co-handler in AF trials.

Self-hunting--A dog which only hunts for itself.

Set up--An effort to match hunting conditions, situations, for dog training which may occur in field trials.

Shock collar--An electronic shocking device (receiver) attached to a dog's collar and set off by a remote transmitter to correct or punish a dog.

Shooting dog--See gun dog. A term used by AF and other associations.

Shut up--A command for a dog to stop barking.

Sickle tail--A tail which curves up and over a dog's back.

Sight points--A dog that establishes point at the sight of a bird.

Singing--A method used to let a dog know the location of its handler. Useful in all-age stakes.

Sire--Male parent of a litter.

Socialize--Giving a dog many different associations and relationships with man, dogs, horses, groups and every experience needed to make it well rounded and balanced for working independently in training and competition.

Softening on point--Insecurity caused by stress or wrong introduction to pointing. Flagging. The behavior often occurs on approach of the handler.

Spay--Neuter of a female dog.

Speak--Command for a dog to bark.

Spotting system--A method of judging where the best dogs are placed (spotted) as the braces in a stake are run. It requires bird dog experience, knowledge, keen observation, a good memory and the ability to make value judgments about performances of all dogs in a stake. It has no hard or fast rules outside of a given standard.

555

Spring—The jumping in of a dog trying to catch game.

Stake—A number of dogs entered in a field trial which are paired and run in braces. Stakes are set up to distinguish between one being for both professional and amateur handlers or just for amateur handlers, or for type and age of dogs.

Stake out—The use of stakes driven into the ground with a chain attached to hold dogs to eliminate, eat or watch training. Horses tied to a stake by a rope threaded through a section of garden hose.

Stand—A point.

Staunch—Stopping on point. Not moving. Stanch.

Stay—A command not to move. To stay in place.

Steady to wing and/or shot—A dog which stands at the flush of a bird and the shot of a gun.

Stealing point—A dog which refuses to honor its brace mate's point and continues to advance in front of it before establishing point.

Sticky on point—A dog which refuses to move when released or asked to relocate.

Stop—A command to stop moving.

Stopping to command—Demonstrated obedience to a command.

Stud book—Official register of dogs and breeds.

Stud dog—A male dog used in matings.

Tail set—The way a dog's tail sets onto its body (croup).

This way—Command for a dog to change direction.

Trap—A device to hold game.

Tongue—Bark.

Trail—Follow game by foot or body scent.

Trial—A contest with pointing dogs.

Twelve o'clock tail—A tail that sets on and is held vertically while on point.

556

Up front--A command for the dog to go to the front.

Upwind--A position relative to wind direction and object. When a dog runs with the wind in his face.

Unproductive--A barren stand. Handler is unable to produce game once a dog establishes point and the game has moved off.

Versatile--A dog with an aptitude to work and point different kinds of game or to handle several different tasks well.

Walk--Following a dog on foot.

Whistle--A device used to direct or control a dog in training and field trials blown by its trainer or handler.

Whoa--A command for a dog to stop moving.

Whup--A command for a dog to change directions.

Wind--Air that moves at a certain velocity and direction.

Winds--The way a dog scents game.

Wild flush--A bird that flushes in front of or near a dog which did not cause it to fly.

Wildness--Caused by a inexperienced or untrained dog when finding game. Caused by the scent of game.

Winner--A dog which places in a field trial stake. A first place award.

Wirehair--Kind of hair on a dog. Word used in a breed's name.

Wrangler--One who furnishes and care for horses used at a field trial.

Yard training--Obedience training. Used for commands used in field trials.

Yo-Yo--A dog that runs out and back.

Index

560

567

W

X

Y